TWENTIETH-CENTURY COLONIALISM AND CHINA

The question of colonialism in modern China is fundamental to the histories of Chinese nationalism, modernity, and revolution. Colonialism in China is a fragmented and distinctive story which achieved its greatest extent in the first half of the twentieth century. Even so, the diversity of the colonial character throughout China's history defied systematic characterization and has posed numerous conceptual challenges.

The cross-disciplinary essays in this volume illustrate the diverse and multivalent character of colonialism in twentieth-century China. Its subjects include a variety of colonizers and locations from Tianjin and Qingdao in the north to Hong Kong, Macao, and French influence in the south. The focus even extends beyond China to studies of overseas Chinese networks and beyond the establishment of the People's Republic of China in 1949 in its claims for national reunification.

Bringing together an international team of experts, *Twentieth-century Colonialism and China* is an essential resource for students and scholars of modern Chinese history and colonialism and imperialism.

Bryna Goodman is Professor of History at the University of Oregon, USA.

David S G Goodman is Professor of Chinese Politics at the University of Sydney, Australia, where he is also Academic Director of the China Studies Centre.

WITHDRAWN
UTSA LIBRARIES

TWENTIETH-CENTURY COLONIALISM AND CHINA

Localities, the everyday and the world

Edited by Bryna Goodman and David S. G. Goodman

LONDON AND NEW YORK

First published 2012
by Routledge
2 Park Square, Milton Park, Abingdon, Oxon OX14 4RN

Simultaneously published in the USA and Canada
by Routledge
711 Third Avenue, New York, NY10017

Routledge is an imprint of the Taylor & Francis Group, an informa business

© 2012 Bryna Goodman and David S. G. Goodman for selection and editorial matter; individual chapters, the contributors.

The right of Bryna Goodman and David S. G. Goodman to be identified as editors of this work has been asserted by them in accordance with the Copyright, Designs and Patents Act 1988.

All rights reserved. No part of this book may be reprinted or reproduced or utilised in any form or by any electronic, mechanical, or other means, now known or hereafter invented, including photocopying and recording, or in any information storage or retrieval system, without permission in writing from the publishers.

Trademark notice: Product or corporate names may be trademarks or registered trademarks, and are used only for identification and explanation without intent to infringe.

British Library Cataloguing in Publication Data
A catalogue record for this book is available from the British Library

Library of Congress Cataloging in Publication Data
Twentieth-century colonialism and China : localities, the everyday, and the world / edited by Bryna Goodman and David S.G. Goodman.
p. cm.
Includes bibliographical references and index.
1. China—Colonization—History—20th century. 2. Europeans—China—History—20th century. 3. China—Relations—Western countries.
4. Western countries—Relations—China. 5. China—History, Local—20th century. 6. Imperialism. I. Goodman, Bryna, 1955– II. Goodman, David S. G.
DS775.8.T84 2012
325.5109'041—dc23
2011036753

ISBN 978-0-415-68798-0 (hbk)
ISBN 978-0-415-68799-7 (pbk)
ISBN 978-0-203-12545-8 (ebk)

Typeset in Bembo
by Cenveo Publisher Services

Printed and bound in Great Britain by the MPG Books Group

CONTENTS

Contributors	*vii*
List of maps	*x*
List of figures	*xi*
Abbreviations	*xii*
Preface	*xiv*

Introduction: colonialism and China Bryna Goodman and David S. G. Goodman	1

PART I
Colonial governance and questions of identity   23

1 'Good work for China in every possible direction': The Foreign Inspectorate of the Chinese Maritime Customs, 1854–1950 Robert Bickers	25
2 Negotiating the nation: German colonialism and Chinese nationalism in Qingdao, 1897–1914 Klaus Mühlhahn	37
3 Things unheard of East or West: colonialism, nationalism, and cultural contamination in early Chinese exchanges Bryna Goodman	57

PART II
Colonial spaces and everyday social interactions   79

4 The Peak: residential segregation in colonial Hong Kong   81
John M. Carroll

5 An Italian 'neighbourhood' in Tianjin: Little
Italy or colonial space?   92
Maurizio Marinelli

6 The colonial space of death: Shanghai cemeteries, 1844–1949   108
Christian Henriot

7 French medicine in nineteenth- and twentieth-century
China: rejection or compliance in far south treaty-ports,
concessions and leased territories   134
Florence Bretelle-Establet

8 Writing home and China: Elisabeth Frey in Tianjin, 1913–14   151
Yixu Lu and David S. G. Goodman

PART III
Late colonialism and local consequences   165

9 Modernism and its discontent in Shanghai: the dubious
agency of the semi-colonized in 1929   167
Yiyan Wang

10 Equality and the 'Unequal Treaties': Chinese émigrés and British
colonial routes to modernity   180
John Fitzgerald

11 Hong Kong and the New Imperialism in East Asia, 1941–66   197
Prasenjit Duara

12 The hapless imperialist? Portuguese rule in 1960s Macau   212
Cathryn Clayton

Bibliography   *224*
Index   *247*

CONTRIBUTORS

Robert Bickers is Professor of History at the University of Bristol and a Co-Director of the British Inter-university China Centre. He is the author of *Britain in China: Community, Culture and Colonialism*; *Empire Made Me: An Englishman Adrift in Shanghai*; and *The Scramble for China*. As well as work on the Chinese Maritime Customs Service, he has recently been leading the Historical Photographs of China project (http://chp.vcea.net).

Florence Bretelle-Establet is a researcher at REHSEIS (UMR 7219, CNRS & Université Paris Diderot, Sorbonne Paris cité, F-75205) and co-editor of *Extrême-Orient Extrême-Occident*. She is the author of *La Santé en Chine du Sud, 1898–1928*. Her current research focuses on the medical practices and theories in three southern provinces in the Qing empire.

John M. Carroll is Professor of History at the University of Hong Kong. He is the author of *Edge of Empires: Chinese Elites and British Colonials in Hong Kong*; and *A Concise History of Hong Kong*.

Cathryn Clayton is a cultural anthropologist of China and Assistant Professor in the Asian Studies Program of the School of Pacific and Asian Studies, University of Hawai'i at Manoa. Her recent book, *Sovereignty at the Edge: Macau and the Question of Chineseness*, is an ethnography of the intersections between conceptions of sovereignty, experiences of colonialism, and questions about the meaning of Chineseness in Macau during its transition from Portuguese to Chinese rule.

Prasenjit Duara is the Raffles Professor of Humanities at the National University of Singapore, where he is also Director of Research in Humanities and Social Sciences. In addition to Chinese history, he works more broadly on Asia in the twentieth century, and on historical thought and historiography. Publications include *Rescuing History from the Nation*; *Sovereignty and Authenticity: Manchukuo and the East Asian Modern*; *Decolonization*; and *Culture, Power and the State: Rural North China, 1900–1942* which won the Fairbank Prize of the American Historical Association and the Levenson Prize of the Association for Asian Studies. His most recent work is *The Global and the Regional in China's Nation-Formation*.

John Fitzgerald is an Honorary Research Fellow in the School of Social Sciences at La Trobe University in Melbourne, and concurrently China Representative of the Ford Foundation in Beijing. His publications include *Awakening China: Politics, Culture and Class in the Nationalist Revolution*, which was awarded the Joseph Levenson Prize for Twentieth-Century China by the Association for Asian Studies; and *Big White Lie: Chinese Australians in White Australia*, which received the Ernest Scott Prize in Australian History from the Australian Historical Association.

Bryna Goodman is Professor of History at the University of Oregon. She is author of *Native Place, City and Nation: Regional Networks and Identities in Shanghai, 1853–1937*; and co-editor of *Gender in Motion: Divisions of Labor and Cultural Change in Late Imperial and Modern China*. She is currently completing a manuscript on public culture in 1920s Shanghai.

David S. G. Goodman is Professor of Chinese Politics at the University of Sydney, where he is also Academic Director of the China Studies Centre. His research has concentrated on social and political change in China since 1900, especially at the local level. He is currently undertaking research on social and political change in the North China base areas of the Chinese Communist Party, 1939–1940; and on the formation of local elites in contemporary China (with Dr Beatriz Carrillo and Dr Minglu Chen). His most recent publication is *The New Rich in China: Future Rulers, Present Lives*.

Christian Henriot is Professor of Chinese history at University of Lyon and currently a Senior Research Fellow at the Institut Universitaire de France. He is the author and editor of several books on modern Chinese history, including *Prostitution and Sexuality in Shanghai: A Social History, 1849–1949*; and *In the Shadow of the Rising Sun: Shanghai under Japanese Occupation*. His latest project is an online research and resource platform on Shanghai history (http://virtualshanghai.net).

Yixu Lu is Chair, Germanic Studies at the University of Sydney, Australia. Her research is concerned with German literature since the eighteenth century and German colonial adventures in China. Some recent publications include 'German colonial fiction on China: the Boxer-uprising 1900–1901' [*German Life and Letters* 59(1): 2006]; *Medea unter den Deutschen. Wandlungen einer literarischen Figur*; and 'The war that scarcely was: the *Berliner Morgenpost* and the Boxer uprising', in Michael Perraudin and Jürgen Zimmerer (eds) *German Colonialism and National Identity*.

Contributors **ix**

Maurizio Marinelli is Professor of China Studies and Director of the China Research Centre at the University of Technology Sydney. He specializes in contemporary China's intellectual and urban history. His research investigates how China's relations with the rest of the world have influenced historical narratives and shaped visual representations within their respective intellectual discourses. He is currently working on the socio-spatial transformation of Tianjin during the foreign concessions era (1860–1945). Among his recent publications are 'Tianjin, a permanent expo of world architecture' (*China Heritage Quarterly* March 2010); and 'Making concessions in Tianjin: heterotopia and Italian colonialism in mainland China (1860–1945)' (*Urban History* December 2009).

Klaus Mühlhahn is Professor of Chinese History and Culture at Free University of Berlin. He is interested in Chinese legal history in the modern period, and the history of imperialism and Sino-Western exchanges in the twentieth century. His most recent publications include *Criminal Justice in China: A History*, winner of the American Historical Association's Fairbank Prize for 2009; 'The concentration camp in global historical perspective' [*History Compass* 8(6)]; '"Friendly pressure": law and the individual in modern China' in Mette Halskov Hansen and Rune Svarverud (eds) *iChina: The Rise of the Individual in Modern Chinese Society*; and 'National studies and global entanglements: the re-envisioning of China in the early 20th century' in Vanessa Kuennemann and Ruth Mayer (eds) *Transpacific Interaction: The United States and China, 1880–1950*.

Yiyan Wang is Professor of Chinese at the Victoria University of Wellington, New Zealand. Her publications focus on modern Chinese literature and culture, and she is currently engaged in research on modern Chinese art history. She is the author of *Narrating China: Jia Pingwa and his Fictional World*.

MAPS

5.1	Foreign concessions in Tianjin, 1910	93
5.2	Coastguard Filippo Vanzini's Tianjin, November 1901	97
6.1	Foreign cemeteries in Shanghai	111
6.2	Pahsinjao Cemetery ('New Cemetery')	112
6.3	Bubbling Well Cemetery	114
6.4	Muslim Cemetery (corner of Pahsienjao Cemetery)	119
6.5	Hungjao Cemetery	127
6.6	The 'resisting' lineage land lot (Bubbling Well Cemetery)	129
7.1	The French sphere of influence in late nineteenth-century China	136

FIGURES

6.1 Pootung Cemetery (Sailors' Cemetery) on Pudong   122
6.2 Squatter huts in Pootung Cemetery   123

ABBREVIATIONS

AS/JYS	Academia Sinica and Jindaishi yanjiusuo (Institute for Modern History, Academia Sinica, Taiwan)
BArch/MA	Bundesarchiv/Militärarchiv (German Federal Archives /Military Archives)
BArchB	Bundesarchiv Berlin (German Federal Archives)
BR	Royal Italian Concession in Tientsin. Local Land Regulations and General Rules, Archivio Storico del Ministero degli Affari Esteri (1891–1916)
Bt	Board of Trade (United Kingdom)
BWC	Bubbling Well Road Cemetery
CADN	Centre des Archives diplomatiques
CAMAE	Centre des Archives du Ministère des Affaires étrangères
CAOM	Centre des Archives d'Outre-Mer
CCP	Chinese Communist Party
CMCS	Chinese Maritime Customs Service
CO	Colonial Office (United Kingdom)
DASM	Directeur Administratif des Services Municipaux (Administrative Director of Municipal Services)
DBC	Deutsche Botschaft China (German Legation China)
DD	*Documenti Diplomatici sugli avvenimenti di Cina presentati al Parlamento dal Ministro Prinetti*, two volumes, Roma, 1901–2
DG	Director General
DQSLXJ	*Deguo qinzhan Jiaozhouwan shiliao xuanbian 1897–1898* (Selected Materials on the German Occupation of the Jiaozhou Bay 1897–98)
ECAFE	Economic Commission for Asia and the Far East

FC	French Concession (Shanghai)
FCO	Foreign and Commonwealth Office (United Kingdom)
FHA	First Historical Archives, Peking
FMC	French Municipal Council
FNAE	First National Arts Exhibition
FO	Foreign Office (United Kingdom)
HJC	Hungjao Cemetery
HKRS	Hong Kong Public Records Office (papers)
IG	Inspector General
IS	International Settlement (Shanghai)
KMT	Nationalist Party, Kuo Min Tang
mu	unit of land area (600 square metres)
NCDN	*North China Daily News*
NCH	*North China Herald*
PHD	Public Health Department
PRC	People's Republic of China
PWD	Public Works Department
RIC1	Royal Italian Consulate. Tientsin-China. Sale by Auction of land in the Royal Italian Concession in Tientsin, 6 July 1908
RM	Reichsmarine/Marinekabinett (Naval Cabinet)
ROC	Republic of China
SEATO	Southeast Asia Treaty Organization
SHAC	Second Historical Archives of China
SMA	Shanghai Muncipal Archives
SMC	Shanghai Municipal Council
SMP	Shanghai Municipal Police
SPBC	Shanghai Public Benevolent Cemetery
SZF	Shizhengfu (Chinese municipality)
Tls	Taels (unit of currency, often approx. 40 g silver)
TRFYT	*Tongren fuyuantang*
UN	United Nations
WSJ	Weishengju (Bureau of Public Health)

PREFACE

The Sydney-based Provincial China Project is dedicated to examining the variety of social and political change across China. The project started in 1994 with a series of annual workshops to examine the impact of China's reforms on the provinces outside Beijing, and since 1999 each annual workshop has had more of a themed focus. The project continues to focus on the provincial and the local in its understanding of China's society, economics, politics and culture. A selection of the papers from each workshop have been published in a series of edited volumes.

In 2007, the Provincial China Project took its first step into China's history to consider the variety of colonial experience during the early twentieth century. This volume results from the Provincial China Workshop held on *Colonialism and China: Localities, the Everyday, and the World* at Ocean University, Qingdao in the autumn. Appropriately, the part of Ocean University where we met was the site of the German school established with the colony of Qingdao at the start of the twentieth century.

The workshop, and this volume, were a collective effort between the UTS China Research Centre and China Ocean University, as well as a series of academic participants from the USA, Europe, Australia and China. In particular, the editors would like to thank Prof Sun Lixun, then of Ocean University (now of Beijing Normal University), Claire Moore of the UTS China Research Centre, and Professor Louise Edwards, then of UTS (now of the University of Hong Kong). We also wish to thank all those who participated in the workshop, and who have contributed their work to this volume.

Bryna Goodman
University of Oregon

David S. G. Goodman
University of Sydney

INTRODUCTION

Colonialism and China

Bryna Goodman and David S. G. Goodman

Colonialism in China was a piecemeal agglomeration that achieved its greatest extent in the first half of the twentieth century, the last edifices falling at the close of the century. The diversity of these colonial arrangements across China's landscape defies systematic characterization. Jürgen Osterhammel (1986: 290) problematized the descriptive capacity of the notion of 'semi-colonialism' by enumerating twenty-six 'variegated historical phenomena' associated with imperialism and an imprecise 'semi-colonialism' in China. There was no coherent whole. This was not simply a matter of quantitative unevenness, but of qualitatively different configurations. Although some sites, like Shanghai or Hong Kong, have served as icons of colonialism in China, these two locations of British colonial presence, the former a treaty-port and the latter a colony, were structurally dissimilar and have engendered different historical narratives.

British victory in the Opium War forced the signing of the Treaty of Nanjing in 1842, the first of the 'unequal treaties' that initiated modern colonial formations on Chinese soil, ceding Hong Kong as a colony and providing for the initial establishment of five ports – Shanghai, Guangzhou, Xiamen, Fuzhou, and Ningbo – to be opened to foreign trade. But Britain, prominent as it was, was neither the first nor the last, and certainly only one architect of the colonial landscape in China. Portugal had maintained various leasehold arrangements in Macau since the sixteenth century.[1] After the global scramble for colonies that marked the end of the nineteenth century, the geography of colonialism in China encompassed actual British, Portuguese, and Japanese colonies (Hong Kong, Macau, and Taiwan) as well as coercively leased territory like the Russian Port Arthur (Lüshun, now incorporated within Dalian), British Weihaiwei (Weihai), German Kiaochow (Jiaozhou, with headquarters in the city of Qingdao), and the French Guangzhouwan. In all of these, Chinese sovereignty was suspended over a delimited area for a lengthy but finite period.

These clearly colonized pieces of China, each of which was governed by a single colonial power, coexisted with a more restricted type of colonial formation, the 'treaty-ports', numbering 92 by 1917. Such cities, forcibly-opened sites for foreign trade, dotted China's coastal areas, inland ports, and railway junctions. The major treaty-ports, such as Shanghai and Tianjin, contained multiple foreign settlements with extraterritorial jurisdiction, formal enclaves of foreign residence and governance that facilitated imperialism without the costs or responsibilities of full colonialism. Other treaty-ports, like Suzhou, sustained only one foreign settlement (in Suzhou's case, Japanese). Others had no foreign settlements at all.

In addition to formal colonies and treaty-port enclaves, there were all manner of inland and peripheral intrusions.[2] These included large and internationally recognized 'spheres of influence' of colonial powers that overlaid regions of Chinese sovereignty. The French zone, for example, included the Chinese provinces contiguous to French Indochina: Yunnan, Guangxi, and Guangdong, where French held rights of residence and of mining and railway development. Despite these diverse and substantial colonial inroads, throughout the nineteenth century and the first three decades of the twentieth century, the vast bulk of China remained under the authority of indigenous governments, surrounding and overshadowing the comparatively insubstantial foreign footholds.

The termination of these varied colonial and colonial-style structures, like their initial formation and accretion, was a haphazard affair, reflecting the contingencies of Chinese and global politics. China's entrance into the First World War ended the extraterritorial rights of Germany and Austro-Hungary in 1917. The Soviet Union repudiated Russian treaty rights in 1919, formally renouncing extraterritorial claims in 1924. Anti-imperialist nationalism and foreign policy changes after Nationalist Party (Guomindang) victory in 1927 achieved some treaty revision by 1929 (most notably tariff autonomy and reduction in the numbers of treaty-ports). The most economically dynamic treaty-ports remained largely untouched, however, even as minor treaty powers such as Belgium and Mexico relinquished particular claims. Extraterritoriality persisted until the decolonization of the European treaty-port settlements in China in the Second World War, in the context of Japanese occupation.[3] Japan's defeat in the war terminated Japanese colonialism, though it meant the resumption of British authority in Hong Kong.

That the British and Portuguese colonies of Hong Kong and Macau survived until 1997 and 1999, respectively, meant that Chinese nationalists could point to enduring stigmata of the colonial past, even as ambivalence over return to China tempered local residents' perceptions of colonialism. The global media event of the ceremonial transfer of the crown colony of Hong Kong to the People's Republic of China on 1 July 1997, ending a century and a half of British rule, is imprinted on the memories of adults today with different inflections, depending on location. If the colonial era is now past, the foreign-dominated parts of China and a history of 'national humiliation' continue to be remembered, reappropriated, and strategically evoked by scholars, activists, and the Chinese state. Both because of the influence of the past on the present, and because of this continuing politics of memory, although the era of colonialism may seem distant, the issues raised in this volume on twentieth-century colonialism and China are not merely academic.

Questions of terminology and colonial formations in China

Throughout the twentieth century and into the present, conceptualization of the profuse forms and distinctive pattern of colonialism in China has been distracted by politics and stymied by clumsy terminology. In 1923, with characteristic hyperbole, if little theoretical precision, Sun Yat-sen, in his second lecture on the 'Three Principles of the People', noted that there was a categorical distinction to be made between full colonies and the situation of China. Although China retained formal sovereignty, its territory was diminished and, Sun argued, it was 'crushed by the economic strength of the Powers *to a greater degree* than if we were a full colony' (emphasis added). Sun rejected the Leninist formula of 'semi-colony' as inaccurate. Such terminology, by suggesting that China was not entirely colonized, misleadingly beguiled Chinese into thinking that their global position was better than that of the colonized peoples whom they denigrated as 'slaves without a country'. Sun grappled for a descriptive term that could bolster his assertion that 'China is everywhere becoming a colony of the Powers', despite the fact that actual colonial enclaves comprised only a tiny portion of its land area. In place of the imperfect appellation 'semi-colony', Sun proffered the label of 'hypo-' or 'sub-colony' (*ci zhimindi*), borrowing the authority of scientific terminology as a cover for his descriptive vagueness:

> Whose 'semi-colony' is China? China is the colony of every nation that has made treaties with her, and the treaty-making nations are her masters. China is not the colony of one nation but of all, and we are not the slaves of one country but of all....So 'semi-colony' is not the right designation for China; I think we ought to be called a 'hypo-colony'. The prefix 'hypo' is taken from chemistry [designating a] lower degree of [a] compound.
>
> *(Sun 1927)*

Lenin had formulated the undeniably imprecise category 'semi-colony', in 1916, to convey what he took to be a 'transitional form'. He placed China in this category, along with Persia and Turkey, suggesting that all three were rapidly becoming colonies. Lenin's intent was not so much to assert a lesser form of domination, *pace* Sun, than to include these countries within his chart of 'Colonial Possessions of the Great Powers', thereby demonstrating the nearly complete partition of the world by the early twentieth century (Lenin 1968: 134–35). Although, Lenin argued, 'finance capital finds most "convenient"…a form of subjection that involves the loss of the political independence of the subjected countries and peoples', he nonetheless insisted that finance capital had become such a powerful international force in the late-nineteenth-century era of capitalist imperialism that 'it is capable of subjecting and actually does subject to itself even states enjoying the fullest political independence' (Lenin 1968: 135).

Unfortunately, Lenin's relative lack of interest in specifying what he took to be transitional, and his use of the prefix 'semi', obscured the precision of his chosen term. Unlike Sun, Lenin was not especially preoccupied with China. He was more concerned to grasp the world through universal categories than to understand the ways in which historical anomalies might refine universal theory. Focusing particularly on China, Sun – by noting the multiplicity of colonial powers active in China – called attention to one aspect of the difference of colonialism in that country. However, his recourse to quantification, and his determined but unprovable claim of *greater* oppression, derailed in a different fashion the specificity of his analysis.

Sun's substituted nomenclature has had generally less currency as a description for China than Lenin's undeveloped idea of the semi-colony (and its official Chinese Marxist adaptation in the formula 'semi-colonial, semi-feudal'); however, continued Chinese references to China's hypo-colonial status persisted under Guomindang rule. A contemporary Western gesture to the lingering 'hypo-colony' notion may be seen in the recent coinage of the neologism 'hypercolony'.[4]

If, in Lenin's original formulation, the semi-colonial was merely transitional and could be classed with the colonial, semi-colonialism was articulated as a somewhat more theoretically and practically complex issue for the Comintern, in murky debates between Stalin and Trotsky, in the context of erupting tensions between the Chinese Communist Party and the Guomindang in 1926–27. For Stalin, China's semi-colonial nature reinforced remnants of feudalism. As a result, the chief internal enemies of the Chinese revolution were the feudal forces of militarists, bureaucrats, and landlords who oppressed the peasantry. Trotsky held, *contra* Stalin, that power was in the hands of a bourgeoisie, and that the Chinese bourgeoisie was tightly linked with foreign imperialism, a diagnosis that prescribed a noncapitalist, social revolutionary path for the Chinese revolution.

These Comintern debates on the character of semi-colonialism and its implications for revolutionary strategy were taken up after 1927 by Guomindang and Chinese Communist Party theorists, who attempted in the following decades to reconcile the accepted diagnosis of 'semi-colonial/semi-feudal' to their differing political goals for China. Guomindang theoreticians generally favored the economic development and state strengthening prescribed by Sun as an antidote to China's 'hypocolonialism', without the debilitating disruptions of class struggle. Communist writers, in the meantime, constructed 'tortuous arguments' in order to explain Chinese social developments 'in terms of Marxian historical categories derived from the European experience' (Dirlik 1978: 81). If imperialism, by nature, oriented China in the direction of capitalism, it also fed upon the feudal oppression of Chinese peasants, prolonging traditional agrarian structures and creating obstacles to progressive development. In the 1937 diagnosis of the CCP writer Wang Xuewen, China 'preserves strong feudal forces, but has entered the path of capitalism in a colony…[O]n the one hand, China has already started developing toward capitalism under the control of international imperialism which is propelling it toward semi-colonialism, while on the other hand, she preserves very strong feudal forces' (Dirlik 1978: 84).[5]

In contrast to Lenin's and Stalin's preoccupation with transhistorical universal principles and an international (or USSR) focus, most Chinese analyses of the 1930s were inclined to bring local preoccupations to bear on the question of semi-colonialism. As Rebecca Karl has noted, this involved attention to 'uneven social relations at the local level that, while not separable from the global/nation-state arena, were nevertheless also not reducible to it' (Karl 2005: 173). Such preoccupations were generally nationally oriented and focused on the state. Karl highlights a popular pamphlet by Chen Hongmin, *Colonialism and Semi-colonialism*, which outlined key aspects of the semi-colonial condition:

> In general semi-colonial countries have a colonial character. Pre-capitalist social relations are superior [*zhan youshi*] in their social formations, and imperialism is in the dominant [*zhan tongzhi diwei*] position…Yet, aside from these general characteristics, semi-colonial countries also have their particularities[:]
>
> 1. The transitional nature of semicolonialism;
> 2. Formal political sovereignty;
> 3. The demand for national unification and the establishment of state capitalism;
> 4. The vacillation between dictatorial and democratic politics;
> 5. The role played by the rejection of global capitalism by semicolonial revolutions.
>
> *(Karl 2005: 177)*[6]

Mao's formulations of the semi-colonial in the 1930s and 1940s, in particular, highlighted the necessity for class struggle and social revolution. Liberation from imperialism, in the context of a weak national bourgeoisie, could only be achieved by the mobilization of the peasants against a feudal rural order through land reform and the linking of national liberation to the revolutionary transformation of the countryside. Though Maoism attended creatively to local Chinese particularities in practice, Mao's writings also reproduced the stock categories of semi-feudal/semi-colonial that would structure subsequent analysis by historians in the People's Republic.

Since the first half of the twentieth century, political theorists and historians alike have generally attached 'semi-colonialism' to China in a formulaic fashion, with little attention to or interest in China's particularity as a terrain for the operations of colonial powers. Consideration for the particular characteristics of semi-colonialism has not developed significantly beyond Osterhammel's observation that there has been no clear mapping of '*where, when, how* and to what *effect* did *which* extraneous forces impinge' on Chinese life. (Osterhammel 1986: 295; Goodman 2000: 889–926.)

Shu-mei Shih has perhaps taken recent theoretical discussion of semi-colonial formations in China furthest, but in another direction, in an inquiry into the cultural and psychological effects of the power rivalries among imperialists in China, the cooperation among them, and the 'multiple layers of domination' to which Chinese were subjected (Shih 2001: 32). Rather than ground her argument historically, Shih follows the rhetorical logic of Sun Yat-sen's assertions that China experienced both a greater intensity of oppression and greater neglect than a formal colony, suggesting that informal empire exempted foreign powers from responsibility for 'colonial benevolence'. While asserting China's greater subordination through 'multiplied controls and augmented exploitation', Shih also emphasizes 'the incomplete and fragmentary nature of China's colonial structure' (Shih 2001: 34–35; Rogaski 2004: 12). This combination of features, she argues, produced a distinctive relationship of domination and subordination. If domination was less formal, it was 'no less destructive and transformative'. At the same time, it 'afforded Chinese intellectuals more varied ideological, political and cultural positions', and unintended spaces for 'multi-directional pursuits'. The effect was a bifurcating mentality through which Chinese intellectuals separated the cultural attainments of colonizers from their colonial projects in China and sanctioned a self-imposed 'cultural colonization'. The presence of multiple colonizers diffused the exercise of power, making it difficult to clearly 'target the enemy', as Shih suggests, and resist (Shih 2001: 35–37). Because the cosmopolitanism of Chinese intellectuals was unrequited and asymmetrical, it was 'self-particularizing' (in that Chinese enacted the universal relevance of European culture without achieving European recognition of Chinese culture). In this context, Shih suggests that Chinese intellectual agency was doubtful, restricted to the 'willing colonization' of Chinese consciousness (Shih 2001: 374).

Shih usefully insists on the combination of multiple but fragmentary control that characterized China's experience of colonialism and the varied options that became available for Chinese intellectuals. Her concern is nonetheless primarily to characterize a generalized 'effect', rather than to pursue the varied workings of particular semi-colonial formations in China in space or time.[7] The discussion proceeds, as well, from several nationalist and postcolonial assumptions: 1) of a sharp colonizer–colonized divide (even if Chinese intellectuals did not see it precisely that way); 2) that intellectuals' adoption of Western or Japanese ideas amounted to 'self-colonization'; and 3) of the efficacy and extensive rupture of colonialism.[8]

Shih's emphasis on semi-colonialism shares common ground with renewed scholarly emphasis in the China field on the broad theme of colonialism and on 'colonial modernity', an emphasis that has been spearheaded, to a degree, by the journal *positions*. Such scholarship – while productive in calling attention to the ways in which China's experience of colonialism was continuous with global European empire-building more broadly – has tended nonetheless to move discussion further from the historical and local specificities that might be conveyed by a terminological distinction between colonialism and what has been variously referred to as 'semi-', 'hypo-', or 'hyper-' colonial (Barlow 2001; Hevia 2003). This recent emphasis on colonialism and China, influenced by postcolonial studies, may be contextualized as a reaction against older historiographical approaches, both the early 'China's response to the West' formulation associated with John Fairbank, and the politically engaged scholarship of the Committee of Concerned Asian Scholars (which sharply criticized the Fairbank school).

Renewed emphasis on colonialism comes also as a departure from historiographical inclinations of the 1980s and 1990s toward what Paul Cohen termed

'China-centered studies', characteristically local studies that emphasized indigenous dynamism and development, often in relation to European markers of modernity, such as the idea of a public sphere (Cohen 1997a). If some local studies (such as those of William Rowe, Mary Rankin, and David Strand) tended to de-emphasize the role of colonialism, others, particularly scholarship on Shanghai, stressed the positive role of the foreign-administered settlements in the cultural dynamism of the city (Wagner 1995; Bergère 2009). Against this historiographical tendency, scholars associated with *positions* have programmatically reasserted the importance of colonialism, focusing most commonly on understanding colonialism's cultural guises, with some highlighting of the full quantum of colonial violence, with little concern for mapping the layout of political, economic, institutional, and cultural configurations of power across the Chinese landscape.

Indeed, China's distinctiveness has been de-emphasized in order to 'bring China into colonial studies' (Hevia 2003: 17).[9] James Hevia's recent examination of colonial violence in nineteenth-century China, for example, emphasizes that, although China was not formally a colony, colonial projects, rhetoric, categories, and practices of violence, plunder, and exhibition nonetheless 'violently plac[ed] China firmly within a colonial world and its forms of power-knowledge' (Hevia 2003: 281). Hevia concludes his study by enumerating systematic resemblances between China and fully colonized settings (lest historians imagine that 'semi-colonialism' meant a gentler form of association) (Hevia 2003: 346).[10] The enfolding of China into the increasingly pervasive, if still vague, concept of 'colonial modernity', which asserts the centrality of imperial domination, a loosely defined colonialism, in the shaping of Asian modernity, has similar effects. 'Colonial modernity', as an analytical concept, does not distinguish qualitatively among localities, since all are subject to the global circulation of a Eurocentric modernity (Barlow 1997). In practice the concept is universalizing and lends itself to an emphasis on the global over the local.

If it is well to be reminded of the violence at the core of colonial enterprises, there is little in such broad evocations of colonialism that specifies the complex operations of multiple enclaves, 'on the ground' in China, points and lines that by their presence (if not express design) substantially reconfigured patterns of power and the circulations of people, capital, and ideas across the Chinese landscape. Attention to some of this complexity may facilitate critical reflection about universal models or abstract theorization of the workings of colonialism across space and time, in China and elsewhere. Recognition of the distinctive character of colonial ventures in China need not be seen as suggesting that these ventures were not also continuous, in various respects, with European empire-building on a global scale.

China's 'contact zones' (Pratt 1992: 4–7), sites of asymmetrical relations created by the exercise of colonial power on Chinese soil, hosted widely divergent local arrangements. In places where a single power held sway, such as Hong Kong or Qingdao, there could be unified administration. The development and fate of each was nonetheless powerfully affected by the looming proximity of 'China' as a neighbouring or surrounding presence. In treaty-ports such as Shanghai or Hankou, on the other hand, where multiple foreign enclaves competed for turf side-by-side and with bordering urban areas of Chinese jurisdiction, the institutions of each delimited the powers of the others.

Different formations emerged from different imperial ambitions. Early colonial powers such as Britain projected different goals for their China toeholds than latecomers such as Germany, Japan, and Italy. Shifting relations among the metropoles changed the colonial topography (for example, the First World War forced Germany to relinquish Qingdao to Japan). Moreover, the evolving character and changing legitimacy of imperialism created distinctive formations on the Chinese landscape at different points in time. As Prasenjit Duara has observed, in the period after the First World War, developing notions of legitimacy and authenticity, in particular the rise of anti-imperialist nationalism, challenged some colonial powers to move beyond the formal colonialism of the previous century as they competed to control global resources. As Japan occupied north-east China in the 1930s, it pursued novel developmental policies by creating the puppet state of Manchukuo, rather than a formal colony (Duara 2003: 19). Different colonial powers responded in different ways to growing challenges to the legitimacy of their hold on pieces of China, as may be seen in the distinctive ideologies of Japanese pan-Asianism and the Portuguese propagation of the myth of 'lusotropicalism', a claim to a distinctively humane and democratic form of colonialism based on racial mixing.

These multifarious, partial, and discrete constellations of colonial power on Chinese soil developed at different historical moments and in interaction with different local population groups and sectors of society. The large areas of China that were geographically remote from areas of contact and untouched by foreign presence were nonetheless permeable to shifting economic developments and flows of news and ideas, albeit indirect and delayed. Such areas also influenced treaty-port life (or life in colonial Hong Kong), providing alternative spaces and models (positive and negative) of Chinese society, culture, and residence, and serving as a source for sectors of the urban population, sending sojourners, students, and refugees.[11] Inland areas of China also depleted urban resources as sojourners sent remittances and funded public works in their impoverished or war-torn native places (Goodman 1995: 219–20).

The cast of colonial institutions operating across China was similarly broad and diverse, encompassing national diplomatic missions, railroad and mining operations, medical and charitable missions, and the strikingly hybrid foreign-administered departments of the Chinese central government: the powerful Chinese Maritime Customs Service that collected duties and policed waterways and administered a post office; and a salt administration, smaller in scope.

The panoply of judicial arrangements across the Chinese landscape required practicing lawyers, Chinese and foreign, to gain expertise in multiple legal systems. In early twentieth-century Shanghai alone, to accommodate the divided jurisdictions of the city, extraterritoriality, and the mixed residence of Chinese and foreigners in the settlements there was a Chinese court for the Chinese residents of Chinese areas of the city; a hybrid International Mixed Court (providing for Chinese residents of the International Settlement joint hearings by a foreign assessor and a

Chinese judge); a similar French Mixed Court for the French Concession; courts exclusively for foreign nationals such as the United States Court for China, and various consular courts. The enduring effects on Chinese legal practice of this spatially uneven multiplicity of legal systems and institutions has yet to be probed.

Additionally, there were supra-colonial formations like the Diplomatic Body in Beijing, which brought together envoys and plenipotentiary ministers from 15 countries. Consular Bodies brought together European and US diplomatic representatives within one treaty-port. That the diverse agglomeration of international treaties that anchored this loosely interwoven web of arrangements is termed the 'treaty system' gives an appearance of agency and coherence to the disorganized logic of global capitalism that expanded fitfully and indirectly through the improvisations of multiple and only loosely coordinated agents. These included metropolitan powers engaged in imperial expansion, sojourning and settler communities, overseas Chinese networks, and local residents.

In view of the diversity of actors and institutions involved, Robert Bickers and Christian Henriot have argued that it may be useful to think in terms of a 'network of overlapping imperialisms' that did not directly serve the imperial interests of colonial powers. They suggest that, within this network of overlapping imperialisms, 'the treaty system effectively replaced the state as the defining organizational frame, and the treaty system and its citizens were international' (Bickers and Henriot 2000: 5). This would seem to go too far. Though forms of international community indeed existed in the treaty-port world, the proliferating nationalisms of the era call into question the idea that states and national loyalties were displaced. Nor could it be maintained that Chinese and non-Chinese subjects of the treaty system occupied positions comparable with citizenship. Scholarship in this vein has nonetheless been pathbreaking in forcing recognition of all manner of liminal identities and collaborations that thrived in the interstices of imperial mappings, and in pressing scholars to go beyond binary and nationally oriented understandings of colonial processes in China, to engage China's difference, and to engage the global complexities that came together historically on Chinese soil.

Colonial interactions: people, communities, and identities

Within China's contact zones, colonial agency created new social actors and attracted others, some deliberately (through the insertion of consular and policing structures), and some by accident (as a result of economic and social opportunities, or new transportation infrastructures). Varied local, overlapping, and at times competing structures of governance contended with and negotiated among these newer and older social groups and networks. Research in the past decade in archives within and outside China – in accordance with interpretive trends in colonial studies more broadly – has increasingly recognized the empirical ambiguities of Chinese and foreign interactions, substantially challenging nationally oriented narratives of subjugation and liberation and abstract binaries of colonizer–colonized. This has included noting the complexities of ethnicity, class, and nationality within foreign populations in China, and the contingent spaces of business opportunity, citizenship, settlement, and privilege opened up by multiple colonial enterprises. (Cooper and Stoler 1997; Bickers and Henriot 2000.)

These spaces were peopled by diplomatic, commercial, missionary, settler, and refugee communities. Within these networks and communities, lines of identity were complex, multilayered, and pragmatic. Reflecting on a variety of colonial, refugee, and immigrant treaty-port communities, Robert Bickers and Christian Henriot have described an 'interpenetration of interests' that blurred distinctions between colonizers and indigenous 'colonized' (Bickers and Henriot 2000: 5).

Several studies have called attention to the different ways that pre-existing regional or ethnic identities and networks among 'indigenous' people affected their interactions with colonizers, and their 'Chinese' identities. People from Guangzhou (Canton), in particular, specialized as early cultural intermediaries, servants, and compradors, moving north with the British as the treaty-ports opened in the mid-nineteenth century (Goodman 1995: 47–83). At the end of the century, rivalries among different native-place networks complicated national identities and could overshadow preoccupation with a Chinese–foreigner divide. Elite identities or commercial interests could similarly prove more significant (Goodman 2000). At another level, minority communities within the Qing empire (for example, Tanka boat people), treated as outcastes by local Cantonese, quickly grasped new business opportunities in colonial Hong Kong, transforming themselves into a local Hongkong bourgeoisie that actively collaborated with the colonial government (Carroll 2005: 22).

Overseas Chinese represented one among several striking and paradoxical, but eminently practical, configurations of identity found in the colonial contact zones of China. Overseas Chinese moved along the circuits of empire as citizens, at times engaging in a reverse form of sojourning, drawn to colonial spaces within China by opportunities provided by their combination of native identity and colonial nationality, and their multiple linguistic and cultural proficiencies as businessmen, translators, and cultural intermediaries (Carroll 2005: 191; Goodman 2004b). Taiwanese, colonized subjects of Japan, for example, took advantage of their status as Japanese within Japanese-colonized areas of China. There, together with migrant Koreans, who enjoyed the privileges of extraterritoriality, Taiwanese migrants contributed substantially – intentionally and unintentionally – to the expansion of Japanese imperial community (Brooks 2000).

Chinese population movements similarly blurred the colonizer–colonized and foreign–indigenous divides, and also complicate interpretations that might attribute the economic dynamism of China's colonial spaces to colonial agency. John Carroll has described how the Taiping Rebellion gave rise to a process of Chinese immigration to and settlement in colonial Hong Kong, without which the economy would have floundered (Carroll 2005: 22). Meng Yue has suggested a similar process for Shanghai, finding 'the city's 'rise' as a cultural center a paradoxical outcome of the catastrophes of the Qing Empire', in that Jiangnan elites fleeing rebellion, together with all manner of 'unruly elements', filled the city (Yue 2006). Both scholars have reconsidered 'the complicit relationship between Chinese society and imperialism' (Yue 2006: xix) from the perspective of Chinese society, finding spaces of considerable freedom, choice, agency, and economic prosperity, without denying the hierarchical power relations of imperialism. Reconsiderations of Chinese agency, and the intertwined tensions, dependencies, and mutual empowerment of Chinese networks and colonial structures, are given transnational scope in Philip Kuhn's recent portrayal of Chinese merchants overseas as 'coadjutors' with Europeans and Southeast Asian monarchs in the machinations of colonial empire (Kuhn 2009).

Plural colonialisms and differential effects

As Osterhammel has observed, colonialism is a 'phenomenon of colossal vagueness'. (Osterhammel 1997: 4) Responding to the renewed scholarly discussion of colonialism that has been spurred by postcolonial studies in the past two decades (and a concomitant tendency to model colonialism upon British India), the Pacific Island anthropologist Nicholas Thomas has emphasized a need to both localize and historicize colonialism. To avoid banality, generalizations that fit only specific cases, or ungrounded assumptions regarding the efficacy or impact of colonialism, Thomas proposes that colonialism 'can only be traced through its plural and particularized expressions' (Thomas 1994: ix, 3, 55). Taking a step further Thomas's critique of globalizing theories of colonial discourse, Africa historian Frederick Cooper has suggested that 'the field has become unmoored from analyses of processes unfolding over time…which makes the identification of structures, agency, and causality fade from view'. Emphasizing diversity and contingency, Cooper also advocates thinking about multiple colonialisms – as opposed to a one-size-fits-all model – in conceptualizing colonial situations, so as 'not to diminish the importance of the specific forms of colonization', and to enable precise analysis of colonial processes (Cooper 2005: 52–53).

This volume is stimulated by recent discussion of the nature of colonialism in China, critical debate in colonial studies more broadly, and a growing base of empirical scholarship, research that now extends beyond a single China site or a single metropole. If Shanghai studies remain especially bountiful, recent impulses to look 'beyond Shanghai' have challenged Shanghai's representational status (Esherick 2000). Drawing on archives across Europe, Asia, and the USA as well as Southeast Asia and Australia (to include overseas Chinese in the picture), the scholarship in this volume highlights the varied and changing articulations of colonialism in China by bringing together studies of a variety of places, institutions, and actors along the itinerary of China's colonial experience. The collection of studies localizes discussion of colonial projects in historically specific twentieth-century sites, and juxtaposes different powers, institutions, geographies, social agents, moments, and colonial spaces. This juxtaposition is important, not simply to provide comparative context, but because, as Frederick Cooper has noted, 'imperialisms existed in relation to one another' (Cooper 2005: 53). Different colonial ideologies and technologies circulated through various colonial networks, and in China, each successive treaty power established its position in relation to the others. A multiplicity of colonial styles was a feature of everyday life. In a city such as Tianjin, in the space of an afternoon, an individual could pass through six or more national colonial enclaves, choosing goods and services as he or she pleased (Hersey 1982).

Although the combination of studies in this volume does permit comparison of particular French, British, Japanese, or German interventions in China, the intent is not to reify national styles of colonialism. On the contrary, juxtaposition of varied portraits of colonial governance, at different moments, in inland and treaty-port sites, or different social spaces (public or domestic), should help to interrogate such characterizations.[12] Multiple views are offered of particular sites in order to avoid the construction of something like 'a Hong Kong model' or a 'Shanghai model'. The project is attentive to local specificities as well as to certain aggregate effects – which went beyond the particularities of the individual contact zones – as a corrective to the type of generalization and imprecision that has often obscured historical understandings of colonialism in China and elsewhere.

Because the individual chapters elaborate local specificities, it is useful here to evoke briefly some of the distinctive effects of the broader pattern of colonial formations across the Chinese landscape. Some of these have already been touched upon in discussion of semi-colonialism, though they have not been systematically assessed.

First, extraterritoriality and the multiplicity and often side-by-side presence of different foreign settlements, along with areas of Chinese jurisdiction within treaty-ports, created multiple, alternate, and interstitial spaces. These attracted a variety of social groups – immigrants, refugees, revolutionaries, businessmen, intellectuals, criminals. Negotiation, accommodation, and contestation among these groups, elements within Chinese society, and the various Chinese and foreign municipal formations were complex, with no party definitively responsible or 'in control'.

The major treaty-ports owed much of their draw to their multiple jurisdictions that offered security beyond the reach of Chinese authorities; new opportunities; and limitations on any overarching control, prior to the 1930s. Although Shu-mei Shih makes the theoretical claim of 'snowballing exploitations', archival research has tended to emphasize the incoherence, improvisation, collaboration, fragmentary governance, heterogeneity, and relatively open character of such spaces (Wagner 1995; Martin 1996; Bickers and Henriot 2000; Yeh 2006; Bergère 2009). Certainly, multiple occupying powers at crucial moments cooperated to compel coercion. This was the case in Tianjin after suppression of the Boxer Uprising in 1900, when a multinational occupying army for two years 'enforced new ways of behavior at gunpoint', as Ruth Rogaski reminds us (Rogaski 2004: 13). Such violent assertions of colonial power were fundamental to the enterprise, but were also localized and relatively short-lived, only temporarily disrupting population flows to such areas. Meng Yue has recently called for renewed attention to the 'ungovernable' elements that flocked into the spaces of Shanghai, 'a haven for outlaws, as well as a cradle of anarchists, anti-Qing revolutionaries, early Chinese communists, radical journalists, and strikers and demonstrators against imperialism' (Yue 2006: xxv).[13] It is worthwhile to recognize these flows and the attractiveness of these spaces, not in terms of colonial intentions, but as an unintended and contingent consequence of particular local formations.

Second, if extraterritoriality hampered the sovereignty of both the Qing and Republican-era governments and created accidental spaces for refugee communities, it was also routinely manipulated to benefit particular Chinese groups or individuals. In the early twentieth century it was well recognized, for example, that prominent Chinese newspapers and newspaper-owners acquired foreign partners (or papers) and registered with foreign consulates. This could be a source of dismay to competing foreign journalists, as attested by an alarm sounded in an October 1924 issue of the English-language *Far Eastern Review*, entitled 'Prostituting extraterritoriality: legalizing the sale of protection to Chinese citizens, a practice involving the ownership of foreign newspapers in China' (Goodman 2004a: 66–67). The author warned gravely that such practices threatened 'to hand over to Chinese control the organs of foreign public opinion' and erode the privileges of extraterritoriality. This is not to say, of course, that there was anything approximating equal opportunity access to extraterritoriality, but it is to note the ambiguities of agency and empowerment that existed within colonial frameworks.[14]

Third, a consequence of the presence of multiple imperialists was the production of multiple models of modernity. As Shanghai Chinese residents sought associational frameworks for citizenship, for example, the local profusion of representative structures and governance led to a 'fanciful, redundant and grandiose variety of associational forms and political initiatives', a superabundance of forms adapted from local European, American, and Japanese formations in the city, in addition to reworkings of earlier Chinese forms of association (Goodman 2003). Whereas more unitary colonial cultures were created in sites colonized exclusively by one power, such as Hong Kong or Qingdao, the smallness of such spaces, and the circulations of people through them, contributed to the particularization (rather than the universalization) of specific colonial discourses and to their general multiplicity across China.

Fourth, the confusions of multiple imperialisms across China necessitated some communication and coordination, leading to the formation of multinational and hybrid mechanisms of administration, as in the Diplomatic Corps, on the one hand, or on the other, the extraordinary, largely British-staffed Chinese Maritime Customs Service that turned customs revenues over to successive Chinese governments while collecting trade information, policing waterways, and constructing a lighthouse system to make China navigable and legible for the interests of global commerce.

Fifth, the fact that China preserved formal independence, retained sovereignty over most of its territory, and was at least nominally recognized as a sovereign nation by international law may be taken to be not simply a quantitative difference from an always incomplete colonialism, but a qualitative distinction that produced a different relation between colonized and colonizer and different experiences of governance. It meant that most Chinese did not consider themselves to be subjects of a foreign power, that a Chinese polity existed in the international pantheon of nations, and that the treaty system that was the instrument of colonial agency in China would be mediated by a Chinese state, however compromised. Anne Reinhardt's recent study of the introduction and gradual expansion of the steam-shipping network in China, as a field of evolving interaction among foreign and Chinese actors, maps the considerable political, economic, and diplomatic agency of successive Chinese governments, an agency that cannot be characterized by notions of either resistance or collaboration (Reinhardt 2002). As Qing and Republican-era governments in turn were held responsible for China's global weakness, the logic of blame turned inward and Chinese nation-building required revolution. In the meantime, colonial enclaves in treaty-ports and on China's margins were especially difficult to sustain, given continuing interactions with the Chinese political polity and Chinese population movements across boundaries.

Sixth, the relative prominence of foreigners and colonial structures in coastal cities and inland ports and their relative paucity elsewhere meant that modernizing reforms took on a particular spatial aspect. For example, pressed to reform its legal institutions as a precondition for the restitution of full legal sovereignty, in the Nanjing Decade (1927–37) the Guomindang government produced new-style Chinese courts and judicial regulations, prisons, and judicial personnel in the major treaty-ports, where they were visible to metropolitan authorities. These coexisted and interacted with the largely unchanged Chinese administration of justice in inland areas, with the result that the Republican era was characterized by two co-existing modes of Chinese judicial administration, old and new, depending on location (Xu 2008).

Finally, foreign nationals in China adopted very different strategies in different locations, depending on local populations, power formations, and structures of support. This was not just a matter of the unevenness of colonialism, that, as Cooper has suggested, was 'arterial' in most contexts, 'strong near the nodal points of colonial authority, less able to impose its discursive grid elsewhere'. In the multiple grids that crossed the Chinese landscape, one finds foreigners marketing their skills at both foreign and Chinese nodes of power (in the latter as lawyers, journalists, and all manner of military and civilian advisors, who often imagined themselves to be working for China or acting as independent agents, rather than representing any foreign power) (Selle 1948; Lewis 1989).

Insufficiently protected foreigners who ventured into Chinese-governed (and ungoverned) territory could become bargaining chips in Chinese internecine power struggles, as when, especially during the 1920s and 1930s, bandit chiefs seized on the value of foreigners as 'foreign tickets' through which they could often negotiate army appointments for themselves from Chinese authorities.[15] These disparate possibilities came together in the remarkable Lincheng Incident of 1923, involving the kidnapping of 27 foreigners of various nationalities by a confederation of Chinese bandits who held up a train. Kidnapped in Chinese territory, their release could be negotiated only by the Chinese government. In the event, the envoy of the Chinese government who negotiated with the bandits was the legendary, if mysterious, Roy Anderson, an American born and raised in China (Nozinski 1990).

Localities, the everyday, and the world

The goal of this volume, and the workshop from which it emerged, was to understand the complexities and subtleties of colonialism in China in the twentieth century. The focus of the project has been to understand the interaction between localities and forces of globalization that shaped the particular colonial experiences characterizing much of China's experience at this time. An emphasis on interaction, synergy, and the development of hybrid (if often hierarchically charged) social and institutional frameworks can add much to an understanding of colonialism in twentieth-century China, for which the binaries of colonizer and colonized and of aggressor and victim, and a one-way transfer of knowledge and social understanding, are inadequate. To order the analysis, the chapters in this volume are arranged into thematic sections that examine: 1) colonial governance, hybridity, and questions of identity; 2) colonial spaces and everyday social interactions; and 3) late colonialism and local consequences.

Colonial governance and questions of identity

This first section examines fields of interaction in a variety of colonial spaces that joined multiple peoples in the improvised social and institutional frameworks of China's contact zones. Three chapters, one on the crucially important but insufficiently analysed Sino–foreign Chinese Maritime Customs Service; one on the German colony of Qingdao as a venue for the formation of organized Chinese nationalism; and the third on the development of Chinese securities exchanges in Shanghai, suggest, in different ways, how distinctive contact zones shaped state, political, and economic formations and, in the process, renegotiated the identities of actors and institutions.

Although seen by some as a structure of British imperialism, one of the best recognized examples of improvised colonial/Chinese hybridity was the Chinese Maritime Customs Service (CMCS), the rich records of which are only recently undergoing systematic examination. In chapter 1 on the development and operation of this central pillar of the treaty-port era, Robert Bickers homes in on the question of *whose* interests and powers were involved in its activities. Bickers traces the ways in which the CMCS served the Chinese state, and the ways in which its ordering of Chinese affairs also served the imperial powers. For the Chinese state, the CMCS brought revenue as well as a measure of regulation in a series of localities. For the imperial powers, and especially for the British, it provided an alternative to settler colonialism, providing a systematic machinery for the development of economic interests. Though exercising a panoply of governmental functions, the diffuse nature and location of its activities essentially prevented it from becoming an autonomous sub-unit of the state itself.

Chapter 2, by Klaus Mühlhahn, on the shift from violent coercion to colonial governance in German Qingdao, 1897–1914, and the mutual formation of colonialism and nationalism, examines questions of metropolitan and native agency and identity in a formal colony that was unusual in a number of regards. Qingdao was originally designed as a naval colony that would showcase the glory of German socio-economic and technological development to the world. Although Qingdao was never intended as a settler colony (there were at most about 4300 Germans in Qingdao before 1914, and always very few women) the German government poured vast quantities of money into developing its 'model' colony. Chinese reactions to Qingdao and German colonization were not as straightforwardly subservient as descriptions of German colonialism would seem to warrant. As Mühlhahn recounts, the development of the colony engendered not simply political resistance from the Chinese, but also structured organized political opposition that played a significant role in the emergence of modern Chinese nationalism. In tracing this process, he draws attention to the chronological trajectory of colonial experience in China and the importance of global influences as well as of local interactions between Chinese and Germans.

In chapter 3, the final chapter in this section, Bryna Goodman takes up the question of Chinese constructions of Western- and Japanese-modeled institutions. Here the highlight is the rapid development and equally rapid demise in 1920–21 of Chinese stock exchanges, an economic institution that proved spectacularly dysfunctional in the treaty-port environment. Western colonial extraterritoriality motivated and facilitated the emergence of local stock exchanges in these years. Goodman examines the development of Chinese exchanges, highlighting the role of semi-colonial encounters in the history of foreign and Chinese stock exchanges in the city. She then considers the ideological ramifications of these semi-colonial encounters, and the way that anti-imperialist rhetoric provided legitimation for stock exchange development and created anxiety over the national purity of Chinese capital, while diverting attention from the structures of extraterritorial jurisdiction that facilitated the multiplication of the exchanges. The discussion of Shanghai's exchanges and the 1920–21 boom concludes with consideration of the cultural particularities of the semi-colonial context. From the desires that underlay their inception to the sentiments aroused by their demise, the early Shanghai stock exchanges were haunted by the nationalist ambitions, mixed company, multiple and fragmentary political jurisdictions, and cultural anxieties that inhabited the interstices of semi-colonial Shanghai.

Colonial spaces and everyday social interactions

The everyday social interactions of European colonialists and Chinese are examined in five chapters dealing with Tianjin, Hong Kong, Shanghai, and areas of French presence in southern China.

Segregation, its consequences, and the ambiguities of maintaining the social aspects of colonialism, especially in housing, are the subject of John Carroll's study of the Peak in Hong Kong (chapter 4). Carroll locates the Peak in its colonial context as a healthy retreat for the colonialists. Unlike other colonial hill stations, common throughout Asia, where expatriates removed themselves from the heat of the summer, the Peak was a year-round operation. In Hong Kong there was undoubtedly a drive for social exclusivity amongst the European communities. At the same time, there were two countervailing pressures. One was the attitude of the British Foreign and Colonial Office, which, increasingly during the twentieth century, did not want to be seen as discriminatory against colonized peoples. The other countervailing pressure was the emergence of rich Chinese and Eurasians, each of whom were seen as being able to make legitimate claims to live in European areas, whether those areas were sanctioned by law (as was the case for a time in the Peak) or by custom. One solution for Hong Kong was to turn at least public discussion into one about 'the right kind of people' rather than relying on racial stereotypes and identities.

As in Hong Kong, the development of housing and accommodation in the Italian concession in Tianjin was predicated on cleanliness and hygiene as a point of significant difference between colonialists and Chinese. The monumental architecture of the former Italian concession – with its nineteenth-century neo-renaissance style, for private housing as well as municipal buildings – has recently been reconstituted as a relic for historical preservation in modern Tianjin. In chapter 5, Maurizio Marinelli focuses on the ways that a once obvious monument to Italian imperial ambition has now become reconceptualized as a marker for economic and cultural interactions between China and Italy. The key to this transformation was in developments soon after the establishment of the concession, when its Italian nature was reinforced by self-description as a community 'neighborhood', deliberately constructed with a different civilizing mission from some earlier outposts of empire. Nonetheless, as Marinelli points out, this was little more than a sleight of hand. The real goal at the time, and especially during the 1930s, remained imperial bragging rights rather than cultural interactions between equals.

If architecture framed and visually organized the circuits of daily life in China's colonial contact zones, an essential aspect of the modernist discourses that engendered colonialism was the claim to control of individual corporeality, in death as well as in life. The management of death and illness is examined in chapters 6 and 7, respectively, on Shanghai and on the French area of influence in southern China. In Shanghai, conflict over burial space framed the expansion of colonial enclaves in the city (Goodman 1995: 158–72). In chapter 6, Christian Henriot details conflict and competition in the history of modern Shanghai's cemeteries. There was of course the obvious divide between the colonialists and their search for burial space, and the Chinese and their own burial arrangements. But at the same time, commercial considerations complicated this relationship as Chinese landowners attempted to benefit from the expanding city's need for burial space, especially for different colonial populations. As Henriot highlights, the various residents of the city might have lived relatively integrated lives, but in death they were rigorously segregated by community, religion, and even, to some extent, class. Rigid hierarchies divided the colonial communities as much as, if not more than, they separated colonialists from Chinese.

The history of the French sphere of influence in Southern China is relatively unexamined, especially in English language sources; however, French materials have much to tell about the spatial dispersion of power and influence. In her analysis of French health care provision to local residents, Florence Bretelle-Establet (chapter 7) examines the impact of French doctors and French medicine. French colonial administrators originally attempted to extend their health care system to these parts of China in order to protect their colony in Indochina. Though the French understood the expansion into southern China of the French medical system as a symbol of expanding French civilization, French doctors necessarily operated differently in the leased territory of Guangzhouwan, where colonial rule pertained, than in the treaty-ports, with their mixed foreign residence. While the colonial administrators might have seen the provision of health care and disease management as a way of expanding influence, the reality was much more limited. For locals, French medicine was more often than not seen as supplementary to more established practices; there was little tolerance for long-term or indirect solutions to medical problems, and conversely more of a demand for immediate, miraculous cure.

Chapter 8, the final chapter in this section, shifts focus to consider colonialism and private and domestic space. European colonialists who came to China at the end of the nineteenth and beginning of the twentieth centuries were often accompanied by their families. Walther Frey was a leading architect in China 1910–38 and a mainstay of the German community in Tianjin before 1914. Yixu Lu and David Goodman present a view of colonial life as reflected in the correspondence of his sister Elisabeth, who visited during 1913 and 1914 from Stuttgart, and who wrote a series of letters back to her mother in Germany. Intended as a diary from the start, these letters reveal many of the ambiguities of the expatriate colonial experience. Elisabeth was determined to enjoy China, but as a convinced expatriate, one of whose aims was to establish a Swabian lifestyle in Tianjin. Her observations on violence are particularly interesting, emphasizing as she did the brutishness of Chinese society, but ignoring simultaneously the violence of her own behavior towards the Chinese with whom she came into contact.

Late colonialism and local consequences

Four chapters in this section take up questions of the local effects of late colonial governance, in four spatial environments: Shanghai's cosmopolitan artistic world, Chinese–Australian merchant pathways, Hong Kong, and Macau. Each author considers a different geography and era, underscoring the distinctive landscapes and chronologies of colonial experiences in China.

Chapters 9 and 10 illuminate the cultural and ideological effects of colonial experience, first, in artistic circles in Shanghai, and second, in the trajectories of highly mobile Chinese–Australian émigrés, who found that Britain's maritime trade routes provided congenial pathways for their enterprises as well as their introduction of 'a new style of commercial egalitarianism'. Both chapters demonstrate the difficulties of analysing the relationship between metropole and colonized in simplistic terms, as a one-way relationship. Chinese increasingly engaged with wider ideas and technologies through interaction with the rest of the world in contact zones and through social mobility. Resistance and attraction coexisted from the Chinese perspective, no less than in the minds of many Europeans.

In chapter 9, Yiyan Wang examines Shanghai as a crucible of modernism and debates over the direction of Chinese art modernization. Specifically, she examines the interaction of the pressures of modernism, colonialism, and national revival on intellectuals through a focus on the events surrounding China's First National Art Exhibition in Shanghai in 1929. Wang demonstrates that Shanghai's cosmopolitan atmosphere was conducive to modernist pursuits in art and literature and led to considerable achievement on the part of China's *avant garde* movement. However, because China's modernization of art was conceived primarily as a means of nation building, the avant garde movement had to give way to realism as early as the 1920s. The broader global frame entailed that choices over artistic styles for Chinese modern art were limited, as they were enacted essentially as responses to colonial presence and Western dominance.

Chapter 10 moves beyond China's territorial borders to the transnational communities of overseas Chinese who inhabited the pathways of British empire. John Fitzgerald examines networks of Chinese–Australians as they negotiated rights and claims through appeals to Chinese and colonial governments, based on both the ostensibly universal ideals enshrined in treaties and a sense of natural justice. Fitzgerald highlights the agency of Chinese–Australians in the transfer of ideas and economic practices in both China and Australia. Despite Australia's later hostility to Chinese immigration, a significant population of Chinese–Australians, especially from the southern counties of Guangdong (notably Heungshan, today's Zhongshan County), played key roles in establishing modern retail enterprises in Hong Kong and Shanghai, as well as in the development of Melbourne and Sydney. While their greater impact on China was in business development, as Fitzgerald notes, this was also a route for the transfer of other modern ideas, such as equality before the law and of citizens. In this context, Liang Qichao's 1900–01 visit to Australia played a central role.

The final two chapters in this section bring the chronological frame closer to the present. Looking at the distinctive environments of Hong Kong and Macao, they examine the processes by which the balance of power between the metropole and the colonized shifted in favor of the latter by the end of the twentieth century.

Although Hong Kong is often taken to be the standard by which European colonialism is measured, its relationship to the metropole did not stay constant, especially in the twentieth century. In chapter 11, Prasenjit Duara examines how Hong Kong's relationship with the United Kingdom began to change dramatically in the immediate post-war era, especially with the advent of the Cold War. In this analysis, he highlights the emergence of an authoritarian capitalism unusual in post-colonial societies, where a more prominent discourse of nationalism usually results in greater state provision of welfare. During the 1930s, a new form of imperialism had emerged, in which new economic empires relied not on totally subservient colonies, but on subordinate territories becoming nominally independent sovereign states. After Japan's defeat, and with the challenge of Communism in Asia, Hong Kong's relationship to the United Kingdom became increasingly subject to similar economic and diplomatic pressures. When added to the Sterling Crisis during and after the Suez Crisis, the result was both the increasing importance of Hong Kong to the United Kingdom's economic stability, and the colony's ability to check the metropole in that relationship. With the Sterling Crisis of the mid-1960s, the colony was able to establish its financial autonomy and substantially shift the relationship in its favor, or at least in favor of its economic elites.

It is fitting that the final chapter looks at Macau, the oldest European colony in twentieth-century China, having been established in the mid-sixteenth century as part of Portugal's attempt to establish a series of fortified ports across the Indian Ocean and South China Seas. Macau was also the last colony, becoming part of the People's Republic of China only in 1999. Anti-government riots during the winter of 1966–67, usually linked to the PRC's Cultural Revolution, resulted in what is often seen as the colonial government's capitulation to the PRC, so that from then on until 1999 it was regarded as a 'half-liberated area'. Cathryn Clayton's research reveals a more complex series of explanations for the events of 1966–67 than simply a clash between the colonized and the colonial power. In chapter 12, Clayton both examines in detail the social groups involved in the colony's immediate politics, and reaches back to Portugal's longer-term relative powerlessness in the colony. The Macau administration had a distinctive and long-established practice of compromise with the Chinese state. It was this capacity for 'apologies and capitulation' that paradoxically enabled it to outlast other colonial entities.

The contributions presented in this volume together highlight the diversity and complexity of colonial interventions and Chinese reactions and interactions, with attention to multiple and fragmentary colonial formations, the persistent agency of a nominally sovereign Chinese state, the making and renegotiation of identities, and a host of Chinese–foreign interactions that defy characterization in the simple (and often anachronistic) terms of collaboration or resistance. While these essays sometimes touch on conflict between mutually exclusive civilizational myths, they also emphasize the inherent syncretism of the colonial environment. In the process, this volume underscores the importance of observing colonial China from the everyday and specifically local perspective, as well as noting the impact of globalization over the course of the twentieth century.

Notes

1 In 1849 Portugal ceased rent payments to China, abolished the Chinese customs, and declared Macau an independent colony.
2 Osterhammel (1997) suggests the concept of 'informal empire' to describe such zones of imperialist intrusion that were distinct from fully organized colonies. Whereas formal empire implies exclusive colonial rule over a territory, informal empire could coexist with an 'Open Door', that is, equal opportunity among metropoles.
3 Sino-British and Sino-American treaties in January 1943 terminated British and American extraterritorial claims. Italy terminated its claims in stages between 1943 and 1945. France abandoned extraterritoriality in 1946 (Bickers 2004; Cornet 2004).

4 Rogaski (2004) correctively substituted 'hyper' for 'hypo' in her book on late Qing and Republican Tianjin as a means of highlighting the multiplicity of (and competition among) colonial powers in that city, which housed more foreign settlements than any other in the first decades of the twentieth century (British, French, German, Italian, Austro-Hungarian, Japanese, Belgian and Russian). The limited definition and scope of 'hypercolony' does not make it broadly applicable beyond major treaty ports. But the term is useful, nonetheless, like the imperfect 'semi-colony', as a potential marker of the historical distinctiveness of colonial formations in China.
5 Wang Hsueh-wen, in *Shehui kexue jiangzuo*, quoted in Ho, *Zhongguo shehui xingzhi wenti lunzhan* [*Controversy on the Question of the Nature of Chinese Society*], Shanghai, 1937, pp. 61–62, translated and cited in Dirlik 1978: 84.
6 Chen Hongjin, *Zhimindi yu banzhimindi* [*Colonialism and Semicolonialism*], Shanghai: Heibai congshu, 1937, translated in Karl (2005): 174. An alternative formulation of the semi-colonial by economist Wang Ya'nan displaced Chen's emphasis on political sovereignty with concern with Chinese 'compradore–bureaucratic capitalism' and other aspects of the semi-colonial, semi-feudal equation. Karl highlights Wang's critique, as distinct from most party theorists, of 'the notion that there were neatly demarcated foreign and Chinese economic sectors in spatially distinct realms', alongside his refutation of Trotsky's conflation of a foreign and Chinese bourgeoisie. Most interestingly, Wang displaced assumptions of the primacy of Euro-American agency in the process and suggested instead that China's particular semi-colonial formation of capitalism necessitated 'structural revisions in capitalism itself, at the same time as it forced structural revisions in China's relations of production/society' (Karl 2005: 177).
7 Because her focus is limited to two decades of literary modernism, she does not attend to the complexities of colonial formations or their transformations on the ground (and she assumes the universality of the cultural effects of semi-colonialism, though she does not look at the mind-frames of those outside of the literary schools that are her emphasis). In the end, the diagnosis of semicolonialism as a psychological pathology appears reductive and formulaic.
8 Although some of Shih's analysis insists on the difference of semi-colonialism, in other parts she relies on generalized notions of the operations of colonialism more broadly, as theorized by postcolonial scholars such as Ashis Nandy (Shih 2001: 137).
9 At times Hevia argues, alternatively, for the broader relevance of the concept of semi-colonialism, because all colonialism was incomplete: 'we might consider all the entities produced in the age of empire as forms of semi-colonialism, especially British India' (Hevia 2003: 26).
10 Though it may be true that all colonial projects were messy and incomplete, and that 'no two colonial enterprises launched by even a single imperial power were the same', caveats Hevia acknowledges (p. 19), it is not the case that the ubiquity of difference simply obscures the fundamental sameness of colonial formations across time and space, a conclusion that might be drawn from the logic of Hevia's study.
11 John Carroll offers an important account of the role of these Chinese spaces in the making of Hong Kong, in particular, the flight to Hong Kong of Chinese merchants who sought to escape the Taiping Rebellion. He suggests, ironically, that if the rebellion was devastating for the mainland, it was good for the colony, indeed, an essential 'cure for Hong Kong's economic woes' (Carroll 2005: 48).
12 George Steinmetz's recent comparative study of German colonialism demonstrates the value of systematic differentiation among colonial sites and the avoidance of broad generalization about the process of colonialism. It is well to ask not simply *whether* or not China experienced the effects of colonialism without being fully colonized, but *how* the pattern of colonialism in China (and pre-existing social, cultural and ideological configurations in China, and among colonialists) created similar – and dissimilar – effects (Steinmetz 2007). The editors recognize the limited discussion of Japan in this volume. We regret the late withdrawal of one planned Japan chapter.

13 Shanghai, of course, offered the most famous of such spaces, but, as Joseph Esherick notes, 'there was hardly a city that was not linked in some way to Shanghai' through flows of ideas, financial institutions, networks of news, fashion, and circulations of population (Esherick 2000: 12–13).
14 Although the thrust of Hevia's *English Lessons* portrays colonial violence, emphasizing primarily colonial agency and Chinese victimization, he does briefly acknowledge Chinese agency in other contexts: 'In the treaty ports, Chinese businessmen were often so successful that one British consul observed that they were the real merchants and the foreigners merely "commission agents"' (Hevia 2003: 14).
15 Foreigners were the most valuable hostages because Chinese authorities could be held responsible for foreigners kidnapped on their turf (Xu and Billingsley 2000: 38–78).

PART I

Colonial governance and questions of identity

1

'GOOD WORK FOR CHINA IN EVERY POSSIBLE DIRECTION'

The Foreign Inspectorate of the Chinese Maritime Customs, 1854–1950

Robert Bickers

In the background of the iconic photographs of foreign residents departing Shanghai in 1949 – Henri Cartier-Bresson's shots in May that year, or those of Jack Birns in September – can be spotted various Chinese members of the Maritime Customs Service, which regulated the arrival and the departure of ship's passengers (Cartier-Bresson 1956: 136; Wakeman and Light 2003: 121). Standing at the bottom of the gangplank in one of Birns's shots, dressed in a uniform modelled on the naval attire of the Anglophone world, is one figure whose presence speaks volumes about the world that is coming to a close. It seems fitting to draw attention away from the too-obvious symbolism of the departing passengers towards this representative of an institution that was pivotal to China's interaction with the world overseas in the century up to the victory of the Chinese Communist Party. A foreign national still led the service that this man worked for, as his predecessors had since 1854, and at least 11,000 foreign nationals had worked for the service at some point in the preceding 96 years. Those departure procedures undergone by foreign nationals leaving in 1949 mirrored those to be faced at the end of their journey, just as the uniforms mirrored those worn overseas. At its points of entry and departure, China seemed disorientatingly familiar. This was the operational achievement of the Chinese Maritime Customs Service (CMCS), the single most important institutional innovation of the treaty era.

Foreign residents left, but the establishment and staff, and in many cases the procedures and norms, of the CMCS remained, both on the mainland and in the rump republic. This states the obvious, but in fact such institutional continuities have generally been occluded by notions that 1949 marked a definitive break with the past, and in the case of the Customs, by an absence of work (in English in particular) on the service after 1937, let alone after 1945 (for recent work see Lyons 2003; Brunero 2006; van de Ven 2006; Bickers 2008a). They are also clouded by misunderstandings of the place of the CMCS within the Chinese state. The Imperial (later simply Chinese)

Maritime Customs Service built up or oversaw much of the infrastructure of that century-long phase of Sino–foreign trade and interaction which was drawing to a close in 1949, reconciling it to overseas norms as they developed (and tracking changes in those). It was also vital to the finances of the Qing and the Republican states until 1941, both in terms of the revenues collected from across the country, whose delivery to the central state it guaranteed, and through its role as security for foreign loans. Although often viewed by observers as a tool of foreign (mainly British) imperialist control, it was always an agency of the Chinese state, and formally responsible to it. Successive Inspectors-General (IG) had wielded great power and a considerable degree of autonomy, but they had each, in their own way, affirmed their fundamental loyalty to the interests of the state that employed them.

The CMCS was always much more even than a simple excise service. Partly as a result of Sir Robert Hart's own vision for modernising China (Hart was the second IG, 1863–1911) – and because of the alliances he established with key figures in self-strengthening circles (Horowitz 2006), but also because there was no other agency which could initially organise the work and that had international goodwill and connections, the Customs extended its range across a wide range of internationalising, self-strengthening or self-consciously 'modernising' activities. As Hart put it in 1885, it did 'good work for China in every possible direction' (China Maritime Customs 1938b: 544). It built up coastal and riverine lights infrastructures; represented China at international exhibitions and in some diplomatic negotiations (and directly funded the early Chinese diplomatic service); and oversaw the development of a key educational institution (the Beijing Tongwenguan). It surveyed China's coasts and rivers; established a national meteorological network and the Chinese Post Office; and built up a significant and lasting body of publications about China, ranging from topographical surveys, medical reports and reams of statistical data through to less obvious monographs such as J. A. Van Aalst's *Chinese Music* (1884). 'The West does not understand China', Hart noted in 1869, 'nor does China understand the West' (Hart, 'Note on Chinese Matters', 30 June 1869, in China Maritime Customs 1938b: 303). Much of the work of the CMCS was deliberately aimed at bridging that gulf. Other branches of the state came in time to contest its roles and to supersede it, but successive local and central administrations had called on the CMCS to undertake a wide range of work, and even at its lowest point – after it was shattered during the Pacific war, and lost much of its *raison d'être* (and many staff) – the National Government used it to help extend the reach of the state into Xinjiang (Bickers 2008b). The service proved itself a useful asset right up to the end of the Foreign Inspectorate.

But the Customs was also clearly a part of British informal empire, that evolving repertoire of practices that secured the levels of advantage, control or influence deemed necessary for implementation of the British state's strategic or economic aims. The latter might at times seem definable as extending free trade by force. Informal influence and presences were prone to ossify into a more formal hold; it was in fact clearly often the first stage in the establishment of a more formal colonial presence, but more often than not the agents of that British power on the ground, or the opportunists who followed the flag (the colonial government in Hong Kong, or the Shanghailander British; Bickers 1998) pursued their own self-interested agendas, pushing to expand, entrench or defend their positions. As long as these coincided with wider British state interests they could be tolerated, even supported, but they were dropped when the necessary moment had passed (Bickers 1999). The CMCS was from the 1850s to 1930s a British asset, but this must be tempered by the fact that firstly it was always a Chinese state agency, and secondly it was always staffed by a multi-national cadre of officials, and if imperial and other rivalries were clearly sometimes in evidence within its ranks, its carefully nurtured ethos of cosmopolitan service usually won through. Looking at the Customs allows us to explore some of the meanings, nature and limits to informal empire in China. This chapter does so through a survey of some issues around the composition and structure of the CMCS, and then looks at its operations in Nanning in south-west China's Guangxi Province, a locality far away from the chattering centre of its operations.

'Our Hart': whose customs?

What could provide a better example of a hybrid institution than the Maritime Customs? The term has its critics, but an institution that deliberately melded together elements of Qing and British administrative practice – literally so in the detailed form of its internal types of communication, which took Chinese official forms as their models (Circular No. 2/1873) – can reasonably and sensibly be so described. The CMCS worked in at least two worlds. Its most influential IG, Ulsterman Sir Robert Hart, who held the post substantively from 1863 to 1908, was routinely lauded as an agent of British influence, if not power, in China, by British observers as well as (less positively) their rivals (Bickers 2006). Hart even accepted the post of British Minister in 1885, although he withdrew, not least of the reasons being that he would prove more useful a British asset as IG (China Maritime Customs 1938b: 544). But Hart was always at pains to impress upon his employees, at all levels, that they served only the Chinese state, and should be loyal to their employers. 'Our Hart', Prince Gong called him in 1861 (Rennie 1865: 264). Hart's important Circular No. 8/1864 is very clear: 'In the first place', it begins, 'It is to be distinctly and constantly kept in mind, that the Inspectorate of Customs is a Chinese not a Foreign Service' (China Maritime Customs 1879: 54). Commissioners were appointed to 'assist the Chinese Superintendent[s] of Customs' (China Maritime Customs 1878: 1). Foreign traders initially entertained 'deep-rooted dislike' of a service that applied British norms and enforced honest practice on traders who routinely criticised what they represented as an ingrained Chinese propensity for corruption, but who preferred nonetheless to deal with Chinese officialdom where they had to, and no officialdom at all if they possibly could (China Maritime Customs 1879: 56; 1938b: 176–77, 183–87). This was also a transfer of resource from the provinces to the modernising central state – 'to an extent never dreamt of before', claimed Hart in 1864 (China Maritime Customs 1938b: 192) – and it was a feature of the effective function of the Customs that was to long outlast its early years, and that, after the post-Qing breakdown of central power, was to provoke a number of political crises as regional power holders or foreign occupiers sought to seize back local revenues.

The outsourcing, enforced or otherwise, of responsibilities such as those taken on by Hart's service was hardly restricted to China. The interpolation of Europeans, whether as technical or other experts and advisors, into the administrative machineries of independent states, or as traders into existing networks of trade, was a central feature of European colonial history and the developing world of globalised trade in the nineteenth century. In particular, the Ottoman empire's sovereignty was impaired in ways that echo China's, and Egypt was subject to what some critics termed 'an administrative army of occupation' (*The Times*, 31 March 1894: 15). Japan, Siam and many other states also took on (or had forced on them) foreign experts and advisors. From the vantage point of those who actually staffed the service, it was also hardly unusual. Catherine Ladds (2008b) has recently demonstrated how tightly intertwined the world of Chinese Customs employment for foreigners was with wider imperial and international career networks. For individuals, landing a post was a somewhat random happenstance. A better examination result might have sent a man to India; a different family connection might have sent him to Argentina. The Customs was just one part of the 'British world' of work and opportunity (Bridge and Fedorowich 2003). But even so, only around half of all those who served in the Customs were British. German, French, Russian, American and, in the twentieth century, Japanese nationals were strongly represented amongst those who served. This had always been Hart's policy, and the composition of the service in any one year was widely publicised. Foreign recruitment of administrative employees (the Indoor Staff of 'Assistants' and Commissioners) was increasingly politicised in the later nineteenth century as intra-imperialist rivalries were heightened in the aftermath of Japanese victory in the 1894–95 war with China, and Hart shaped his hiring patterns with a view to forestalling criticism and pressure which might follow from diplomats to recruit more of their own nationals (Ladds 2008a). Certainly, this cosmopolitan face of the Customs to an extent masked the hold of the British, or at least Britons, but as successive IGs deflected attempts by diplomats to assert the privileging of specific nationalities, it can reasonably be concluded that the Customs usually kept all interested parties sweet.

Foreign men who staffed the service had different calls on their loyalties, and these sometimes conflicted sharply. 'The personal sympathies of Mr Mansfield are more those of a Foreign Consul as of a Customs Employé', noted a Commissioner of his Assistant in 1907, recommending the transfer of the man away from the sensitive newly opened treaty-port of Nanning.[1] Others were certainly capable of acting with violence or racism towards Chinese colleagues or subordinates, although the CMCS aimed to prevent this. But an analysis which assumes that a foreign national in Chinese employ faced a simple binary choice, and put his homeland first every time, is inadequate even with this and other examples to hand. Firstly – insidiously in some lights – most of the administrative staff saw a fairly clear congruence of interests between their loyalties to the work of the Customs and its contribution to

China's development, and their own national interests. Moreover, from the 1890s, the Customs revenue provided the security on which successive and multiplying foreign loans to China were pledged, and protecting the interests of foreign bondholders became for some individuals the rationale underpinning their work. Secondly, Hart buffered them by fostering a cult around his own person, which was perpetuated by his successors (Bickers 2006). As sometime Commissioner and historian H. B. Morse wrote, it was impossible to impugn 'the absolute loyalty' of the Customs administrative cadre 'to their chief and the government they serve' (Morse 1920: 408). The ordering is revealing. But we must also take into account, at face value, the likelihood of a clear identification of many staff with the disinterested ethos of the service. We need not always be cynical about the loyalty to the service and its Chinese masters of those who ate its salt.

The treaty-port communities across which the Customs operated were marked by such apparent contradictions, unusual solidarities and tangled loyalties. The communities of interest which developed were often out of step with the global tensions of empires. Frenchman and Briton worked side by side as their empires came close to war over the Fashoda incident in 1898. The clearest case is the Anglo–German *entente* that long outlasted the declaration of war in 1914. German and British business had developed strong ties in the treaty-ports. Their joint enterprises were often based on the pragmatic alliance of German capital and expertise, and English company law and its China regulations. Sundering such ties was the task of British diplomats and activist journalists, worried by the seeming indifference of many in their communities to national interests. But for others, this civil strife amongst the Europeans would spoil things for all in China. As Hart's successor, IG Sir Francis Aglen, wrote to one of his German commissioners in August 1914, 'It is a thousand pities [the war]…must invade the Far East where our countries have so many mutual interests and where we English have so many German personal friends'.[2] This is part pleasantry, and many of Aglen's staff rushed to join up and fight for their homelands, but the underlying sense, exhibited here and elsewhere, of a transnational community of interests rooted in the particularities and opportunities opened up by the treaty system, is palpable.

There are of course caveats to add. Firstly, the CMCS was structurally a less homogeneous service than it pretended. Hart's first task on succeeding formally to Horatio Nelson Lay in 1863 was to weld together a service that was working fairly autonomously and in a different fashion in each of the existing Customs districts. The Commissioners were new, often – like Hart – recruited from consular services, and independent in approach and sensitivities. Hart worked to fashion an integrated administrative machine in which he exercised sole and undisputed authority. In time, he came to be criticised for autocracy, and for damaging the service overall as a result (Bickers 2006; Horowitz 2008). But even so, the CMCS reflected in some of its own arrangements not only China's wider impaired sovereignty, but also the diffuse nature of authority within the late Qing state. With the Russian and then Japanese administration of Dalian (Darien), and the German and then Japanese seizure of Jiaozhou (in Shandong), the Customs had to negotiate separate agreements with the colonial authorities which sharply limited its autonomy of action. The service agreed to appoint nationals of the colonial power to the staff at all levels, but then again, their status as Chinese state officials still raised suspicions in the eyes of colonial authorities at the same time as their nationality could raise suspicions in Chinese eyes. In other ways, the Customs itself was less fully coherent than it claimed, not least in the north, where Gustav Detring, with Li Hongzhang's patronage, held sway in Tianjin for over 25 years after 1877 as Commissioner and in other roles (van de Ven 2006). Moreover, local political realities during the Republic meant some stations, such as Chongqing, were consistently denied access to their nominal revenue streams (Reinhardt 2008). Other temporary crises damaged the integrity of the Customs system (at Canton in 1926, at Tianjin in 1930 and elsewhere), as did the Japanese occupations of Taiwan (1895), Manchuria (1931) and the invasion after 1937.

Secondly, Chinese staff were not an equal part of this establishment. That man on the Shanghai wharf was one of about 4800 mostly Chinese employees of the service in 1949. Over the previous 95 years, about 22,000 men and women had worked in the upper-level 'Service Listed' echelons of the service. Half of these were Chinese, and many thousands more worked at lower-level posts. Hart had always stated that, in due course, the Customs would evolve into an institution wholly staffed by Chinese, but it was nearly 50 years before training commenced of what became a cadre of Chinese who could rise to take over all senior positions, and that initiative was not instituted by the CMCS. Alongside other categories of Chinese employee, 'Linguists' were initially recruited to function as translators and as clerks (for economy, as Europeans were paid more), and with the aim of training up 'able and trustworthy Native officials'. But such hopes, Hart noted as early as 1868, proved 'ill-founded' (Circular 12/1868 in China Maritime Customs 1879: 143). Missionary schools were the only institutions which could be looked to, to provide men with the first two attributes; men of talent and orthodox educational achievement would not join the service. Chinese officials distrusted those who joined; and that missionary flavour was unhelpful. A less ambitious structure of Chinese clerks was instituted in 1875 and remained in place thereafter, with some promotion into the Foreign staff structure only in the early twentieth century (and that initially driven by salary economies). Institutional inertia played a part, but raced notions of Chinese abilities to function within a system built up on English lines, as well as conceptions of Chinese corruption and the power of social and kinship ties over individuals (who might, it was routinely assumed, corruptly – or at least unethically – make decisions as a result), also held sway amongst most foreign observers. This was often turned around as an argument – extraterritoriality, opponents of Chinese promotion argued, meant that these foreign employees of the Chinese state had a level of protection against local power holders that Chinese nationals simply could not call on. That revenue being channelled into the central state – 53.5 per cent of it in 1929 – was secured, they argued, solely through extraterritoriality (Woodhead 1925: 140–41).

Reform began with the establishment of a Customs College in 1908 by the new Shuiwuchu (Bureau of Fiscal Affairs), which supervised the CMCS from

1906 onwards. This held entrance examinations at Peking, Hankou, Shanghai, Fuzhou and Guangzhou, and its graduates competed for formal entrance into the structure of assistantships from which the executive was drawn, alongside the clerks (China Maritime Customs 1938a: 91–96, 189–91). But it was not until the Inspector Generalship of Frederick Maze (1929–43) that Chinese were promoted into the senior ranks (Brunero 2006). In 1929, the formal distinction between 'Chinese' and 'Foreign' staff was abolished, but the politics of nationality remained a consideration thereafter. And even in the last years of the foreign inspectorate, when nationalistic considerations had been considerably heightened, an earlier, pragmatic notion of the usefulness of the disinterested foreign servant of the Chinese state (or faction) could be found. Song Ziwen, whose influence over the service long outlasted his formal responsibility for it when he served as Minister of Finance, lobbied in 1946–47 to retain a foreign national as Commissioner at Shanghai. IG L.K. Little responded that this was now politically impossible, and that 'the time had come to place a Chinese in the top post in the top port'. 'T.V.', he concluded, 'finally agreed, but not too graciously'.[3]

Through its recruitment and induction programmes, the CMCS eventually aimed to bring together men from Manchuria and Italy, Guangdong and Germany, and develop staff cadres who could meet, efficiently and effectively, the needs of the Chinese state, the foreign powers, and the multifarious Chinese local administrations that called on the formal and informal services it provided. The range of activities the CMCS undertook changed over time, but in the 1940s it was still being offered new responsibilities, and while the treaty system had been impaired by the Sino–Japanese war, and surrendered by the wartime and postwar Sino–Foreign treaties, the Foreign Inspectorate survived into post-war China (Bickers 2008b). It still offered, through its foreign dimension and personnel, some of the potential access to expertise and resource that was needed to strengthen the country – in this case for the post-war economic rehabilitation of the Chinese economy and the reconstruction of its maritime communications infrastructure. The echoes even after 1945 of the Customs of Hart's first frantic decade as IG are worth noting.

Whose Customs then? Men (99 per cent of its employees were men) made the CMCS serve their own career interests. It was theirs. It was British: in 1898 the Foreign Office extracted a agreement from the Zongli yamen that a Briton would hold the Inspector-Generalship while British trade in China predominated. Hart did not think this a wise or an enforceable claim. Hart and his successors kept the hustling diplomats of the other powers whose nationals served in the CMCS sweet by recruiting their nationals. It was theirs too. However, the asymmetries of interest in many of the relationships needs to be remembered alongside asymmetries of power. Britain was far more important in China than ever China was important to Britain – British relations with continental Europe, the United States and the wider formal British empire overshadowed all others (Cain and Hopkins 2001), even when China was the subject of those relations (Otte 2007). Moreover, the CMCS acted through its various programmes and activities to provide the infrastructural basis for Sino–foreign trade, while through its *Medical Reports* and meteorological activity, Hart had offered its resources to science and knowledge. The CMCS systematically served the interests of the Qing state and its successors, nationally and locally. Its centrality in the state's foreign relations diminished over the course of its career, and this was recognised structurally as it was moved from the control of the Zongli Yamen, to the Shuiwuchu, and then to the Ministry of Finance and its Guanwushu (Office of Customs Affairs).

'This *Ultima Thule*': the Customs at Nanning

It is necessary to augment any discussion of the international and institutional history of the Customs by looking at its operational activity in the localities it served. It affected major trading cities as well as tiny, isolated rural villages (through its lighthouse network). The CMCS is most familiar as part of the landscape of the great urban centres that have dominated recent scholarship, but the number of stations almost reached 50 (with many sub-stations), and most treaty-ports had their Bund and Customs House. It needs to be remembered that the service was a feature of the localities as much as it was of Qing and Republican international politics. Nanning, a port opened to foreign trade as a 'voluntarily opened mart' in 1907, presents a telling case study. It reminds us of the ways in which the central state used the Customs to extend its reach in to local economies in search of revenue; of the prevalence of the internationalising entrepreneurship that was also to feed that revenue; but also of resistance, indifference and simple failure. The contrast with the obvious successes – with the big trading ports – is also instructive, and scholars could more usefully think more routinely about imperial and settler failure.

Located 100 miles from the border with French Indo-China, Nanning was the focus of French railroad ambitions which aimed to tie south-west China into the French colonial orbit. The driving force was not the French government, but the men on the spot in Indochina, not least the 1897–1902 Governor-General, Paul Doumer (Lee 1989). The potential riches of south-west China's economy had long excited British and French observers out of all proportion to reality (Walsh 1943; Lary 1974: 25–26). But as the Wuzhou Commissioner noted in a 1901 report on the prospects for opening up Nanning, doing so was 'not at present a commercial necessity', and it was not even entirely certain that it was technically feasible for steam vessels to run regular services that far along the river. It was not likely to bring on stream a new source of revenue (rather it would divert Wuzhou's), but it would certainly help to keep Yunnan's trade in Chinese hands, and not those of 'a foreign country' – the French. Local sentiment, he noted, also hoped that a visible (non-French) foreign presence, the arrival of 'Consul and Commissioner', would bring peace and stability to a disturbed and threatened region.[4] The opening of Nanning, Customs historian Stanley Wright noted, 'bid fair to be a complete frustration to [French] plans' (Wright 1950: 702). It certainly set the seal on Doumer's defeat, although the capture of south-west China's trade through railway construction from Indochina was still being mooted in the 1930s, as imperial dreams long lingered on the frontiers of formal empire (Ennis 1936: 122–24).

Inland Nanning, 560 miles and one junk-month upriver from the sea, was, like the Yangzi ports, hardly a logical site for collection of revenue on foreign trade, but aside from strategic considerations – countering the French and appeasing the British who had demanded it be opened (and for whom countering the French was a good) – opening the port potentially served to further the interests of the central state on the ground. An increase in foreign flagged trade facilitated by the establishment of a Customs station and procedures, as well as a foreign settlement, could potentially increase revenues in the long term. In the short term, reflagging of existing vessels (which would thereby secure Maritime Customs papers and so avoid transit taxation barriers) would divert local revenues to the centre (and every additional landing point those inter-port traders were allowed to use – the authorised 'Ports of Call' – enabled the Customs to tap into more potential revenue; Tsai 2005). Maritime Customs stations reached inland as far as Chongqing on the Yangzi, 1400 miles from the sea. The Customs Marine Department surveyed the river, and developed and maintained its navigational infrastructure. All these benefits could potentially be derived from opening up Nanning. The West River system, whose main southern tributary flows through the city, had, like the Yangzi, what Hart termed a 'hybrid character', both inland highway and 'continuation of the sea'. This was certainly true for Wuzhou, downstream from Nanning, and might thereby benefit development of the port.

But the Yangzi provided more fertile openings than did the West River. Poverty-stricken Guangxi thwarted even the most sanguine hopes. Disillusionment set in from the start – 'a backward country town, the people are slow without enterprise', claimed the first commissioner, German E. A. W. von Strauch, in one of his earliest reports.[5] (A British appointee might have been too much a provocation for the French.) The only foreign residents were nine missionaries, and the community barely grew thereafter. The Bund kept falling down. The foreign settlement site lay undeveloped. Strauch felt himself exiled at the edge of the world, that '*Ultima Thule*'. Floods in 1913 devastated the local economy. One foreign Customs assistant killed himself (1914) and another narrowly failed to do so (1919) (Ladds 2007a). The only significant branches of foreign firms were established by Standard Oil and the Asiatic Petroleum Company. The ongoing resistance (or indifference) of local merchants, as well as the antagonism of other taxation authorities towards the interpolation of a central state agency, made for many other Customs headaches. Up to 1912, it was concluded in a later report, merchants did in fact see positive advantages in taking out CMCS documents, but these advantages declined thereafter, and by 1927 there was no advantage to be gained.[6] After 1930, no foreign employee was appointed to any position at the station. The French had once feared that the West River would become an 'English river' feeding Hong Kong; in reality it became at most a British backwater, and only ever as English as the motley whiskey-soaked mariners who nominally crewed its British-flagged, Chinese-owned steamers (Benson diary, 1929–30 *passim*; Philips papers, *passim*).

But the Customs presence had had an impact, if small at first. 'I write to report a first sign of life', reported von Strauch in April 1907, when three junks brought in the station's first revenue.[7] Private enterprise had scented an opportunity, and shipping company began to run launches from the port to feed shipments on its Wuzhou to Hong Kong steamers. Ten vessels were engaged in this trade four years later (China Maritime Customs 1913: 218) and 45 in 1922 (but most were likely to be smuggling opium (China Maritime Customs 1924: 299). Reports across the following decade indicate the incremental changes wrought by Nanning's integration into what we might term Maritime Customs China. The Governor requested that the Customs survey the river, and sought advice on various issues, especially on acquiring foreign technology (for the sugar industry). Consuls visited; Japanese military advisors passed through; and a Japanese-trained military commander arrived. A Belgian engineer arrived to survey the planned Guilin–Nanning railway line (1910), but this project never developed, and Nanning had air services before it had railways. There was a statistical increase in foreign trade over the first four years of the Station's work, although most of these 'foreign goods' were actually Chinese products coming from colonial Hong Kong (China Maritime Customs 1913: 217). Hope sprang eternal, and private concession hunters – foreigners in search of economic opportunity that often involved them renting out their extraterritorial status to Chinese backers – became a local feature.

There was, of course, a booming economy (or transit trade at least) if opium is factored in. Reports from Commissioners provided much detail about the extent of the trade, not least after its nominal suppression in 1911–12, but this does not show in the Customs statistics, except in terms of seizures. Ultimately, the aim of fully integrating Nanning into Maritime Customs China was in one sense a failure: for the British who lobbied for its opening; for the Customs, which added it to the network of stations; and to the central state, which derived little ultimate benefit. Communist insurgency and civil strife hardly helped before the 1930s (Lary 1974), and thereafter the province's reformist militarist leadership imposed their own vision of development on the economy, and secured their own revenues on trade (Levich 1994). Successive commissioners in the 1920s and after recommended the Customs station be closed. 'No very useful purpose is served by maintaining this office' concluded one 1930 report.[8] The attempt to reshape the local economy to suit national purposes had been frustrated. Political considerations kept it open, however, as they had caused it to open in the first place, but now they were domestic rather than diplomatic. The later wartime retreat of the National Government to the west brought more work to the Customs, but twofold disaster to Nanning, in 1939–40 when it was seized and then burned by the Japanese, and during the Ichigo offensive in 1944.

The Nanning story highlights the way in which the CMCS and its staff operated at the intersection of centre and locality, between the Chinese state and the foreign powers, and between imperialist rivals. Foreign customs officers initially found themselves advising Nanning officials on local economic development plans and overseeing the construction of a new infrastructure for trade. They operated on their local scenes in much the same way that Hart had operated in Peking amongst the reformers in the 1860s. They were not the only such new voices in Nanning (and Hart's was not the only new voice in Peking). They were part of a wider, slow and fluctuating influx of foreign advisors and chancers, as well as Chinese interests from outside the city and province, and indeed from Hong Kong, but they were central to that development. Such habits died hard. They might still be lecturing local power holders on China's faults in the late 1920s, as private diaries testify, but they were by then an irrelevance compared with their status and usefulness 25 years earlier, and Guangxi would find its own way forward (Benson diary, 10 April 1930, and *passim*). They were also an irrelevance as far as British interests were concerned. Nanning's opening had served a momentary purpose, but the rivalries of the turn of the twentieth century had moved on, and within a decade the Anglo–French *entente* had defused the two states' global imperial rivalries.

Informal Empire – Formal State

The place of the Maritime Customs Service in the shifting repertoire of British informal empire has been one theme of this chapter. It marked the high tide of the British advance into the Chinese state; and it was far as the British needed to go, and could safely go, without provoking intra-imperial conflict or Chinese resistance. Alongside the offshore base at Hong Kong, diplomatic representation, extraterritoriality, a fixed tariff and a range of ports opened to trade and residence, it rounded off the fundamental requirements (as the British saw them) for effective protection of British interests in China. That its activities aided transitions in the Qing state and its successors that were necessary to manage the new threats and challenges of the treaty-port era was also for the British a directly related good. That its multinational character and disinterested service of the trade and interests of all treaty powers, let alone its formal incorporation within the Chinese state, all took the edge off its British character, was also vital. There was never any real British hunger for the Chinese melon, for all the jingo talk of men on the spot and imperialists at home. The 'good work for China' of the Customs – at Shanghai, Hankow, Nanning and the dozens of other local sites – satisfied the appetites of most parties, most of the time.

The Customs at Nanning, at the intersection of French and British ambitions, was the outcome of a fevered moment of colonial bluster. The threatened forays towards the city by rail or river came to nothing, and the attention of the parties involved moved elsewhere. The moment passed; von Strauch and his successors were left to while away their lonely hours as best they could. This Customs outpost served its purpose for a few years, but although politics had underpinned its establishment, political and economic realities curtailed its development. More widely, the CMCS itself grew out of a particular moment of crisis in 1854, a broader colonial moment during the Taiping rebellion, which saw the establishment of other institutions in Shanghai – notably the Shanghai Municipal Council and its police force – which also became pillars of the British and international presence in China. It survived, prospered and grew as a pragmatic institution working at the intersection of Chinese authority and the foreign presence, which recast the business of the treaty-ports, greatly reducing the daily potential for conflict between foreign traders, consuls and Chinese officials. As with many such initially *ad hoc* arrangements of informal empire, it had a predisposition to permanency, even though it was a Chinese state agency, and even though its leading lights all accepted the inevitability of evolution. It can indeed look like a colonial bridgehead, like an administrative army of occupation, and contemporary Chinese and other critics saw it as such. But it was, for the British for example, ultimately expendable. China was not within the formal world of British empire, and it was a far less important market than most others. When the long colonial moment was passed, when the British in particular re-ordered their China policy to adapt to the successes of nationalism and the Guomindang in the later 1920s, then the importance of the Customs in their eyes started to decline.

Notes

1 Second Historical Archives of China (SHAC), 679(1), 32516, Nanning Semi-official letters, 5 September 1907.
2 SHAC 679(1), 32834, IG Semi-official Letters to General Public Vol. 8, 1914, Aglen to Wilzer, 14 August 1914.
3 L. K. Little, 'Footnote on Customs History', Hoover Institution Archives, Arthur Young papers, Box 29.
4 SHAC 679(9), 19475, Wuzhou despatches No. 585, 29 August 1901; No. 593, 31 August 1901.
5 SHAC, 679(1), 32516, Nanning Semi-official letters, 2 February 1907.
6 SHAC 679(1), 17405, 'Considerations governing closing of Nanning as an independent port', Nanning No. 1366, 11 October 1932.
7 SHAC, 679(1), 32516, Nanning Semi-official letters, 10 April 1907.
8 SHAC, 679(1), 32519 Nanning Semi-official letters 1928–30, 30 September 1930.

2

NEGOTIATING THE NATION

German colonialism and Chinese nationalism in Qingdao, 1897–1914

Klaus Mühlhahn

In the fifteenth and sixteenth centuries, the rule of colonial powers often relied on unconstrained use of force and violence in subjecting indigenous populations and exploiting resources and riches supposed to be hidden overseas. Compared with the early period of the European conquests, nineteenth-century colonialism was a more complex and subtle enterprise. Sophisticated state machineries had been developed in order not only to subject, but to govern and to administer indigenous populations. Nineteenth-century colonial rule relied less on physical force, but more on a broad range of legal, cultural, educational and administrative technologies to maintain control over subject populations. The emerging colonial 'governmentality' (Foucault 1976: 143, 195) was a complex assemblage of 'institutions, procedures, analyses and reflections' aiming at maintaining the colonial state's control over society and extracting diverse resources. Education, medicine and science were therefore considered to be, in the words of the later German colonial minister in Berlin, Bernhard Dernburg, 'the most important auxiliary field of learning (*Hilfswissenschaft*) for the colonizer' (Dernburg 1907: 11).

As recent scholarship has argued convincingly, colonies were terrains where projects of power and concepts of superiority were not only imposed, but also engaged and contested by the colonized (Cooper 2005: 3–32). In fact, political activism within, about and against colonial rule has engendered not only the possibility of accepting or rejecting the application to colonial worlds of ideas and structures asserted by Europe, but also the possibility of changing the meanings of the basic concepts themselves. The problem of translation and transfer looms large in any such inquiry. As Lydia Liu has shown, one does not translate between equivalents; rather, one creates tropes of equivalence in the fluid middle zone of translation between the host and guest languages (Liu 1999: 137). This middle zone of hypothetical equivalence, which is occupied by neologistic imagination, becomes the very ground for change of meanings, for modifications and for negotiations.

These interstices also contain the possibility for the forming of new concepts and new knowledge. It is here where Chinese projects of defending or saving the nation against imperialism were engendered and articulated. It allowed for borrowing concepts and terms from the global and for appropriating these concepts for the local. The colonies became fluid, unstable zones of contact where identity lines and cultural borders were blurred through exchanges and transfers.

This chapter explores the interactions between German colonial authorities and the Chinese population in the colonial society in Qingdao, 1897–1914. In particular, it looks at how various actors maneuvered within this particular colonial space; how the dislocation of colonial rule was experienced, resisted, accommodated and manipulated by Chinese groups; and what imprint the colonial state left on local society in Qingdao and Shandong. In each of the cases under discussion, the goal of resisting, accommodating or modifying German colonialism was connected with larger Chinese strategies and rhetoric that transcended the framework of local colonial governance. The colonial contact zone, with its complexities, gradations and blurred identities, became a site where the project of Chinese nationalism was negotiated and gained profile.

Ambiguities of colonial governance in Qingdao

Recent studies have stressed the diversity of colonial manifestations and forms (Thomas 1994: 11–32; Wolfe 1997). Nineteenth-century colonies, in particular, constituted highly complex and dynamic social spaces. Colonies were culturally and socially diverse worlds, distinct from both metropolitan and indigenous societies. Far from being monolithic and uncontested, the development in the colonies was characterized by dynamic processes, which resulted from tensions, conflicts and collaborations between various social groups of different cultural backgrounds. In these contentious and contested worlds, power and rule needed to be negotiated between the various agents. As Ann Stoler maintained, empire and colonial states were not steady states, but 'states of becoming' (Stoler 2006: 135–36), where constant formation and flexible adaptation was based on ongoing transfers of ideas, practices and technologies across fixed boundaries, and on interactions between various groups in the colony and between the metropolitan regions and their colonies.

The case of the German leasehold territory of Kiaochow is well suited to demonstrate that nineteenth-century colonialism was a multifarious, diverse and variable enterprise. The murder of two German missionaries in November 1897 gave Germany the long awaited excuse for the occupation of the Kiaochow Bay area in the North China province of Shandong. The Chinese Empire was forced to sign a treaty in March 1898 that granted the German Reich a 99-year lease of a small territory around the bay. With this treaty, Germany also secured so-called concessions or rights to build railways and to exploit coal mines in Shandong province. The province was now considered by the German Reich as her 'sphere of influence' in China. Although Kiaochow, as the new colony was called, was formally a leasehold, Germany treated it as nothing less than a colony. German interests in China were by no means limited to the leased territory itself. The construction of a railway line to the provincial capital Jinan and the opening of coal mines along the railway was intended as only the beginning of a larger German 'sphere of influence' to secure economic, cultural and political dominance over Shandong province.

After the occupation, Kiaochow was placed under the jurisdiction of the Naval Ministry (in Leutner and Mühlhahn 1997: 181–84; documents 42 and 43).[1] Kiaochow was in fact the only German colony ever run by a branch of the military. The naval minister, Alfred von Tirpitz, explained his interest in the new colony in a note from January, writing that 'if the Navy is on the top of the colonial movement, the colonial successes as well as the results will benefit the Navy'. (Note by Tirpitz, 4.1.1898, in: BA/MA, RM3/6699, fol. 1–11.) The occupation of Kiaochow was designed to mobilize support for the Navy in general, overcome objections by the opposition party, and help to realize the ambitious naval plans of Tirpitz. The calculations of Tirpitz proved right. In March, a German newspaper commented: 'The events in Kiaochow and the new hopes for commerce and the missions increase the willingness to make sacrifices for the navy.' (*Centrumskorrespondenz*, 2.3.1898, quoted in Canis 1997: 273). One month later, in April, the Reichstag finally approved the so called Tirpitz plan, which provided funding for the building of a large German naval force. This triggered an arms race between the leading sea power, Great Britain, and Germany, which of course was one of the most important long-term factors leading to the outbreak of the First World War.

There can be no doubt that the main architect behind Kiaochow's development was Alfred von Tirpitz. Tirpitz took a personal interest in Kiaochow, reading and commenting on almost every report from China. He had far-reaching goals in mind. As early as 1896, when Tirpitz spent a year in China as Commander of the German Squadron in East Asia, he proposed strong German colonial expansion in China. In private correspondence, he argued: 'The accumulation of giant nations like Panamerica, Greater Britain, the Slavic race or the Mongolian race under the leadership of Japan will destroy or almost extinguish Germany [...] in the course of the next century, if Germany does not become a great power outside the borders of the European continent. The imperative basis for that [...] is a fleet.' (Quoted in Deist 1976: 111). Like many other contemporaries, especially in the military, Tirpitz had a Darwinistic understanding of international relations in the modern age, seeing it as a fight for survival between races (according to contemporary theories, a modern nation was supposed to be formed by a race). Tirpitz was convinced that only colonial outposts could effectively support a flexible, global and powerful military force, and that only in this way could the survival of the German race be guaranteed in the long run. From these remarks, it is clear that neither economic nor diplomatic but military considerations were at the very center of Tirpitz's colonial blueprints for China.

Because Kiaochow was of highest priority to Tirpitz, he carefully tried to steer the colony form Berlin. Tirpitz was always aware of any possible disruption of his policies by local colonizers, domestic political groups or Chinese groups. Tirpitz limited the powers of the Governor of Kiaochow.[2] The Governor, a Navy officer, had to present monthly reports about the development of the colony. Every ordinance issued by the Governor was countersigned by Tirpitz. When governors failed to carry out the policies expected by Tirpitz, they were dismissed. This happened with Governor Rosendahl in 1898 because Tirpitz felt Rosendahl had neglected the economic development of the colony (Tirpitz to Wilhelm II, 7.10.1898, in Bundesarchiv/Militärarchiv (BArch/MA), RM2/1837, Bl.126–28, reprinted in Leutner and Mühlhahn 1997: 352–53). Governor Truppel was dismissed in 1910, when he failed to support the German–Chinese College favored by Tirpitz (Pyenson 1985: 258). In addition, by declaring Kiaochow a imperial 'protectorate' (*Kaiserliches Schutzgebiet*) in April 1898, the constitutional organs of the German Reich such as the Reichstag and Bundestag were barred from passing legislation for Kiaochow.

The strong role of the Navy had consequences for the German colonial project in China. According to Tirpitz's plan, Kiaochow should be turned into a 'model colony', a colony that would demonstrate a specific, innovative and effective approach to colonialism. 'Model colony' meant making Kiaochow a showcase for modern cultural, scientific and technological achievements. The Navy was investing huge resources into the development of the new city of Qingdao and a new urban infrastructure, including railway connections and port facilities. More importantly, perhaps, this concept also implied the establishment of an exemplary economic and social order. The Navy saw in Kiaochow the opportunity to realize its economic and social ideals and to demonstrate its efficiency in running a colonial society along military lines. Unlike Hong Kong, the British crown colony in China, Kiaochow was under tight supervision by the Naval Ministry, with almost no room left for any form of self-administration.

The colonial economy was centrally managed by state authorities focusing on the establishment of large-scale industries (coal, iron and steel) of military significance. On several occasions, the colonial authorities tried to have the leading iron producer in Germany, Friedhelm Krupp, open a shipyard in Qingdao. The company, however, declined the offer in 1899, 1900 and 1904, because it saw no commercial basis for a profitable shipyard in Qingdao (Schrecker 1971: 226f; Seelemann 1982: 271). Although a smaller company in Qingdao, Franz Oster, was willing to take over the shipyard, the authorities decided to operate the shipyard as a state enterprise. They feared that a small private entrepreneur would not be able to invest the large amount of capital necessary to build large-scale facilities.

In other sectors such as electricity, too, authorities preferred 'big business' like Siemens. When Siemens decided to withdraw from Qingdao, the authorities founded a state enterprise despite the fact that local businesspeople were interested in taking over the power station in Qingdao (Seelemann 1982: 295–97). Smaller private commercial firms and businesses were welcomed, but their economic activities were restricted. They had to apply for various concessions before being allowed to go into business. There were also operational guidelines set up by the bureaucracy. In the colonial economic order, large-scale industries, colonial authorities and the Navy mutually supported each other and cooperated to the common goal of realizing a 'permanent expansion' (Arendt 1951: 260) of state and economy. The intent was that at the end of this development, a military–industrial base in Qingdao would emerge, which would constitute the basis for the future military prowess of Germany in East Asia.

Parallel to the intention of establishing a model economic order, Tirpitz also wanted to socially engineer the colonial society in Kiaochow and to develop it along systematic lines. Life in Qingdao's colonial society was tightly controlled. The colonial administration followed a heavy-handed approach with the goal of establishing clear-cut social structures. In particular, the administration wanted to avoid a mingling of different races or different social groups (like soldiers and civilians). Kiaochow was divided into different zones for the various ethnic and social groups (Warner 1998: 89). The main city of the colony, Qingdao, was exclusively reserved for Europeans, while Chinese workers were settled in newly constructed suburbs.

The legal system reflected this fundamental distinction between Chinese and Europeans.[3] Local common law would apply to the 'natives', while German law (with its courts and legal proceedings) was exclusively reserved for Europeans. The legal system was fundamentally based on a racial distinction between Chinese and Europeans. District commissioners were asked to explore and codify the local common law for use by the German administration. Lesser litigation cases were to be settled in the traditional way by the village heads. Only if there was no solution through traditional Chinese bodies was the case brought to the district commissioner, who delivered a final sentence. In criminal cases, the colonial administration authorized the commissioners to apply the Qing code. However, the administration also issued its own criminal laws. It included an unclear catch-all provision which stated that all actions 'which constitute an offense' are punishable. There was neither a definition nor an explication of what would be considered to be an offense. This paragraph is an obvious violation of the essential legal principle law of *nulla poena sine lege* (no punishment without law). There was no discussion of what kind of offense would result in what form of punishment. This meant that, even for a minor offense, one could in principle be sentenced to severe penalties. Most cases involving Chinese were dealt with by the district commissioners, usually sinologists with no judicial training. The judges in the Kiaochow court would deal only with European and mixed European–Chinese cases, while also trying the appeals against the judgments of the district commissioners.

For the colonial judges, one important question emerged: who was to be considered a 'native' in Kiaochow in a legal sense? In a speech at the Colonial Institute in Hamburg in 1912, High Judge Crusen said that the natives in Kiaochow 'are Chinese in an ethnological–cultural sense' (Crusen 1913: 5). Crusen went on to explain that the reason for not applying the modern German law to the so-called 'natives' rests with cultural difference: 'The application of the German law to people who lack the basis for such an application should be avoided.' Lashing was therefore allowed as the most frequent form of punishment for Chinese, but not for Europeans. For minor offenses such as spitting or urinating on the street, a policemen could impose a punishment of ten strokes on the spot without any trial. Although there are no reports that the administration resorted to extraordinary severe and violent punishments, it was the overall psychological effect that was important here. The Chinese population certainly was aware of the threat that a small offense could, in theory, lead to severe punishment. For the colonial authorities, the goal of such provisions was less to practice them, but to use them as symbolic power. The Chinese population was forced into an insecure position, dependent on the goodwill of the colonial administration. Legal exceptions, graded rights and inequitable treatment served as the basis for the disciplining of the everyday life of the Chinese population.

The administration of Kiaochow was also organized into two separate structures, for Europeans and for Chinese (Norem 1936: 107ff; Schrecker 1971: 70f). While in the countryside the district commissioners tried to avoid any changes in jurisdiction and administration (and therefore cooperated with traditional community leaders such as village heads, who remained in power), a whole set of new regulations was issued for the Chinese population living in urban areas, most importantly after June 1900 (Mohr 1911: 22–29). Part B of this legislation dealt with the 'Maintenance of Public Order and Security'. The paragraphs prescribed in detail that every Chinese living in Qingdao had to register with the Civilian Commissioner for Chinese affairs. §7 forbade any gathering without approval from the administration. §6 stated that all public proclamations in Chinese must have official approval by the colonial administration. §5 ordered that after nine o'clock every Chinese had to carry a lantern while walking on the street. The major and most important instruction, however, is found in part C: 'General Regulations for the Maintenance of Public Health'. §10 forbade any Chinese to settle in the European city of Qingdao, supposedly for sanitary reasons.

The legal regulations for Chinese, the building regulations, as well as the land system (with the monopolization of land in the hand of the colonial administration) (Matzat 1985, 1986; Leutner and Mühlhahn 1997: 173–76) together produced one of the most essential features of the society in Kiaochow, the consequent, pervasive segregation of Germans and Chinese. In the following years, the old Chinese villages in and around Qingdao were razed and the population was moved to the newly built towns Taidongchen and Taixichen. This was justified as necessary 'sanitary measures'. Obviously, Chinese were considered to be 'unclean' and 'infectious' because of their 'promiscuous' and 'unhealthy' way of living, as described in many contemporary medical treatises. German physicians argued that the traditional Chinese customs and way of living inevitably led to the spread of epidemics (Uthemann and Fürth 1911: 35–36). The naval physician Kronecker wrote, for example, in an article in the magazine *Medizinische Presse* in 1913: 'The densely populated living quarters, dirt and vermin, above all the revolting sexual excesses, in which especially Chinese men indulge, make the separation of the Chinese city from the European city inevitable. Buggerie with geese and ducks, […], homosexuality, sexual abuse of children of both sexes, rape in its dreadfullest forms are the order of the day all over China and are almost never prosecuted by the Chinese authorities.' He came to the conclusion: 'Not only Europe, but all parts of the world have a serious duty to fight against an invasion of Chinese proletarians' (Kronecker 1913: 11f).

This is one of many examples of colonial racism, expressed also by other 'scientific' treatises and reports. The allusions in the example previously cited to the fear of a 'yellow peril' reflect colonial racism, too. The *Hunnen-Rede* by Kaiser Wilhelm II is perhaps the best known example of a wide-spread 'yellow peril' effect in Germany at the time. After 1900, there were many popular publications that expressed similar feelings of both anxiety and racial superiority (Gollwitzer 1962). Many of these articles and small booklets stressed the threat to the general public health and racial purity posed by Chinese and other immigrants. Medicine and ethnography created a dominant discourse, in which descriptions of habits, customs and morals of the Chinese population served as an argument for the necessity of racial segregation in the name of sanitation and hygiene. At the same time, it also served as a justification to apply strict rules and regulations to the Chinese population within the colony in order to educate and to improve the habits of the Chinese population. The medical and ethnographic discourse thus was a potent method for subjecting the indigenous population using rhetoric and stigma.

The colonial society in Qingdao that emerged under these circumstances was distinct. Unlike other German colonies in Africa, Kiaochow was never considered to be a colony for German settlement. Kiaochow served primarily as a colonial outpost for the navy. Whoever came from Germany and wanted to settle in the colony had to apply first to the Governor of Kiaochow.[4] Only Germans with special skills and experience in trade, engineering or construction were allowed to move to Qingdao. The German society within the colony consisted mainly of soldiers, merchants, professionals and specialists who had been recruited to fulfill certain tasks.[5] There were few German families or women. The Chinese population was mostly male too.[6] Merchants and workers lived only seasonally in Qingdao. Even in the urban areas, there were very few women and families. As a result, prostitution was rampant throughout the whole period of German rule (Eckart 1989: 31–33).[7] Within a short time, a large Chinese pleasure quarter came into being. In general, the social universe of the colony bore the characteristics of an artificial world. This was due to the fact that the colony was not a historically grown organism, but created by foreign intervention. In the colonial society in Qingdao, different cultures and social worlds might co-exist, but they were to be separated by social, legal and cultural barriers. There were, of course, also contacts and interactions between Chinese workers and German businessmen, students and teachers, officials on both sides, but all these interactions unfolded within a framework of difference and asymmetry.

Yet colonial governance is contradictory: racism led to the exclusion of the Chinese population, but the colonial government's desire to govern made it necessary for the Chinese population also to be engaged. The German colonial project was not unitary, extending from the metropole and cast across passive spaces, unmediated by localities or encounters. The colonial project was construed, misconstrued, adapted and enacted by actors with very different strategic interests and different backgrounds (Stoler 1989). Rivalries and conflicts among groups and individuals, whether of the same nationality or not, led to a *de facto* fragmentation of European efforts and created the dynamics that altered the formulas of colonial governance.

Between resistance and accommodation: Chinese strategies towards German colonialism

In the beginning, the occupation of Kiaochow was met with fierce Chinese resistance. Boycotts, protests, as well as violent upheavals in the surrounding areas all document the resentments against foreign occupation in the first years of German rule. In later years, relations with the Chinese population improved as the colonial authorities started to be more willing to accommodate the Chinese population and give their representatives a say in colonial affairs. After the completion of major infrastructure construction in the colony and its hinterland (railway, mines, harbor) around 1907, an economic upswing began which started to transform the colony into a busy marketplace connecting the hinterland to national and international markets reaching from East Asia to Europe. This development was, to a considerable degree, contingent on Chinese business circles. By the final years, Kiaochow had become a 'contradictory formation' (Steinmetz 2007: 506) where segregation and discrimination were practiced in the legal, administrative and spatial order of the colony, but where at the same time contacts, cooperation and exchanges started to undermine the barriers erected by the colonial state.

From the Chinese side, different social groups promoted different strategies to deal with German encroachment. These strategies were always intended to be more than mere efforts of anti-colonial resistance. Each of the strategies was inextricably intertwined with the promotion of more constructive goals for the whole of China. In this way, the act of resistance acquired a wider meaning, which related the actual anti-colonial action to a strategy for future social and political development. Clearly, this was a key to winning political support.

From the very beginning, the existence of a foreign colonial outpost in the 'sacred province' of Shandong was a matter of high concern for Chinese literati and officials of the dynasty. After he learned of the occupation in November 1897, Kang Youwei immediately broke off his journey to Japan and traveled to Beijing in order to present the emperor with his famous Fifth Memorial, written in January 1898. Kang started by stating that China now faces the serious threat of its partition as he had foreseen it in his earlier memorials, which repeatedly called for ambitious reforms. According to Kang, the German occupation of Kiaochow would lead to a crisis for China, in which its whole existence would be gravely endangered: 'Since 1895, the western states despise us. They used to view us as a half civilized nation, today they compare us with the negro slaves in Africa. They used to speak of our arrogance, today they treat us as a deaf-mute and blind person. According to their treaties only civilized nations have a right for protection. Barbarian peoples shall be eradicated in order to save humanity. [...] Kiaochow is the start of a chain reaction. The first move was now made by Germany.' (Tang 1981: 201–10.) Kang concluded that only the imminent introduction of far-reaching and radical reforms could fend off the invaders, otherwise this step would result in the separation of China. Without reforms, China would be doomed to perish. The alarming tone of the memorial impressed Weng Tonghe, member of the Grand Council and of the Zongli Yamen, and educator of Emperor Guangxu. Weng Tonghe, who had negotiated the lease of Kiaochow with the German legation, signed the treaty for his emperor. He wrote in his diary: 'To leave Shandong to the stinky foreigners, is to be at fault with one's ancestors. [...] This is a day of the greatest shame in my life.' (Kong 1997: 48.) Weng Tonghe then played a pivotal role in bringing about the Hundred-days Reform. The German occupation of Kiaochow was the single most important factor which led to the implementation of an ambitious, though short-lived, reform policy in 1898. Kang Youwei had argued that the best way to resist imperialism would be an overhaul of state and society. The specter of full colonial control served Kang as a powerful argument for Chinese renewal and rebirth.

Local officials in Shandong, such as Li Bingheng, Zhang Rumei and Yu Xian, were alarmed too by foreign encroachment (Esherick 1987: 198–200; Wang 1987: 139–52). They, too, viewed the situation as dangerous and they also agreed that the German occupation constituted a serious crises. But they considered a different strategy to deal with the German encroachment. The premise of their strategy was 'Use the people to control the barbarians' (*Yong min zhi yi*), which eventually bought them to tolerate and even promote the self-mobilization of the rural population through the spread of popular societies.[8] Local officialdom did not seek reform, but restoration through popular mobilization.

Among the officials in the central government in Beijing, a third approached gained currency. In particular, Li Honzhang was inclined neither towards reforms nor toward restoration (Zhang 1991: 75–77). He rather advocated maintaining the status quo. Diplomacy was the tool that should help avoid further military conflicts. The Qing ministers of the Zongli Yamen felt compelled to sign the Kiaochow treaty, because China obviously lacked military means to resist the German invasion. In general, the government officials of Qing China were deeply split over the question how to handle foreign imperialism. This opened up a vacuum which allowed for critical and more radical voices to be raised.

Amidst the tensions and fears in the years following the occupation, violent conflicts between the colonial power and the rural population arose on several occasions in the hinterland of the colony. This region and its supposed large coal seams in Boshan and Weixian represented the focus of German economic interests. In order to exploit the coal resources and to build a railway connecting Qingdao with Jinan, the capital of Shandong, two German syndicates were formed in 1899 by major German enterprises and banks.[9] The syndicates then founded the Shandong Railway Company (*Shandong Eisenbahn-Gesellschaft*) and the Shandong Mining Company (*Shandong Bergbau-Gesellschaft*). The construction of the railway and the mining operations were not only the most profitable economic opportunities granted by the Sino-German treaty, their quick completion was also seen as a precondition for a successful commercial development of the harbor in Qingdao. The colonial authorities and the companies alike wanted the mines and the railway to go into business as soon as possible. Every delay would cause losses for the companies and at the same time endanger the economic future of Qingdao.

But from the start, German companies encountered a number of problems. Peasants were unwilling to sell their land to brokers who were making purchases on behalf of the company. They asked for higher prices, or were unwilling to sell because of the location of burial grounds where the railway company wanted to purchase land. Despite protests, the company decided to press ahead with the construction work, although the purchase of some plots had not been completed. The uncompromising progress of the Shandong Railway Company led to a general feeling of anger among the rural population. In this situation it took only a minor provocation, such as a small dispute between a local peasant and railway worker at the market in the small village of Dalü, to lead to the open outbreak of violence. Angry peasants gathered and decided to hinder the workers from continuing their work (Ge Zhitan to Yu Xian, 20.6.1899, First Historical Archives, Peking (FHA) 5012/0–2, No. 292). As news of a popular unrest spread to Qingdao, the Governor of Kiaochow (Jaeschke) decided 'to teach the peasants a lesson'. The consequent action by German troops was designed to discourage further resistance in the future. Jaeschke ordered about 100 soldiers to move to Dalü and nearby Tidong and to quell the unrest. The troops stormed three villages killing 25 people (Leutner and Mühlhahn 1997: 248).

Following these events, German soldiers occupied the city of Gaomi for two weeks (Yang 2007). Here an incident occurred which drew the attention of officials all over China. Gaomi was the seat of a magistrate. As a wealthy city it was well known for its high share of successful examination candidates and many degree holders.[10] On many houses, signs of academic honors or official appointments were displayed. The German troops took up quarter in the academy (*shu yuan*) of Gaomi, which had a famous old library. On leaving Gaomi, German soldiers destroyed the academy and burned the books of the library (Ge Zhitan to Yu Xian, 3.7.1899, FHA 501/0–2, No. 292). The *autodafé* of Confucian classics symbolically expressed the widespread belief among Germans in Qingdao that in this conflict there was more at stake than the mere construction of a railway line. Rather, they believed in the need to fight not only rebellious peasants, but also Confucian civilization in general. According to their conviction, the enlightened progressive civilization of the West must overcome the backward Confucian civilization, if necessary with arms. In 1900, Jaeschke wrote to Berlin: 'At the moment there is a fierce struggle between two different ideologies in China: the national Chinese Weltanschauung, which rests on century-old traditions, and the cosmopolitan occidental Weltanschauung' (Memorial of Governor Jaeschke, 9.10.1900, BArch/MA, RM3/6782, Bl.276–308).

Despite the German military action in June 1899, Chinese resistance continued unabated. Again and again surveyors' rods were ripped out, but there were no further major incidents until spring 1900. In the lowlands of the Haoli district north of Gaomi, the population feared that the railway would block the drainage of the lowlands and cause floods. The railway company saw this response as a mere pretext to prevent the construction of the railway at all.[11] The company urged the Governor to resort to military measures to protect construction work. In the meantime, the people of Haoli invited leaders of the Boxer Movement to teach them the fighting techniques and magic of the Boxers. The Boxers, too, saw the conflict with imperialism in terms of a clash between civilizations. They believed that the presence of foreigners, and especially the construction of a railway, would disturb the natural balance and upset ancestors and gods. The disturbance of the cosmic harmony was seen by the Boxers as the real reason for the drought and other natural calamities in Shandong in 1900.[12] Facing the rapid spread of the Boxers over North China, the growing attacks on foreigners, and the declaration of war by the Qing dynasty (Cohen 1997a: 14–56), the colonial authorities decided to retreat for the time being. Jaeschke ordered all German personnel back to Qingdao. The railway construction was stopped. The peasants of Haoli celebrated their victory.

The situation changed with the arrival of an international relief force in the hot and dry summer of 1900. In late September, under the leadership of Generalfeldmarschall von Waldersee, a large German force disembarked at Tianjin. On October 6 and 7, Waldersee and Governor Jaeschke met in Tianjin to discuss further German military actions in China. They agreed that the Chinese resistance in the hinterland of Kiaochow had to be suppressed as soon as possible in order to avoid further delays in railway construction. German troops should carry out so called 'punitive actions' against the Chinese population. On October 15, 200 German soldiers moved to Gaomi. On October 23 and on November 1, without any previous warnings, three villages were brought under artillery fire and completely destroyed. More than 450 people were killed, among them many women and children (Leutner and Mühlhahn 1997). The devastation of whole villages as a 'punitive action' was intended to punish the Chinese population and deter others from any resistance in the future.

In 1899 and 1900, a series of violent conflicts strained the relations between the German colonial authorities and the Chinese rural population. The escalation of violence led to tension in and around Qingdao. Both sides felt themselves not only engaged in an economical and political conflict, but more fundamentally in a clash of civilizations. This obviously eased the use of force and brutality. Popular resistance against colonialism, while originally encouraged by local officials, had spun out of control, further increasing tensions.

These violent conflicts between the native population and the foreigners severely affected Shandong during the Boxer uprising. Foreign encroachment facilitated the influx of Boxer fighting techniques and magic into rural Shandong. The spread of heretical teachings and practices began to threaten the social order in the villages, in particular in those regions where the German colonial troops were active. Therefore, after 1900, local Chinese officials systematically tried to carry out a strategy of de-escalation. In 1900, Yuan Shikai, and later his most important successors as Governor of Shandong, Zhou Fu and Yang Shixiang, developed a 'new policy'. In Shandong, the 'new policy' implied a strategy to limit the impact on Chinese society of both imperialism, and popular resistance against it, by restoring traditional order and reaffirming imperial hierarchy. The diplomatic dimensions of the 'new policy' included efforts to establish communication in order to deal with the Germans.

Besides solving disputes arising from the railway construction or mining operations, one central focus of the Governors of Shandong was the Chinese population in and around Kiaochow. Starting in 1902, there were regular visits by the Governor of Shandong to Kiaochow. Lower-level civil and military officials were even more frequent official visitors to Qingdao. Zhou Fu, who was the first Chinese governor to visit the German colony, described in a memorial to the throne the construction projects under way and the enormous amount of money the German administration was investing [Memorial of Zhou Fu to the Grand Council, 31.12.1902, Academia Sinica and Jindaishi yanjiusuo (AS/JYS) 02-11-13 (1)]. Like him, many other officials expressed admiration about the large scale of the German plans. On their visits to Qingdao, they wanted to investigate the German system carefully. Another equally important goal was to take care of the Chinese population in Qingdao. In the above-mentioned 1902 memorial, Zhou Fu also reported that he had sent agents who tried to reorganize the imperial *baojia*-system (part policing, part self-protection) among the population. In this way, the interests of the Chinese population were to be protected against the colonial authorities. A functioning *baojia*-system could also make sure that spontaneous actions of violent resistance could be avoided.

When German authorities noticed these efforts to establish informal structures representing the Chinese interests or extending Chinese control over the native population, Governor Oskar von Truppel was alarmed. He used the opportunity of the visit by Zhou Fu to question him about this. Truppel stated the German position, according to which the Chinese population of the colony was subject only to the German colonial authorities. Zhou Fu disagreed. His point of view was that the 'Chinese people in Qingdao still belonged to their families and clans, they therefore were still under Chinese law, and should and must seek help from there' (Letter of Truppel to Tirpitz, 30.12.1902, in BArch/MA, RM3/6718, Bl.71–74). He went on to demand an official mission, a Chinese representative in Qingdao, who would represent Chinese interests and deal with the Germans. At the official dinner, Zhou Fu then gave a speech and said, 'Although the territory of Qingdao is leased to Germany, it is still Shandong earth' (Truppel to Naval Ministry, 12.12.1902, in BArch/MA, RM3/6718, Bl.13–15, reprinted in Leutner and Mühlhahn 1997: 334). Zhou Fu's proposals were not acceptable to Truppel, who held the view that this would be a severe limitation to German sovereignty in Qingdao.

The domestic dimensions of the 'new policy' included the establishment of 'self-opened commercial zones' (*zikai shangbu*) in Jinan, Zhoucun and Weixian in 1906.[13] In the late Qing, provinces were urged to open cities for international trade in order to bring commercial development to provinces in inland China. Foreigners should be allowed to buy land and open businesses in so-called commercial zones (*shangbu*). In contrast to the foreign settlements in the treaty-ports, these zones were under Chinese administration ('Lease and building regulations for the commercial zone in Jinan', in AS/JYS 03-17-1). Yuan Shikai and his successors intended to bring commercial development to rural areas in Shandong. For this reason, roads and canals were built connecting these areas to the supra-regional infrastructure. In addition, the provincial government established a shipping company to operate on the Xiaoqing River (Zhang 1987: 475). A 'dendritic market system' (Bun 1996: 189) of economic relations was established, where rural areas and opened cities with manufacturing facilities and bulking centers at the coast interacted with each others at various levels of the market structure. The 'new policy' signified a sharp break with the traditional politics of non-interference in the economic sphere. Under the pressure of imperialism, Chinese officials saw the systematic development of the economy as the foundation for the accumulation of state power. The state was thereby being assigned a pivotal role in directing economy and society (Wakeman 1991: 77). The state set developmental–political goals and criteria according to which economic resources should be re-allocated. This state-sponsored development of the inland economy was intended to allow efficient resistance against a German monopoly in Shandong.[14] On the level of political discourse, this economic resistance was intertwined with the promotion of mercantilist and étatist concepts, which propagated the building of a strong state with the unquestioned capacity of surveillance and regulation over economy and society.[15]

Despite German objections, Chinese officials continued to take care of the native population in Qingdao. Excellent relations existed between the merchants in Qingdao and the officials in Jinan. Many of the merchants possessed official rank and the associated status. But despite mutual assistance, the merchants had their own interests and goals, which differed from those of the officials. As in all commercial cities, the Chinese merchants in Kiaochow formed guilds to represent their interests. In 1900, three guilds were founded: the Jiyan Guild represented merchants from Tianjin and Shandong; the Sanjiang Guild was organized by merchants from the Lower Yangzi; and the Guangdong Guild was formed by merchants from Canton (Guangzhou). In 1913, two more guilds appeared: the Changyi and Haiyang Guilds. Both had members who undertook international trade.[16] Thus traditional patterns of activity formed the backbone of the merchant self-organization in Qingdao. At the same time the merchants tried to establish new structures. After lengthy discussions, Governor Truppel approved the demand by Chinese merchants and shopkeepers to form a committee in 1902. The so-called Chinese Committee was designed to comment on specific economic questions. The representatives on the Committee were elected by merchants through votes in the guilds. The Governor wanted the Chinese merchants to cooperate with the German administration in order to stabilize German rule.

Problematically, the committee became very powerful. In 1908 the Committee apparently stood behind a well organized boycott by Chinese merchants and workers. Such a collective and politically charged action against the colonial power shocked the administration. The cause was a sharp rise in depot tariffs in the now completed harbor. The new tariffs clearly were intended to favor large German trading corporations. The committee mobilized the Chinese population. Chinese workers were asked to stop buying German products or visiting German shops. Merchants refused to trade with German firms. It was only after essential concessions by the administration that the boycott against German enterprises was finally terminated.

Recapitulating the boycott of 1908, the German Governor stated with disappointment: 'The population still feels and thinks Chinese' (Truppel to Naval Ministry, 4.11.1908, BA/MA, RM 3/6721, fol. 220–23). Because of these events, the Chinese Committee was dissolved in 1910 and replaced by counselors who were selected by the Governor.

The Chinese merchants in Qingdao played an active role in the 'rights recovery movement' in Shandong, too. In and after 1900, local merchants and business people had protested against that part of the German–Chinese treaty according to which the Qing ceded the exclusive rights and concessions for the building of two railway lines (Qingdao-Jinan and Qingdao-Yizhou) and for the opening of coal mines along the railway lines to German syndicates (Li 1963: 364; Zhao Zhenmin 1986: 90–95). In 1908, at the time of the boycott in Qingdao, a Rights Recovery Association was founded in Shandong. While its immediate concern was to claw back the rights for building railways and undertake mining operations in Shandong, it also had long-term goals. One of those goals was to inform Chinese people about the wrongdoings of the colonial power and the economic losses they brought to China. They saw an effective weapon for forming and influencing public opinion in newspapers and magazines. At the same time, they deprecated the Qing's policy toward Kiaochow as too lenient. Their founding document read: 'The population increases constantly and every empire suffers from overpopulation. Even the stupid peasant knows that agriculture alone is not sufficient. The most important sources of wealth are railway and mining. If these are seized by foreigners, how can the indigenous population make a bare living?' (BArchB, DBC, Nr. 1251, Bl.150–52, reprinted in Leutner and Mühlhahn 1997: 410–14). At the end of the document, two strategies are suggested to recover the lost rights. First, the printing and distribution of newspapers in order to inform the people on the significance of political events and economic issues: 'Our intention must be: Educate the uneducated, urge the educated to act.' Popular culture, in the form of articles, folk stories and songs, contributed to that movement by shaping and expressing popular anti-imperialist attitudes (Li 2004). Second, the document concluded that newspapers will have no impact if people do not love their native place. In this context, it is very important to note that the document speaks only of the people of Shandong. No mention is made of China as a whole, not to speak of the rights of the central government. The rights recovery movement did not promote ideas of a central state, but on the contrary argued for the necessity of local self-administration and self-government.[17] At the same time they demanded a free press. Here, too, visions for the future played an eminent role in articulating the underpinnings of anti-colonial action.

In the first decade of the twentieth century, a political press emerged which was read by intellectuals, students and businessmen.[18] The rise of the press represented a growing interest in political affairs on the part of the educated. Articles on German-occupied Kiaochow appeared repeatedly in a number of newspapers and magazines. These reports offered very critical views on the German colony. They represent a remarkable different point of view on the colonial system as compared with that of the officials. In an article from 22.4.1907 in the *Beijing Guanhua Bao*

(*Beijing Mandarin Paper*), a commentator criticized the legal system in Kiaochow. He denounced the fact that different laws were applied to Europeans and Chinese; that lashing was imposed for Chinese as a form of punishment; and that Chinese had to kneel down before the court, while Europeans could stand (*Shandong jindaishi ziliao* vol. 3, 126). Another article by a journalist (Zhu Ji) who had lived in Qingdao for some years appeared in 1909 in the *Peking Daily News*. The first part of the article offers a vivid description of how Chinese are 'raped and ill-treated' by the Germans. He ends his article with a call for solidarity: 'The people in Shandong are our compatriots! Can we be quiet, when they are oppressed by foreigners? […] The Chinese people have the same talents as other races' (Leutner and Mühlhahn 1997: 233–35). To quote a final example, a Chinese journalist wrote about Kiaochow: 'The worst thing is that Chinese and Europeans were treated differently. The Germans said that they are civilized, while the Chinese are uncivilized barbarians. They issued different laws for Chinese and Europeans. They didn't even call us Chinese, but 'natives' (turen).' (Xie 1922: 26–28).

The growing awareness of discrimination against Chinese people in Qingdao as well as the calls for racial equality reflected the emergence of a new political rhetoric and consciousness. It differed sharply from the terms used by the officials of the dynasty, who stressed family ties and clan relationships, which would bind all Chinese people together. Within this new political discourse, the Chinese people are being imagined as a 'race' (*minzu*) who demand the same rights as other races. This concept implies that the political solidarity and coherence within a race is stronger than among a state composed loosely of clans and families. If the people were aware of racial equality and possessed political self-consciousness, then an organic society founded on racial nationalism could be established. This in turn would enable China to fight effectively against colonialism.

This discourse has much in common with nationalist ideas promoted by Liang Qichao and others.[19] The concern with the common fate of the race and the nation is at the center of the new discourse, which is revolutionary by nature. Although the establishment of a strong state is the prominent goal, this strong state is a revolutionary state, based on the capacity to mobilize the 'racial people' (*minzu*). The racial-nationalist state will be created from below. It is interesting to note that the invention and promotion of racial nationalism in China was accompanied by an increasing awareness of being part of larger global structures and developments. As Rebecca Karl (2002) pointed out in her study on Chinese nationalism, after China's defeat by Japan in 1895, and especially the failure of the Reform Movement three years later, there was a growing sense that China's predicament was not uniquely Chinese, nor was it solely the result of its relations with the Western powers. Indeed, the fact that the fate of colonized people was seen as being similar to the treatment of black workers, Indian workers and so on made the emerging Chinese public keenly aware that China's colonial problem was shared by many emergent nations in a world of colonizers and colonized. Reports from overseas led at least some Chinese to extoll the courageous struggles of these nations against much more powerful enemies and hail them as apt models for China's own struggles. They had an immense impact on the nationalist discourse, so much so that by the early twentieth century, more and more Chinese had come to accept the revolutionary praxis as the norm for building a new nation. The experience of colonialism in the formation and rise of nationalism facilitated links connecting the perceived Chinese plight to similar struggles around the world. Moreover, recognition of these dynamics demonstrates the hidden global consciousness present in Chinese nationalism, as well as the intrinsic dialectics between integration into global structures and the discursive demarcation of boundaries.

Most of the Chinese groups just described were more or less critical or even outrightly hostile to the German colony. But towards the end of the first decade of the twentieth century, groups emerged that had a different and more amicable attitude. While they, too, in principle condemned foreign privileges and domination, certain elements in the colonial system were attractive to them. In 1909, for example, a German–Chinese College was founded in Qingdao. This was one of the first foreign-led educational institutions to be co-sponsored and officially recognized by the Qing government. Students were selected by the Chinese Government. The school had a German director and a Chinese inspector. Western education by German teachers in the morning was supplemented by teachings in the Confucian classics in the afternoon by Chinese instructors. A factor in the establishment of the school was, of course, the changing political climate in China. As the influx of new political and partly radical ideas grew stronger, many members of the elite of Qing society started to see the German Reich, a constitutional monarchy, as a model and partner for cooperation, especially in the politically sensitive educational sector. After 1911, many high officials under the Qing fled to the German leasehold and purchased houses there.[20] They had begun to send their sons to Kiaochow and to let them attend the German schools even earlier.

Another political force to be considered in this context is the Nationalist Party. After the Xinhai Revolution, Sun Yatsen was elected Provisional President of the Republic of China. However, he resigned in favor of Yuan Shikai in 1912. Sun became head of the Railway Ministry and made many inspection tours around China during the rest of the year. In September 1912, much to the surprise of the German authorities, Sun Yatsen indicated that he would like to visit Qingdao in October. Since Germany had not even diplomatically recognized the Chinese Republic, the German authorities had very mixed feelings about this plan. Therefore it was decided to send Sun Yatsen a telegram in which it was pointed out that his visit would be treated as a private matter and that he could not expect to receive any official reception. Nonetheless, Sun Yatsen remained eager to visit Qingdao. When the 400 Chinese students in Qingdao learned about his planned visit, they immediately determined to give him a reception at the Chinese theater in Dabaodao. But the director of the school (Keiper) intervened, calling the reception a political event, which according to the school regulations meant students could not participate. In reaction, all the students unanimously withdrew from the school and gave back their student identity cards. Tensions were running high when Sun Yatsen finally arrived in Qingdao on October 2. After his arrival, he urged the students to end their protest and to go back to school. He explained that, like officials and soldiers, students have to serve their country and could not fully enjoy all the freedoms granted by the new republic. On his second day he paid a visit to the College. In a speech to the students, he called Kiaochow a 'model settlement for China' (Mayer-Waldeck to Naval Ministry, 14.10.1912, BArch/MA, RM3/6723, fol. 316–22). Sun continued: 'In three thousand years China has not achieved what Germany did in Kiaochow in 15 years.' He was so impressed that he later read the book of Commissioner Wilhelm Schrameier about the land system in Kiaochow. In 1924 he invited the former colonial commissioner Schrameier to Canton (Guangzhou) to work out a land policy for Guangdong Province. So it was that the most positive image of Kiaochow ever made came from Sun Yatsen, the revolutionary leader of a nationalist movement. In interviews he gave after his visit, no mention was made of any discrimination or mistreatment of Chinese in Kiaochow. Nor did he speak of the loss of rights or sovereignty. Obviously he was fascinated by the organized and bureaucratic capitalism developed by the German Navy, at a time when he as Railway Minister was considering the future economic and social development of China.

Conclusion

The colonial world in Qingdao was complex and multifaceted. Different social groups, each pursuing their own interests and goals, were competing with each other in the dynamic, fluid social space of the colony. German colonial rule did not succeed in unifying the German population, let alone the Chinese. Unification and conformity are but two of the myths of nationalist or colonial historiography. On the contrary, the push for exclusive control by the colonial state led to social and political fragmentation on all sides. Different groups emerged that promoted different strategies to deal with and respond to colonial governance. Qingdao became a highly contested space where, under foreign domination, different social groups struggled to protect or improve their position. It is essential to note that the practical results of the colonial project of refashioning indigenous society were contradictory. Colonial government was partial and inequitable. It did not exist in a hermetic domain, but was revalued and distorted through the participation of the colonized.

The diversity of colonial governance is one of its key features. Another is that this diversity created equally diverse responses and strategies within the Chinese population. Similar complexities have been demonstrated for other colonial or semi-colonial spaces.[21] In this shifting and fractured colonial space, different projects of Chinese nationalism emerged and were negotiated. This is not to deny the central role of complex sets of national traditions and longer trajectories in China. Apart from those long-standing traditions that have been foregrounded by nationalist historiographies, however, the global interaction that had occurred since the appearance of imperialism added an external dimension to the otherwise domestic story. The synchronic articulation of national issues with larger trends and processes allowed social actors to link up with global contexts. These contexts did not create nationalism, but they influenced – and perhaps even fundamentally shifted – the way in which the nation was conceived and the ways in which its mechanisms of inclusion and exclusion were practiced.

The colonial experience and Chinese nationalism were then dynamically interrelated within a fluid global setting. The sense of nation emerged at least partly in response to the colonial encounter. The existence of Chinese communities under foreign domination prompted questions concerning the cohesion and composition of the nation and fed into discourses of nationalism. The trajectories of nationalism in China were significantly altered and acquired sharpness and profile in colonial or semi-colonial contexts.

This, then, amounts to a revision of common assumptions about the history of Chinese nationalism. While an earlier trust in the long traditions and continuities of a national 'essence' has long been deconstructed, most current theories of nationalism nevertheless privilege the temporal dimension of modern 'imagined communities'. While it is recognized that most national genealogies were indeed constructed in retrospect, the analytical focus remains on the connections of past, present and future conceptualized strictly within national borders. However, the example of Qingdao has shown that the particular forms that nationalisms and the various representations of the nation-state took in a colonial context were not mere invented traditions, but rather at least partly the effects of interactions and entanglements in colonial contexts. The shifts and changes in the discourse of nationalism thus appear not only as effects of internal and diachronic modernization, as the familiar picture would suggest, but also just as much effects of more diverse synchronous processes.

Notes

1 Following normal procedure in other colonies, Kiaochow would have been assigned to the Chancellor's office or later the Colonial Ministry. But because of the personal intervention of the powerful Secretary of State for the Navy (*Reichsmarineamt*) Admiral Alfred von Tirpitz, Wilhelm II placed Kiaochow under the jurisdiction of the Naval Ministry in mid-January 1898. This was highly unusual and without any precedent, because the Naval Ministry was thought to be a political government office existing primarily to represent the navy's interests and financial claims in the Reichstag. The daily supervision of the navy was the responsibility of the supreme command of the German navy. In 1889, Kaiser Wilhelm II had reorganized the command structure of the navy. He created three institutions of equal standing: the Naval Cabinet (led by adjutant Gustav von Senden-Bibran), responsible for all affairs concerning naval personnel; the Naval Ministry (directed by the Minister of the Navy Alfred von Tipritz), with the duty to represent the political interests of the navy; and the supreme command (with a commander-in-chief at the top), which was in operational command of all naval units. See Hubatsch (1983): 188ff.
2 Relations between Berlin, the administration in Qingdao and the local German population were often strained. Local colonizers and business people complained that they were not given the right to participate in decisions concerning local affairs. After 1907, four elected civil representatives could comment on current affairs, but they had no real power since their decisions were not binding on the Governor. In later years, criticism by the civilian population on this point grew stronger. See Hövermann (1914): 29.
3 By issuing an ordinance in April 1899, different civil and penal laws for Chinese and for Europeans came into force (see 'Ordinance concerning the legal position of the Chinese

population', 15.4.1899 in Mohr 1911: 72–77). The legal system is discussed by Seelemann (1982): 76–96, but he is unaware of the discrimination and disciplining aspects of this system. The more important relevant ordinances are printed in Leutner and Mühlhahn (1997). While not identical, the judicial system is comparable with that of other German colonies (see Wolter 1995).
4 In a letter to the chief of the Naval Cabinet, Senden-Bibran, the Secretary of State of the Navy, Alfred von Tirpitz, stressed that everybody had to make an application before settling in Qingdao (Tirpitz to Senden-Bibran, 2.6.1898, BA/MA, RM 2/1836, fol. 237).
5 Throughout the whole period 1897–1914, the German population of Qingdao remained relatively small. It did not exceed 1855 people in 1913 (see Wang 1922: 94, using German statistic materials, which are lost today). In addition, German military personnel amounted to 2400 people (see Mohr 1911: 442).
6 This is, of course, not true for the peasants living in the rural regions. In 1914, Kiaochow had a Chinese population of 187,000 people. Of these, approximately 55,000 lived in urban areas. They were mostly workers, who lived in Kiaochow only periodically. See Leutner and Mühlhahn 1997: 238f.
7 The colonial authorities tried to cover up this aspect of colonial society (see Truppel to Tirpitz, 12,12,1903 in Leutner and Mühlhahn 1997: 220–22). Despite censorship, prostitution was occasionally mentioned by German newspapers, see for example *Tsingtauer Neueste Nachrichten* 9.3.1911, p. 9. The paper reported that 'in the large pleasure quarter' many children and young girls were forced to prostitution.
8 See for example the telegram by Li Bingheng to the Zongli Yamen, 19.11.1897, in DQSLXJ (1986): 257.
9 A detailed account on the German companies and their activities is found in Mühlhahn (1997).
10 Sixty per cent of the degree holders of Shandong came from Gaomi or Jiaozhou (see Esherick 1987: 30; Wang 1922: 1).
11 The fears of the Chinese population proved right. In 1902, the whole region was flooded, destroying the harvest and washing away whole villages. The German Governor sent a specialist to the Haoli district to investigate the causes. In his secret report, Engineer Born came to the conclusion that the flooding was beyond doubt caused by the railway. He accused the railway company of having built too few and narrow bridges, in order to cut costs. See report of Engineer Born to Governor Truppel, 4.9.1902, in Leutner and Mühlhahn (1997): 300–02 (Doc. 83). After that, Truppel urged the company to add more bridges to the railway line in the Haoli district. The company did so, and no further flooding occurred.
12 For the belief system of the Boxers, see Cohen (1997a):84f. See also Sun Lixin (2007) and Sabine Dabringhaus (2007).
13 While the foreign-dominated treaty ports have been fairly well studied, this important Chinese counter-model and economic innovation has by and large been ignored in Western and Chinese historiography. A overview is given by Zhang 1994; scarce information is also provided by Schrecker (1971): 155–57; Buck (1978): 51–54; Zhang Yufa (1987): 596–98.
14 German officials were well aware of this. Governor Truppel wrote to the Naval Ministry: 'the opening of commercial zones (...) has the purpose to paralyse German superiority' (in Barch/MA, RM3/6729, Bl. 1–2).
15 The promotion of a strong state is discussed by Hunt (1993): 63; Duara (1995); Tsin (1999); 159.
16 On the guilds, see Zhang (1986): 835–36. Similar conditions existed in the 'Hyper-colony' of Tianjin, see Bun (2001).
17 These were the same groups, who were also active in the new provincial assemblies and demanded more provincial autonomy *vis-à-vis* the central government, especially in financial matters (see Thompson 1995).
18 On the rise of the press and journalism, see Vittinghoff (2002); Mittler (2004).

19 See the excellent discussion by Fitzgerald (1996): 85. Nationalism was supposed to awake the Chinese people and make them aware of colonial cruelties.
20 In 1912, there were 12 Qing Governors and Governors-general living in Qingdao, see Mayer-Waldeck to Naval Ministry, 24.2.1912, BArch/MA, RM3/6723, fol. 84–85.
21 A number of recent studies on Hong Kong or Tianjin can be read in this way. See for instance Ngo (1999); Rogaski (2004).

3
THINGS UNHEARD OF EAST OR WEST

Colonialism, nationalism, and cultural contamination in early Chinese exchanges

Bryna Goodman

> 'My countrymen are so clever, they are capable of doing things that are unheard of in the world, both East and West.'
>
> Yu Huancheng (in Zhu 1947: 142)

In the wake of Engels's remark that colonization was 'purely a subsidiary of the stock exchange', it is not surprising that more scholarly inquiry has engaged links between colonialism and metropolitan stock markets than has sought to understand the role of colonialism in the global spread of stock exchanges beyond the colonial metropole. Examination of Shanghai's securities bubble of 1921–22 suggests, however, that it may be productive to interpret the emergence of a native stock exchange in China as a semi-colonial encounter.

In 1921, between 136 and 150 Chinese stock exchanges opened for business in Shanghai, most of these in the second half of the year. As Shanghai residents rushed feverishly to invest, the Yale and Columbia-trained Chinese economist Ma Yinchu viewed these local financial apparitions in the cold light cast by a global perspective. In a lecture he gave in February, Ma commented: 'We know the total number of stock exchanges in the entire world does not exceed one hundred. Yet now in China, where industry is weak and business is undeveloped, there are surprisingly 40–50 exchanges. Most of them are located in just one corner of the country, the city of Shanghai. Without further reflection it is evident that we are experiencing a potential crisis that could wreak havoc at any moment.' (Ma 1999: 415). Months before the height of Shanghai's 'stock and trust storm', Ma warned that the new exchanges were undercapitalized, poorly managed, excessively numerous, and insufficiently regulated (Ma 1999: 417). Within a year, by early 1922, all but a handful of the Shanghai exchanges had indeed collapsed.[1] Although Shanghai's stock market bubble might simply be interpreted through Ma's concern with deficient economic management, or by means of Chen Duxiu's characterization of the city as utterly corrupted 'with the stink of New York money-worship', such approaches would neglect the ways in which the emergence, character, and popular understanding of these exchanges were intertwined with the semi-colonial structure of the city (Chen Duxiu 1920: 595).

The limited scholarship on the early Shanghai stock market has emphasized economic rather than cultural or political history. Although not all historians have diagnosed the early Shanghai exchanges as symptomatic of a 'sprout' era of modern capitalist finance (Liu 2004: 1), they have typically understood this episode of Shanghai history in terms of economic immaturity.[2] Efforts to explain the operation, or dysfunction, of Shanghai exchanges with reference to normative economic trajectories tend – like assumptions about modernity that associate European institutions with rationality – to cast the modernist aspirations and institutions of Chinese as poor replicas of Western models. This was indeed the perspective of some notable contemporary Shanghai businessmen and economists who, like Ma Yinchu, attempted to make sense of Chinese vernacular formations of global capitalist modernity. The eminent industrialist Nie Qijie (C.C. Nieh, Nie Yuntai), for example, blamed both China's deficient material circumstances and Chinese business morality for the 'economic suicide' constituted by the Shanghai exchanges, concluding that it was destructive 'to adopt non-native practices without considering factors of time and space' (Nie 1922: 6–7).

This chapter re-examines Shanghai's stock market bubble by considering factors of time and space through the prism of colonialism. In Shanghai, the transplanted financial institutions took root in semi-colonial soil, where various, limited, and unequal political authorities configured the urban landscape with elements of extraterritorial jurisdiction and sectors of Chinese governance. In this semi-colonial space, global and local forces, and colonial and local financial institutions, framed the distorted mirror of popular market capitalism that loomed and shattered in the bubble of 1921–22.

The narrative that follows emphasizes the particularities of the Shanghai 'contact zone', a zone in which the institutions and practices of Chinese and foreign residents and authorities were all shaped by the unequal terms of their reciprocal encounters. The Chinese stock exchanges that arose in Shanghai in 1921 were, in several respects, canny appropriations – not of an abstract, idealized, Western stock market – but of the actual, extraordinarily speculative contemporaneous Euro–American stock market in Shanghai, and a deliberate displacement of a Japanese exchange that had just opened in the city. In this respect their provenance was not solely economic. Lofted by the globalized forms and promises of market capitalism, in concert with the anti-colonial rhetoric of Chinese economic nationalism, the Chinese exchanges were oddly disconnected from the global marketplace. Amid controversies over their connection to industry or commerce, Chinese stock market proponents necessarily concealed the fact that Chinese exchanges were not even exclusively Chinese, and that flows of capital could not be policed for national purity. The polarized terms of nationalism, and of nationally-oriented historiography, have obscured the complex identities, hybrid institutions, and transnational flows and networks that infused the city.

The first section of this chapter offers an overview of events and players in the establishment of Chinese exchanges, highlighting the role of semi-colonial conjunctures. The second section considers the way that anti-imperialist rhetoric legitimated stock exchange development and created anxiety over the national purity of Chinese capital, while diverting attention from the structures of extraterritorial jurisdiction that facilitated the multiplication of the exchanges. The final section examines discussions in the Shanghai press of the morality of economics that reflected the cultural particularities of the semi-colonial context. The Chinese conceptualization of economics as *jingji*, a nineteenth-century Japanese contraction of the classical Chinese phrase *jingshi jimin* (to regulate the affairs of the world to succor the people), meant that classical notions of statecraft and morality haunted the imported Western science. The collapse of the stock exchanges raised questions about the cultural and moral purity of the Chinese, whose contamination by monetary desire produced such devastating results. From the desires that underlay their inception to the sentiments aroused by their demise, the early Shanghai stock exchanges were formed by the nationalist ambitions, mixed company, multiple and fragmentary political jurisdictions, and cultural anxieties of semi-colonial Shanghai.

A brief history of the early Shanghai stock market

The Chinese exchanges of 1920–21 grew out of a conjunction of factors: Shanghai economic growth, the presence of foreign enclaves, and a marriage of nationalist vision and pragmatic revolutionary financial necessity. To tell the story, it is necessary to juxtapose the more commonly separate histories of indigenous securities trading in Shanghai, foreign financial institutions in enclaves of extraterritorial jurisdiction, and the murky unofficial histories of the financial calculations and speculative aspirations of Sun Yat-sen and Chiang Kai-shek.

Although formal Chinese stock exchanges were not established until 1920, venues for securities trading existed in Shanghai since the late nineteenth century. An ephemeral Chinese shares market developed in the 1880s along with a short-lived company that specialized in stock trading in 1882 (Zhu 1998). After this, Chinese enterprise stocks were traded informally in 'teahouse meetings' (Feng 1947: 146). As early as 1907, a group of Shanghai businessmen proposed to the government the creation of a Chinese stock exchange modeled on the Tokyo Securities Exchange. The business community was not united behind this plan and it did not receive government support. Informal Chinese trading gradually coalesced into the Shanghai Stock and Bonds Trading Association, which listed approximately 20 securities in 1914. Individual trade guilds (flour and gold, for example) established offices with detailed rules for the buying and selling of securities (Shanghai shi difang xiehui 1933: 43–44; Feng 1947: 147). Because such venues were constrained to limited communities, however, more Chinese investors in late nineteenth- and early twentieth-century Shanghai gained their understandings of the market in the contemporaneous and highly profitable foreign shares trade.

Coinciding with these Chinese developments, and preceding the establishment of a fully fledged Chinese stock exchange, a foreign shares market in Shanghai formalized with a Stock and Sharebrokers Association (around 1898) and a Shanghai Stock Exchange in 1904/05. The Shanghai Stock Exchange, like its foreign community, was multinational and based its rules on various Euro-American models, enforced by the extraterritorial legal framework of the International Settlement. It traded in stock and bonds in Western companies (including rubber companies in Southeast Asia) (Hong and Zhang 1989: 139). From its inception, discipline was lax, records were loose, and speculative forward transactions were common (in short, it bore the signs of corruption, manipulation, volatility, and lack of regulation commonly associated with an immature market). As W. A. Thomas (2001) has noted, whereas in European countries stock markets formed in response to a need to finance mounting national debts, in the Western exchange in Shanghai, speculation alone was a primary motivating factor. Company directors did not refrain from using insider information to 'short sell' shares in their own companies. This speculative market attracted numerous Chinese investors. Although trading did not reach deeply into Chinese society, Chinese compradores as well as clerks in foreign establishments speculated in foreign shares, financing foreign shipping and other commercial ventures. Chinese capital made up 40 per cent or more of the total in major joint stock enterprises launched from the 1860s by Jardine's, Russell's, and other leading firms. Despite substantial Chinese investment, the exchange, like other Western institutions in Shanghai, was openly discriminatory. Chinese were excluded from membership until 1929 (Thomas 2001: 71–90, 103, 112).[3]

With investment in the Western stock market came exposure to global economic currents. In 1910, as the automobile industry in Great Britain and the USA created the expectation of a vast rubber market, rubber plantations multiplied in Southeast Asia. Many of these companies, some of which existed only on paper, advertised heavily in Shanghai. Shanghai investors, foreign and Chinese, responded enthusiastically. Reportedly, 70–80 per cent of rubber shares purchased were Chinese. Chinese investment losses in the global downturn were compounded by local semi-colonial frameworks. As the rubber bubble burst in July 1910, insolvent exchange brokers worked out a settlement with the powerful Shanghai foreign banks and finance houses. Chinese native banks, with limited capital resources, were vulnerable. As many as half of the approximately 100 native banks in business prior to the crisis became bankrupt as they tried to cover their losses and foreign banks refused to accept rubber stock as security on loans.[4]

After experiencing exclusion from the Western exchange, falling susceptible to the fraudulent rubber schemes of Western companies, and witnessing the vulnerability of Chinese financial institutions, Chinese businessmen, political reformers, and revolutionaries pressed for the creation of a Chinese stock exchange as a prerequisite for national modernization.[5] In 1914, the new Beijing government formulated the first stock exchange law, providing for the legal registration and regulation of Chinese stock exchanges and limiting each locality to a single exchange in securities and each type of goods. Differences of opinion remained over whether exchanges should be managed independently by merchants or jointly with the government (Liu 2004: 6).

In the event, the initiator of the ensuing Shanghai drama was neither a businessman nor an official of the Beijing government, and the stimulus for the formation of the first Chinese stock exchange in Shanghai under the new law was less economic development than political expediency. In late 1916, anxious to fund his revolutionary movement, Sun Yat-sen – whose prior fiscal innovations included selling revolutionary bonds (Bergère 1998: 191) – solicited the help of Shanghai businessman Yu Xiaqing. Together they drafted a proposal for a Shanghai exchange for submission to the Ministry of Finance (Shanghai shi difang xiehui 1933: 43). As Yang Tianshi recently detailed, adding flesh to earlier oral histories of Guomindang finance, in this move Sun Yat-sen worked with a Japanese associate, a Kobe shipping magnate, 'a supporter of the Chinese revolution', who wanted to develop a Sino–Japanese exchange and offered Japanese capital in return for a division of profits.[6]

In January 1917, Sun, Yu, Zhang Jingjiang, and Dai Jitao traveled to Beijing and petitioned the government to establish the exchange. They argued that as China's commercial, financial, and industrial center, Shanghai needed an exchange to standardize prices, facilitate the circulation of capital, regulate brokers, attract investment for new enterprises, and prevent panic. Without a Chinese exchange, they reasoned, Chinese investments would not serve China, and foreign brokers could manipulate the prices of manufactures (Yang 2000: 159). The nationalist tone of the petition precluded mention of Japanese capital and technical assistance. In the meantime, however, Dai Jitao traveled to Japan and established a preparatory office in the Tokyo Securities Exchange.

Various obstacles arose to the fulfillment of this plan. In spring 1918, while Dai Jitao was still engaged in organizational work, Japanese in Shanghai pursued an alternate course and established their own exchange, the Oriental Trust Guarantee and Exchange Company (*Shangye quyinsuo*), in the International Settlement, with Japanese government support. The Japanese presented the Shanghai exchange as a branch of an Osaka-based exchange to avoid Chinese legal constraints.[7] The opening of this Japanese concern in December 1918 provided a competitive urgency that Yu Xiaqing exploited to persuade the Beijing government to approve a Shanghai Chinese exchange.[8] The Japanese exchange traded in both commodities (particularly cotton yarn) and securities (in Japanese and Chinese enterprises). Japanese penetration of Chinese financial markets alarmed Chinese financial circles. Articles in *Chinese Bankers' Weekly*, for example, declared that the Japanese concern violated both the new Chinese securities law (which prohibited foreign purchase of Chinese securities) and Japanese law, and decried what the Japanese called 'guidance' as 'economic colonialism', and 'a way of acquiring a colony without changing the colors of the map'.[9]

Asserting that the Japanese exchange endangered the Chinese economy and treated Chinese investors unfairly, Chinese exchange promoters pressed for action to resist Japanese market manipulation (Zhu 1994: 13; Liu 2004: 8–9). While they negotiated the scope of the fledgling Chinese exchange that the Ministry quickly approved in principle,[10] the new Japanese exchange fell prey to anti-Japanese sentiment that had been building in China since the 1915 publication of Japan's Twenty-One Demands. At the end of 1919, in a widely publicized symbolic strike at a site of Japanese economic penetration, Yu Xiaqing purchased the land under the Japanese exchange (prime real estate, on the corner of Avenue Edward VII and Sichuan Road) and served notice to vacate the property.[11] Yu's Securities and Commodities Exchange (*Zhengquan Wupin Jiaoyisuo*), established on this site, opened for business in July 1920. Yu reportedly won support from 'zealous anti-Japanese exponents' by declaring that his aim was to challenge the Japanese concern (Tong 1921: 419).

The creation of a second Chinese exchange soon complicated Yu's careful orchestration of Chinese unity in resistance to Japanese economic colonialism, challenging the business of Yu's exchange and attesting to the weakness of Chinese law in the face of factional politics. A dispute in the stock-trading community led the Chinese Ministry to approve two Chinese exchanges in Shanghai. Yu tried to incorporate members of the pre-existing Shanghai Stock and Bonds Trading Association into his operation, but he was rebuffed.[12] That association successfully opened its own competing concern in early 1921, the Shanghai China Merchants' Securities Exchange (*Shanghai Huashang Zhengquan Jiaoyisuo*) (Liu 2004: 11–12).[13] Each exchange had backers in Beijing who forced through ministry approval, contrary to China's new law that stipulated that there should be only one securities exchange in each locality (Qi Liang: 39–42).

Although the specter of colonialism (and the local experience of semi-colonial institutions) fueled the globalization of economic nationalism and spread of the universal institution of the stock market, the Chinese vernacular institutionalization of stock exchanges was novel in several respects. A peculiarity of these early Shanghai exchanges was their 'three-in-one characteristic'. Their members were at the same time founders, shareholders, and brokers, a situation conducive to, if not designed for, speculative manipulation. Both of the new ventures issued their own stock (Liu 2004: 12). The two exchanges were immediate money-trees, exceeding expectations. However, their profitability led to competition, imitation, and speculation:

> Shares in the exchange skyrocketed. People who wanted to get rich hit on the idea of starting stock exchanges….People were crazy about stocks. If they heard an exchange was being created, they would book stocks in advance, as if getting hold of stocks equaled getting hold of wealth….Even those without a specific trade created exchanges out of the blue. There were no laws for exchanges at the time….
>
> *(Yu 1947: 142)*

By summer 1921, stock exchange euphoria permeated the city. The next months saw the rapid appearance of as many as 150 exchanges and a dozen trust companies, all competing in a frenzy of speculation and popular ignorance. Most traded stock only in themselves.

Multiple sources attest that these new economic institutions were accessible and open to investment from members of Chinese society who had even a paltry bit of capital. Small exchanges competed to entice petty urbanites, including women. The Shanghai General Chamber of Commerce worried as 'people from all walks of life, peddlers and hawkers, even lowly people in the remote countryside busily engage[d] in buying and selling stocks' (*Shangbao* 7 September 1921). At least 20 exchanges operated at night. One of these, the Shanghai Night Market Commodities and Securities Exchange (*Shanghai yeshi wuquan jiaoyisuo*) was located within the Great World amusement palace (*Da shijie*) to attract office workers. French consular documents describe another night-time exchange that operated an on-site pawnshop so that women could turn their jewelery into cash for quick investment.[14] As the bubble developed, speculation 'wiped out prostitutes, actors, servants and soldiers in one furnace'.[15] Peasants in the nearby countryside reportedly sold houses and land to cover stock losses (Cang 1922: 1–2).

If the new institutions were accessible to the Chinese population, they were far from transparent. Small groups behind closed doors manipulated outcomes and absconded with funds at the expense of the larger population. Even insiders had trouble seeing clearly, as is evident from the speculative activities of Chen Guofu, Chiang Kai-shek, and Zhang Jingjiang. Chen Bulei similarly reported deep involvement in the stock market and catastrophic losses (Chen 1949: 2; Lu 1964; Yang 2000). Foreign and Chinese commentary suggests that the profits and losses in this bubble were overwhelmingly Chinese.[16]

In the event, the urgent logic of nationalism conveyed greater legitimacy than the logic of capitalism. The discussion that follows highlights the way that newspaper commentary and serialized fiction voiced concerns over foreign intervention, national purity, economic modernity, and Chinese morality.

Anti-imperialism, semi-colonialism, and economic libertarianism: fearing Japanese contamination but embracing the market

Historically, the abstractions of capital and market-exchange relations, as they replaced face-to-face and familiar habits of exchange, have given rise in different locations to fears of hidden financial associations with groups that were considered disloyal, dangerous, or disreputable. Such targeting of ethnic, national, gendered, or racial scapegoats displaces cultural anxiety over the morality of capitalism.[17] In Shanghai, concerns over Japanese colonialism stoked anxieties about foreigners, specifically Japanese. Whereas anti-Japanese boycotts, beginning in 1915, targeted relatively identifiable Japanese products and companies (and 'traitorous' Chinese merchants), intrusions of foreign capital were less visible. Rumors were rife. In the semi-colonial city, the new stock exchanges rose and fell on waves of popular fears of foreign manipulation of Chinese finance.

Because one rationale for Chinese exchanges was their efficacy as a means of warding off foreign economic penetration, the Beijing government attempted to pre-empt unruly transnational capital flows with assertions of national economic sovereignty.

The Chinese stock exchange law of 1914 prohibited foreign shareholders from the Chinese securities market and excluded non-citizens from employment in Chinese exchanges.[18] On this basis, Chinese commentators declared the Japanese exchange a violation of Chinese law and political sovereignty.[19]

The context of popular nationalism gave rise to suspicions that the new financial institutions – which reduced individual and national identities to universal units of capital – masked foreign infiltration. These fears were present from the inception of the first exchanges. While organizing a stock-purchasing company in June 1920, Chiang Kai-shek fretted in his diary about foreign manipulation of Chinese finance and exploitation of the Chinese people (Yang 2002: 81). Immediately after the July 1920 opening of the Securities and Commodities Exchange, rumors circulated in the Chinese press. When stock prices rose in a few days from 12.5 to 70 yuan, the *Shibao* reported – providing no specifics – that a foreign speculator was manipulating naïve Chinese investors. When the foreigner stopped buying, the price fell, incurring Chinese losses (*Shibao* 15 August 1920).

Widely publicized and incendiary charges affected the public image and profitability of individual exchanges. The first characters in the name of the second Shanghai exchange, *huashang*, identified it as Chinese and implied that the rival Securities and Commodities Exchange was contaminated with Japanese capital (Qi Liang: 39).[20] Rumors circulated that an unseen Japanese expert 'resided in the Exchange', whose power was 'infinite'. Details emerged of arrangements between Yu Xiaqing and directors of the Osaka Fuji Weaving and Spinning Association, whose efforts to establish a second Japanese exchange in Shanghai had been turned down by the Japanese government. Yu's opponents alleged that the Osaka group had provided a capital loan in return for 80 per cent of the shares (Tong 1921: 419). In early November 1920, a letter was published in the most widely circulating English-language newspaper, *China Press*, attacking the Securities and Commodities Exchange for connections with the China Enterprise Society (*Zhonghua Qiye She*), a Japanese corporation, claiming that the exchange camouflaged Japanese shareholders by listing them by Chinese names. The charge was refuted in the Chinese press by representatives of the Securities and Commodities Exchange. Similar charges were soon made against the China Merchants Securities Exchange, followed by threats of legal action. On 18 November 1920, for example, Chinese papers reported that a lawyer representing the Shanghai Cotton Exchange had denounced the China Merchants' Exchange in a telegram to the central government and to Jiangsu provincial authorities, claiming that the exchange had illegally borrowed 3 million yuan from Japanese (*Shibao* 11 November 1920; 18 November 1920; *Shanghai Gazette* 9 November 1920).[21]

Although revelations of Japanese involvement were idiomatic in public debate, observers also criticized the way patriotic rhetoric legitimated Chinese speculation and corruption (*Shanghai Gazette* 9 November 1920). Controversy was fuelled by the practical problem of policing transnational capital flows, the profitability of patriotism for the establishment of new exchanges, factional divisions within the Shanghai business community, and the strategic use of the press by all parties in the affair. By January 1921, as reported in *Millard's Review*, the Securities and Commodities Exchange was 'doing everything within its power to convince the public that it has been financed by the Chinese, managed by the Chinese and operated for the benefit of the Chinese'. However, its critics, including Nie Qijie, chairman of the Shanghai Chamber of Commerce and the industrialist Zhang Jian, announced that it was 'financed by alien capital and established to serve alien interests' (Tong 1921: 418).

The controversy took a toll on the business of the exchange, which initially listed 'cotton, yarn piece goods, gold and silver, cereals, oils and skins and hides'. As suspicions arose of Japanese connections, businessmen handling particular commodities withdrew and organized their own exchanges. In the words of the journalist Hollington Tong, the Stock and Produce exchange was 'fast disintegrating' (Tong 1921: 418). In the meantime, because information flows, like capital flows, were transnational in the newspaper environment of Shanghai, opponents of the Securities and Commodities Exchange substantiated their accusations with evidence from the Japanese press. Clippings from the Tokyo journal, *Finance and Economy*, identified the Chinese exchange as 'in reality, a Sino–Japanese enterprise', with majority interests held by Japan's China Trading Company (Tong 1921: 420).[22]

After the bubble burst, the theme of the secret impurities of Chinese securities markets was reprised and satirized in contemporary fiction. Jiang Hongjiao's social novel, *Revelations of the Stock Exchange* (*Jiaoyisuo xianxing ji*), serialized in *Xingqi* (*The Weekly*) in 1922–23, provides a window onto contemporary apprehensions of economics and the stock market.[23] In the novel's opening pages, Chinese businessmen become interested in a Chinese exchange after observing the Japanese exchange in Shanghai, in which Chinese could not compete. Yu Qianbo, a Guangdong businessman,[24] opens an exchange out of pure greed; however, he emphasizes Chinese economic rights and sovereignty (p. 27). Unable to comprehend stock exchange organization on his own, he relies on a Japanese acquaintance, an inauspiciously named wanderer with the surname Gui (turtle), who designs the new exchange. Yu hides Gui's involvement from his Chinese collaborators. When Gui's presence becomes unavoidable, Yu gives him a Chinese name and identifies him as a Japan-returned Chinese student. Yu's exchange milks patriotism for profit. Persuaded that Chinese should purchase stock to protect their country, even Chinese who originally had no interest in the market invest, boosting prices (p. 37). Despite its agile manipulation of the Chinese public, however, the new exchange is also victimized by rumors, circulated by the *Plain Talk News* (*Ping yan bao*) that it is trading in foreign securities. As satirized in the novel, fears of foreign competition and infiltration of Chinese finances are the currency of stock exchange promotion, as well as of attacks on individual exchanges.

Concern with Japan is unsurprising in both the novel and in the public discussion it satirized; nonetheless, both elided analysis of the semi-colonial administrative structure of the city, which created the framework for the multiplication of the exchanges. Although some commentators bemoaned the fact that, with foreign enclaves in the city, 'the power to administer or prohibit [exchanges] now falls into the hands of other countries instead of our own',[25] there was in general little inclination to dwell upon the recognized effect of foreign enclaves in the city.

The multiple political jurisdictions of the city created structural obstacles to effective regulation. What was hard for Chinese exchange promoters to foresee and impossible for the Chinese government to control, once Chinese exchanges came into being, was the way in which Western authorities in the city first allowed for and subsequently abetted – by virtue of extraterritorial privilege, if not always conscious intent – the multiplication of the Chinese exchanges.

If all bubbles are facilitated by a failure or absence of regulation, the semi-colonial setting of Shanghai provided a particular type of loophole that permitted exchanges to mushroom. If Chinese law had been enforceable, it would have limited Shanghai to one securities exchange and one exchange in each commodity.[26] But as people realized the profitability of exchanges, organizers of new exchanges took advantage of extraterritoriality and registered with foreign consulates. The journalist George Sokolsky, writing at the end of 1921, identified 'pernicious registration in foreign consulates' as the fundamental factor in the excessive establishment of exchanges, providing a convenient 'back door' that freed exchanges from adherence to Chinese law.[27] A November 1921 British report on some 70 exchanges listed only six that were registered with the Chinese Ministry. Others 'were registered with the military governor of Shanghai, the French and Italian Consulates-General', or they were not registered at all (FO 228/3175).

The Beijing government attempted to stop the wild proliferation of exchanges, not just in Shanghai, but also in Tianjin, Hankou, Guangzhou, Ningbo, and other treaty-ports.[28] A letter sent in early November from the Chinese Ministry of Foreign Affairs to the French Legation in Beijing attests to the poor reception of these efforts:

> The Ministry of Commerce and Agriculture and various administrative offices and commercial groups of Beijing and the provinces have repeatedly begged the Ministry of Foreign Affairs to take steps to close the exchanges. [But] the Commissioner of Foreign Affairs in Shanghai has informed me that the French General Consul is not willing to order the closure of the exchanges... Such a state of affairs bankrupts individuals and perturbs the local market.[29]

Rather than accede to the Chinese request to close the exchanges in the French Concession, the French authorities chose to register them in return for a fixed payment of 100 taels per exchange per month. The fees were calculated to maximize French receipts without driving exchanges to take refuge in other jurisdictions.[30] Irregular correspondence ensued between Xu Yuan, Jiangsu Commissioner of Foreign Affairs, and French General Consul Wilden. In December, Xu noted that falling prices had led to financial crisis and suicides.[31] Wilden rationalized his dismissal of the Chinese government's earnest demands to suppress exchanges by noting that, despite Chinese government policy, Chinese government personnel 'do not cease asking, as personal favors, for favorable treatment for the establishment of [particular exchanges]'. Beyond this anecdote of unprofessional and personalistic behavior by Chinese bureaucrats (which, together with his claim that Chinese government functionaries demanded bribes of 5000 taels to register exchanges, helped rhetorically to diminish the legitimate claims of the Chinese government), Wilden deemed it 'impossible to satisfy the Chinese government' for three reasons, each following a different logic:

> First, it would be very dangerous to permit the intervention of the authorities in the administration of a terrain in which we have jurisdiction. Second, the closing of exchanges not registered in Peking…would provoke a panic on the Shanghai market…We might thereby take upon ourselves the responsibility for failures that would eventually be brought about by the immutable laws of economics. To conclude…a decision to close the exchanges would [send] the large number of exchanges into foreign jurisdiction, thereby shielding them from all Chinese authority. The Spanish and Italian consulates are unfortunately too inclined to provide their protection to the most irregular establishments.[32]

In other words, cooperation with the Chinese authorities would infringe on the principal of extraterritorial jurisdiction and interfere with the immutable laws of the market, and finally there was nothing the French could do – even with the best intentions – when it was evident that the Spanish and Italians would not cooperate.

The French in fact made more serious efforts than other consular authorities to regulate the exchanges.[33] Perhaps for this reason, only 33 exchanges established themselves in the French Concession in fall 1921, as against approximately 100 in the International Settlement.[34] In the International Settlement, as a British report lamented, 'with our divided jurisdiction and lack of plenary powers, [we] cannot follow so good an example'. The British, like the French, also found ideological reasons to ignore the appeal, concluding that accession to Chinese requests 'would constitute an interference by the Chinese Government in the internal administration of the Settlement'.[35]

The fundamental role of extraterritoriality in sheltering dubious exchanges and the complicity of the foreign powers was obvious to Chinese observers. Nonetheless, journalists writing for Shanghai's commercial newspapers were reluctant to support Chinese government claims against the foreign settlements if this entailed constraining the rights of Chinese businessmen and legitimating the unpopular Beijing government's efforts to ban excessive and illegal exchanges. Indeed, in their opposition to government regulation, Shanghai journalists and businessmen were outspoken, not only in articulating their faith in the ability of the market to correct itself, but also in defense of the *status quo* of extraterritoriality.

Shao Lizi, writing in the Guomindang newspaper *Minguo ribao* (*National Daily*) in July 1921, argued that free market competition, left to itself, could resolve the problem of the increasing numbers of exchanges:

> Chinese people can claim no other freedom but the freedom to make money. For this, the conditions have been rather accommodating. Even if the officials

really mean to ban [excessive exchanges] it would be difficult....However, we needn't be too pessimistic. Through the free competition that characterizes capitalism, unsuccessful exchanges may be eliminated and economic reform promoted [without government intervention].[36]

Commentary in the *Shangbao* (*Journal of Commerce*), a paper that advocated a politically mobilized middle class, worried that the Beijing Government might ban excessive exchanges.[37] A characteristic editorial written at the peak of the bubble deployed patriotic rhetoric to oppose government supervision and regulation, asserting the rights of the Chinese 'masses' against oppressive government:

> [The government] did nothing to prevent the existence of the Japanese exchange in Shanghai, letting the foreigners undermine our sovereignty. Now it wants to recover national sovereignty by stopping the exchanges our own countrymen have organized....Since the respectable officials have forgotten about protecting sovereignty, why should they reproach the masses?
> (*Shangbao* 11 August 1921)

Another editorial argued that since the Ministry of Agriculture and Commerce violated its own law limiting exchanges, Chinese laws themselves had no force:

> Up to today, there hasn't been a legal exchange law...The regulations the present official refers to should actually only be taken as provisional rules. The officials and the masses should equally be subject to the rules. As the Ministry violated the regulations in the first place, why should business people be scolded?
> (*Shangbao* 4 September 1921)

Prominent businessmen were outraged when news circulated that a memorandum recommending the banning and suppression of unauthorized exchanges had been sent to Chinese authorities in the name of the Shanghai General Chamber of Commerce (*Shangbao* 31 August 1921), in which the Chamber suggested that the organizers of illegal exchanges could be arrested when they stepped beyond the limits of the foreign settlements (where they were protected by extraterritorial jurisdiction). The pharmaceutical manufacturer, entertainment entrepreneur, and 'advertising king' Huang Chujiu and others engaged in an war of words with the Chamber, carried in the major Shanghai papers, criticizing the Chamber for 'helping the government to suppress merchants'. Huang argued that the Chamber's treatment of exchanges was hypocritical since, 'according to the customs of the foreign settlements', Chinese merchants routinely registered their businesses with the foreign consulates or settlement authorities. He and his colleagues also railed against the incompetence, illegitimacy, and hypocrisy of the Beijing Government. Finally, Huang suggested somewhat disingenuously that, if the Chamber incited the Chinese government to punish those who resided in the foreign settlements, this could anger foreign nations, leading to new humiliations for the Chinese nation and further damage to Chinese sovereignty (all of which would be caused by the Chamber's proposal that Chinese exchange organizers follow Chinese laws) (*Shangbao* 7 September 1921; see also *Xinwenbao* 3, 4, 5, 6, 7, 8, 9, and 10 September 1921).

These commentators preferred self-regulation through the efforts of Chinese businessmen, banking institutions, and public associations. They embraced the global form of the market and the competitive development of Chinese capitalism against Japanese infiltration of the Chinese economy. When assertions of national sovereignty threatened Chinese businessmen's ability to make profits, they firmly opposed compliance with the Beijing Government.[38] Because of this public record of ardent Chinese advocacy and agency in the multiplication of Chinese stock markets, when the bubble burst, Chinese businessmen and market promoters could be understood as a traitors from within, undermining the Chinese economy under cover of the specter of Japanese intervention.

Economic modernity, colonialism, and cultural ambivalence

This final section considers ramifications of the translingual notion of *jingji*, economics, which incorporated classical Chinese, Japanese, and Western elements in a fashion that was characteristic of the mixed cultural repertoire of the semi-colonial contact zone.[39] The imported toolkit of economic modernity in the form of global capitalism was subject to reworking. Chinese meanings for economics in the early 1920s were multiple and uncertain, assimilating globalized Western models of scientific nation-building, fiscal planning and prosperity, and older notions of benevolent statecraft and anti-mercantile bias. Different moments in the bubble called forth different rhetorical packages.

In semi-colonial Shanghai, from the late nineteenth century, dreams of national capitalism in a competitive global order provided new rationales for Chinese businessmen to embrace profit-making. Contemporary stock market guides and economic reportage attest to the strategic construction by interested parties of positive notions of capitalist economics. This work was necessary to counter coexisting moral reservations that were uncongenial to capitalism and European-modeled notions of modernity. National capitalism also necessitated the stock exchange. According to proponents of the new economic modernity, only by strengthening China's industry and commerce could China challenge the colonizing appetites of the world powers:

> With global communication, competition becomes fierce. Military confrontations are joined by commercial warfare....Those who wish to develop industry and commerce must have power, substantial capital, good organization and systematic economic institutions....The stock exchange is a specialized institution to guarantee credit, stabilize commodity prices, regulate supply and demand, guide capital investment, and reduce the dangers of business....The stock exchange is an institution that those in economic, industrial, commercial and financial circles cannot afford to do without.
>
> *(Wang 1921: 3)*

The idea of a harmonious and protective market elided the troublesome issue of individual profit-making and speculation. In such guides and commentaries, stock exchanges emerge as institutions for the national good.[40]

Such notions could be sustained only through the temporary erasure of earlier conceptualizations of money-making, though these were hardly consistent either. The romance of capitalist modernity, as presented in the commercial press in the May Fourth/New Culture era, was built on the vision of a discredited Chinese past, one that was weakened by an array of 'traditional' cultural weaknesses. These problems needed to be rooted out before Chinese culture could be remade to fit the needs of a strong nation that could end the nightmare of imperialist humiliation. Among China's cultural flaws were decadent pastimes, particularly those – like gambling – that dissipated rather than built up Chinese wealth. The press was awash in editorials attacking lotteries and advocating the suppression of all forms of gambling.[41] Economic modernizers opposed gambling because it wasted resources that were needed to build the national economy. The popular association of stock exchanges with gambling created moral problems for market promoters who had been vocal opponents of gambling but who also advocated the new exchanges.

As the bubble swelled, premonitions of disaster brought questions of gambling and morality to the fore, and businessmen castigated their class. At the height of the bubble, in the 21 July 1921 inaugural issue of the *Journal of the Chinese General Chamber of Commerce*, the cotton magnate Mu Ouchu (Xiangyue, H.Y. Moh) diagnosed Chinese exchanges as a false response to China's vulnerability to the global economy. Mu argued that the post-war depression had led Chinese businessmen 'to rush into the stock market, staking everything on a single venture'. Although the economy had prospered during the war, 'exchanges are now numerous and commercial morality has declined'. The result was disaster: 'Those that died, died, and those who fled, fled. Then scholars grandly informed people that the exchanges were nothing but large-stakes gambling houses.'[42] Rampant speculation was soon so evident that comparisons with gambling and references to suicide were everywhere.[43] Nie Qijie joined others in decrying the corruption of businessmen 'who have no moral values to speak of in this situation' (Nie 1922: 2).

Rhetorical defenses of the market lost ground in the context of the burst bubble. State-building and patriotic policing of the purity of national capital against foreign contamination had provided a convenient anti-colonial gesture that distracted from concerns about the moral impurity of capitalism. After the collapse, however, a revivified anti-mercantile moralism surfaced powerfully to rebuke the Chinese exchange fever. A Chinese contractor's report for the International Settlement cataloged the damage wrought by the 'mushroom finance' of 1921, and the demise of the first third of the exchanges by January 1922. Rents in the downtown district increased ruinously by 20 per cent as speculation possessed the city. Stock exchange promoters absconded with cash investments. Businessmen lost fortunes. Many committed suicide. Enterprises folded. Promising young men had been led astray.⁴⁴ Jiang Hongjiao's novel, *Revelations of the Stock Exchange*, concludes with a scene of destruction:

> Only three or four exchanges remained, tottering in the midst of the raging storm…Former elementary school teachers had abandoned their profession. Former shop clerks had thrown themselves into exchanges, and in less than six months, where were they?…Shanghai's business had been destroyed by stock exchanges and many became destitute. Truly one could say, in a field of calamity, the words 'stock exchange' were on everyone's lips.
>
> (Jiang 1994: 158)

The modern terms 'stock exchange' and 'economics' became vessels for negative cultural apprehensions about greed. Writing about the suicide of a woman who lost money in the stock fever, the pioneering Shanghai film director Zheng Zhengqiu asked rhetorically who was to blame. Surveying the social destruction wrought by the stock market, Zheng concluded that it was unfair to blame the woman (Xi) for her 'death by speculation' (Cui 1922).⁴⁵ Zheng concluded, as did others at the time, that a crime had taken place, and that Xi, like other stock market-induced suicides, was an unwitting victim. The guilty party was a foreign-tinged abstraction: 'Whose crime is this? If it isn't the crime of economics, what is it?' (Cui 1922: 10). Zheng's question highlights the inability of the imported notion of economics to maintain its progressive aura after the bubble burst.

Stock market fiction bloomed as a genre in the wake of the bubble, recoding the imported institutions of economic modernity with associations of death and destruction. In Jiang Hongjiao's satirical exposé of the corruptions of the market, the exchange – like the late imperial demon god of wealth, Wutong – tempted good women to go astray.⁴⁶ Like the lascivious Wutong, who dazzled maidens with gifts of golden trinkets that evaporated in their hands, the stock market both took back what it seemed so freely to bestow, and ruined its seduced victims. The following passage highlights one suicide in a panorama of destruction:

> Most pitiful was the suicide of the wife of the Western-medicine doctor, Pan Huzhen…When she saw stock prices rising, she relied on someone to purchase 100 shares, and in four days she earned 700 *yuan*…Who could have known that four brokers had cornered the market?… In less than two months she lost a total of 17,000 *yuan*. At first she didn't tell her husband, but when he found out she couldn't think what to do. She went to the Midnight Exchange and hid in a dark corner. After midnight, when the exchange closed and the people went home, she tiptoed onto the trading floor. There she took out a cloth, fastened it on a post in the brokers' section and hung herself.
>
> (Jiang 1994: 155–56)

In a similar vein, a short story by Lu Shouxian, 'The Suicide Hanging of a Woman Who Failed', suggested that women were targets for brokers who understood that 'women's money could be easily loosened from their grasp, with promises of profit'. This story recounts the financial seduction of an insufficiently guarded wife, whose husband was periodically away on business in Hankou, unaware of her secret and deadly financial relations with a broker. The narrative presents the impersonal economic consequences of the woman's speculative market activity in terms of her interpersonal relations with her broker: 'Morning and night the broker demanded payment, not permitting even a slight postponement. Madame Hu begged the broker for mercy…' Desperate, Madame Hu went to the stock market director and knelt humiliatingly before him. Even though the fictional Madame Hu was not sexually promiscuous, her financial transactions appear as marital improprieties (Lu 1922: 41–42).[47]

In these moral tales, the stock market is an agent of moral contamination. Investors progressed rapidly from moral deterioration to self-destruction. This happened as quickly as the new exchanges 'turned what was formerly gold and silver into paper with characters on it', and ultimately to 'waste paper'. (Lu Shouxian1922: 54, 74)

If the stock market was hailed initially in a robust discourse of national economic strengthening on a global stage, the traumas of the burst bubble displaced the expansive promise of capitalism with claustrophobic images of self-destruction. Newspaper cartoons moved from mild cultural ambivalence to images of danger and suicide.[48] The cover of Lu Shouxian's satirical anecdotes of the Shanghai stock market, *Revelations of the Stock Exchange*, was festooned with skulls (Lu 1922).

One might explain the interpretive association of the stock market with suicide as a simple reflection of the extent of the economic disaster and the suicides it incited. No statistics document the actual incidence of suicide in Shanghai at this time, so the question cannot be answered empirically.[49] An analytical focus on literal suicides, in any event, cannot do justice to the problem of understanding the prevalent merged images of suicide and the stock market. Some foreign observers questioned the preoccupation with suicide in Chinese accounts after the bubble. A British report on the market collapse concluded that, while there was much damage, 'it is easy to exaggerate. Though the Chinese press constantly reports cases… such reports are not to be relied upon except as an index to the course of public opinion.'[50]

Historically, suicide in China was an arena for the production of moral truth. For opponents of the stock exchange, the spectacle of suicides committed by ruined investors provided poignant evidence of the evils of the institution. In the end, the stock market was apprehended in moral terms that were both uncongenial to capitalism and innocent as well of a systematic language of global economic or class analysis.

If it is not surprising to find rehearsals of cultural ambivalence toward profit-seeking in the aftermath of the bubble, it must be noted that the Shanghai public did not refer to older diabolical embodiments of greed (like the late imperial demon Wutong) in their efforts to make sense of the event and identify a culprit. For those who did not hold the suicides themselves responsible, beyond the abstract notion of economics and the dubious mechanism of the stock exchange, two other culprits came readily into public discussion.

The first of these was the suspect foreigner, familiar from the discussion above, the agent of economic colonialism. But in semi-colonial Shanghai, Chinese had not only embraced the market, they had taken refuge from the Chinese government by registering in the foreign settlements. Precisely for this reason, a foreign scapegoat alone did not suffice. It was also necessary to locate and identify an internal offender, the traitorous Chinese businessman. The market traumas of 1921–22 stained the image of the business community that had so avidly promoted the destructive exchanges, revealing the fragility of business and profit-making as reputable modern pursuits.[51] Indeed, the positive façade of the new modern businessman had never entirely effaced notions of the immorality of greed, which haunted the Chinese exchanges from the moment of their inception. Even as Chiang Kai-shek began trading stocks and commodities in 1920, he expressed his deep moral disgust for capitalists. He asked in his diary, 'how can we not sweep away all these profiteers and philistines?' (Yang 2002: 85). Essays and poems published in the daily papers reviled 'poisonous snakes who created the stock exchange' (*Shishi xinbao* 18 September 1922), blaming 'traitorous merchants' for the stock market crash (Cui 1922: 16). These accusations refer to businessmen as 'fat bellies' and 'demons in human clothing' (*Shibao* 14, 16, 18, and 19 October 1922), images that would be redeployed in various ideological contexts over the course of the next half-century.

While newspaper readers and pundits selected their culprits as they pleased, an imaginative focus on suicide may have helped to displace suspicions of stained virtue with the greater honor of victimization. If most people in Shanghai were still too poor to have risked their money on the market, it was still shocking how many families of modest means had succumbed to the temptations of the market. The inevitable collapse that followed the orgy of market speculation elicited soul-searching public reflection upon the disturbing loss of Chinese morality. The semi-colonial framework ensured that the moral searching that followed the crash would be experienced as a cultural inadequacy as well. Insofar as a sense of Chinese morality had been one secure source of cultural superiority in comparisons with foreign imperialists and colonizers, the figure of the naïve suicide was perhaps a way of displacing cultural guilt over Chinese agency in what had happened.

Notes

I am grateful for the challenging comments of Brett Sheehan, Cynthia Brokaw, and Wendy Larson.
1 At the height of investment fever, the total capital in the Shanghai stock market was more than double the amount held by all foreign and native banks in the city. A November 1921 report calculated that, whereas the amount held by native and foreign banks in that year totaled $75 million, as much as $163 million was in the exchanges [Public Record Office, Foreign Office (United Kingdom) (FO) 228/3175]. George Sokolsky estimated $200 million in 140 exchanges in early December 1921 [G. Gramada (pen name), 'Gambling in produce exchanges', *North China Daily News*, December 6, 1921]. Liu Zhiying calculates approximately 148.5 million yuan plus US$10 million in stock

exchanges, and another 8 million yuan in trust companies (Liu 2004: 19). Losses exceeded 30 million yuan (Caizhengbu caizheng kexue yanjiusuo 1997: 713). In 1922, 1 yuan was approximately equal to $0.56.
2 These studies assume a logic of normative market development that has, until recently, dominated the field of economics (Feng 1947: 146; Bergère 1986: 86; Zhu 1998: 3; McElderry 2001; Thomas 2001; Liu 2004).
3 Because Chinese investments in foreign companies were not recognized by the Chinese Daotai (Intendant), such investments were riskier for Chinese shareholders than foreigners (Hong and Zhang 1989: 138–39; Thomas 2001: 89).
4 Pressured by the Chinese business community, the Daotai secured a low-interest loan from the foreign banks to preserve Shanghai trade, palliating the crisis in Chinese financial institutions (Shanghai renmin yinghang shanghai shi fenhang 1978: 74–78; Zhu 1998: 62–65; Thomas 2001: 153, 162).
5 Sun Yat-sen attributed the huge Chinese losses in the rubber speculation to foreign exploitation of Chinese weakness for gambling (Liang 1910; Sun 1927: 51–52). On fraudulent Western companies, see Yu (1947): 141; Hong (1989): 140–41; Zhongguo renmin yinhang, *Shanghai qianzhuang shiliao*, pp. 74–88.
6 The Japanese associate is identified as shipping magnate Mikami Toyotsune. On December 5, Dai Jitao negotiated and signed a contract setting the capital basis for the exchange at 5 million silver dollars. Because the Chinese side lacked funds, the Japanese side agreed to provide an interest-free loan of at least half of the sum, in return for 80 per cent of the profits. An agreement was signed that the exchange would hire experienced Japanese advisors. Sun Yat-sen, Yu Xiaqing, Dai Jitao, and Zhang Jingjiang all signed (Yang 2000: 158). Hong Jiaguan suggests that the initial, unrealized Sino–Japanese exchange was envisioned as a Chinese, Japanese and US cooperative effort that would be registered as a US company (Hong 1989: 143).
7 According to Shao Lizi, an article in the *Tokyo Economic Journal* admitted to legal uncertainties (Shao Lizi 1918).
8 The first Chinese exchange, which traded primarily in government bonds, was established in Beijing in 1918. For an expression of the competitive urgency aroused by the establishment of the Japanese exchange in Shanghai, see 'Quyinsuo yu jiaoyisuo zhi zhengzhu' ['Competition between the quyinsuo and jiaoyisuo'], *Shenbao* September 17, 1918 (Hong 1989: 143).
9 *Yinhang zhoubao* [*Bankers' Weekly*] 2: 46 (November 26, 1918), 'Lun Shanghai quyinsuo' ['On the Shanghai quyinsuo']; 'Cang, Jingji zhanzheng yu jingji tixie' ['Economic war and economic guidance and help'], *Yinhang zhoubao* 2: 47 (December 3, 1918).
10 The Ministry favored the creation of three exchanges, rather than one with combined functions. Yu Xiaqing argued for the latter, on the model of the Japanese *quyinsuo* (Yang 2000: 160).
11 'Japanese exchange loses its quarters to Chinese combine', *China Press* January 1, 1920; 'Chinese form stock exchange: institution formally inaugurated after 20 years of agitation', *China Press* February 3, 1920; 'Chinese exchange oust Japanese: by the simple plan of purchasing the site', *Shanghai Gazette* January 2, 1920. The Japanese exchange moved and operated until 1922 or 1927, when it was forced to liquidate its assets (Feng 1947: 152; Hong 1989: 144).
12 Resentment of Yu's actions led to legal challenges and a successful motion in the Jiangsu Provincial Assembly to shut down his exchange. This tactic was useful only for publicity in the context of the fragmented Chinese government and Shanghai's extraterritorial jurisdictions. 'Assemblyman would close Chinese stock exchange', *China Press* November 7, 1920; 'Motion to close Chinese exchange passes assembly', *China Press* November 13, 1920.
13 According to Chen Guofu, he and Chiang Kai-shek established the Maoxin brokerage in the Securities and Commodities Exchange. Chiang and his associates initially lost heavily, but gradually profited. Chiang was also involved in the unprofitable Hengtai brokerage, with Zhang Jingjiang. Chen Guofu's correspondence with Chiang Kai-shek indicates

remittances to Sun Yat-sen, but no details regarding the amounts (Lu 1964; Yang 2000: 161–64).
14 Nantes, Ministère des Affaires Étrangères, Archives Diplomatiques, Shanghai Consular Papers, Série A, Box 59, letter dated December 23, 1921.
15 This reference to the lowest social classes appears in 'Xinjiao kuangchao zhi fandong' ['Reaction to the exchange madness'], *Yinhang zhoubao* 5: 50 (December 27, 1921). Feng (1947: 147) mentions the involvement of butchers and peddlers.
16 Foreigners' aversion to the risks posed by the Chinese exchanges largely contained the 1921 Shanghai bubble to Chinese investors (in contrast to the rubber bubble). 'Havoc wrought in Shanghai by new stock exchanges is bared in police reports', *China Press* November 17, 1921; 'Big fraud is charged in stock exchange case', *China Press* January 26, 1922.
17 In eighteenth-century London stock trading, popular fears focused on Jews and Scots, who were understood to endanger the English economy with their speculations and swindles (Andrew and McGowen 2001: 155–57). In nineteenth-century France, women were considered more likely to betray French interests and dissipate French capital by foreign investments (Thompson 2000: 131–62). On women and Chinese exchanges, see Goodman (2005a): 351–75.
18 'Zhengquan jiaoyisuo fa', December 29, 1914, reprinted in Shanghai shi dang'an guan (ed.) *Jiu Shanghai de jiaoyisuo*, pp. 274–81.
19 'Lun Shanghai quyinsuo' ['The Shanghai exchange'], *Yinhang zhoubao* 2: 46 (26 November 1918); Shao Lizi, editorial, *Minguo ribao* (2 November 1918).
20 This charge was also made in the Jiangsu Provincial Assembly: 'Motion to close Chinese exchange passes Assembly', *China Press* November 13, 1920.
21 Such attacks were as likely as not to be based in fact. Not long after its establishment, mismanagement and speculation caused a financial setback at the Securities and Commodities Exchange. The problem was resolved through a large loan from a Japanese citizen, the Taiwanese Lin Maoru (Zhu 1994: 16.)
22 Another Japanese journal (*Diamond Economic Journal*) identified the exchange as Japanese, described Yu as a 'Japanese catspaw', and indicated that secrecy was necessary in an atmosphere of Chinese anti-Japanese feeling (Tong 1921). On the Shanghai press, see Goodman (2004a): 55–88.
23 The novel, written ten years earlier than Mao Dun's epic stock market novel, *Midnight*, is reprinted in Tang (1994).
24 The early exchanges were actually dominated by Zhejiang and Jiangsu merchants.
25 'Qudi jiaoyisuo zhi san da yaosu' ['Three essential reasons to prohibit exchanges'], *Qianye yuebao* 1: 8 (August 1921): 35–36.
26 This is not to say that the Beijing government would have effectively controlled the numbers of exchanges. As noted above, Ministry approval of a second securities exchange in Shanghai that was contrary to law indicates the corruptions of factional politics.
27 Sokolsky argued that some Chinese bought shares in exchanges believing that, should troubles arise, they would be protected by the American consulate. He argued that the consular powers should act responsibly because 'foreign honor' was at stake: 'for it may be claimed that businesses which would not be tolerated in their own countries have been permitted to exist and multiply in Shanghai under the protection of foreign flags' (G. Gramada, 'Gambling in produce exchanges', *North China Daily News* December 6, 1921).
28 Various Chinese also remonstrated with foreign consuls to terminate registration of Chinese exchanges. The British archives contain appeals from Zih Likung, Hong Kong and Shanghai Bank Compradore, and S. K. Chow, Glenn Line Compradore (FO 228/3175).
29 Nantes, Archives Diplomatiques, Shanghai Consular Papers, Série A, Box 59, letter dated November 7, 1921.
30 Nantes, Shanghai Consular Papers, A-59, letter dated October 25, 1921, and enclosures. Comments on the revised regulations (which lowered the projected tax) argued against

putting the French Concession exchanges in an unfavorable position 'to the profit of their competitors in the International Settlement or the [Chinese] city...This would go against our goal which is to increase our receipts.' Receipts were to fund public welfare projects in the French Concession.

31 Nantes, Shanghai Consular Papers, A-59, letter dated December 12, 1921.
32 Wilden to Fleuriau, Nantes, Shanghai Consular Papers, A-59, letter dated December 19, 1921.
33 In addition to the monthly fee, the French imposed fines of $5–1000 for breaches of regulations (FO 228/3175 Enclosure No. 1).
34 Nantes, Shanghai Consular Papers, A-59, letter dated December 19, 1921.
35 Fraser, report dated January 31, 1922, USDS 893.52/37
36 'Mei fa bimian de jie yun' ['Ill-fortune which cannot be avoided'], *Minguo ribao* July 24, 1921.
37 *Shangbao* was established in the wake of the May Fourth mobilization of business circles in Shanghai. Chen Bulei was general editor, and was himself involved in market speculation (*Chen Bulei huiyilu*).
38 'Jingji shibian yu shehui zeren' ['Economic accidents and the responsibility of society'], *Shangbao* February 27, 1922; 'Konghuang zhi fangzhi' ['Preventing panic'], *Shishi xinbao* August 13, 1921).
39 *Jingji* was a return graphic loan, the *kanji* term *keizai*, derived from classical Chinese. Other translations were also used, including *fuguoce* (means to enrich the country), *fuguoxue* (national enrichment-ology), and the transliterations *aikangnuomi* and *yikanglaomi* (see Liu 1995: 268, 315, 360).
40 In the context of Chinese cultural norms, the absence of subscribers to Adam Smith's faith that individual economic self-interest contributed to the public good is unsurprising. Even among the Shanghai business class, the individual profit motive was considered injurious to the group. The delicacy of Chinese stock market promoters' descriptions of the market may be contrasted with a contemporaneous speech on the stock exchange presented to British residents of Shanghai. The speaker, A. J. Hughes, argued that the stock exchange was indispensable to general social welfare. His assertion of the social value of individual incentive in the stock exchange would not have easily persuaded a Chinese audience. 'Mr. Hughes discusses "The Stock Exchange as a Factor in Social Evolution"', *Shanghai Gazette* November 30, 1920.
41 Examples translated from the *Shishi xinbao*, *Zhonghua xinbao*, and *Shenbao* appear in *Shanghai Gazette* November 15, 1919 and February 15, 1921; see also 'Caohehing shangmin qing yanjin dubo' ['Caohejing businessmen call for the strict banning of gambling'], *Shangbao* April 3, 1922.
42 Mu Ouchu, 'Lun jiaoyisuo zhi li bi', *Shanghai zongshanghui yuebao* 1(1) (July 1921): 1–2.
43 See, for example, *Jingbao* June 17, 1921; June 18, 1921; August 9, 1921; August 27, 1921; July 30, 1922. 'Wei jiaoyisuo ji xintuo gongsi wenti da Yang Chu jun' ['Response to Mr. Yang Chu in regard to exchanges and trust companies'], *Shishi xinbao* August 17, 1921.
44 'Shanghai's stock and produce exchanges', *Chinese Engineer and Contractor Bulletin* (supplement, January 1922), US Department of State Archives, 893.52/37.
45 This case is detailed in Goodman (2005b).
46 On Wutong, see Von Glahn, *Sinister Way*, pp. 242–46. More men than women fell victim to the market in the novel, and in real life. But female suicide victims were particularly highlighted (see Goodman 2005a).
47 Lu's collection bears the same title as Jiang Hongjiao's novel.
48 See, for example, cartoons published in *Shenbao* August 19, 1921; August 23, 1921; September 15, 1921; September 17, 1921; *Jingbao*, July 20, 1922; September 18, 1922.
49 Suicide statistics are not available prior to 1928. Shanghai shi difang xiehui, *Shanghai shi tongji* (*Statistics for Shanghai Municipality*) (Shanghai, 1933).
50 USDS 893.52/37, Fraser, report dated January 31, 1922.
51 Lawsuits filled the courts after the collapse, exposing egregious business practices. When called to comment or provide evidence, business journals and institutions such as the

Chamber of Commerce chose words with care. Rather than expose the broad guilt of the business community by coming to the assistance of colleagues who had simply followed common practices at the time of the bubble, the Chamber appears to have made a calculated decision to let individuals fall as scapegoats. Appeals to the Chamber to provide exculpatory evidence – or to clarify commercial practice – went unanswered, even when directors of the Chambers themselves admitted privately that a particular individual had only followed what had become standard business practice [Shanghai Chamber of Commerce archives, Gong-Shang-Lian Archives, 200-1-008 (1922)]. For a discussion of both the developing social legitimacy and fragility of the new business class in the Republican era, see Yeh (2007).

PART II

Colonial spaces and everyday social interactions

4

THE PEAK

Residential segregation in colonial Hong Kong

John M. Carroll

Few visitors to Hong Kong have failed to be impressed by its skyline, defined by rugged, verdant hills. Describing the sights and wonders of Hong Kong, a guidebook published in China in 1938 noted how watching the sunset from one of the colony's peaks was 'as good as seeing Mount Tai' (Chen 1938: 23), one of the 'five sacred mountains' of Taoism. The best known of these summits has always been Victoria Peak on Hong Kong Island. An English guidebook of 1893 explained how 'the visitor will probably select Victoria Peak as the first place of interest to visit after his arrival in Hongkong, particularly if the day is fine and the hills are clear of mist' (Kelly & Walsh 1893: 86). Usually referred to simply as 'the Peak', it became known both for its beauty and its salubrious climate. After Governor Richard MacDonnell's summer home was built there in the 1860s, some 20 years after the British occupied the island of Hong Kong during the Opium War, the Peak quickly became a full-time residence for European elites. As the 1893 English guidebook noted (p. 86), the area was full of villas 'erected by merchants and others to escape from the heat during the summer months and enjoy a night's sleep in the pure and cooler air of the mountains'.

Perched high above the rest of the colony, the Peak was often compared with Simla, the hill station and summer capital of British India. Complete with its own police station and water supply pumped from below, and connected to the main business district by the Peak Tramway, the Peak had all the features of a quaint English town. In a colonial society obsessed with social rank and hierarchy, living on the Peak also became the pinnacle of social status, 'a visible manifestation of class and position' (Gillingham 1983: 8). In a series of imaginary letters published in the local *China Mail*, a pseudonymous 'Betty' (1905, reprinted in White 1996: 147) described the Peak as 'a would-be mountain dotted over with bungalows and villas wherein live the elect'. As 'Betty' put it, 'the Peak looks down on everything and everybody'. Crucial to this sense of superiority and control was the area's separation from the rest of Hong Kong. In 1903, Governor William Des Voeux recalled in his memoirs (p. 222) how 'neither sight nor sound gave any token of human existence, and it seemed difficult to realise that within so short a distance was a dense population'.

Because the Peak was the year-round home to Hong Kong's European elite rather than only a summer resort, it differed from other hill stations in Asia. As in most hill stations, however, residence was restricted to Europeans. In ordinances enacted in 1904 and 1918, Chinese, except for the servants, cooks, *amahs*, houseboys, and drivers in their special uniforms, were excluded from living there. Amidst the fears of increased contact with Chinese and Eurasians, and economic competition from these rising upper classes, such restriction movements were attempts to preserve the status and social structure of the elite European community. More important for this volume on colonialism in China, the Peak residence ordinances show how formal colonialism in Hong Kong differed from the type of imperialism or semi-colonialism practiced elsewhere in China, where Europeans simply did not have the power to enforce such rigid forms of residential segregation. Unlike in China, where hill stations came to include Chinese populations, and despite some concerns from the Colonial Office in London, the Peak remained closed to Chinese and other non-Europeans until after the Second World War.

Hill stations in Asia

Hill stations could be found everywhere Westerners settled in Asia. The most famous was Simla, but the British had a string of resorts in Ceylon, Burma, and Malaya. In Indochina the French summered in Dalat, while in Indonesia the Dutch decamped to Bogor, Brastagi, and Bukittinggi. Baguio became the summer capital of the American colonial government in the Philippines and housed the summer residence of the governor-general (Reed 1976; Crossette 1999; Jennings 2003). Only two parts of China, Hong Kong and Macau, became formal colonies, but China also had its hill stations, most of which began as summer resorts for missionaries. The best known was Kuling (Guling), atop Mount Lushan in Jiangxi, but there were others: Mokanshan (Moganshan), in Jiangsu; Kikungshan (Jigongshan), on the Hubei–Henan border and especially popular with foreigners in the riverine trading ports; and Kuliang (Guliang), a more rustic mountaintop retreat in Fuzhou (Johnston and Erh 1994).

To outsiders, hill stations could be quaint, even comical – yet another example of how far expatriates would go to distance themselves from the 'native' communities. As Anthony King (1976) and Dane Kennedy (1996) have argued, however, hill stations tell more about colonialism than their appearance suggests. Although their ostensible purpose was as sanitaria and resorts, grounded in the ethnomedical beliefs that diseases such as cholera, malaria, and typhoid occurred less often there, hill stations also helped Europeans retain a sense of community and identity in their alien environments. The large number of women meant that the stations helped reproduce the empire, both biologically and ideologically. Such places were also attempts to preserve some semblance of colonial prestige against the rising socio-economic status of non-whites. In India, for example, fears of contact with upwardly mobile Indians were frequently encoded as concerns about hygiene, sanitation, and disease. Especially after the Great Rebellion of 1857–58, the Indian hill stations were also strategic centers of colonial power. The transfer of political and military power from the Indian plains to the hills demonstrated how the British rulers had become convinced that the best way to rule India was from a distance, physically removed from their Indian subjects.

Hill stations in China fulfilled similar functions. The resort at Kuling, for example, was founded to escape the heat of Jiujiang, just as the altitude and mild summers of Mokanshan offered a perfect retreat. The resort at Kuliang enabled missionaries to evade the malaria and typhoid of Fuzhou. The Chinese hill stations also played a similar socio-cultural role to their counterparts in the colonies. With its English and American street names, Kuling was home to several year-round British and American boarding schools, and families came to join their children in the summer for picnics, swimming, tennis, hiking, and camping. Even for missionaries, who had more contact with Chinese and often tried to define themselves against their more secular counterparts in the treaty ports, notes Jane Hunter (1984: 186), such resorts 'ended up institutionalizing the habits of life of the European concessions'. Especially for those who spent most of the year in the inland mission stations, hill stations were a chance to 'recharge national and racial identities through association with "our own kind"'. However, perhaps because they had often been founded by missionaries, but more significantly because the pressures of Chinese nationalism prevented them from excluding Chinese elites, many of these resorts eventually included sizeable Chinese populations. Kikungshan, where Chiang Kai-shek kept two homes, had two Chinese communities – one consisting mainly of railroad executives and military leaders, the other of Kuomintang officials. Advertisements in the 1930s for Kuling, 'China's premier health resort', featured attractive young Chinese couples. Of the more than 150 stone houses built in Mokanshan by the early 1930s, some 30 belonged to Chinese, including Chiang Kai-shek and Shanghai kingpin Du Yuesheng. Mokanshan 'grew from a few scattered houses to a community, a small microcosm of the cities from which the westerners had fled the heat' (Johnston and Erh 1994: 12).

European concerns about residential space in Hong Kong

In Hong Kong, the attempts to restrict wealthy Chinese from moving to the Peak represented the culmination of several decades of efforts by Europeans to insulate themselves from the Chinese community and to preserve the best real estate for themselves. These efforts had been challenged in the late 1870s and early 1880s, when the more liberal-minded Governor John Hennessy allowed wealthier Chinese to move into areas previously reserved for Europeans. It was also Hennessy who, in 1880, appointed the first Chinese to the Legislative Council: Ng Choy, a British-educated barrister who later, as Wu Tingfang, became a legal advisor to the Qing government and then the first Chinese minister to the United States. Since 1843, when Hong Kong officially became a Crown Colony, it had been administered by a governor appointed by the British Crown, with help from a lieutenant governor and colonial secretary, and an Executive Council and Legislative Council. These two councils each consisted of official and non-official members appointed by the governor. Although Ng Choy's appointment was only temporary, it reflected the increasing influence of the Chinese business community, which in 1879 had requested more representation. After 1883, when Governor George Bowen appointed Wong Shing, a locally and American-educated journalist and businessman, there would always be a Chinese member on the Legislative Council; a Chinese was not appointed to the Executive Council until 1926.

In the face of this rising Chinese business elite, in May 1888 Governor Des Voeux's Legislative Council passed an ordinance aimed at reserving part of Victoria, on Hong Kong Island, for Europeans by prohibiting the building of 'any Chinese tenement within the European District' and by forbidding any 'non-Chinese tenement' to be occupied by more than one person per thousand cubic feet of internal space. As the preamble to the ordinance explained, 'the health and comfort of Europeans in a tropic climate' demanded conditions 'inconsistent with the neighbourhood of houses crowded with occupants and otherwise used after the manner customary with the Chinese inhabitants'. The 'rapid influx of Chinese' able to purchase property 'not universally present in their own country' had encouraged landowners to demolish European houses to make room for Chinese ones, which could house more people and thus offer higher rental profits. Soon only the richer Europeans would be able to afford to live there. Given that a 'large leaven' of Europeans was vital to the 'well-being of the Chinese themselves', excluding those who had 'transformed a bare uninhabited rock into a beautiful city and an emporium of trade second to very few others in the world, would be not merely a sentimental grievance, but a real calamity'. Nothing in the ordinance, noted the preamble, forbade Chinese to live there, as long as their dwellings met the requirements. On the contrary, the ordinance would benefit the Chinese as well by preventing the overcrowding so common elsewhere in Hong Kong (*Sessional Papers* 1888: 25–26; *Government Gazette* 1888: 319, 375–76).

Such proposals often met with skepticism from the Colonial Office, which at least overtly was wary of any measure suggesting racial discrimination. Thus Des Voeux had to assure Lord Knutsford, Secretary of State for the Colonies, of the gravity of the situation and the soundness of the ordinance. The Governor had tried to cause 'as little disturbance as possible of existing interests', and there had been 'no protest against the measures from any quarter', even though he had delayed the final passing of the ordinance 'so as to give all reasonable opportunity for objection'. He assured Knutsford that the ordinance 'creates no exclusive privilege to the detriment of Chinese', as 'people of any race are permitted to live in what, for sake of convenience, is termed the European District, and the only obligation placed on them is that their houses shall be other than of a certain specified character and shall not be unduly crowded'. The ordinance had cleared the Legislative Council 'without opposition', the only modification, suggested by the Chinese member of the council,

Wong Shing, being a clause allowing the 'erection of buildings of Chinese type in the European District, when satisfaction is given that they are intended for a useful public purpose' (CO129/237, 8 May 1888, Des Voeux to Knutsford, 399–405). Although some in the Colonial Office condemned the ordinance as 'class-legislation', Knutsford sanctioned it, arguing that if the ordinance indeed constituted class-legislation, it was 'against a class of buildings rather than against the Chinese community' (CO129/239, 6 January 1889, CO comments on Stewart to Knutsford, 322).

Encouraged by the 1888 ordinance, in 1899 a group of Europeans in Kowloon requested a reservation 'there within which no Chinese houses should be permitted to be built'. As Acting Governor William Gascoigne explained to Secretary of State Joseph Chamberlain in July 1902, the section of Kowloon where Europeans generally lived was intersected by vacant strips of land where owners could build 'Chinese houses or any other class of houses' they wished. Attempts had been made to persuade the owners to sell the vacant strips, but the majority refused unless they were compensated for the difference between the value of the land for Chinese houses and European ones – the latter being significantly higher. In April 1901, a subcommittee of the Sanitary Board recommended that a section of waste land be used for a European reservation 'where inexpensive dwellings could be erected for Europeans of the middle class'. Excluded would be not only the Chinese lower classes, whose living conditions were said to be more favorable for the transmission of malaria by mosquitoes, but also the richer Chinese, 'who, if they invaded the area, would by competition in rents gradually oust the poorer white population'. The Executive Council approved the proposal in October 1901, but advised that the governor should have the power to grant permission in 'special cases' to Chinese to live in European-style houses within the reservation (CO129/312, 18 July 1902, Gascoigne to Chamberlain, 52–55). As with the 1888 ordinance, opinions in the Colonial Office were mixed. Although most officials supported the measure for health reasons, they rejected its goal of reducing competition for rents from 'in many cases better-educated' Chinese (CO129/312, 27–29 August 1902, Colonial Office comments, 51). Chamberlain sanctioned the proposal in September 1902, on the condition that the reservation would be 'open to all persons whether Europeans or Chinese who are approved by the Governor' (CO129/312, 4 September 1902, Chamberlain to Blake, 57–58).

The 1904 Peak District Reservation Ordinance

These earlier ordinances may have prevented the construction of Chinese-style houses in mainly European areas, but they could not stop the rise of a Chinese upper class. In February 1904, European property owners petitioned the government to preserve the Peak 'for the exclusive residence of non-Chinese inhabitants'. Because of the 'vast increase' in the size and wealth of the Chinese population, rich Chinese had moved upward until areas previously inhabited by Europeans were now 'mainly in the occupation of Chinese'. If even more Chinese moved to the Peak, the Europeans would be forced downward, which would be 'highly prejudicial to their health'. Not only was the Peak 'undeniably' the best place for Europeans unused to such an 'unnatural environment', it was the only place in Hong Kong 'fitted to be a healthy residential quarter for people accustomed to a temperate climate'. Prohibiting all Chinese, except for servants, from living there would not cause any 'hardship' to the Chinese, who had never shown any great interest in residing there since they were already in their 'native climate'. It was 'for the advantage of a community as a whole' that each racial group should reside in 'the environment to which it is best adapted'. Furthermore, the 'future welfare' of the colony, and its 'consequent value to the Empire', depended greatly on 'the well-being of the European section of the community', a community whose health it was 'essential' to preserve. The Peak must be preserved as a place where the 'rising generation' of Europeans could spend its childhood in the 'healthiest obtainable surroundings' (CO129/322, 4 May 1904, May to Lyttleton, 638).

The petitioners had little trouble convincing Acting Governor Henry May of the necessity of the ordinance and the expediency of passing it. Unlike those in 1888 and 1899, however (which – although aimed at keeping out Chinese – did so indirectly by prohibiting Chinese-style buildings), the proposed 1904 ordinance explicitly prohibited Chinese from living on the Peak. This meant some finessing, both within the Legislative Council and subsequently to the Colonial Office in London. 'We welcome the Chinese who like to come here, and we put no limit upon their numbers', Attorney General H. S. Berkeley insisted to the council. 'It is obvious to anyone who reads the Bill that it does not restrict Chinese from building on the Peak....The object is not to prevent Chinese as such from living on the Peak, but to preserve a place that cannot be overcrowded' (*Hansard* 1904: 17–18). Council member H. E. Pollock, a long-time resident and original supporter of the petition, insisted that the petitioners had 'no intention at all' of introducing anything in the way of class legislation against the Chinese'; the reason was 'simply and solely the question of the public health'. Although there had been a 'regular rush of non-Chinese' to the Peak since the opening of the Peak Tramway in 1888, 'not a single Chinaman', except the servants exempted, were now living on the Peak. This, Pollock, argued was 'very good proof indeed that the Chinese gentlemen' had never felt 'any desire to live up at the Peak' and that the measure would inflict 'no hardship at all' (*Hansard* 1904: 19).

Although the two Chinese council members, Ho Kai and Wei Yuk, did not contest the ordinance, they could not let it pass completely unchallenged. Ho explained that the bill had 'a decided savour of the nature of class legislation, and especially against the Chinese', but he was 'quite convinced of the reasonableness and expediency' of the bill because the wealth and wellbeing of Hong Kong depended on the European community. Such a 'concession from the Chinese', Ho argued, 'would not only be graceful but justifiable'. Ho had discussed the matter with other Chinese leaders at several meetings; although a minority had been 'dead set' against the principle of the bill, the majority saw no objection. They did, however, 'unanimously' agree with Ho and Wei on the need to 'alter somewhat the phraseology' of the bill, which resulted in the addition of a clause giving the governor the right to grant exemptions for Chinese he considered fit to live on the Peak (*Hansard*, 1904: 18). Relieved, May told the council that Ho and Wei's support for this 'somewhat delicate subject', which reflected the Chinese community's 'sound practical commonsense', had given him 'a great deal of gratification' (*Hansard* 1904, 19). Happily, May reported to the Colonial Office, the ordinance passed on 26 April, 'without evoking friction or ill-feeling' (CO129/322, 4 May 1904, May to Lyttleton, 633–36).

A bill passed in the Legislative Council still required the approval of the Colonial Office. As in 1888 and 1899, the Hong Kong Government had to convince the Colonial Office, which argued that the new ordinance was aimed not at sanitation but at keeping Peak rents low for Europeans already living there. May admitted to the Colonial Office that he could not 'plead Sanitary necessity' for the ordinance, as there was 'no danger of coolie houses being built on a mountain like the Peak'. But he denied that the ordinance was about keeping rents low for Europeans, for the owners of the properties on the Peak were among the main supporters of the ordinance. Nor was this a case of class legislation; it was 'Climatic Legislation'. The Peak was the only place where Europeans could 'live in health'. Even the Chinese community had recognized this and, through its representatives on the Legislative Council, had accepted the ordinance. Although May's predecessor, Henry Blake, had worried that the Chinese government would object to such an ordinance, this concern need not be 'seriously concerned'. The Chinese government would not be likely to 'trouble its head' about a 'comparatively trifling domestic arrangement' in Hong Kong. Besides, May argued, in Chinese provincial capitals, Manchus and Chinese lived separately, while in Peking the foreign diplomats and the officials of the Imperial Maritime Customs lived in the Legation Quarter – 'a European Reservation'. Nor did the Qing government seem to mind that Chinese were excluded from the British concessions in the treaty ports. It had 'cheerfully' assented to the 'British Municipalities which administer those Settlements and Concessions'. Was it conceivable that the Chinese government would object when the Chinese of Hong Kong had already accepted the ordinance as a 'reasonable measure'? (CO129/323, 19 June 1904, May to Lyttleton, 135–39). In the end, the Colonial Office decided not to 'pick the obvious holes' in May's argument (Colonial Office comments, 25 July 1904, in CO129/323, 19 June 1904, May to Lyttleton, 136).

The Peak District Ordinance of 1918

The 1904 ordinance succeeded in preventing the 'influx' of Chinese that the Europeans had feared, and by 1917 the only exemption granted had been to the Eurasian tycoon Robert Ho Tung, who owned three homes on the Peak. But in September of that year, May reported to the Colonial Office that a legal loophole had been discovered in the wording of the ordinance: a Chinese living in his own house on the Peak could not possibly be 'permitting' anyone to live there, Chinese or otherwise. Ho Tung's brother, Ho Kam Tong, had also recently purchased a Peak house at public auction. Citing the 1904 ordinance, May asked Ho Kam Tong to sell the house to the government, which Ho, a well known philanthropist, did, and he agreed to give the profit to the War Charities Fund. But now, May wrote in alarm, Ho was trying to buy another property. Only a few days earlier, Robert Ho Tung had bought two semi-detached homes and planned to make them into one home for his daughter, who would soon marry a Chinese. Other Chinese had expressed interest in similar properties, and Ho Tung was planning to build a large place for his own residence on 'the one really good site still vacant on the Peak' (CO 129/433, 5 September 1917, May to Long, 384–85).

Like in 1904, the controversy in 1917 was as much about race and class as about health. As May explained, Chinese had become wealthier than the Europeans, making the need for keeping them away from the Peak 'considerably stronger' than in 1904. Wealthy Chinese businessmen, 'living with their wives and concubines in semi-European fashion', had been 'steadily ousting' the Europeans from the Mid-Levels, where men like Ho Tung were purchasing land from Europeans who could no longer pay the rents. The Portuguese had been the first to go, followed by the other Europeans. If the Chinese were allowed to settle on the Peak, they would set a trend of buying homes at 'fancy prices far beyond the European purse'. These 'displaced' Europeans would be forced into the 'less desirable and less healthy parts of the Colony' (CO129/433, 5 September 1917, May to Long, 386–87).

Although the 1888 and 1899 ordinances had been phrased in terms that disguised, albeit only barely, their racist intentions, and whereas the 1904 ordinance had been couched in talk of health and sanitation, the new ordinance was aimed squarely at protecting Europeans from Chinese. Regardless of their wealth, May wrote, Chinese families on the Peak would have more contact with less privileged Chinese, greatly increasing the likelihood of 'the carriage and dissemination of communicable disease'. With more children than ever on the Peak, European parents were 'bitterly opposed to any contact between their children and Chinese children'. Wealthy Chinese men would bring their wives, concubines, and 'numerous progeny', who would be 'thrown into daily contact with the European children in the children's playground and the few shady spots to which the Europeans are now taken by their nurses and amahs'. It would thus be 'little short of a calamity if an alien and, by European standards, a semi-civilized race were allowed to drive the white man from the one area in Hong Kong, in which he can live with his wife and children in a white man's healthy surroundings'. May now requested permission to give 'legal force' to the 'obvious intention' of the 1904 ordinance by modifying it so that, except with the consent of the governor, 'no Chinese may reside at the Peak'. Although he had been assured by the secretary for Chinese affairs (a Briton) that the Chinese members of the Legislative Council would not disagree with the proposed modification, May suggested that 'it might be politic' to offer well-to-do Chinese their own reservation, similar to the one granted (but which never materialized) to the Portuguese in 1912 (CO129/433, 5 September 1917, May to Long, 388–90).

The new residency controversy also highlighted the rise of a group of Eurasians, who posed a threat to Europeans because of their vague racial and social status, and who exacerbated fears about miscegenation, disease, and biological and moral contamination. As described in a 1908 guide to Hong Kong and the Chinese treaty-ports,

Eurasians in Hong Kong held a 'precarious position between the foreign and native elements' (Wright and Cartwright 1908: 341). Usually the progeny of relations between European men and Chinese women, Eurasians, writes May Holdsworth (2002: 186) were 'neither fish nor fowl'. As in other Asian colonies, Eurasians in Hong Kong often filled important commercial and government clerical posts, some becoming wealthy businessmen and leaders of the Chinese business community. And because Eurasians were usually locally born and spoke English and Chinese, Europeans often considered them more trustworthy, loyal, and reliable than the 'pure' Chinese. Unlike the Portuguese in Macau, however, the British in Hong Kong never saw miscegenation as a means of promoting racial harmony and social stability. Many Europeans considered Eurasians to resemble the 'mean whites' of the American South, while colonial officials frequently worried that colonial mixing produced a new category of 'wavering classes'. Eurasians, notes Vicky Lee (2004: 24), were 'liable to a double distrust, for having a different identity in the first place, but also for not really having an identity at all, being neither one thing nor the other, and consequently sneaky and opportunistic'. In the 1920s, Governor Reginald Stubbs would report that because 'pure' Chinese disdained Eurasians as 'the Bastards', the government had been reluctant to appoint them to official positions (in Miners 1987: 128). Socially ostracized by both Europeans and Chinese, many married into other Eurasian families, creating a distinct Eurasian community with its own cemetery.

The 1904 ordinance, May explained to the Colonial Office, had failed to define 'Chinese', thus enabling Eurasians such as Robert Ho Tung and Ho Kam Tong to slip through. May now sought to expand 'Chinese' to include Eurasians – 'to all intents and purposes Chinese in their habits and customs' – proposing to define the term as 'a person of Chinese race on the side of one parent only' or to refer in the ordinance to 'persons of Chinese extraction' instead of to 'Chinese', with power vested in the governor to 'decide what constitutes Chinese extraction' (CO129/433, 5 September 1917, May to Long, 389). As in 1904, May wrote, the Chinese members of the Legislative Council were 'sympathetic'. But although they 'did not dispute the reasonableness' of the bill, they realized the difficulty of 'securing whole-hearted support' for it. Other members of the Chinese community had objected, and when some Eurasians called a meeting of the Chinese General Chamber of Commerce, the chamber passed a resolution against the ordinance and the Eurasians voiced their objections in the local press. And even though the Chinese members of the Legislative Council did not disagree with the 'justice and reasonableness of the proposed legislation', they could not deny that the 'alternations of the law would be derogatory to the prestige of their race'. After all, May wrote, 'the time-honoured fear of "loss of face" is too strong for the modicum of moral courage with which the Chinaman is endowed' (CO129/447, 24 January 1918, May to Long, 69–70).

Further complicating matters was the increasing number of Japanese residents in Hong Kong, which intensified European concerns about another Asian population and showed the rise of another power in East Asia – one that British diplomats often viewed with disdain, yet were also eager not to offend. The colonial government could not grant concessions to these Japanese without alienating its Chinese subjects. The Chinese members of the Legislative Council offered two possibilities: exclude all Asians from living on the Peak without permission from the governor, or prohibit anyone from living there without permission from the governor. Because the Japanese government would protest the first option, May suggested the second. Not making any amendment or addition to the ordinance 'would give the undesirable impression of a moral victory on the part of the Eurasian population'. The second option, a general prohibition, would also solve another problem: the possibility of 'an undue invasion of the Peak by the rapidly growing Japanese population', who might not remain content for long with the 'little Colony' they had already formed just below the Peak. Although the Colonial Office generally supported the new ordinance, Britain and Japan had signed a commercial and navigational treaty by which residents in the other's territories should have the right to live 'in the same manner as native subjects'. The Japanese government had recently invoked this treaty to prevent its citizens from being barred from the rich rubber fields of Malaya. Once Foreign Secretary Arthur Balfour had approved the ordinance, Secretary of State Walter Long reminded May to ensure that the ordinance was not administered 'in such a way that legitimate ground may be given for complaint as to the infringement of the Spirit of the Treaty of Commerce and Navigation with Japan…or any similar treaty to which assent has been given by the Colony' (CO129/451, 8 May 1918, Langley to Long, 346, and 15 May 1918, Long to May, 347).

The new bill, the Peak District (Residence) Ordinance of 1918, passed without amendment or opposition. The Peak was thus again reserved for Europeans, a restriction that lasted until after the Second World War. As Norman Miners (1987: 54–55) has observed, the ordinance was used to exclude Chinese and other non-Europeans without writing this discrimination into law. Only one Chinese was given permission to live on the Peak from 1918 to 1941: Madame Chiang Kai-shek, who was granted permission by an Executive Council decision in 1936. In 1919, a similar bill created a vacation preserve for British and American missionaries on the outlying island of Cheung Chau. Acting Governor Claude Severn explained to Walter Long in October 1918 that the area had been 'made by the missionaries and pioneers' and should thus 'be kept for those whose habits of life are sufficiently in harmony to form a Community' (CO129/450, 23 October 1918, Severn to Long, 148–49). This time, however, the Chinese members of the Legislative Council objected. Lau Chu-pak expressed surprise and disappointment that even missionaries could have made such a move. Ho Fook, Robert Ho Tung's brother, criticized the bill as little more than 'racial legislation'. But only Lau and Ho opposed the bill (Wesley-Smith 1994: 100–101).

The Peak ordinances repealed

Unlike in China, where European privilege came under widespread attack in the 1920s, the Peak ordinances were challenged only twice, both during the strike-boycott of 1925–26, and neither serious. One of the demands of the strike committee was for Chinese to be treated as the equal of Europeans and to be able to live on the Peak. But Hong Kong's Chinese and Eurasian elites abhorred the disruption caused by the strike and worked closely with the colonial government to end it. In November 1925, during the strike, the India Office enquired whether Indians were allowed to live on the Peak. Still in its summer capital at Simla, the Government of India wanted to know how such an ordinance came to be, and whether any Chinese or non-Europeans had requested an amendment (8 October 1925, Bajpai to India Office, enclosed in CO129/491, 2 November 1925, 207–8). Embarrassed, especially since an Indian politician had raised the matter in the Legislative Assembly after reading about the 1918 ordinance in a popular British almanac, the Colonial Office assured the India Office that the ordinance had been passed to 'regulate excessive competition for houses in the Peak District and to prevent the exclusion of Europeans from one of the few areas in the Colony which are healthy for them and their children', noting that it was unaware of any protests by Chinese or other non-Europeans (24 December 1925, CO comments on CO129/491, 2 November 1925, 205).

As in other Asian hill stations, non-Europeans were eventually able to move to the Peak. But only after the defeat of Japan, which had ruled Hong Kong from late December 1941 through August 1945, and the return in 1946 of Governor Mark Young, were the Peak ordinances repealed. In what became known as 'the 1946 outlook', both British government officials and local colonial administrators realized that Hong Kong could not return to the pre-war days of racial discrimination. 'The conquest of December 1941', writes Philip Snow (2003: 303), 'had given the old colonial rulers a sort of enforced sabbatical in which to sit back and take stock of their pre-war deficiencies'. The impulse for change also had a strong pragmatic basis, for the British realized that they needed to win over the local Chinese to legitimize and maintain their continued rule in Hong Kong. Ironically, part of the impulse for these changes came from the Japanese, who in their wartime propaganda had drawn unflattering attention to Hong Kong's racial discrimination.

Although the magnitude of these changes should not be exaggerated – many elite clubs remained closed to Chinese and Eurasians – they were nonetheless significant. Alexander Grantham, governor from 1947 to 1957, observed a 'marked decline in social snobbishness' and a 'greater mixing of the races' compared with when he had served in Hong Kong during the 1920s and 1930s (Grantham 1965: 104). Whereas before the war, visitors from Shanghai and from other colonies had frequently commented on the width of the racial divide in Hong Kong, visitors after the war were often surprised to see both Chinese and foreigners using buses and trams. On 26 July 1946, the colonial government repealed the 1918 Peak ordinance as well as that which had reserved part of Cheung Chau for Europeans. Just before the repeals were passed one week later, Lo Man-kam, a Eurasian council member who, as member of the Chinese General Chamber of Commerce, had opposed the 1918 ordinance, told the Legislative Council that the ordinance had been 'a source of resentment to the Chinese ever since its enactment'. The repeal of this and the Cheung Chau ordinance, Lo hoped, indicated the government's 'recognition that Ordinances of this nature are out of harmony with the spirit of the times' (*Hansard* 1946: 78).

5

AN ITALIAN 'NEIGHBOURHOOD' IN TIANJIN

Little Italy or colonial space?[1]

Maurizio Marinelli

The only Italian concession in China was located in the Hebei district of the modern municipality of Tianjin from 1901 until 1947. It was also the only example of Italian colonialism in Asia. Through the historical investigation of the former Italian concession, from its acquisition to its socio-spatial reorganisation as a 'laboratory of modernity' (Stoler 1995: 13–26), this chapter emphasises the imposed notion of the concession as an Italian-style 'neighbourhood': a miniature Disneyland-style venue of 'Italianness' or 'Italian spirit' (*Italianità*). Focusing on the conceptualisation of the concession as a 'neighbourhood' and not a colony, Italy tried to give shape to a short-lived, although in colonial terms glorious, project: the 'neighbourhood' was meant to establish Italy's status and prestige among the other colonial powers operating in China at the time.

Between 1860 and 1945, the Chinese port city of Tianjin was the site of up to nine foreign-controlled concessions. Ruth Rogaski (2004: 11) argues that Tianjin's distinctiveness deserves the appellation 'hyper-colony'. This contrasts with the traditional, dominant Chinese historiography based on Sun Yatsen's claim that the incomplete colonisation process in China created a 'hypo-colony': a weak country which, due to its 'semi-colonial' and 'semi-feudal' condition (Tianjin 1987: I) struggled to negotiate its national identity *vis-à-vis* the foreign powers (Sun 1923; see also De Bary and Luffrano 1960).

Rogaski's image of hyper-colony, 'drawing attention to the potential implications that arise when one urban space is divided among multiple imperialisms' (Rogaski 2004: 11), is more in line with the socio-spatial and political intricacies of Tianjin.

Space and power in Tianjin

In his 1967 lecture 'Des espaces autres', Michel Foucault defined his era as 'above all the epoch of space' where the key element is juxtaposition: this refers to the projective

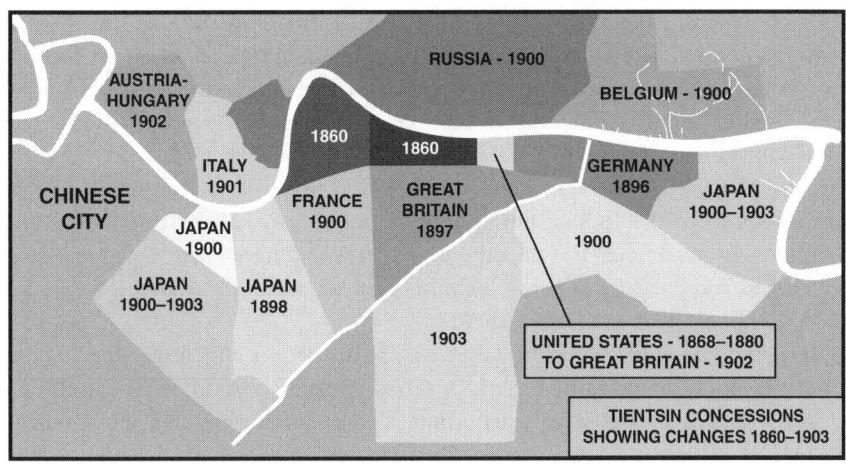

MAP 5.1 Foreign concessions in Tianjin, 1910
By Philip R. Abbey. With permission.

dimensions of near and far, side-by-side. He describes our experience of the world using the image of 'a network that connects points and intersects with its own skein' (Foucault 1984: 46). Foucault conceptualises space as a social process:

> Space was treated as the dead, fixed, undialectical, immobile. Time, on the other hand, was richness, fecundity, life, dialectic…The use of spatial terms seems to have the air of anti-history. If one started to talk in terms of space that meant one was hostile to time. It meant, as the fools say, that one 'denied history'…They didn't understand that these [spatial terms]…meant the throwing into relief of processes – historical ones, needless to say – of power.
> *(Foucault 1980: 149)*

Foucault is not dismissing the value of time, but he directs the historian's attention towards the often overlooked intersection of time with space, since it is within the conceptualisation of space as a social process that strategies of power and signification jointly operate.

The multi-layered identity of hyper-colonial Tianjin is a clear example of the juxtaposition of near and far spaces, side-by-side, as demonstrated by American journalist John Hersey, who was born in Tianjin to missionary parents in 1914:

> What a weird city I grew up in. For three or four Chinese coppers, I could ride in a rickshaw from my home, in England, to Italy, Germany, Japan, or Belgium. I walked to France for violin lessons; I had to cross the river to get to Russia, and often did, because the Russians had a beautiful wooded park with a lake in it.
> *(Hersey 1982: 54)*

Each concession developed its residential area for the expatriates of the colonial power (and for wealthy Chinese citizens) using building styles that were reflecting, reproducing and imposing the stylistic traditions of each individual country. Cultural reproduction contributed to the emergence of hagiographic representations. The Italian 'imagined community' (Anderson 1991: 7) in Tianjin capitalised on the rhetoric trope of the 'civilizing mission' attributed to the newly created Italian nation: this was based on the 1890s claim that 'Italy's was a "proletarian" colonialism' and therefore less pernicious than the others, since it would have been 'aimed to secure better land and greater prosperity for its indigenous citizens.' (Andall and Duncan 2005: 11; Ben-Ghiat and Fuller 2005).

Imagining an entity like the 'modern' Italian nation and projecting it onto China, through the construction of the Italian 'neighbourhood' in Tianjin, was a way of building up a positive story around the Italian citizens and, intentionally, beyond: this took the form of a master narrative of benign colonialism, where the colonial agents became the positive characters of a specific national success story. The Italian concession in Tianjin had the characteristics of a hybrid community, with foreign and Chinese citizens living in a small area *de iure* defined as a permanent foreign possession but *de facto* dwelling on the Chinese soil. Yet it was a community 'imagined' according to a specific scheme of projective self-perception, and therefore represented as a 'neighbourhood' bridging multiple worlds: Italy and China, but even more so, Italy and the other foreign powers operating in Tianjin.

The origin of the concession

In his 1921 report,[2] Consul General Vincenzo Fileti offers the first historical reconstruction of the Italian concession (Fileti 1921: 8–9). With the signature of the 'Final Protocol for the Settlement of the Disturbances of 1900' (Xinchou Treaty) on 7 September 1901, following the repression of the Boxer Uprising,[3] Italy received an allotment of 5.91 per cent of the Boxers' indemnity (*Documenti Diplomatici sugli avvenimenti di Cina presentati al Parlamento dal Ministro Prinetti*), extraterritoriality privileges in the Legation Quarter in Beijing, as well as the concession in perpetuity of a small zone on the northern bank of the Hai River, in Tianjin, on which to develop an Italian concession. The area had been *de facto* occupied by Italian troops in January 1901, and was set between the Austro-Hungarian and the Russian concessions, the left bank of the Hai River, the Beijing-Mukden (today's Shenyang) railway track, and the remnant Chinese-controlled territory.

Apparently, Vessel Lieutenant Valli, commander of the Tianjin garrison, was the person responsible for the military operations and he chose 'to occupy the next best thing' (*quanto restava di meglio*), probably the only part still left untouched by the other colonial powers. An Italian source indicates that government's thinking that the British would have reserved the best area for themselves (Bertinelli 1983: 218). But Salvago Raggi, the Royal Minister in Beijing in 1901, proudly argued that the concession's territory was the best area, with prospects for rapid and successful development. The Italian Consul in Tianjin, Cavalier Poma, noticed instead that the area consisted of a populous Chinese quarter, a cemetery, and wetlands, which did not seem to be very promising (Bertinelli 1983: 218–20).

The Sino–Italian agreement was signed by the Director of the Chinese Maritime Customs Tang Shaoyi, and Giovanni Gallina (successor to Salvago Raggi), stating that: 'The Italian Government will exercise full jurisdiction in the same way established for the concessions obtained by the other foreign powers' (Agreement 1901). The agreement clarified that the concession was ceded 'to promote the development of Italian trade in the northern part of China, and in the Zheli (Chi-li) province in particular' (Agreement 1901). This corresponded to the acknowledgment of the long-sought-after 'equal' treatment of Italy at the same level of the other colonial powers in China. The acquisition of the concession was perceived as a historical nemesis, after the repeated failures, which had characterised both Italian colonial policy in Africa and diplomatic relations between Italy and China from the 1866 bilateral Treaty onwards (Bocca 1961). On 1 March 1896, Italian troops had suffered a devastating defeat in the final battle of the first Italo–Ethiopian war, which was fought near Adwa, against Ethiopia's Negus Menelik II (Henze 2000: 170). This defeat led to the resignation of Prime Minister Francesco Crispi, amidst a profound disenchantment with 'foreign adventures' (Vandervort 1998: 164). The new Prime Minister, Giovanni Giolitti, referring specifically to the Italian experience in China, defined the former unsuccessful Italian attempt in spring 1899 to obtain the official Chinese Government's recognition of the Sanmun bay as a naval station and Italian influence zone in Zhejiang, as 'a waste of a few millions (of lire) and a national humiliation' (Giolitti 1922: v. I, 154).

This rejection by the Chinese Government when it received the 1899 Italian request, and the ensuing ultimatum, caused a serious wound in the imagined community of the newly created Italian nation, especially since that rejection occurred at a historical moment when all the other foreign powers (Great Britain, France, Germany, but also Japan and Russia) were obtaining concessions and settlements in locations strategically important for their political presence and economic penetration in the Chinese territory. The wound was even more profound because the 1899 Italian request and ultimatum were not supported by Great Britain (Pistolese 1935: 305–6; Bocca 1961: 157–88), revealing that the other foreign powers were not keen on seeing Italy exerting its influence in China.

Cicchiti-Suriani, writing in 1951 to commemorate the fiftieth anniversary of the acquisition of the concession, pointed out that 'After the unfortunate prelude of Sanmun, that gesture represented the epilogue of the 1900 international events' (Cicchiti-Suriani 1951: 562).

The voices of the advocates of Italian commercial interests in China had been particularly intense in the decade 1890–1900. Amongst academics, Professor Ludovico Nocentini from Rome University wrote articles to launch petitions in its favour from the pages of magazines such as *Nuova Antologia*, *Rivista d'Italia* and *Rivista Geografica Italiana* (Nocentini 1904). Journalists such as Giovanni Vigna del Ferro (1901) were also active to this end.

The territory

The area originally ceded to the Italian Government consisted of approximately half a square kilometre (Pistolese 1935: 306; De Antonellis 1977: 52; Li 1986: 135; Tianjin 1987: 209).

Proceeding from the south (where the river flows) to the north (where the railway station is now located), the territory consisted of four parts.

1. A higher-rising area used as a salt deposit (approximately 100,000 square metres).
2. The Chinese village (approximately 200,000 square metres) consisting of, according to Navy Lieutenant Mario Michelagnoli, 867 dwellings (quoted in Cardano and Porzio 2004: 26). These were mainly huts, built by the salt workers. Fileti's description reveals the high degree of poverty of the dwellers: misery and indigence are the key words used (Fileti 1921: 13).
3. North of the village there was wetland, where the water could be as deep as 3–4 metres, and which was usually completely frozen in the winter.
4. On the more elevated parts of this wetland, the dwellers used to bury their dead, so the place had assumed the aspect of a 'vast abandoned and flooded cemetery'.

Gallina justified the immediate expropriation of what he referred to as the 'filthy Chinese village', arguing that 'all the other powers had proceeded to expropriation as soon as they occupied the area of their concession' (Archivio Storico Diplomatico del Ministero degli Affari Esteri).

There is no unanimous consent concerning the Chinese population living in the area at the time of the transfer: 13,704 according to the 1902 census; around 17,000 people according to Fileti (1921: 15) 16,500 according to Arnaldo Cicchiti-Suriani (1951: 562). The 1922 census reports 4025 Chinese citizens, 62 Italians and 42 from other nationalities (Nankaidaxue zhengzhixuehui 1926: 6–7). In 1935 the total estimated population was 6261, of whom 5725 were Chinese and 536 foreigners, including 392 Italians, but Gennaro Pistolese argues that the Italians were 'about 150 people' (Pistolese 1935: 306). F. C. Jones, in a few lines dedicated to the Italian concession, says: 'The population in 1937 was 373 foreigners and some 6,500 Chinese' (Jones 1940: 128).

These figures indicate how spatial reorganisation determined a significant decrease of the population, from 16–17,000 (1902) to 4–6000 (1922–35), and a clear predominance of Chinese citizens living in the Italian concession. Nevertheless, Italian sources tend to obscure any hybrid character and annihilate the presence of Chinese citizens in the concession, relegating them to the role of invisible subalterns. This tendency reached its climax in 1935, when Pistolese affirmed: 'Our concession has a demographic consistency superior to the other concessions in Tien-Tsin', and he reports the data of the Japanese concession (5000 people), British (2000) and French (1450). This mystification contributed to the fascist regime's

MAP 5.2 Coastguard Filippo Vanzini's Tianjin, November 1901
Vincenzo Fileti (1921): 13. Courtesy of Ministero degli Affari Esteri di Roma.

construction of a self-congratulatory image based on cultural reproduction: the successful infrastructural projects that beautified the area were indicative of the outstanding success of the Italian spiritual and civilising mission in this 'faraway extension' of the motherland (Pistolese 1935: 305–10; Bassi 1929).

Concession, neighbourhood or heterotopia?

The concession 'imagined' as an 'Italian neighbourhood' allows its past (Fileti 1921) and present re-presentation as 'the witness of the implementation of a common work between Italians and Chinese that today, after more than sixty years, is somehow rediscovered and re-evaluated in its value and its own meaning' (Cardano and Porzio 2004: 7). 'Common work', 'value' and 'meaning' have become the key features of a continuous attempt to obliterate the idea that Italy, for almost half a century, had a concession in Tianjin, not a 'neighbourhood'. One could argue that the compound word for concession – *zujie* – does not indicate a real colonial status (since 'colony' in Chinese is *zhimindi*) or a settlement. Nevertheless, the compound word *zujie* embodies both the idea of 'leased territory' (*zu* means hire, rent or lease) and the concept of territorial demarcation (*jie* is boundary.) Chinese historians emphasise that, from an administrative, juridical, police and fiscal perspective, the concessions were 'states within the state' (*guozhongzhiguo*) (Shan and Liu 1996: 1). The linguistic replacement of 'neighbourhood' (*qu*) belongs to a colonial process of formal renaming: the modification of the form mystifies both the content and the context, producing an edulcorated image of the colonial presence. Renaming is an essential component of benign colonialism, which aims at offering an ultra-positive, and often narcissistic, image of Italian colonialism. The Italian term for 'neighbourhood' is *quartiere* (quarter): it conveys both the sense of a defined residential district and the idea of a community characterised by some forms of vicinity and familiarity. The inhabitants of a quarter share both the fact of co-inhabiting a space and also certain habits and customs.

Almost one century later, various exhibitions held in Italy and Tianjin between 2004 and 2006 have tried to narrow the spatial, temporal and ultimately hermeneutical distance, reinforcing the portrayal of the Italian concession as a 'neighbourhood'. The goal of course is to emphasise that, at the time, the concession was intended 'to encourage and expand the commercial relations between the two countries, and export and diffuse the best image of urban, architectonic, and artistic culture at that point of time to a country so faraway from Italy like China' (Cardano and Porzio 2004: 7) and, in so doing, to emphasise that continuing relationship even more today.

On the one hand, the fictitious re-presentation of a 'neighbourhood' that would have been 'received' from the Chinese Imperial Government masks the tone of the Italian colonial experience in China. On the other hand, the 'neighbourhood' narrative is in line with the current Chinese official intention to re-evaluate the concessions era as the beginning of Tianjin's internationalisation, capitalising on those seeds of global capitalism instead of demonising them. From the year 2000 onwards, Tianjin Municipal Government has approved a progressive renovation of the former Italian concession. Today the area is called *Yishifengqingqu*, an expression whose etymological translation would be 'scenic *area* or *neighbourhood* of Italian style' even though it is officially known as the 'Italian Business Park' (Guo 1989; Como *et al.* 2006).

A more appropriate conceptual redefinition of the former concessions area could be a space characterised by the juxtaposition of contradictory elements: what Foucault calls *heterotopia*. He derives his definition of *heterotopia* from his interest in sites 'that have the curious property of being in relation with all the other sites, but in such a way as to suspect, neutralize, or invent the set of relations that they happen to designate, mirror, or reflect' (Foucault 1994: 755). Foucault clarifies that these spaces belong to two main types: *utopia* and *heterotopia*. The Italian concession in

Tianjin, as well as the whole foreign concessions area, was not a utopia, since it was not an unreal space ideally constructed as a perfect analogical projection of an existing society. Both physically and emotionally, the concessions area can be more adequately defined as a multi-layered *heterotopic site* since, *de facto*, the concessions, via translingual practice[4] (Liu 1995: 24), fall into the Foucauldian category of 'real places – places that do exist and that are formed in the very founding of society – which are something like counter-sites, a kind of effectively enacted utopia, in which the real sites, all the other real sites that can be found within the culture, are simultaneously represented, contested and inverted' (Foucault 1994: 755). The legitimate question is whether this definition is still valid for post-colonial/globalising Tianjin, since, as Foucault argues, heterotopic sites are '…outside of all places, even though it may be possible to indicate their location in reality' (Foucault 1994: 755). In terms of physical and emotional construction of a collective space, the concessions area in Tianjin is a paradigmatic juxtaposition of the 'absolutely real' with the 'absolutely unreal' – one in which the convex mirror function of colony-motherland (based on the mechanism of reflection, distorted perception and projective duplication) allows the colonial subject to play.

The *Yishifenqingqu* that one experiences today in Tianjin is not a utopian re-presentation or a simulation of a miniature Italy. Walking around the former Italian concession 'area', one witnesses a commodity: a glocalised entity with all the characteristics of a commoditised space and its relevant discourse of power. The *Yishifenqingqu* is an open-air mall much more than an open-air museum. The signs naming and indicating the *Yishifengqingqu* are naming and defining the space, trying to point out the 'reality' of the 'Italianness'. Yet, paradoxically, they are reminiscent of a historical precedent: the arrogance of street signs imposed by an Italian colonial power in the period 1901–47. After the annihilation of the former site, the appropriation and reinvention of the urban form. In those days, Piazza Regina Elena and Corso Vittorio Emanuele III were signs claiming 'reality' in the Italian concession, in a similar way to the signs indicating Victoria Road (today *Jiefangbeilu*) and Victoria Park with its Gordon Hall[5] in the British concession in Tianjin.

Spatial transformation: a 'laboratory of modernity'

In 1905, the Italian Foreign Ministry approved the concession's town plan, drawn up by Lord Lieutenant Adolfo Cecchetti. The priority was the levelling of the territory, implying both the removal of the cemetery and the draining of the marshes.

On 5 July 1908, a public auction programme tried to attract potential buyers for the allotments of the Italian concession [Royal Italian Consulate. Tientsin-China. Sale by Auction of land in the Royal Italian Concession in Tientsin, 6 July 1908 (RIC1)]. At the same time, the police regulations were issued, together with the first Building Code signed by Consul Da Vella [Royal Italian Concession in Tientsin. Local Land Regulations and General Rules, Archivio Storico del Ministero degli Affari Esteri (1891–1916) (BR)]. The Building Code clearly indicates the intention to annihilate all the signs of Chinese identity, and replace it with the superimposition of the layout of a 'neighbourhood' consisting of Western-style roads, maximum two-storey houses, and 'European style, elegant residences'. The 1908 Building Regulations specified that:

> ...All the buildings facing the Vittorio Emanuele road must be in European style and exclusively occupied by Europeans of good character and standing or by Taotais[6] or other high Chinese Officials who must obtain a permit from the Royal Italian Consulate. (BR I)

The Consul had 'full power to order any alteration of any building not put up in accordance with the plan rendered to him for sanction; or order any repair with regard to safety and hygiene.' He also had 'full power to have any house or building pulled down', should it not be strictly in accordance with the Building Regulations (BR III, XI). A precise association existed between class status, morality and hygiene. Restrictions imposed Chinese inhabitants to obtain written approval 'previous to weddings, funerals or any other function' (BR XXIV, 10). In general, 'All kinds of public entertainments must be authorised by the police' (BR XXIV, 13), while special permission was required to open Chinese theatres, where the proprietors should 'guarantee the morality of the artists as well as the public safety' (BR XXIII). Furthermore, the 'Chinese inhabitants on the unexpropriated portion of the concession' were required to keep their houses clean, including 'the portion of the road in front of their houses' (BR XXIV, 1). Discretional discrimination applied since 'Any native of bad character may be expelled from the concession' (BR XXIV, 13), but the same rule did not apply to foreigners.

The 1908 public auction was not successful. In 1912, the Italian Government finally decided to allocate 400,000 lire to promote the development of the Italian concession (Law 707, 1912).

The period 1912–22 witnessed the creation of all the major streets and the construction of the most important buildings, among them the Consulate (1912), the hospital (1914–22) and the municipal council (1919).

The Italian concession became the imagined community depicted in extremely positive terms by Italian sources, which in utter unison praised the enlightened city planning intervention that totally transformed what the Italian Ambassador in Beijing, Count Carlo Sforza, described on 22 April 1912 as 'a whole Chinese village, and around it, rotten [*putrefascente* in Italian] marshes, and as far as the eye can see layers and mounds of Chinese caskets' into a deeply contrasting image where 'the wetland had been reduced to a minimum, and not a single tomb can be found in the concession' (Cardano and Porzio 2004: 32–33).

The concession assumed 'the role of showcase of Italian art, with the import of decorating and building materials from the motherland', especially for 'the most representative objects, like the public buildings and the monumental fountain located at the centre for Queen Elena Square' (Cardano and Porzio 2004:34).

The new street layout and European-style houses received unconditional praise. The *grazioso villino* (nice little villa) hosting the Consulate and the *villino* hosting the municipal council (Sforza 1922, quoted in Cardano and Porzio 2004: 32–33) are among the best examples anywhere of colonial buildings intended as symbols of power. They defined a spatial-political identity and legitimised the affirmation of the Italian national discourse in hyper-colonial Tianjin.

The neo-Renaissance-style Italian council building[7] echoed fifteenth-century Italian villas, characterised by a square shape, consistent floor plan and hip-roof surmounted by a turret. Built in 1925 by the company of Tianjin resident Egidio Marzoli, in 1929 the building was expanded, according to the plan of architect Bonetti, with the addition of a heated verandah used as a reception room. This building was destroyed around 1990. The former Italian Consulate building has become the headquarters of the Chinese People's Political Consultative Conference for the whole of Hebei District, where the *Yishifenqingqu* is located in Tianjin.

The export to China of the Italian neo-Renaissance style was a way to affirm the nation's prestige and self-positioning as a colonial power on the same level as others, despite Italy's late entry into the game of European colonialism. In fact, a self-consciously neo-Renaissance manner had rapidly expanded and become popular throughout Europe, especially between 1840 and 1890, and by the end of the nineteenth century it was a commonplace sight on the main streets of thousands of towns, large and small, around the world. An example of inter-foreign hybridity derives from the presence of Italian neo-Renaissance style in the French concession, in particular in the church of St Louis, which combined a Florentine neo-Renaissance interior with the romanesque Renaissance façade. There are similarly strong architectural echoes in the former Zhongfu and Guohua banks, both situated today on Jiefangbeilu (Liberation North Road).

The creation of the concession as a sort of miniature Italian architecture display resonated deeply with colonialists from other countries and helped to raise the international recognition of the newly created Italian state, both internationally and domestically. Foreign journalists such as H.G.W. Woodhead stated:

> The German concession…was the most favoured residential area for foreigners of all nationalities.…The British concession and extension contained the most important foreign banks, offices and shops, and a considerable Chinese population…The Italian concession.…was becoming the most popular centre for the palatial residences of retired Chinese militaries and politicians.
>
> *(Woodhead 1934: 65)*

The Italian colonial discourse of power was also reflected in the choice of the names for the major streets. The use of Matteo Ricci to name a road where the barracks dedicated to national 'hero' Ermanno Carlotto[8] were located reveals a clear intention to use historical precedents to legitimate the existence of a long-term exchange and communication between Italy and China. Moreover, within the 'faraway' and idealised borders of the Italian 'neighbourhood' in Tianjin, the Italian nationalistic tropes could be exported and reinvented, assuming a powerful symbolic value for the Italian audience at home. The matrix of names such as *Fiume* or *Trento Trieste* belongs to the rhetoric of Italian nationalistic ideology, since they are explicit references to the process of Italian unification (officialised in 1871) and indicate the emphasis on reclaiming the north-eastern 'just borders' (namely Trento, Trieste, and the Dalmatian coast with the city of Fiume). This was a crucial motivation for Italian intervention in the First World War: in order for the country to become complete, it was necessary to regain those bordering areas. The dream of unity was then also being recreated in Tianjin.

After the establishment of the People's Republic of China in1949, the appropriation and naming processes were reversed, and today the surviving Italian-style villas are located on *Minzulu* (Nationalities Road) and *Ziyoudao* (Freedom Road), while Matteo Ricci Road has been reclaimed as *Guangmingdao* (Road of Light – indicating the New China), but taxi drivers still know the main square of the former concession by its earlier name, Marco Polo Square. According to the new geography of space embodied by today's map, the former Italian concession is contained between *Bei'andao* (Northern Peace Road) and *Ziyoudao* (Freedom Road) on the north, the Haihe on the south, *Wujinglu* (Five Elements Street) on the east and *Xinglongjie* (Flourishing Street) and *Jianguodao* (Street of the Foundation of the Republic) on the north-east.

Images of benign colonialism

During the fascist period, the hagiographically tinged master narrative of benign colonialism reached its climax, emphasising the dichotomy between the bleak prospects of the past and the unique achievements of the present in the concession's territory. In 1936, in line with the fascist regime's dream of empire-building,[9] engineer Rinaldo Luigi Borgnino wrote an enthusiastic article, arguing against the possibility of ceding the territory back (Borgnino 1936: 363–66). The alleged legitimacy of keeping the concession was based on the highly civilising motivations demonstrated by Italians, as revealed by the progressive 'evolution' of that 'small territory'. Before the Italian intervention, the area was 'miserable', 'noxious', 'desolated' and 'sad'. After the Italian acquisition, the area had become a stage display of 'Italianness': a model of modernity and hygiene. Among the achievements, Borgnino boasted an advanced civil engineering and infrastructural projects, such as wide roads, elegant buildings, a modern hospital, electricity and potable water in all the houses, an advanced sewage system and public landscaping:

> Vittorio Emanuele III Boulevard, 24 metres wide, was the main arterial street of our concession. This boulevard, crossed through by a tram line managed by a local company, absorbs all the traffic from the Chinese city to the Tianjin east railway station and the other concessions. Obviously, the public buildings should have been erected on this Boulevard.
>
> *(Borgnino 1936: 363)*

Italy provided leadership for the neighbouring colonial concessions to modernise, stimulated to implement similar measures to improve their overall aspect and conditions.

A local British newspaper, mentioned by Borgnino, defined the Italian concession as 'the most pleasant residential neighbourhood among all the concessions' (Borgnino 1936: 365). The representation of the concession as a 'neighbourhood' became a recurrent colonial rhetorical trope.

Borgnino had a personal interest in the production of this successful image, ultimately due to his own personal contribution. Borgnino was in charge of the drawings of the Italian municipal council building, that was aimed at 'creating an example, the most complete, of Italian art, a showcase of thought, technique and materials, a representative building in the most comprehensive sense of the term' (quoted in Cardano and Porzio 2004: 44) He was also the supervisor of the hospital's building – inaugurated on 21 December 1922 – following the drawings of engineer Daniele Ruffinoni. Borgnino used most of the information contained in Fileti's 1921 report, but intentionally shifted away from Fileti's emphasis (Fileti 1921: 8–9) on the economic opportunity for the Italian companies (represented by the penetration in the Chinese 'large and virgin market'[10]) to an emphasis on the built form: a unique sign of distinction and prestige for the Italian concession, and a clear indication of its 'Italianness'. Nevertheless, Borgnino's attempt to avoid the colonialism as a theme reveals significant anxieties about Italy's imperial identity. These anxieties are also reflected in the subjective rewriting of the East and West encounter, offered by the lesson delivered on 26 April 1927 by Dr Ugo Bassi at the Fascist University of Bologna. Bassi stated that:

> First, even in China, as in every other part of the world are the Italians, who went there for that desire of adventure, for that almost mystical sense of the unknown that in the Middle Ages, pushed the light and well built Italian ships to face new routes, towards Africa or America, searching for the legendary Saint Brandano's islands or looking for gold.
>
> *(Bassi 1929: 9)*

Bassi remembered Giovanni da Pian del Carpine (1245–47), Marco Polo (1261–95) and Matteo Ricci (1552–1610), and concluded: 'Magnificent progeny this our Italian one, that has offered to the whole world vast continents and new knowledge, affirming herself always and in every field, first among all the others.' (Bassi 1929: 10.)

Bassi praised England for opening up China and putting an end to the Chinese superiority complex (Bassi 1929: 12–13). With reference to the international military expedition to suppress the Boxer Rebellion, Bassi first remembered the deceased Ermanno Carlotto as a national hero (Bassi 1929: 15), then argued that the Italian soldiers distinguished themselves from the other troops, who committed the most tremendous cruelties and created an overwhelming chasm between 'white and yellows'. According to Bassi: 'the Italians proud as usual of the humanist tradition of their motherland and the roman civilisation brought to the indigenous people, where they could, aid and rescue' (Bassi 1929: 16). The alleged magnanimous behaviour of the Italian 'liberators' is contradicted by the first-hand account of Medical

Lieutenant Giuseppe Messerotti Benvenuti. In 58 letters and 400 photographs to his mother (written and taken between September 1900 and September 1901), he documented the relations between the different military troops, mentioning the killing, looting and other atrocious excesses, and in the end he sadly concluded:

> If our soldiers did less harm than the other armies it is due to the fact that, even though they (the Italians) always went everywhere, they always got there late, when the villages had already been burned and plundered. The few times they arrived on time, they behaved like the others.
>
> *(Benvenuti 2000 [1900]: 17)*

But Bassi was more interested in reiterating a crucial element of Fileti's 1921 report: Italy could not miss the opportunity to mark off China 'as an actor and observer in that world where probably new global destinies were developing' (Fileti 1921: 20–21). His aim was to emphasise Italian remarkable achievements, from urban architecture to missionary schools portrayed as 'Centres of Italianness'. The Italian neighbourhood became the ideal ground for experimentation in the Italian notion of modernity and reinvention of the collective identity of Italy as a glorious and unified nation. The Catholic cathedrals functioned as the metonymic trope of 'Italianness': masculine symbols of space conquest, dominating heaven and earth, they 'recall the faraway motherland, in the simple but typically Italian style'. Bassi praises the 'silent apostles' in the Chinese and other foreign lands, who act 'in the name of Christ, but also in the name of Italy' and 'turn on the vivid human light, Latin, in the lighthouses of the most remote lands' (Bassi 1929: 29). The climax of his lecture is an absolute and religiously tinged pledge of allegiance: 'It is not possible for an Italian to forget his Nation, unless this Italian is so degenerate to deserve the loss of his nationality as extreme punishment' (Bassi 1929: 29).

Conclusion: the 'neighbourhood' as a 'zone of dominance'

Mary Louise Pratt defined 'contact zones' as:

> The social spaces where cultures meet, clash, and grapple with each other, often in contexts of highly asymmetrical relations of power, such as colonialism, slavery, or their aftermaths as they are lived out in many parts of the world today.
>
> *(Pratt 1991: 33)*

Coining the term 'contact zone', she challenged the model of community perceived by the coloniser as an idealised construction, which tends to suppress the alternative and marginalised voices as a means of affirming the assumed unity of a group. The representation of the Italian concession as a 'neighbourhood' tends to legitimise the construct of an allegedly homogeneous idealised 'community', and to prevent shedding light on the possible existence of a 'contact zone'. The issue at stake with the 'contact zone' is that it is not a reassuring space; it forces us to challenge our predominant views and to express the otherness that intrinsically exists inside ourselves. The rhetorical situation revealing the 'contact zone' in the printed culture can arise only when two or more interlocutors, coming from very different backgrounds and characterised by very different positioning processes, show their willingness to learn how to communicate with each other. As Pratt states, we need to 'figure out how to make that crossroad the best site for learning that it can be' (Pratt 1991: 40). Transculturation (Pratt 1992) is missing in the idealised projection of a culturally reproduced Italian 'neighbourhood' in Tianjin. The result is a Manichean representation of the Italian 'laboratory of modernity' in contrast to the backwardness of the indigenous population.

This narrative reached its climax during the fascist era, when Benito Mussolini portrayed this 'eye in the faraway Orient' as 'an extremely advanced sentry of Italian civilization' (quoted by Cesari 1937: 23), and the Italians were depicted as extremely popular and welcome in China. An esteemed (but not identified) Chinese literati even exclaimed: 'Oh! If our compatriots had trusted Marco Polo!' (Catalano 1936, quoted in Cesari 1937: 23). This providential representation capitalised on the derogatory image of misery, poverty and filth before the Italian arrival. Benvenuti's description of the exact moment when the Italian troops entered Tianjin in January 1901 is an example:

> As soon as we entered the remains of the city, the smell of burned was replaced by a special stench that we call Chinese smell. It is a stink of fat, aromas, and soil, dissimilar from any good and bad smell which is known among us: this is the reason why we call it Chinese.
>
> *(Benvenuti 2000 [1901]: 17)*

In his correspondence, Benvenuti insisted on the Chinese dirtiness, especially in the houses of the poor, but also among the well off, even though he vaguely concluded: 'it seems that the wealthy are clean' (Benvenuti 2000 [1901]: 18). His references to Chinese women reveal a racially connotated misogynist tone: 'I haven't seen a single Chinese woman who is beautiful or pleasant, or at least not repulsive' (Benvenuti 2000 [1901]: 28). This leads Benvenuti not only to consider the presence of the European concessions as a blessing, but also to express sympathetic understanding for the Chinese men who show little respect to their wives, since 'they are so horrible'. Chinese women become the object of his mixture of 'colonial gaze' (Fanon 1967, 1986; Gilman 1985) and 'colonial grasp' (Kelly 1997). Their derogatory depiction, which allegedly justifies Chinese patriarchal social hierarchy, is a metaphorical projection of power relations between the foreign occupiers and the indigenous occupied.

The interaction with the locals is described positively in only two cases. The first is self-referential: when Benvenuti meets an 'educated official' who demonstrates 'particular sympathy for the Italians' and 'knowledge of Italian Risorgimento's history' (Benvenuti 2000 [1901]: 40). The second case, although vague, leaves more room for dialogue. When Benvenuti describes Chinese architecture and civil engineering, he admits the possibility to learn from them:

> If I stayed in China a bit longer, I would leave enthusiastic (about it). The Chinese are called barbarians since it would be convenient if they were such, while in many and many things they could be our teachers' since in many ways they outrun us (Benvenuti 2000 [1901]: 44).

In 1921, Consul Fileti described the concession's Chinese dwellers as 'fairly mild'. His emphasis on the 'great respect that Chinese have for the principle of authority…when treated with justice and dignified firmness' (Fileti 1921: 15) was ultimately instrumental to praise (and justify) the Italian forces of occupation, since both during the occupation and the transformation of the concession the Chinese dwellers did not cause any 'unpleasant accidents' (Fileti 1921: 22).

The contact zone requires both a temporal–spatial interaction between groups, and a mechanism of blending and interpenetration between systems of meaning formation (Pratt 1991). There is no room for this in the ultra-positive conceptualisation of the 'neighbourhood'. The representations remain substantially self-referential, created by the speaker to address the speaker's selected audience.

The imagined community of the Italian concession in Tianjin became an imagined 'zone of dominance' with a precise symbolic capital. It represented a triple historical nemesis for the Italian Government. Italian colonial policy had suffered a major reversal after the 1896 devastating military defeat near Adwa, which the Tianjin concession could, if only partly, help set aside, as was also the case in China after the unsuccessful attempt to obtain Sanmun in 1899. Tianjin represented international recognition of Italian prestige among the other foreign powers involved in the 'scramble for concessions'.

Notes

1 Preliminary research was facilitated by a small research grant from the British Academy in 2007. This chapter was completed with the support offered by the Economic and Social Research Council, whose help is gratefully acknowledged (grant number RES 062-23-1057).
2 Fileti's report is particularly important for the photographs, which represent a sort of witness to the first stage of development of the Italian concession, setting in this way a *terminem post quem*.
3 The Boxer Uprising was directed against foreign influence in areas such as trade, politics, religion and technology. The uprising crumbled on 14 August 1900 when 20,000 foreign troops entered Beijing. See Joseph W. Esherick, *The Origins of the Boxer Uprising* (Berkeley, CA: University of California Press, 1987); Paul A. Cohen, *History in Three Keys: The Boxers as Event, Experience and Myth* (New York: Columbia University Press, 1997); Diane Preston, *Besieged in Peking: The Story of the 1900 Boxer Rising* (London: Constable, 1999).
4 I borrow this definition from Lydia Liu, who uses it to refer to the necessity to reinvent the meaning of words in a different context.
5 It was built in 1889 in the northern side of the park to commemorate the British general Charles George Gordon who helped the Qing dynasty to repress the Taiping rebellion.

6 *Taotai* (*Daotai* in pinyin) refers to an official at the head of the civil and military affairs of a circuit, which consists of two or more or territorial departments (*fu*). A possible translation is 'Intendant of circuit'. Foreign consuls and commissioners associated with *taotai* as superintendants of trade at the treaty-ports are ranked with the *taotai*.
7 The equivalent of this style in England is the so-called 'Renaissance Italian palazzo'. Inspired by John Ruskin's panegyrics to architectural wonders of Venice and Florence, a shift occurred around 1840 with 'the attention of scholars and designers, with their awareness heightened by debate and restoration work' (Pavoni 1997: 73).
8 Carlotto was the naval lieutenant who had died in Tianjin on 15 June 1901 while defending, together with a group of navy men, the so-called Italian Consulate. De Antonellis informs us that 12 Italian soldiers died in the military expedition 1900–01.
9 On 9 May 1936, Benito Mussolini proclaimed the foundation of the Empire. This event occurred three days after the Italian troops, commanded by Marshall Badoglio, had entered Addis Ababa after the eight-month-long military occupation campaign of Ethiopia.
10 'China is a vast virgin land for economic exploitation that can be opened to human activity and the effort to overcome the difficulties is well justified…all the nations that feel strength, due to their commercial and industrial development, have always looked with active and growing interest to the vast and virgin Chinese market and seized every favourable opportunity to breach the wall enclosing such a treasure, to avoid being second or overpowered in the exploitation of that vast new market' (Fileti: 1921, 8–9).

6

THE COLONIAL SPACE OF DEATH

Shanghai cemeteries, 1844–1949

Christian Henriot

With the signing of the Treaty of Nanking in 1842, the fate of Shanghai took a new course. The establishment of foreign settlements – originally conceived as no more than foreign enclaves where 'barbarians' would be kept at bay by the Chinese authorities – opened a new space that ultimately led to the emergence of three separate administrations within the same city: the International Settlement (IS), a result of the merging of the British and American settlements in 1863; the French Concession (FC); and the Chinese city.[1] Although land usually remained the property of China, the foreign enclaves in treaty-ports, especially in Shanghai, Tianjin, and Canton, developed as quasi-colonial territories. Due to their size and role in the city, the two foreign settlements in Shanghai became the epitome of foreign rule on Chinese land.

The original plan of limiting residence in the foreign enclaves to foreign settlers (except for their Chinese servants) proved illusory. With the civil war that ran havoc in Central China after the mid-1850s, streams of refugees sought safety and protection in the foreign settlements. Extraterritoriality and gunboats offered a relative haven from the raging war between the Taiping and Imperial forces. This was the first population onslaught that put an end to the 'foreigners only' rule. Natural disasters and subsequent warfare in the lower Yangzi area through the late Imperial and Republican period fed a constant surge in population.

The economic success of Shanghai also brought increasing numbers of foreign immigrants. Westerners figure most prominently in the early decades, but with them actually came along a mixed lot of colonial subjects, especially as soldiers in times of crisis. The Japanese arrived much later, but their community soon overshadowed all other foreign communities altogether. Finally, there were a few cases of refugee-seeking Westerners – Russians in the 1920s and Central European Jews in the late 1930s – who came in sudden waves.

The composition of the population in Shanghai became truly international. At the same time, there was more at stake than a too-often glamorized cosmopolitanism.

Foreigners administered two major areas of the city and ruled, regulated, and even passed sentences on all matters of urban life. But as much as for life, they had to regulate on issues of death or, more precisely, the management of death. Foreigners came with all kinds of creed, belief, and religion, which meant a lot when it came to death. The urban space was fragmented as much as the social landscape was segregated. Depending on nationality, people did not enjoy the same rights, dead or alive.

This chapter is concerned with the issue of the management of space for the dead. This is a curious angle, from which one can also get a sense of how colonialism operated in Shanghai. It concentrates on the foreign settlements, as both had to deal with the issue of mortality among their increasing populations. It is not a general study of how death was managed in Shanghai, but a study of how the Shanghai Municipal Council and the French Municipal Council defined policies on death and marked out territories with various privileges to accommodate the dead. An examination of cemeteries reveals much about colonialism's spaces of inclusion and exclusion, tension and contestation, and urban transformation.

Cemeteries as colonial markers of death

The reading of Western imperialism seizing Chinese territory with a ready-made blueprint to parcel it out and conquer more land over time requires some revision. The establishment of 'settlements' in treaty-ports was conceived by both sides as an expedient, for foreigners, to have a foot on Chinese territory with a large degree of autonomy and, for the Chinese authorities, to manage an alien population by conventional means of setting them apart and making them responsible for their own kind (Cassel 2008). Within these enclaves, especially in Shanghai, foreigners acquired far more autonomy and power than was written in the treaties, while the settlements evolved into full-blown towns with millions of residents. If the Chinese and foreign authorities had probably foreseen problems with the living foreigners, the dead also had to be taken care of. And as the Chinese moved into the foreign enclaves, they also became part of the social and human equation.

The extent to which death required the attention of the authorities resulted first from population growth. If we follow the classic study by Zou Yiren, Shanghai's population grew from around 540,000 in 1852 to 5,400,000 in 1948, a tenfold increase over a century. In the foreign settlements, before the first census in 1865, the population numbered from a few hundred in 1853 to 20,243 in 1855 in the British Settlement. (There is no figure for the French settlement.) Between 1865 and 1942, the population in the two areas grew from 92,884 (IS) and 55,925 (FC) to 1,585,673 (IS) and 854,380 (FC), respectively (Zou 1980: 90–91). Foreigners, except in the very early years, were no more than a tiny minority within the whole population. There were about 50 residents in the British settlement in 1845, a couple of hundred by 1855, and more than 500 in 1860. After a surge in numbers in 1865 (2297), the foreign population actually decreased and did not regain its initial level until 1880 (2197). It resumed its growth, doubling between 1900 (6774) and 1910

(13,536), again in 1930 (29,997), and almost again in 1942 (57,351). In the FC, there was a similar though more modest movement upward, from 460 in 1865 – it remained basically at that level until 1900 – to 831 in 1905. It increased at a quicker pace thereafter, with the foreign population doubling from the 1910 level (1476) in 1920 (3562), 1925 (7811), 1931 (15,146), and 1942 (29,038) (Zou 1980: 141).[2]

In terms of deaths, the annual number among foreigners in the IS was never very substantial compared with that among the Chinese population. It is impossible to compare the figures until 1902, when finally some statistics were kept for the Chinese population. Among foreigners, the number of deaths almost doubled between 1880 (55) and 1900 (97), while the mortality rate decreased. Thereafter, with a fairly stable rate, the yearly number of deaths was multiplied by five from 138 in 1902 to 560 in 1936. Over the same period, the number of deaths in the Chinese population was multiplied by three between 1905 (6443) and 1936 (17,594) (Zou 1980: 138). Due to its role as a harbor, there was a large foreign transient population, among whom some unfortunates unexpectedly passed away during their stay. Periods of political tension or outright military confrontation also brought large contingents of foreign troops. Between 1887 and 1907, there were often as many, or even more, visitors who died than there were adult residents (Stanley 1908: 435). What these rough data reveal is that from the beginning, several dozen to several hundred foreigners died every year in Shanghai and required local burial.

The birth of foreign cemeteries in Shanghai

There were initially no provisions for deaths and burials in the agreements signed between China and foreign countries. This came at a later date, in the second round of treaties signed in 1858–60. Yet people did not wait until such agreements were made to die in the foreign settlements, both Chinese and foreigners. The case of Chinese residents was addressed in a very simple and straightforward way. They were not allowed to be buried in the foreign settlements, in accordance with the initial rule of non-residence by the Chinese in the settlements. Although that rule was not enforced, the prohibition on burials was maintained. The only exceptions were the existing cemeteries that came to be part of the territory of the settlements as the latter expanded westward. In such places, burials were allowed, although with restrictions. These Chinese cemeteries, for the most part, were established by and for sojourners or charities.

The first piece of land (8.25 *mu*) acquired for the purpose of establishing a cemetery was purchased in 1844 at a cost of Tls 730. The title deed of the 'Shanghae Cemetery' stated it was meant for 'the use of British subjects at this port as a place of interment'.[3] The creation of a cemetery by private individuals followed the new pattern established in Great Britain proper, with the move away from parish graveyards and the rise of cemeteries as municipal or private ventures (Brooks 1989: 38–42). In the context of settling in an alien land at a time when there was, as yet, no formal municipal authority beyond the management of 'roads and jetties', the birth of foreign cemeteries in Shanghai came out of nothing more than the concern by private individuals to provide a decent burial to those who happened to die in the city. The 'Shanghae Cemetery' was located in the countryside, outside the limits of the settlement, replicating the same pattern as around the walled city. Urban development, however, soon placed the cemetery in the heart of the city (Map 6.1).[4]

Although the foreign community was small, the number of deaths among visitors, mostly sailors, had immediate consequences for space in the 'Shanghae Cemetery'. In 1855, with 50 foreign sailors interred in the portion of land allotted for that purpose, the cemetery was running out of space. The Committee of the Shanghae Cemetery decided it was time to find another location to accommodate these dead, 'out of regard for the health of the community'. In 1859, a new subscription bill was circulated among the community to collect the $3000 necessary for the purchase of a piece of land on Pudong across the Huangpu River [*North China Herald (NCH)* 15 September 1855]. The Pootung Cemetery was twice as large as the first cemetery (16.22 *mu*). Yet, as we shall see, the Pootung Cemetery was closed well before it reached its capacity.[5]

The establishment of a joint cemetery in 1865 was a unique experience that the two settlements did not repeat. In the course of 1865, a Committee for the New Cemetery (a name one finds on maps for a long time) was established to organize the purchase of a large piece of land well into the Chinese countryside, beyond the limits of the two settlements (Map 6.2). This was the first involvement by the French authorities in municipal cemeteries.[6] During the first two decades of the settlement,

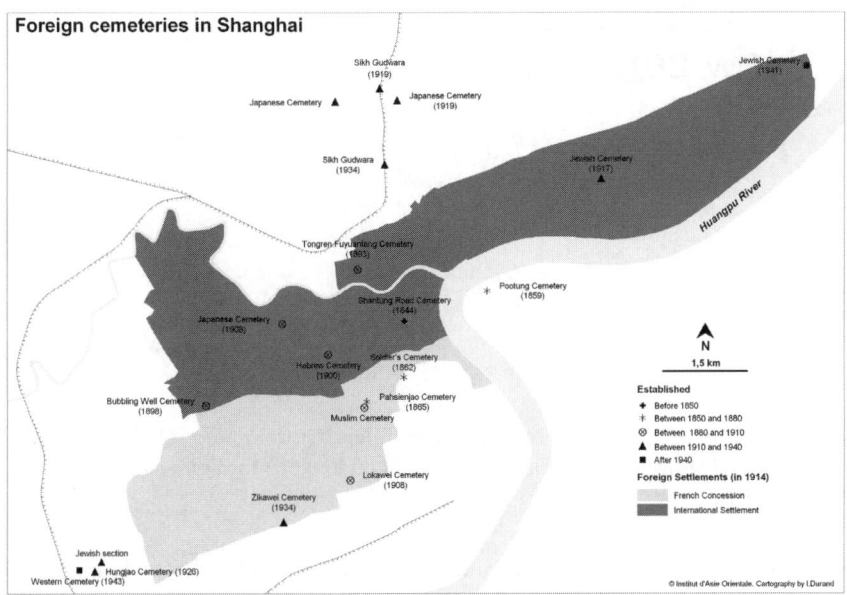

MAP 6.1 Foreign cemeteries in Shanghai
© @*Virtual Shanghai Project*

112   Christian Henriot

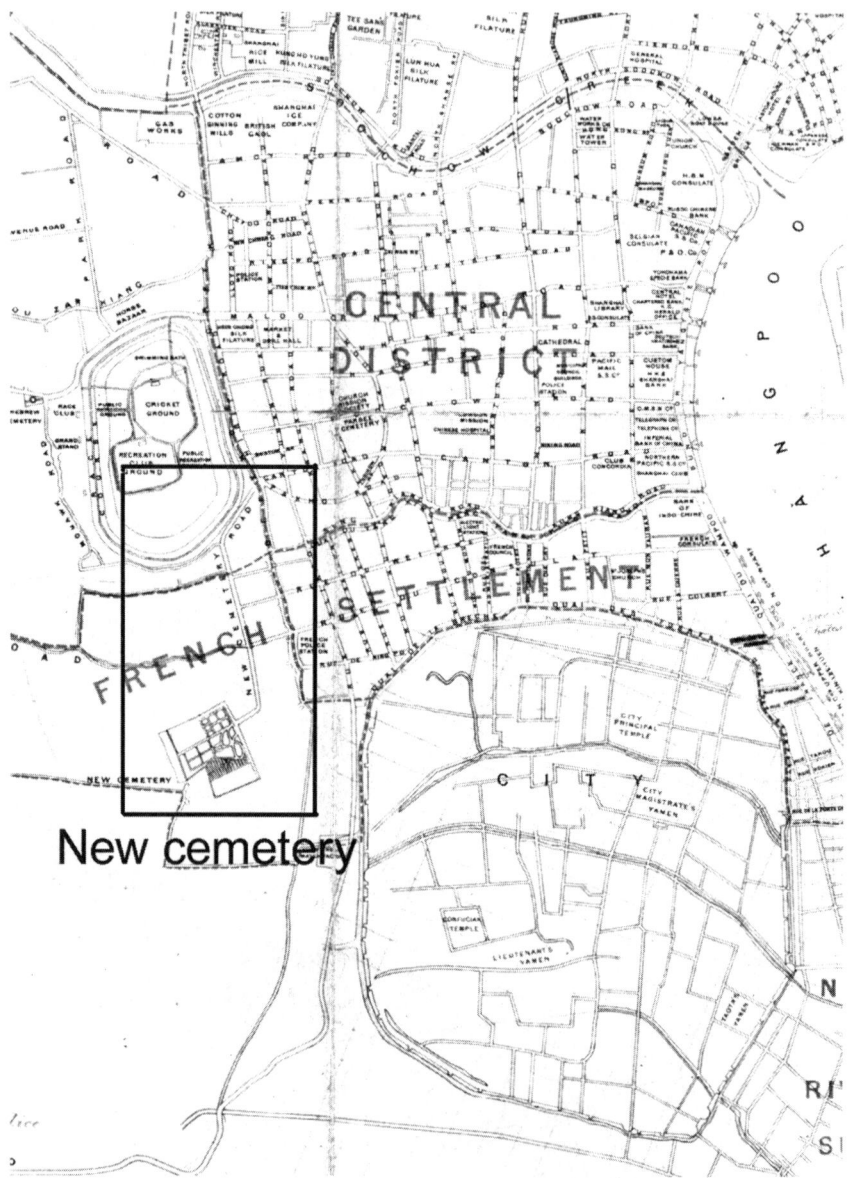

MAP 6.2 Pahsinjao Cemetery ('New Cemetery') (extract from Map ID: 342; Original title: *A map of the foreign settlements at Shanghai*, London: Stanford's Geographical Establishment, 1900)

the very small size of the French community hardly called for the establishment of its own burial ground. The New Cemetery was divided into two sections, each settlement taking care of its own. The extension of the FC in 1900 placed the cemetery in the middle of its territory, with full control over its use. It created an uneasy situation for the Shanghai Municipal Council (SMC), with repeated disputes over mostly minor issues, except about the Muslim cemetery. The two municipal administrations opted for an autonomous development thereafter.

Over time, the private initiatives found it more difficult to cope with the increasing responsibility of providing burial ground for the expanding local community, especially with the rapid turnover of residents in the early decades of the foreign settlements. For another part, the movement toward a greater involvement of municipalities in the supply and management of cemeteries in Europe implicitly called for an intervention of the SMC in the management of cemeteries. Eventually, by mutual consent, the two cemeteries – 'Shanghae' and 'Pootung' – were transferred to the SMC in February 1866 [*North China Daily News (NCDN)* 8 November 1926, 8 March 1927].[7] This marked the end of the privately run foreign cemeteries and the beginning of a larger process of regulating death in the foreign settlements. In the same period, the two settlements took over the 'New Cemetery' – the Pahsienjao (Baxianqiao) Cemetery – which also became joint municipal property.

Apart from the early private initiatives, cemeteries were also created as a result of circumstances, usually military events that left numerous dead among the troops. Those who died from their wounds during fighting or from disease would be buried close to their initial encampment. The first such cemetery was established near the wall of the walled city, on its southern side, in Chinese territory. It came to be known as the 'Soldiers' Cemetery'. The cemetery served for only two years, between 1862 and 1865, and accommodated some 300 bodies of soldiers from British regiments who died in 1862–63.[8] The site somehow fell into oblivion as the soldiers were buried without individual tombstones[9] (*NCH* 24 January 1908). The SMC also inherited this cemetery, which proved difficult to maintain with a decent appearance. Nevertheless, the SMC was relentless in preserving this area.[10] While this burial ground went on record, other burial grounds were established for the colonial subjects of British and French troops, but no record or memory of them was preserved.[11]

Population growth and the expansion of municipal cemeteries

The provisions for the burial of foreign residents soon proved inadequate for the size of the population. In 1896, the SMC decided to acquire 64 *mu* of land along Bubbling Well Road to establish a new cemetery (Bubbling Well Road Cemetery, BWC) and a crematorium.[12] The new cemetery was located much further west, in Chinese territory, far away from the built-up area, although eventually the urban sprawl caught up with it (Map 6.3).[13] By 1928, however, the BWC was running out of space.[14] According to the Public Health Department (PHD), there was a strong sentimental attachment among [foreign] residents to the cemetery, rather than to the Hungjao Cemetery opened a few years earlier (1926). In fact, the BWC was considered 'prime burial ground' by the foreign community due to its proximity. In 1939 the BWC was still in operation, though meeting with the same problems of space.[15]

In the FC, pressure on the Pahsienjao Cemetery led to the establishment of a new cemetery in 1905 outside the settlement's boundaries, but right next to it.

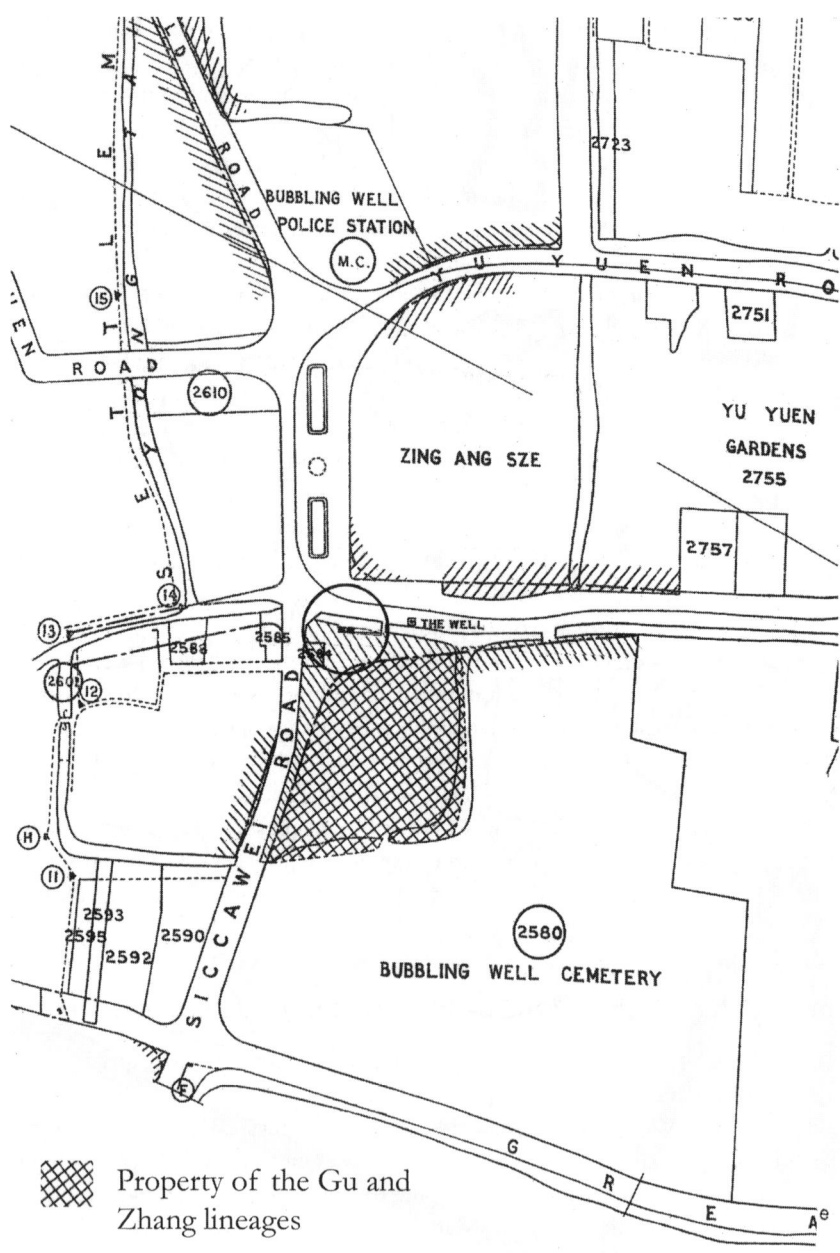

MAP 6.3 Bubbling Well Cemetery (Shanghai Municipal Archives, File U1-14-6913)

The new cemetery was located in Chinese territory, in Lujiawan (Lokawei), to the south of the settlement. The French managed space in their new cemetery as in France. The Lokawei Cemetery offered grave spaces with various terms: perpetual (506 graves), 25 years (40), and 15 years (247). This regime allowed a certain degree of flexibility and renewal of the graves. The removed bones from the expired concessions were exhumed and reburied in a collective ossuary. This rule applied to the Vietnamese (Annamese) tombs (424 graves) in the Lokawei cemetery and to the tombs of indigents in the West Cemetery (see below).[16] There was also a separate section for soldiers (36). Although there was nothing made consciously, the French authorities and residents literally grounded themselves in Chinese soil with a view to stay for ever.[17]

The French Municipal Council eventually decided to open a third cemetery further west, also outside its boundaries, in Zikawei in 1934, for free pauper burials.[18] By 1939, the Lokawei Cemetery was running out of space unless existing graves were suppressed. The margin for expansion was found in the Vietnamese section. The previous rule had been to exhume the graves after 20 years and to remove the remains to an ossuary. It was decided to anticipate on the disinterment of Vietnamese remains and to implement a program of early removal to make room for new perpetual graves. Yet there was no end to this process with population increase in the settlement.[19] In November 1939, the Director of Municipal Services proposed to purchase a new tract of land for a new cemetery in the external road area, but this was not followed up.[20] By September 1942, the Secretary General advised again to use municipal property to create a new cemetery for paupers. The last addition to municipal cemeteries – the Cimetière de l'Ouest (West Cemetery) – was established in July 1943 to receive the bodies of indigents, mostly foreigners without resources, such as Russian refugees. The right to a burial place rested upon a clear hierarchy based on wealth and ethnicity.

In the IS, the SMC followed the same pattern of moving the location of its cemeteries west and establishing them outside their official boundaries. In 1926, the decision was made to acquire a large tract of land that would be prepared and used as demand arose. The new cemetery was located in the Hongqiao area, and came to be known as the Hungjao Cemetery (HJC). The SMC implemented a subtle rate policy that made the BWC more expensive and the HJC more affordable. As in other aspects of social life in foreign Shanghai, the rate policy drew lines between the best off and the rest of the population. This policy did not follow the general pattern in Great Britain or France, where such differences were eliminated. On the contrary, the pressure on burial space and the conditions of war combined to reinforce the differential rates and actually reserved the BWC for the richer segments of the foreign population.[21]

As the city expanded, cemeteries followed a pattern of migration westward, where farm land was available at a low cost. Death contributed to 'colonizing' land beyond the limits of the foreign settlements. The urban space was dotted with these permanent burial grounds that came to be fully included in the city, except for the last two additions. As we shall see, other 'dots' appeared over time, but their lack of official status made them vulnerable to destruction.

The general policies of cemetery management

Cemeteries for whom? On the surface, the answer to this question seems simple. After all, cemeteries were created for the benefit of Shanghai residents. Yet, in life as in death, rights were not the same among Shanghai residents, due not only to ethnic divisions, but also to religious differences and residential patterns. The Western settlers created spaces for their enjoyment, to which one was admitted according to ethnicity, wealth, religion, etc. When it came to death, each settlement cared for its own residents although, of course, reality was more complex. Among Westerners, issues of religion drew hard lines when it came to burial. The general rule that applied was the exclusion of the Chinese from the municipal cemeteries. The cemeteries were reserved to the foreign population, actually to the Western residents. Over time, however, it became problematic to exclude *all* Chinese, even if no policy was ever designed to take care of the dead among the Chinese population. The Japanese were not welcome either, and by virtue of their own self-organization they established their own burial grounds.

In the FC, for example, the authorities tried to limit access to the Lokawei cemetery to its residents, but it also had to take into account the transient foreign population that happened to die on its territory. To sort out 'right-holders', a different set of rates applied for residents and non-residents. This rule was introduced in 1926 and maintained until 1943.[22] The same held true in the IS, but defining 'residents' and 'non-residents' proved to be a tricky question. In 1933, the PHD proposed a text that would first define residents according to nationality.[23] The French residents, therefore, would have been excluded from IS cemeteries, as well as other foreign nationals living in the FC and, of course, all Chinese. Yet the SMC realized that many of its former residents had moved to the FC and might die there, even if they could claim a right to a burial in the IS.[24]

In the 1930s, excluding the Chinese – actually Christian Chinese – also proved politically and religiously sensitive and even offensive. Eventually, the SMC came to the conclusion that a formal scheme would cause too much trouble if made public. But it did not shelve it entirely, and decided to use it within its own bureaucracy. Basically, it favored restricting cemeteries to Christian burials, even if it admitted: 'on a strict municipal basis, non-Christian ratepayers are entitled to be treated on parity with Christian ratepayers'. To manage a way out of this dilemma, the SMC reserved for itself the right to make such rules as it saw fit to restrict the use of cemeteries to the burial of Christians.[25] This issue was not discussed again until 1937, when pressure on burial ground increased as a result of war.[26]

Chinese had been 'admitted' in the BWC by way of reservations of burial ground. By 1913, however, the increase in such applications caused some alarm to the PHD, who asked for instructions. Prior to 1913, occasional burial of Chinese had been made, 'all having professed Christianity'. Since 1912, population increase and the success of conversion also meant that more Chinese wanted to be buried in the BWC. The health inspector reviewed three options, with only one that appeared workable: to limit the number of burials of Chinese to around 20 per year pending the creation of a cemetery for the Chinese.[27] The SMC found it advisable to purchase a suitable site, as and when opportunity offered, as a burial ground for the Chinese.[28] Thereafter, the existing cemeteries would be reserved for foreigners only. Ten years later, however, the SMC had not done anything in that direction.[29]

In the FC, the general policy toward the Chinese was not different. The Chinese had to take care of themselves. The French authorities actually applied a policy modeled after the practices established in the home country after 1881, when a law secularized all municipal cemeteries (Lassere 1994: 117). All non-Chinese residents were subject to the same rules as French citizens, whatever their origin, nationality or religion. The cemeteries in the FC were genuine municipal cemeteries, except for the Chinese residents. At the same time, however, the French authorities buried all their dead in Chinese territory. When the French obtained a new extension of their territory in 1900, they decided to ban any more burials within their boundaries. The rule was applied strictly, even after the large 1914 extension.[30] All new cemeteries were established around the settlement, south and west. No coffin repositories were allowed, except for the Ningbo Guild. Only one funeral parlor was allowed to operate in the settlement, even during the Sino–Japanese war.

A place for each, but each in its own place: ethnic cemeteries

In terms of foreign population, Shanghai was home – albeit often a temporary one – to a myriad of nationalities. The 1935 census listed 51 different national groups in the two foreign settlements. Yet nationalities do not tell the whole story, as colonial subjects of the major powers were sometimes listed under the 'main' nationality. Some communities were permanent and acquired a certain size, while some came to Shanghai for a short time, usually with the military, and went home. Yet, in between, they also left behind their dead who, more often than not, were buried in specific places and forgotten. Even the more stable communities like the Japanese or the Baghdadi Jews had 'rotating' burial grounds before they settled in one final resting place (Map 6.1). The geography of death in Shanghai, therefore, was a constantly unfolding process, with new and vanishing places, to meet the needs of individual communities.

The SMC as well as the French Municipal Council actually never wanted to be involved in establishing and running cemeteries for specific communities. There were issues of cost, but also of principles, even if these principles were bent when it came to the majority group of Western Christians. The only community cemeteries sponsored by the SMC were one for the Muslims and one for the Jewish refugees. In both cases, the SMC made a free gift of a piece of land. It justified its lack of concern for the Chinese population out of respect for its 'traditions':

> By custom of long standing, cemeteries in China are provided by families, guilds and benevolent societies – it is because it is not in the established

custom for municipal authorities to provide cemeteries for Buddhists that the SMC has refrained from attempting anything of the kind, knowing that to disregard this custom would involve interference with the authority and influence exercised by families, guilds, and benevolent institutions.[31]

This was obviously an *ex post facto* rationalization of a complete disregard for the needs of the Chinese population, even if we take into account the practice of shipping back the coffins to the native place (Hiroyuki 1994: 1–32; Goodman 1995: 6–7, 90–92, 252–25). The foreign settlements never made any arrangement for the burial of their Chinese residents.

Colonial subjects

With the French came colonial troops, mostly from Indochina. Vietnamese ('Annamites') were assigned to Shanghai in times of crisis as part of the colonial contingents sent to protect the settlement. They were also recruited as permanent officers in the Garde Municipale (French police), playing somehow the same role as the Sikhs in the Shanghai Municipal Police (SMP). Many of these transient or temporary Vietnamese residents, as well as members of their families, died in Shanghai.[32] The policy toward the burial of colonial subjects in the FC followed the principle of inclusion with all other foreign residents in the settlement, but with different rights. They were interred in a separate section of the Lokawei cemetery. After a period of 20 years, however, their remains were excavated and placed in an ossuary.[33]

The Sikhs were also a prominent element of the British colonial presence in Shanghai. They worked in the police force, but also as private guards and in various menial jobs. They constituted a permanent community of substantial size with specific burial practices. A major feature in Sikh religion was the cremation of dead bodies. The first cremation site – *guardwara* – was established outside the city, north of Hongkou.[34] The *guardwara* was poorly maintained, but above all it was located in an unfavorable environment, low land often covered with water. In 1911, a Sikh assistant superintendent of police asked the SMC to do some work on the site.[35] The SMC actually installed the *guardwara* in another place close by, opposite to the Hongkew Park. The development of housing nearby made it difficult to maintain it, and two years later a new location was proposed along Rifle Range (Map 6.1).[36] By 1923, however, shooting practice required another move. This was the last displacement. The *guardwara* was a simple installation described as 'merely a concrete slab in the open air'.[37] After the outbreak of Sino–Japanese hostilities, the place was actually abandoned.

Muslims were present in Shanghai among the Chinese population. Many, however, came as members of British colonial troops, mostly from India. The French also brought troops drawn from their colonies in North Africa. Since the early cemeteries were established for 'British subjects' of the Christian faith, Muslims had to be accommodated elsewhere. Maps show a spate of 'Muslim cemeteries' on both sides of the post-1900 southern limit of the FC. Since the map that lists them was established shortly after the 1900 extension, the cemeteries must have been established much earlier, to bury members of either British or French troops. They could also be Chinese Muslim cemeteries. These burial grounds created out of expediency were soon neglected, forgotten and overrun.

The first mention of a Muslim cemetery appears in a correspondence in 1910. We learn that a piece of land was purchased at the south-western corner of the Pahsienjao Cemetery some years before (Map 6.4). One-third was filled by Muslims who had come at the time of the Boxer Rebellion. In 1910, the representative of the mosque, R. Rajabally, asked the SMC to purchase an additional piece of land to enlarge the burial ground for Muslims. After some quibbling, the SMC eventually agreed to provide three *mu* of land. Yet the final decision about on which land the cemetery was located rested with the French Municipal Council.[38] There began another trail of correspondence that clearly revealed the reluctance of the French authorities to accept an extension of the Muslim cemetery. They flatly refused to grant an extension 'for reasons of public interest of which the effect has been that since the extension of the Settlement in 1900 all deposition of coffins has been

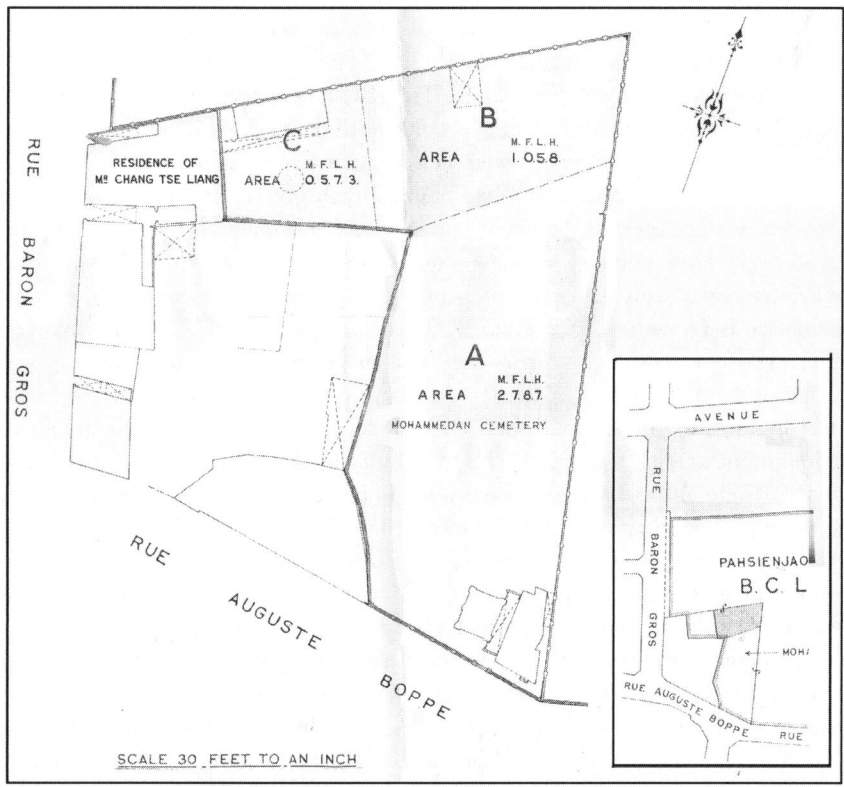

MAP 6.4 Muslim Cemetery (corner of Pahsienjao Cemetery) (Shanghai Municipal Archives, File U1-16-2453)

prohibited'.[39] The French Council remained adamant about not authorizing another extension. By 1940, the SMC still had in its hands the piece of land it had bought to extend the cemetery, but had to leave vacant.[40]

Non-Christian foreigners

Jewish settlers were among the very first to come to Shanghai. Several of them became exceptionally successful. The names Sassoon or Hardoon are the most famous, but a much larger community developed over time. A second significant wave of Jewish Russian refugees came on the heels of the Bolshevik Revolution in the late 1910s. Finally, a third wave came from Central Europe, Germany, and Austria to flee Nazi persecution. (Kreissler 2000; Ristaino 2002; Betta 2003). Of course, the very different conditions under which these various groups came – the difference in size, too – implied different forms of accommodation when it came to burial. As with other minority communities, a permanent ground was not found until late. A map of 1900 shows a 'Hebrew Cemetery' along Bubbling Well Road, next to the race course. It was still listed 18 years later on a 1919 map of the city, but not on subsequent maps.[41] The first stable Jewish cemetery was established by the community itself off Baikal Road. It served the whole Jewish community well until the late 1930s.

After 1939, however, the SMC had to face the issue of the high number of deaths among the Jewish refugee community. The Jewish cemetery on Baikal Road had space, but it was open to people who could afford the cost of burial spaces therein. The SMC debated whether it would set a 'dangerous precedent' by setting aside a portion of the Hungjao Cemetery for the Jewish refugees. It feared that other communities would expect similar favorable treatment and apply for their own specific section. The SMC considered giving money to the community to purchase a piece of land, but eventually the PHD's view prevailed to reserve a corner of the Hungjao Cemetery as a Jewish burial ground.[42] That decision was made against the avowed principle of the SMC not to provide cemeteries for specific communities.

The opening of this burial section failed to solve the problem of a Jewish cemetery in the long run. In December 1940, the representatives of the 'Jewish Liberal Community' applied for a piece of land to bury the dead according to Jewish customs.[43] There was an argument about the land made available free of charge within the Hungjao Cemetery in December 1939.[44] The major problem, however, was that of distance between Hongkou, where most of the Jewish refugees lived, and the Hungjao Cemetery at the other end of the city. The matter was finally settled in March 1941, when the PHD and Public Works Department (PWD) won the argument to give out a piece of land located at the corner of Point Road and Liping Road at the far end of the Eastern district.[45] While this provided a temporary respite, the cemetery proved inadequate to meet the high mortality rate among the Jewish refugee community.[46] In September 1943, the *Juedische Gemeinde* informed the SMC that there were only six burial spaces left in the Jewish cemetery.[47] The SMC tried to stick to its principle, but eventually it gave in and authorized the PWD to sell an additional three *mu* of land.[48]

Despite the importance of the Japanese community in the city, little evidence remains about its cemeteries. At the turn of the century, a cemetery existed to the west of the pre-1899 limits of the IS, along what would become Carter Road. This burial ground was still visible on 1908 and 1919 maps, but it disappeared thereafter.[49] As the community actually concentrated in the Hongkou area, a new burial ground was established in the north of Shanghai.[50] Yet it has not been possible to find documentary evidence about Japanese cemeteries until the early 1930s. In 1932, the SMC signed an agreement with the 'Japanese amalgamated association of street unions of Shanghai' to rent a piece of land of 2.9 *mu* for 20 years, on the east side of Kiangwan Road in the Chinese municipality, to be used as a Shinto shrine.[51] Yet, whether out of financial trouble or on purpose, by 1938 the association had defaulted on the payment of the rent.[52] After the occupation of the IS by the Japanese army, the shrine expanded by 18.8 *mu* with a new 20-year lease, starting in 1942. Eventually, the site of the Shinto shrine was one of the largest foreign cemeteries in Shanghai (31 *mu*).[53]

What emerged from these developments and policies was a pattern of juxtaposition of burial grounds for each sub-group. All claims to 'cosmopolitanism' notwithstanding, cemeteries reflected the ethnic and social dividing lines that ran through the social body in the foreign settlements. Hybridity could be found, to a certain extent, in the cemeteries designed for Westerners, although the hard core for admission remained set on a mix of religion (Christianity) and ethnicity (Westerner). French cemeteries allowed for more encompassing hybridity, but with unequal rights (Vietnamese, North Africans). With slightly diverging views on cemetery policy, the two foreign administrations actually imposed their own cultural and political hegemony on the territories of death in the city, including those outside their own boundaries.

The preservation of colonial memories

Cemeteries are meant to last, though not necessarily for ever. In the case of Western cemeteries in Shanghai, issues of religion, memory, and law contributed to the preservation of cemeteries a long time after they had been closed. In 1918, the SMC projected to reinter the remains in the Shantung Road Cemetery (the original 'Shanghae Cemetery') and rebuild the Shantung Hospital on the site.[54] Although the trail of documents is thin, it appears the matter was dropped due to legal complications. In 1925 again, the SMC consulted its legal adviser about using the burial ground for a new fire station. The adviser stated that the removal of graves and remains was open to contestation by the heirs of the deceased. Even if the chances were low – the cemetery had been closed since 1871 – the SMC decided to give up.[55] In 1939, the PWD turned down a new proposal by a private company to turn the cemetery into a parking lot.[56] The last document found is about an unsuccessful attempt to turn the cemetery into an open space and sell frontage for buildings.[57]

The Pootung Cemetery was also the object of regular solicitations to use part of its ground. For a long time, the SMC abided by a strict line of not allowing any infringement and protecting the nature of the site as a burial ground (Figure 6.1). The location of the cemetery, however, caused some problems when the area came to be covered with factories and wharfs. The presence of the cemetery that cut the frontage of the river into two disconnected sections created an obstacle to circulation between the factories and the wharfs. The SMC denied both right of passage and pathway to the foreshore.[58] Even the application of a Protestant parish was rejected.[59] Eventually, the SMC softened its position – in part under the pressure of the companies, in part because it found advantageous to have them pay for the cost of erecting and maintaining a fence and a gate at each end.[60] The erection of illegal Chinese huts forced the SMC to consider selling the foreshore part to avoid further colonization.[61] In 1932, after a negotiation with the municipality, the Chinese police expelled the 59 families of squatters (Figure 6.2) who, however, received a financial indemnity.[62] The SMC wasted no time in putting the land on sale, which brought a large sum of money to the SMC's funds.[63]

The Soldiers' Cemetery, next to the former wall that surrounded the city, proved far more complex. Despite its small size, it represented a much higher stake in terms of memory among Western residents. Whereas the Pootung Cemetery was somehow treated as a second-rank burial ground, the Soldiers' Cemetery held a privileged status in the eyes of the SMC leaders. It had proved difficult to maintain since the 1860s, but the destruction of the wall in 1912 brought serious concern about its preservation. The press related the poor condition of the cemetery, forgotten and neglected. In 1907, the SMC had leveled the enclosure and converted it into 'a little

FIGURE 6.1 Pootung Cemetery (Sailors' Cemetery) on Pudong (Shanghai Municipal Archives)

FIGURE 6.2 Squatter huts in Pootung Cemetery (Shanghai Municipal Archives)

green sanctuary amidst a wilderness of squalor' according to the *NCH* (3 February 1912). There may have been some exaggeration in this idyllic description of the place because this remote portion of land amidst a highly densely populated area was exposed to various forms of encroachment. The major issue was its use as a dumping ground, which remained a constant problem. In 1924, a Chinese company put up advertising signboards which the SMC also found intolerable. It pressured the Chinese authorities and obtained their removal.[64] Because of these repeated incidents, the SMC considered removing the graves to one of its own cemeteries in 1929, but was unable to solve the thorny issue of rights over the remains.[65]

In 1938, the Superintendent of Cemeteries reported once more on its deplorable conditions after the hostilities in late 1937.[66] The SMC approached the consulate with its proposal to remove the remains to the Hungjao Cemetery and provide them with a memorial.[67] After a lengthy process, the operation was done in November–December 1938.[68] Instead of the 2,000 bodies claimed by Lanning and Couling (1921), the SMC workers found 316 adults bodies and two children.[69] The English-language press was ecstatic about the removal: 'New graves for Taiping heroes', 'Romantic old burial ground has now been abandoned' (*NCDN* 14 December 1938; *China Press* 1 March 1939). The removal of the remains turned into an ode to the great sacrifices made by Westerners [British] to protect and save Shanghai. It became part of an exercise in 'memory-building' based on the reading of Shanghai history exclusively through Western eyes. The memorial was unveiled at a grand ceremony on 3 October, 1939. The English-language press reported extensively on the event, which brought together civic, religious, diplomatic, and military representatives of Western countries (*Shanghai Times* 27 September 1939; *NCDN* 30 September 1939; *China Press* 4 October 1939; *NCDN* 4 October 1939). Neither the list of guests nor the photographs seem to include Chinese dignitaries.

Cemeteries carved out spaces in both the urban physical ground and the social landscape. The colonial subjects and the minority groups, except for the large, self-contained Japanese population, did not enjoy the same rights as the members of the majority. They had to take care of themselves or to depend on the reluctant benevolence of the authorities. Even in the more public-minded FC, access to burial ground followed a clear hierarchical pattern. On the other hand, the 'feature' cemeteries were the objects of constant care and protection. Attempts to recover their space for other purposes, as with the Shantung Road Cemetery, were foiled by the fear of encountering legal and religious challenges. Cemeteries that were part of the 'history' of Westerners in Shanghai, like the Pootung Cemetery or, more evidently, the Soldiers' Cemetery, provided the occasion for small or large ceremonies when it came to transferring the remains of their occupants. Such ceremonies nourished the colonial memory and vision of the city.

Cemeteries as spaces of contestation

Burial grounds created all kinds of friction. In the early days of the foreign settlements, the individual tombs scattered all around the walled city were a constant problem for the management of land. The area outside of the wall served as a place of burial for the local population, pretty much as was the rule throughout the countryside around Shanghai. The presence of a large population, of course, increased the density of tombs in the area that became the settlements. This was especially true in the FC, although the westward extension of the foreign enclaves absorbed hamlets and villages around which graves were to be found. Most of the time, the removal of the individual tombs was negotiated with the owner if the family was still around. It rarely created a problem. As for cemeteries, however, their removal or transformation was more delicate. The French authorities were able to negotiate the removal of the Fujianese cemetery after they obtained the section of the riverfront south of their original limit (Maybon and Fredet 1929: 61) Yet, as shown in Bryna Goodman's study, the handling of the Ningbo Cemetery became a tug of war that escalated several times into riots (Goodman 1995: 159–69). Even in less violent forms of opposition by the Chinese population, the foreign authorities were sometimes unable to have their way.

As with the Ningbo Cemetery, the SMC was powerless over Chinese cemeteries that existed prior to the existence or extension of the foreign settlements. While it avoided a confrontational approach, the SMC maintained a strong grip on a piece of land it would have liked to disappear. In 1893, a cemetery owned by the Tongren fuyuantang (TRFYT) – a charitable institution devoted to collecting and burying exposed corpses and abandoned coffins in the city – happened to have been included within the newly demarcated boundaries of the 'American Hongkew Settlement'.[70]

The SMC signed an agreement with the TRFYT establishing that it would not build roads across or interfere with the cemetery. The TRFYT, for its part, had to maintain the place in good order and avoid anything offensive or injurious to health.[71] In 1902, the SMC proposed to purchase the land to build a Chinese public school. While the TRFYT initially gave its consent, influential members within and outside the organization expressed considerable opposition, including a demonstration before the seat of the county magistrate. The SMC backtracked and purchased another piece of land. Yet it also imposed a new agreement on the TRFYT, by which the latter was prohibited from using the land for another purpose or from selling it.[72] This marked the beginning of a quiet but persistent tug-of-war between the TRFYT and the SMC.

In 1906, we learn from a report by the Chief Engineer that the cemetery was dirty and neglected.[73] The file on the cemetery in the subsequent years shows mostly correspondence or reports by SMC inspectors that usually point to the 'considerable quantity of garbage and debris dumped over cemetery walls'.[74] In 1930, the SMC made a new attempt to obtain the cemetery to turn it into a public park. The plan was to make a swap with the Chinese municipality (SZF) in exchange for the Soldiers' Cemetery in Nanshi. The proposal failed.[75] Two years later, the same offer to create a public park was made to the TRFYT through the SZF, but the SMC was not successful.[76] The cemetery continued to be used as before in a way that brought constant criticism from the health inspectors of the SMC. A 1933 detailed colored map of the cemetery shows a stall for the sale of second-hand goods, dwellings of squatter type, human excrement, and so on.[77] In March 1936, a report noted the use of the cemetery as a playground for football, the presence of squatter huts, and even that of a woman dying her wool.[78] A company contacted the SMC about the possibility of building on the cemetery, following a request by the TRFYT to vacate all the graves. The TRFYT may have tried to test the SMC's dispositions indirectly, but the SMC reasserted its position that no change could be made to the use of the land.

In fact, it appears the cemetery was never put to another use, at least up to 1940. A school applied to use it as a playground in spring 1937, but the proposal was turned down by the SMC. The school principal described the cemetery 'like a wilderness, as before the war…[it] has become filthier than ever. Residents in the neighborhood use the place to dry their laundry and rowdies […] frequently put up gambling stalls. Garbage is dumped all over the place.'[79] In February 1938, the Shanghai Federation of Charity Organizations was allowed to establish sheds for refugees on the cemetery.[80] In 1940, the cemetery was no longer a refugee camp and had reverted to its original usage as an 'open space'.[81] Despite its pressures and regulating powers, the SMC was able neither to obtain the sale of the cemetery land for its profit, nor to regulate the use of the land in a satisfactory manner. The restrictions imposed in 1893 and the failed attempt to purchase it in 1902 left a legacy of implicit animosity that both sides expressed by neutralizing the other. On the whole, however, the TRFYT was the main winner in these strong-arm tactics that left the organization with actual control on the use of its burial ground (Fuma 1989: 294–95).

Another example of cemeteries as place of contestation and competing claims is that of the Hungjao Cemetery. After its initial purchase of land, the SMC acquired successive lots to extend the capacity of the cemetery. In 1934, after two previous extensions, it offered to buy Lot no. 11184. A round of negotiations followed with the owner, who still found the proposed price too low, even if, according to the SMC, it was above market value. In 1939, the issue of purchasing the lot came up again, but no move was made.[82] The targeted lot became a bone of contention between the SMC and the owner, who took no care of his land. The reason why the SMC was unhappy is that the lot was located in the middle of the cemetery area (Map 6.5). In 1941, finally, a new round of discussion was opened through a comprador, but the owner kept asking for more each time a deal had been struck with the SMC. The PWD suspected the owner to have bought the land for the sole purpose of speculating on its value and to 'put us in a hole'.[83] A new offer was made, but the owner asked four times more. Out of frustration, the PHD suggested removing the path that gave him access so as to inconvenience him. Yet no action was taken.[84] One last attempt was made in early 1943, but it seems to have failed.[85] Quite clearly, clever landowners could anticipate cemetery extension and bet on the rise in the land price for otherwise little-valued farm land.

The SMC also met with serious difficulties even with ordinary peasants, especially with land owned by a lineage. Despite all the rhetoric about colonial abuses, it appears that the 'vested powers' the SMC enjoyed under the Land Regulations had their limits. One must also acknowledge that the SMC actually also abided by the rule of laws and regulations it enforced on the population within its territory. In 1907, the SMC planned to purchase the whole piece of land adjacent to the BWC so as to cover the whole block (Map 6.3). In February, after initial contacts, the PWD reported its failure to convince the owners to negotiate with the SMC.[86] The matter was dropped for a few months, but the Works Committee renewed its instructions to proceed. The PWD approached the head priest of the Bubbling Well Temple (Jing'ansi) to seek his collaboration in the discussion with the villagers. From the minutes of the interview, we learn that opposition by the landowners was related to the refusal by the SMC to let them repair their local temple; one landowner was willing to sell, but the other refused because it would cut access to their own land; the landowners had a definite idea about the value of their land (no less than Tls 5000 per *mu*).[87]

A second meeting took place between the PWD, the head priest, the local headman (*dibao*), and the district headman. They concurred that it was pointless to deal with individuals, and suggested a general assembly of the villagers.[88] The PWD prepared a list of the 20 owners – among them seven Zhang and nine Gu – and called a meeting on 15 November 1907. During the meeting, the SMC representatives explained that the SMC was prepared to purchase their land at market value and use its power to claim the land. The villagers were given three weeks to formulate counter-claims. Past this deadline, the SMC would post a proclamation and use its powers of land condemnation.[89] On 12 December 1907, the proclamation was posted in Chinese and English to inform the villagers that the land commissioners

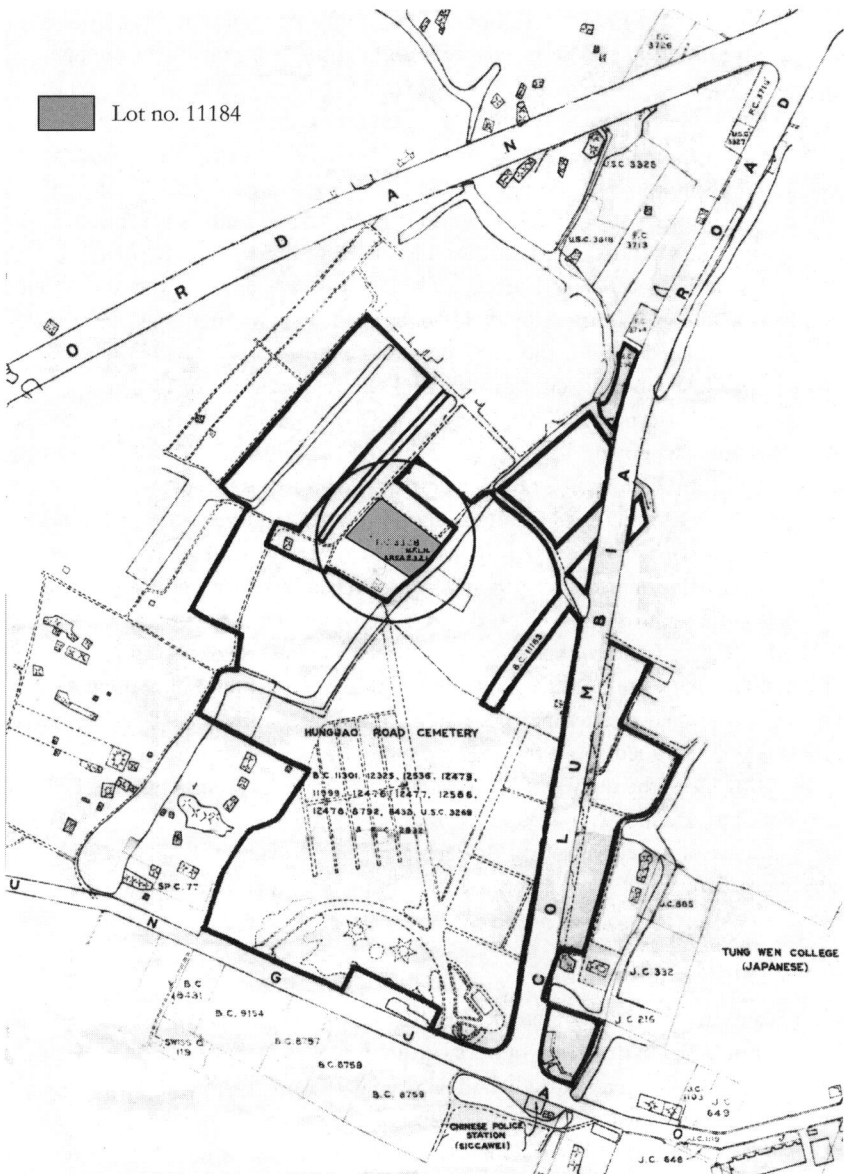

MAP 6.5 Hungjao Cemetery (Shanghai Municipal Archives, File U1-16-2450)

would proceed to assess land for its acquisition by the SMC.[90] Yet by March 1908, the PWD reported that the villagers had taken no notice of the proclamation. The Works Committee decided to take no further steps.[91] Obviously, the threat to use its 'vested powers' had failed to impress the villagers. Probably, the SMC realized its planned purchase relied on shaky legal ground. Moreover, it also had to count with the resistance not of individuals, but of two tightly knit communities around the Zhang and Gu lineages. The passive resistance of the villagers forced the SMC to shelve its project.

In 1911, however, the SMC planned again to resume the land purchase. There was a serious internal debate within the SMC about its strategy. The PWD argued that it was pointless to try again unless the SMC was prepared to go all the way toward the completion of the purchase. If, for the second time, it was to withdraw as in 1908, this would convey to the villagers the impression that the SMC was weak.[92] A careful and detailed survey of the area was made with a view to seeing whether the lineages could be divided between rich and poor members (Map 6.6).[93] Although nothing like this appears in the documents, the PWD had little reason to check the socio-economic status of each landowner for the sake of academic knowledge. Despite these preparations, and although the planned purchase was to take place at a time when the local Chinese authorities were in shambles due to the revolutionary movement, the SMC eventually decided not to pursue this.[94]

The SMC felt it did not have the force to press the villagers to sell and did not want to put its face at risk. As in the case of the TTFYT cemetery, however, the SMC retaliated by refusing all permits for the repair or construction of houses in the area.[95] The failure to purchase the land remained like a burning scar. In April 1916, the Works Committee again gave directions toward the acquisition of the land, but nothing seems to have happened. There is no further trail of documents.[96] The PWD resumed its attempt to purchase the land in February 1920. In a letter to the Secretary, it argued about the advantage of having the area scheduled for acquisition. The tone of the reply amply revealed the frustration of the SMC: 'the Council does not require and will not buy this land under any circumstances'.[97] Thereafter, the relevance of purchasing this lot decreased, first because the area had become largely urbanized, and second because the Hungjao Cemetery had opened.

Conclusion

The expansion of the foreign settlements westward created a trail of cemeteries. This particular 'journey to the West' of burial grounds reveals that population growth and urban expansion always exceeded the capacity of anticipation of the municipal authorities. New locations had to be found further west to accommodate the increasing number of graves for the various foreign communities. Over time, the western area of Shanghai became *de facto* a 'cemetery area', a phenomenon which the Sino–Japanese conflict reinforced dramatically. There were indeed more than the two large western cemeteries. Next to them was a large Chinese cemetery visible on a 1932 map. After 1937, this is where the Shanghai Public Benevolent Cemetery (SPBC) and TRFYT found land to bury the paupers' bodies as well as all the exposed corpses and abandoned coffins they found in the streets. Hongqiao also became a temporary burial ground for all the Chinese whose bodies could no longer be shipped back to their native place. Eventually, more than 100,000 coffins were stored in that area (Henriot 2007). When the nationalist authorities regained

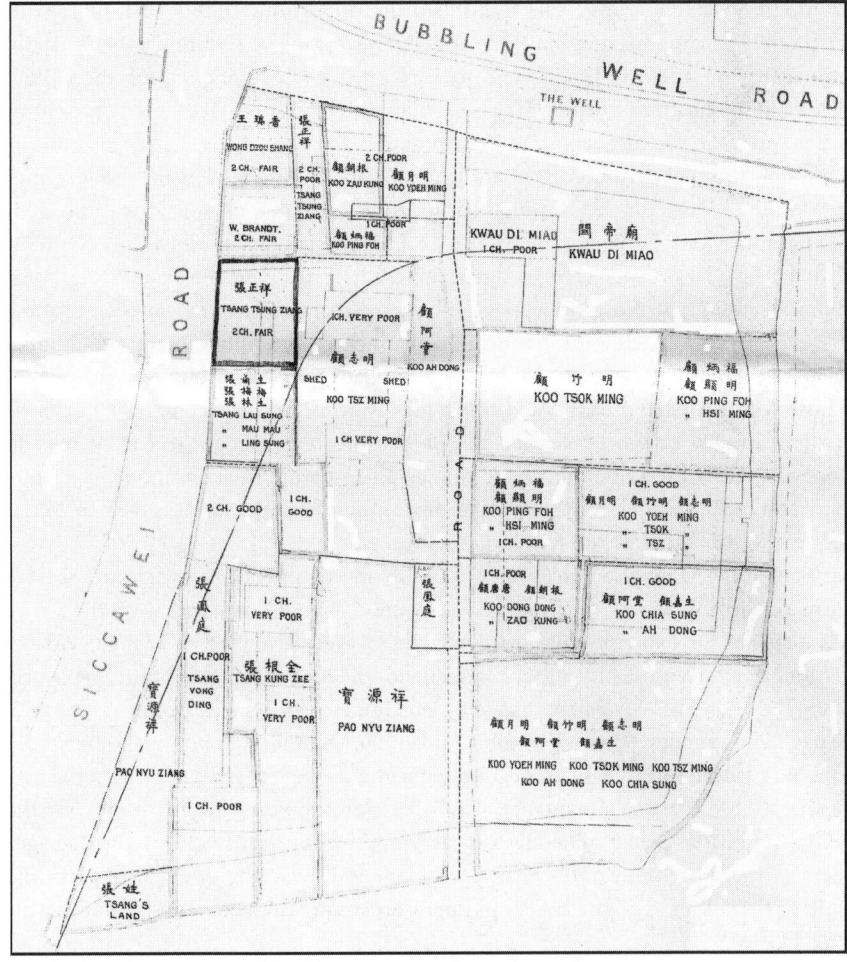

MAP 6.6 The 'resisting' lineage land lot (Bubbling Well Cemetery) (Shanghai Municipal Archives, File U1-14-6913)

control over Shanghai after the war, they designated three 'cemetery areas' (*gong-muqu*) around Shanghai. Hongqiao was one of them.⁹⁸

Cemeteries were initially created on an *ad hoc* basis to meet the biological consequences of death among the foreign settlers or sailors. There was nothing planned or designed for the burial of foreigners in Shanghai. Burial grounds were created by private initiative until it became obvious they required public attention. The control of cemeteries by the SMC and the French Municipal Council, however, introduced a new dimension as they became the object of policy and regulations. Such public involvement contributed to making cemeteries increasingly serve as social markers defining who belonged – and who did not – to a given community or sub-group. The living had the opportunity either to mingle with each other or stay separately in their respective working or leisure places. In death, however, one came back into the fold of one's community or, for those who belonged to subaltern groups (Sikhs, Vietnamese, Jewish refugees, etc.), had no or little agency on the disposition of their remains.

While the foreign authorities took great care of the dead from the majority groups, they were much less involved in providing burial grounds for those from their colonies or who had come to Shanghai as refugees. It was almost under duress that the SMC usually agreed to distribute land for the purpose of creating community cemeteries. No money was paid for the maintenance and upkeep of these places. The cost rested entirely on the concerned communities. Access to a burial ground, therefore, followed the hierarchy of nationality, race, religion, and wealth. Those with financial means could find a graveyard in a decent cemetery, but those without money or who belonged to colonial subaltern categories had to rely on benevolence or their own limited resources. Even within the colonial subjects, one can sense a subtle hierarchy, as in the more careful consideration given to Sikhs' requests versus those of the Muslim community.

Cemeteries were also places of contention and competition. It did not take the form of violent action, but quite clearly the Chinese landowners tried to take advantage of the expansion of burial grounds on their farm land. It brought 'urbanization' away from the city and increased land values. Yet, outside of sheer speculation, the main issue was the capacity of Chinese organized groups – lineages, benevolent societies – to stick to their land and prevent foreign power-holders from purchasing it, to force a sale, or even to regulate the usage of their land, as in the case of the TRFYT. Passive resistance was a far more powerful tool to block off the SMC's ambitions than is generally assumed. Yet the dominant mode in the management of the space of death in Shanghai before 1949 was one of exclusion – of the bulk of the Chinese population – and division among unequal communities.

Notes

1 The term 'foreign settlements' is used throughout this chapter to designate the International Settlement and French Concession. The Chinese-administered areas came under the authority of the county magistrate, with proto-municipal administration after 1905. Yet it was only in 1927 that a unified modern municipality was established (Henriot 1993: ch. 1).
2 In 1942 there were altogether 150,931 foreigners in Shanghai, of whom two-thirds were Japanese. By 1946 the figure had come down to 65,409 when all the Japanese were repatriated to their home country (Zou 1980: 146–47).
3 'Brief history', 4 May 1939, U1-14-6912, Shanghai Municipal Archives (SMA).
4 Letter PHD–Sec., 23 February 1925, U1-14-6912, SMA.
5 See documents 58–61, 1924, U1-14-6921, SMA
6 As this was not yet a municipal venture in the International Settlement, the cost was borne by a subscription. Extract from *Annual Report 1865* (17 March 1865), U1-16-2453.
7 Letter, H. W. Dent – SMC, 8 February 1866, U1-14-6921; extract from *Annual Report*, 1865–66, U1-16-2452, SMA.

8 Lanning and Couling (1921: 254–55) mention the 31st and 67th regiments of the Royal Artillery and Royal Engineers, and the Commissariat Corps, as well as many Belluchis. Many had died of wounds or cholera.
9 The cemetery was actually never used to its full extent. In 1867 there remained 80 burial spaces. Letter to SMC, 27 May 1867, U1-2-1111, SMA.
10 Letter to SMC, 27 May 1867, U1-2-1111, SMA.
11 *North China Daily News (NCDN)* 30 September 1935.
12 Extract from *Annual Report for 1896*, p. 167.
13 Technical note, 2 December 1938, U1-14-6913, SMA.
14 Letter PHD–Sec., 26 June 1928, U1-16-2443, SMA.
15 Letter PHD–Sec., 4 May 1939; PWD–Sec., 11 May 1939; Superintendent of cemeteries–PHD, 4 March 1941, U1-16-2443, SMA.
16 'Plan du Cimetière de Lokawei', U38-4-3282, SMA.
17 Letter, DASM-DG, 11 December 1939, U38-4-3280, SMA.
18 In September 1939 there were 738 individual graves, but the cemetery also served for paupers' burials. The 560 unclaimed victims of the Great World bombing on 14 August 1937 were all buried there. Letter DASM-DG, 11 December 1939, U38-4-3280 (1).
19 Letter DASM-DG, 11 août 1939, U38-4-3280 (1).
20 Letter DASM-DG, 8 November 1939, U38-4-3280 (1).
21 1932: PWD–Sec. – 11 August 1932, 1933 (documents 18–22), 1935 (documents 23–35, including map), U1-16-2450.
22 Letter PHD–Sec., 20 October 1931, U1-3-1183.
23 PHD, 16 June 1933; Memo, no author, 29 June 1933, U1-16-2423.
24 Superintendent of Cemeteries–PHD, 23 Nov. 1937; list, undated, but 1940, U1-16-2423.
25 On this issue see Note, PHD, 16 June 1933; memo, 29 June 1933, U1-16-2423. See new regulation 'Municipal notification' no. 4361, dated 4 May 1933, *Municipal Gazette*, U1-16-2423.
26 Letter, Superintend of cemeteries–PHD, 23 November 1937, U1-16-2423.
27 Letter, Health inspector-Sec., 14 March 1913, U1-14-3195, SMA.
28 One could read here a parallel with public parks, from which most Chinese were excluded until the late 1920s. To make up for this exclusion, a public park for Chinese was created along Soochow Creek in 1890. On this issue see Bickers and Wasserstrom (1995).
29 Letter Sec.-PWD, 5 September 1924, U1-14-3195, SMA.
30 Letter FMC–SMC, 24 Feb. 1911, U1-16-2453, SMA.
31 Letter PWD–Sec., 28 December 1942, U1-4-712, SMA.
32 Letter DASM-DG, 11 August 1939, U38-4-3280, SMA.
33 Letter DASM-DG, 11 August 1939, U38-4-3280 (1).
34 Minutes of the Watch Committee, 7 November 1907; Letter, Park keeper–Chief municipal engineer, 5 April 1908, U1-14-6907, SMA.
35 Letter, Sikh assistant superintendent, 12 April 1911, U1-14-690, SMA.
36 Sec.-SMP, 4 May 1911; SMP-Sec., 10 September 1913, U1-14-690, SMA.
37 Letter PWD, 10 September 1923, U1-14-690, SMA.
38 See correspondence in File U1-16-2453, SMA.
39 Letter FMC–SMC, 13 February 1911, U1-16-2453, SMA.
40 Letter PWD–Sec., 29 July 1940, U1-16-2453, SMA.
41 *A map of the foreign settlements at Shanghai*, 1900 (Virtual Shanghai, Map ID 342); *Plan of Shanghai 1919*, compiled from surveys made by the Shanghai municipal council, 1919 (Virtual Shanghai, Map ID 28).
42 Sec.–PHD, 11 Dec. 1939; Superintendent of Cemeteries–PHD, 14 December 1939; PWD–Sec., 15 December 1939, U1-16-2422.
43 Letter Jewish Liberal Community–SMC, 11 December 1940; PWD–Sec., 5 March 1941; PWD–Sec., 15 January 1941, U1-14-6927, SMA.
44 Minutes, Council meeting, 19 February 1941, U1-14-6927, SMA.
45 PHD–Sec., 28 February 1941, U1-14-6927, SMA.

46 Note, undated, 'visit to Jewish cemetery on 27 June 1942', U1-14-6927, SMA.
47 CAJR-PWD, 3 July 1942; Letter Juedische Gemeinde-PWD, 4 November 1942; *Juedische Gemeinde*–SecGen, 1st Special District – 21 September 1943, U1-14-6927, SMA.
48 PWD–Sec., 6 October 1943; PWD–Juedische Gemeinde, 8 October 1943; Juedische Gemeinde-PWD, 8 November 1943; Sec.-PWD, 15 December 1943, U1-14-6927, SMA.
49 *Saishin Shanhai chizu* (*The New Map of Shanghai City*), 1908 (Virtual Shanghai, Map ID 269); *Plan of Shanghai 1919*, (Virtual Shanghai, Map ID 28).
50 *Plan of Shanghai 1919* (Virtual Shanghai, Map ID 28).
51 There were three minor extensions in 1934 (0.7 *mu*), 1935 (1.65 *mu*), and 1936 (1.64 *mu*); 'Agreement', U1-14-6931; see extension documents in U1-14-6931, SMA.
52 Memo, PWD, 14 September 1938, U1-14-6931, SMA.
53 See documents and map in U1-14-6931, SMA.
54 Memo on Shantung Road Cemetery, 23 February 1940, U1-14-6912, SMA.
55 Letter Sec.–Legal adviser – 2 February 1925; Legal adviser–SMC, 22 May 1925, U1-14-6912, SMA.
56 Letter E. S. Little–SMC, 28 March 1939; Letter SMC–Legal adviser, 2 February 1925; Letter Legal adviser–SMC, 22 May 1925, U1-14-6912, SMA.
57 Memo on Shantung Road Cemetery, 23 February 1940; Memo on Shantung Road Cemetery, 26 February 1940, U1-14-6912, SMA.
58 See documents numbered 38–40, 1913, 1917, U1-14-6921, SMA.
59 See documents numbered 45 and 47–50, 1920, U1-14-6921, SMA.
60 Letter SMC–Shanghai Dock & Engineering Co., 14 September 1927, and agreement, U1-14-6921, SMA.
61 Letter PHD & PWD, 18 June 1928, U1-16-2452, SMA.
62 Letter PHD–Sec., 29 January 1932; Letter SMC–SZF, 21 November 1932; Letter SMC–Gong'anju, undated [1932], U1-16-2452, SMA.
63 Letter Superintendent of cemeteries–PHD, 1 November 1938, U1-16-2452; Report, Superintendent of cemeteries–PHD, 17 September 1942, Letter Sec.–PHD, 23 October 1942, U1-16-2443, SMA.
64 Letter PWD–Sec. 15 July 1924, U1-16-2454; Letter Superintendent of cemeteries–PHD, 27 May 1926; Letter Consul–SMC, 5 July 1926; Letter SMC–Consul, 21 January 1927, U1-4-711, SMA.
65 Letter PHD–Sec., 4 February 1938, U1-16-2454; Letter PWD–Sec., 28 March 38, U1-16-2454, SMA.
66 Minutes of meeting, 6 April 1938, U1-16-2454, SMA.
67 Letter SMC–Consulate, 9 April 1938, U1-16-2454, SMA.
68 Letter Consulate–SMC, 13 August 1938, U1-16-2454, SMA. The SMC even consulted the East Surrey Regiment about the design of the memorial. Letter PHD–PWD, 9 January 1939, U1-16-2454, SMA.
69 Letter Superintendent of cemeteries–PHD, 9 December 1938, U1-16-2454, SMA.
70 The case of the TRFYT cemetery is studied in detail by Fuma 1989: 287–90.
71 'Agreement', 18 July 1893, U1-14-6928, SMA.
72 'Site for Chinese Public School', extract from *Annual Report for 1902*, U1-14-6928, SMA.
73 Letter, Engineer & Surveyor–TRFYT, 5 January 1906, U1-14-6928, SMA.
74 Map of TRFYT cemetery, 27 January 1927, with notes by PWD inspector, U1-14-6928, SMA.
75 Letter PHD–PWD, 28 July 1930, U1-14-6928, SMA.
76 Memo 'Fu Yun Tang Cemetery', 6 October 1932, U1-14-6928, SMA.
77 Report and map, PWD, 22 November 1933; Letter SMC–TRFYT, 14 April 1934; Note, PWD, 8 June 1934, U1-14-6928, SMA.
78 Note, 19 March 1936, U1-14-6928, SMA.
79 Letter Zhonghua School–SMC, 25 March 1937; 22 December 1937; Letter SMC–TRFYT, 17 January 1938, U1-14-6928, SMA.

80 Letter Federation–SMC, 10 February 1938; Letter SMC–Federation, 15 February 1938, U1-14-6928, SMA.
81 Memo, PWD, 3 October 1940, U1-14-6928, SMA.
82 PWD–PHD, 21 November 1939, U1-16-2450, SMA.
83 PWD–PHD, 11 August 1941, U1-16-2450, SMA.
84 PHD–PWD 15 August 1941, U1-16-2450, SMA.
85 PHD–Sec., 3 February 1943, U1-16-2450, SMA.
86 Departmental report, 1 February 1907, U1-14-6913, SMA.
87 Memo of interview, 16 October 1907, U1-14-6913, SMA.
88 Memo of interview, 18 October 1907, U1-14-6913, SMA.
89 Memo of general meeting, 15 November 1907, U1-14-6913, SMA.
90 Proclamation poster, 12 December 1907, U1-14-6913, SMA.
91 Minutes, 23 March 1908, U1-14-6913, SMA.
92 Sec.–PWD, 23 December 1911; PWD–Sec., 27 December 1911, U1-14-6913, SMA.
93 See maps 62 and 63 in File U1-14-6913, SMA.
94 Minutes, Works Committee, 8 January 1908, U1-14-6913, SMA.
95 Sec., 25 November 1914, U1-14-6913, SMA.
96 Works committee minutes, 20 April 1916, U1-14-6913, SMA.
97 PWD–Sec., 14 February 1920; Sec.–PWD, 26 January 1926, U1-14-6913, SMA.
98 Report, undated [November 1949], B242-1-226-62, SMA.

7
FRENCH MEDICINE IN NINETEENTH- AND TWENTIETH-CENTURY CHINA

Rejection or compliance in far south treaty-ports, concessions and leased territories

Florence Bretelle-Establet

This chapter examines interactions between the French physicians appointed in the final decade of the nineteenth century on southern Chinese soil and various members of the local society. More precisely, it focuses on the ways Chinese people reacted towards French doctors' prescriptions, and thus addresses the issue of authority and power at the core of the present volume. As different scholars working on contemporary societies have pointed out, attitudes of acceptance or rejection towards medications depend on a set of factors far more complex and diverse than the notion of efficiency only, a complex notion yet. The status of the physician in society and thus the legitimacy of his power, the less or more critical attitude of people towards those who claim having the power to transform the others, and collective and individual conceptions of disease and health improvement are all elements that can explain the different regimes of compliance towards medications that one can observe in any society (Lee 1980; Kleinman 1982; Fainzang 2001). None of the sources that are available to us can be compared to the modern ethnological or sociological inquiries that allowed recent scholarship on this issue in contemporary societies. Nevertheless, French archives, together with Chinese gazetteers and local medical treatises, offer valuable insights into this question, raised in the context of nineteenth- and twentieth-century China, when the Qing empire came to be shared among different political entities that bestowed on foreign physicians and native patients different but interrelated status.[1]

This chapter first offers a brief reminder of the context of the presence of French military doctors in the far south of China (Yunnan, Guangxi and Guangdong). It then explores the political and scientific authority on which these physicians could rely, in an area that combined not only different political entities – treaty-ports, concession and leased territory – but also geographical sites located in the hinterland as well as in the more obvious heartland, for convincing their Chinese patients to abandon their familiar strategies against disease.

Political context for the arrival of French physicians in southern China

The project of appointing French physicians in southern China emerged at the end of the nineteenth century, when European powers were competing for a share of the Chinese empire. For a long time, the French Government had been coveting the far south of China for the easy access it provided to the Chinese market from the French possessions in Indochina. In the final two decades of the nineteenth century, the French explorations of Yunnan, Guangxi and Guangdong revealed riches in raw materials and made these provinces even more attractive. After Indochina's conquest and the end of the Sino–French war (1884–85), the French Government negotiated a profitable result. It obtained the opening of towns on the border between Tonkin and China (Mengzi, Manhao and Longzhou), in Yunnan and Guangxi provinces, where French residents were not only permitted to reside, but also enjoyed extraterritoriality and favorable tax rates.

In order to secure these achievements, the French Government established consulates in Mengzi and Longzhou in 1889, which were expected to inform the colony about the local agitation against the French in the area. Soon after Japan's victory in the Sino–Japanese war (1894–95), the French authorities actively worked to strengthen their influence in the area. The appointment of Paul Doumer as Governor-general of Indochina (1897–1902), supported by Gabriel Hanoteaux, Minister of Foreign Affairs (1894–98), who was all for an imperialist policy, actively served the French project of extending the Indochinese colony to the south of China. By different treaties and conventions, the French Government gained access to more towns located on the frontier, where it acquired the right to create consulates. It also obtained railway and mining rights in Yunnan, Guangxi and Guangdong, and the leasing for 99 years of a small portion of Guangdong province, the bay of Guangzhouwan (or in French the *Territoire de Kouang-Tchéou-Wan*). This territory consisted in part of land in the Gaozhou sub-prefecture, on the eastern coast of the Leizhou Peninsula, and in two small islands, Donghai and Naozhou (Brocheux and Hemery 1995; Lorin 2004).

In the final decade of the nineteenth century, the French authorities had thus succeeded in building a sphere of influence they regarded as very useful (Map 7.1): it would notably protect the French colony of Indochina against hostilities on its northern frontier, and it could be the starting point for further expansion of the colony in case the break-up of the Chinese empire would result in the creation of fully colonized territories.

Two elements combined to lead to the appointment of physicians near the French consulates created in the area: Paul Doumer's policy of 'a peaceful expansion', and the regular outbreaks of plague in the area. Paul Doumer indeed considered the appointment of physicians and the foundation of free medical dispensaries, like schools or the mail service, as a good means to alleviate the tension provoked by the recent expansion of French imperialism. But the appointment of French physicians in the area also responded to another need: the protection of public

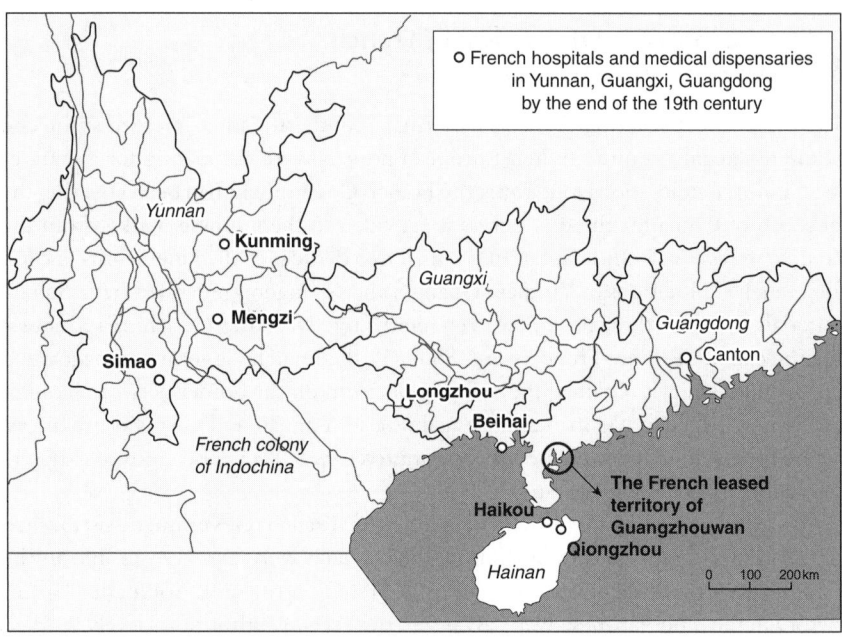

MAP 7.1 The French sphere of influence in late nineteenth-century China

health in Indochina and France, threatened by regular bubonic plague outbreaks in the Chinese area bordering the colony. Named *sentinelles avancées* (advance guards) or *ceinture de sûreté* (safety bands) by the French authorities (Kermogant 1907), these physicians were appointed to inform the Indochinese authorities about the epidemics that were developing on and across the northern frontier of the colony, so that appropriate measures could eventually be taken to protect the health of the French, both in Indochina and in France. Quarantine was also expected to protect the health of the Indochinese native labor force, working for the French interests (Monnais-Rousselot 1997).

The protection of French lives and the reinforcement of a French influence thanks to peaceful benevolence – the physician and teacher were, in the words of Paul Doumer, the 'most powerful levers of expansion of a nation' (CAOM.GGI. doc.32741, 8/1/1902) – were the motives that lay behind the appointment of French physicians in the far south of China. These motives were not very different from those that led most European countries to appoint physicians in their colonies. However, the status of these physicians diverged (Turin 1971; Arnold 1988, 1993; Macleod 1988; Vaughan 1991; Marks 1997; Monnais-Rousselot 1997).

French physicians' status and authority in treaty-ports and in the leased territory of Guangzhouwan

The physicians appointed in the French sphere of influence had different status. Because the Qing court and the subsequent republican governments retained formal sovereignty in treaty-ports, the French physicians appointed to Kunming, Mengzi, Simao, Longzhou, Beihai or Haikou had no official authority towards Chinese people. 'In carrying out their obliging activity, in providing free health care to the mandarins and to the populace', these physicians were just expected 'to make people like the French and to increase the prestige of France', explained Paul Doumer to the Minister of the Colonies in 1898, the year when physicians were first officially appointed in China (CAOM.SOM.NF.doc. 297, 20/07/1898). And from this perspective, the French colonial authorities provided those physicians with the financial means to create dispensaries or hospitals so that they could receive Chinese patients.

The status of the French physicians appointed to the leased territory of Guangzhouwan was very different. Placed under the authority of a French administration that itself was answerable to the rule of the Governor-general of Indochina, physicians had a status close to that of their colleagues working in the fully colonized Indochina. They were expected to apply the rules issued by the Governor-general of Indochina. Their mission was less to 'make people like the French' than to ensure an effective *cordon sanitaire* around the French colony and the Indochinese troops stationed in the territory. One physician, working on the gunboat *Estoc* stationed in the bay, openly declared in 1903: 'We just have to take care of the Europeans living on the Territory and mostly of the military garrisons in Fort-Bayard' (CAOM. GGI.doc.23852, 18/5/1903). And despite local disagreements about what the French administration should do in the field of disease prevention and medical assistance in the territory, and despite the claims to provide medical assistance to the natives formulated by a few physicians, no medical establishment was created for the natives until 1920. The French medical assistance provided there mainly consisted in giving health care to the French colony and to the soldiers, and as far as possible in isolating from the French the Chinese suffering from plague, by building lazarets and issuing coercive 'hygienic' measures or launching vaccination campaigns (Bretelle-Establet 1999: 87–90; Bretelle-Establet 2009).

French physicians appointed to treaty ports thus had a very different status to those appointed to the French-leased territory of Guangzhouwan. This difference gave them different kinds of authority. In Guangzhouwan, the French physicians were the intermediate agents of a French administration that had the right to issue commands backed by sanctions. The following public announcement, made in 1904, about fighting the plague illustrates well the nature of the French administration's authority:

> In the area comprised between the sea and the frontier indicated by red flags…inhabitants are obliged to follow the following prescriptions:
>
> 1/ Do not bury any corpse without covering it with quicklime and spread lime on the ground in order to make tombs visible.
>
> 2/ Clean meticulously the surroundings and inside of the houses…sprinkle quicklime on the floor and extinguish immediately or simply spread straw on the ground and burn in order to burn fleas and dust that carry the sickness of plague.…

These measures are necessary to protect Fort-Bayard against the epidemic of the plague. The Administration is convinced that these measures are for the sake of indigenous people as well as for the sake of Europeans and nothing will lead it to give them up until all the directions are fully followed.

Consequently, corpses that are buried inappropriately will be unearthed and burnt, and those responsible for burial will be seriously punished; Houses where no cleansing work has been undertaken before Monday 25th April will be burnt…Police tours will visit houses in order to check how prescriptions have been followed.

(CAOM.GGI.doc.5105, 21/04/1904)²

By contrast, the French physicians appointed in treaty-ports had no *de facto* authority. Esserteau, a physician who spent more than ten years in the French hospital of Haikou, expressed it very clearly in 1925:

Concerning hygiene and public prevention of disease, the action of the French physician is necessarily limited. In a country where France exercises neither sovereignty nor a protectorate, […] a foreign physician has neither administrative nor financial means to replace them [national authorities] in the task of enforcing the measures that could stop epidemics or would limit the expansion of endemic or contagious diseases. It is only within the clientele that trusts him or within the services that already resort to him that he can carry out such actions.'

(CADN Série A, Légation de France à Pékin, 1925)

Deprived of *de facto* authority towards the Chinese, the French physicians appointed in treaty-ports at the end of the 1890s started to work in a hostile climate. Although the Boxer Rebellion was confined to northern China, hostility between Chinese and Westerners also arose in the far south, where different conflicts turned into riots against foreigners. In the small open town of Mengzi, south of Yunnan, and after the replacement of the French consul, a conflict that opposed two Chinese people working mines turned into a riot in 1899 that finally affected the foreigners: in June 1899, the English and French facilities, notably around and including the railway, were destroyed and burnt. The French consulate of Mengzi was plundered and the Imperial Customs burnt. In June 1900, a rebellion against the French broke out in the provincial capital of Yunnan, after the arrival of the first French consul: the consulate was plundered, the church destroyed and the consul, together with the French residents of the town, was obliged to leave hurriedly. In summer and autumn 1900, hostility against foreigners was so intense in Canton that the French physician who had just arrived had to wait six months before opening his medical dispensary in the Chinese town (CAOM.GGI.doc.21842, 21/7/1899; CAOM.GGI.doc.2184, 18/8/1900; GGI.doc. 32789, 1/10/1901).

However, the French physicians, who had been sent to the area partly to alleviate the exasperation of the Chinese provoked by the French imperialist expansion, rapidly gained the favour of local elites, civil and military. The French hospital of Canton, built in 1903, was inaugurated under the patronage of a committee that included the highest Chinese officials of the province. It received Chinese subsidies from dignitaries, local notables and rich merchants of the town. Two years later, a few Chinese students, all grant holders from the provincial government, were educated there. In Kunming as well, and as early as 1901, the General Governor of Yunnan urged the French consul to create a medical course for Chinese students in the French hospital. In1905, out of the eleven students, seven had been selected and appointed by the Vice-Governor of Yunnan and four by the Vice-Governor of Guizhou (CAOM.GGI.doc.42396, 1905; CAMAE.NS, 6/3/1902; CAOM.SOM. NF.doc.315, 21/9/1901). In Longzhou and Mengzi, local military authorities established contacts with French physicians as early as 1902. In Longzhou, the French physician Pélofi was urged to cure the malaria contracted by some soldiers requisitioned by local authorities from Hubei province in order to eradicate piracy. In Mengzi, the *Daotai* (the Chinese Intendant) asked the physician to provide medical assistance to soldiers (CAOM.GGI.doc.20034, 11/03/1910; CAOM.GGI. doc.28433, 16/01/1904).

In the very first years of the twentieth century, sporadic contacts were thus established between French physicians and local elites on the initiative of a handful of local officials. These contacts, the French physicians recognized, increased their authority. Doctor Feray, who had just arrived in Hainan Island, noted: 'A few dignitaries came to receive health care for diseases that were easy to cure. They recovered very quickly and immediately the number of my patients increased. The Chinese likes to take the rulers as his model', and three months later, he confirmed 'I received the officials quite often. Their visit increased the confidence of the people to the extent that I came to cure forty people a day' (CAOM.GGI.doc.32756, 1/4/1900 and 2/7/1900).

The reforms undertaken by the Court during the first decade of the twentieth century amplified these contacts. Weakened by its defeat against Japan in 1895 and against the multinational coalition that had stopped the Boxer Rebellion in 1900, in 1901 the court of the Qing launched a series of reforms that touched different fields such as education, the army, the tax system and political organisation. In the field of medical assistance, as early as 1906 the court tried to centralize the sporadic actions undertaken by a few local governors. It entrusted the newly created police force with health matters. Between 1905 and 1911, in different places, local police bureaux, public thoroughfares, hospitals, medical research institutes and universities were thus created and managed by the police. Local police bureaux were created in provincial capitals, as in Canton or in Kunming (1905 and 1908), but also in a few minor towns such as Longzhou, Beihai (1907) or Nanhai (1908). Physicians educated in Western medicine, either in China or in Europe, America or Japan, were often appointed to head the major medical institutions.[3]

If the presence of foreigners still provoked local riots during the first 20 years of the century, Western medicine had definitely gained the favour of the ruling imperial and then republican elites who relied on it to lay the foundations of a public health system. Wang Daxie's attempt as Minister of Education to suppress Chinese medicine in 1913, or the drawing up of a law allowing dissection in order to facilitate the study of modern anatomy, attest to this general movement (Wu 1936; Xu 1997).

The favour granted to Western medicine by the ruling elites, in an institutional landscape that was still flexible and not overly coercive, undoubtedly increased the authority of the French physicians. This authority was reinforced by the fact that some local governors offered them posts and functions in local medical activities. Vadon, head of the French hospital in Kunming, was entrusted with the direction of a temporary Red Cross hospital created by the military authorities in 1916. Casabianca, director of the French hospital of Canton, was offered the post of medical consultant to the Chinese Marine force in Whampoa Military Academy, in 1918. Vallet, in Kunming, was offered the post of official physician to Yunnan province, in 1919. His successor, Mouillac, from 1922 until the end of the 1930s, in addition to his job as chief physician of a hospital that employed more than 40 people, held the functions of official physician to the province, medical consultant to the Yunnanese Government, and technical director of a Chinese lazaret. He was, furthermore, elected as a member of the newly created Sanitary Society in Kunming (CAOM.GGI.doc.40898, 27/06/1914; CAOM.GGI.doc.18737, 22/06/1918; CAOM.SOM.NF.doc.285, 02/06/1919; CAOM.GGI.doc.40895, 19/5/1922). A few also received Chinese symbolic-substantive awards such as the 'Double Dragon' in 1906 for Barbezieux; and the 'Golden Ear fifth class' for Vadon in 1914, who afterwards received the republican military distinction of 'Civil Tiger' in 1916 (CAOM. GGI.doc.32839, 1/10/1906; CAOM.GGI.doc.40898, 27/06/1914).

Although, when the French physicians first arrived, they had no official authority to deal with the Chinese people, they rapidly became valued not least by the ruling elites, imperial then republican, who engaged the country in various attempts at 'modernisation'. While their political authority to act was relatively speedily delivered, what scientific authority could the French physicians call on to convince their Chinese patients to follow their prescriptions?

Nineteenth-century French medicine in a context of scientific innovation and pharmacological expansion

French physicians sent to China at the end of the nineteenth century were quite different from those sent 50 years earlier to colonial Algeria, who only had a few efficient drugs available to them, such as quinine sulfate, potassium iodide and eye lotions (Turin 1971). After the extraction of morphine from poppies in the first decade of the nineteenth century, a large number of other alkaloids had been discovered during the century – quinine, strychnine, cocaine, codeine, atropine – that allowed physicians a large range of therapeutics, including analgesics, anti-emetics, cardiotonics, antipyretics, antirheumatics, anti-inflammatories, anaesthetics and sleep-inducing drugs. Moreover, during the final three decades of the century, germ theory had opened two fields of therapeutics: chemotherapy, which resulted in an improvement of antiseptic therapeutic strategy followed by the discovery of efficient chemical substances against infectious diseases during the final decade of the century; and vaccination, which until then had been limited to Jenner vaccination against smallpox. There was, as the historian Léonard points out, a medical synthesis that articulated different heritages (Bernard's experimental method, chemotherapy, Roentgen's discoveries, Pavlov's researches and germ theory), and that permitted physicians at the beginning of the twentieth century to improve their effective therapeutic action, in metropoles at least (Léonard 1981: 242–58, 1992: 228–29; Collin 1999).

But what kind of drugs were available to the French physicians appointed in hinterland China for dealing with a sanitary situation that, though difficult to evaluate *a posteriori*, seemed to have been particularly bad, riven with plague, cholera and smallpox epidemics until at least the 1930s and affected by endemic malaria and expanding syphilis and tuberculosis? In the first place the French doctors had access to the most common drugs available in France, which they could buy either in the French pharmacies of settled Indochina or in France directly. In addition, after 1910 the French physicians, even in hinterland China, had access to salvarsan, a preparation made with arsenic, developed by Paul Ehrlich (1854–1915), which could be injected to fight against the bacterium responsible for syphilis. Serums and vaccines that were mainly provided by the Pasteur institutes in Saigon and Nha Trang were also included in French physicians' medication. Smallpox vaccine and Yersin serum for plague were available at the very beginning of the twentieth century. After 1904, physicians had serums against diphtheria and tetanus; after 1906, they could use the Haffkine vaccine against the plague. More generally speaking, they benefited from the creation of new serums and vaccines: by the beginning of the 1930s, they were using serums against gangrene, streptococcus infections, gonococcus and staphylococcus.[4]

At the turn of the twentieth century, the French physicians appointed to southern China were thus able to access the most up-to-date drugs to secure their scientific legitimacy. However, different problems linked to the geographical and political remoteness of these physicians, to medical knowledge and to the drugs themselves, cast shadows over the whole enterprise. Firstly, shortages of plague serum regularly occurred and delays in supplying drugs were often highlighted. In 1923, physicians were still complaining that serums regularly arrived a few weeks after the direction had been given that they should be injected immediately in emergency. While a terrific epidemic was ravaging Kunming in 1921, the French Antirabic and Bacteriologic Institute of Hanoi even refused at first to send serum against diphtheria, in order not to deprive the hospitals within the colony (CAOM.GGI.doc.40931, 21/11/1923; CAOM.GGI.doc.40897, 2/3/1922). Secondly, despite the progress realized in identifying infectious diseases since the 1870s, some diseases still gave physicians trouble 50 years later. This was the case with the disease that expanded widely and very quickly in Kunming between March 1921 and May 1922. Microscopic analyses were carried out in place that revealed the presence of rods similar to Klebs–Loeffler bacillus, responsible for diphtheria. Serum against diphtheria was thus widely used, but ineffectively. Disappointed, the French physicians reconsidered the disease they subsequently identified as cholera. Serum against cholera was then widely injected, but with no greater effect. Further analyses were carried out that found neither the Klebs–Loeffler bacillus nor the cholera vibrio, but identified the presence of scarlet fever. In one year, and in spite of numerous but inappropriate injections of serums, the epidemic killed 50,000 people, a quarter of the town's population (GGI. doc.40934, 1922). Finally, as recent works have pointed out, therapeutic inventions in this time of 'drugs fever' were in fact very often disappointing and without a future: the beginning of serum and vaccine development was always very insecure (Sournia 1992: 258–59; Porter 1997: 443; Bonah and Rasmussen 2005: 41).

It is impossible to evaluate *a posteriori* the efficiency of serums and vaccines in China at the beginning of the twentieth century. Testimonies are contradictory, and the success rates for curing disease change according to whether they are announced as predictions or as statements of fact. In 1899, Dr Reygondaud praised Yersin serum for its ability to cure 80 per cent of people with plague in the face of the Chinese authorities of Mengzi. But other success rates, calculated admittedly on small-scale experiences, were much lower. In 1900 in Haikou, two out of three patients treated with a particular serum died. Two years later, the success rates obtained in Longzhou and in Fuzhou were 47 and 45 per cent, respectively. In 1908, A. Yersin in Nha Trang had a 58 per cent success rate (CAOM.GGI.doc.19947, 15/01/1899; CAOM.GGI. doc.32756, 15/5/1900; CAOM.GGI.doc.32741, 1902; CAOM.GGI.doc.18319, 1902; Yersin 1908).

To summarize, French physicians working at the turn of the twentieth century in southern hinterland China had access to the most up-to-date drugs in different material forms: pills, capsules, tablets, injections, plasters. For the most part, they were effective in treating symptoms such as pain or fever, or simple physiological functions such as digestion. But until the end of the 1920s, few of them were able definitely to cure diseases. The only chemical substances effective against infectious diseases were mercury; salvarsan and its variants for improving syphilis's symptoms; antimony, effective against bilharzias; and quinine against malaria (Porter 1997: 452). Vaccines and serums had only a limited effect in preventing or curing a handful of diseases which, before antibiotics, were nearly always fatal. The Yersin serum was generally not very effective, but it was clearly better than nothing: 97 per cent of those infected died when plague broke out in Haikou in 1900, and 100 per cent in Nha Trang in 1908.

How did the Chinese people react to these medications that, according to Doumer's 'peaceful expansion' policy, were provided free to the natives?[5]

French medication: rejection and compliance

There was a widespread belief that the Chinese patients used to resort to French physicians only after they had first tried more familiar medications. Nonetheless, the analysis of serial statistics left by the French hospitals, together with the analysis of statistics left by missionary dispensaries and by the newly created Chinese hospitals, show that resorting to Western medicine expanded rapidly and widely at the turn of the twentieth century. Attitudes towards Western medicine and medication were not uniform, however, and there was both resistance and rejection, related not only to social group and background, but also to the medications prescribed (Bretelle-Establet 1997, 2002: 160–90). Although French archives do not permit analysis of the degree of compliance towards medication, taking into account patients' social origin and genre, there is anecdotal evidence to suggest that attitudes towards French prescriptions varied according to social milieu. At the very beginning of the twentieth century, for instance, preventive inoculations against plague or smallpox were not only well accepted, but even highly appreciated by educated people belonging to those social groups close to the reformers and progressives – the General Governor of Canton, the staff of the naval school, pupils from the new schools. On the other hand, such medical interventions generally provoked fear and resistance in the poorest social groups located far away from urban centres (CAOM.GGI.doc.42396, 1906; CAOM.GGI.doc.56359, 5/7/1900).

Thanks to recorded narratives and serial inventories of the different diseases suffered by patients, the French sources allow analysis of variation in compliance towards French medications and prescriptions in the population in general. In this respect, they clearly indicate the lure for medications that had rapid and easily noticeable effects on symptoms. In addition to quinine and purgatives, which seem to have been widely accepted and appreciated by the Chinese people, antiseptic washing of infected injuries, infected eyes, and more generally surgery were among the medical interventions that were well accepted. Foreign observers unanimously noted that salvarsan and neosalvarsan, then used against syphilis and other skin diseases, were highly appreciated. The general enthusiasm for this medication was surely motivated by its apparently 'magical' effects on external symptoms, and by its mode of administration, by injection, perceived as not very different from acupuncture: 'I never saw them frightened by the syringe of Pravaz that they consider as an improved tool for acupuncture', noted Dr Richard in 1906 (CAOM.GGI.doc.23859, 1906). The introduction of medicine into the skin had above all been used since the beginning of the nineteenth century for smallpox vaccination, and it might have embodied the values of modernity and of science that a part of the population, at the beginning of the twentieth century, wished to adopt (Dikötter 2004).

Vaccination against smallpox had been practiced sporadically in China since the beginning of the nineteenth century, and was one medical intervention that the Chinese people accepted rapidly. Although smallpox vaccination was adopted everywhere by the Chinese, to the extent that by the 1920s it had replaced, in urban centres at least, the ancient and familiar practices of variolization, it still provoked resistance. French physicians all deplored the fact that the Chinese did not accept revaccination. 'The Chinese easily accepts vaccination [...] But he considers revaccination as useless' writes Dr Dupuy in 1906, while Dr Esserteau, in Hainan, continues to deplore in 1930 'the lack of concern of the adult towards revaccinations' (CAOM.GGI.doc.42396, 1906; CAOM.GGI.doc.40934, 27/5/1930). Moreover, the Chinese generally accepted vaccination only in the spring, a period that had previously been normal for variolization and that usually matched with smallpox epidemic outbreaks.

Medications were thus particularly well accepted when they could provide immediate evidence of their appropriateness, or when they did not conflict too much with Chinese therapeutic strategies. On the other hand, there was resistance to those medications prescribed for a longer period, and where the effects could not be quickly perceived by the patient. In this respect, physicians all noted that internal diseases were very few compared with diseases that surgery could cure quickly.

Rejection was even more noticeable towards prescriptions that were not directly related to the patient's symptoms. This was the case with diets or advice that concerned small children. 'A patient with albumin, put on a milk diet, thinks that he is condemned to die of starvation' noted Dr Abbatucci in Beihai in1905; while a colleague in Canton wrote, a few years later, 'The question of special diets…is a very difficult problem and it is usually insoluble. It is nearly impossible to ask a Chinese to accept a diet that he dislikes […] The Chinese […] will never admit the limitation of his appetite and he will easily see in it a punishment, the fancy of the physician, of these European devils.' (CAOM.GGI.doc.32773, 1905; CAOM.GGI.doc.32792, 1914.)

Prescriptions concerning newborns were equally rejected. In order to reduce infant mortality rates, which, according to the physician of Mengzi, appeared very high yet difficult to establish with precision, the French physician Tardieu undertook to establish a special service of 'Goutte de Lait'. Following the general principles of the French institution of the same name, created in France in 1894 by Léon Dufour, the objective was to give advice to young mothers, particularly to those living in poorly educated milieus, promoting breastfeeding and regular control of the newborn.[6] Very soon he was disappointed. At the beginning of 1925, he was still visiting two newborn children a day, but by the end of the year no newborn babies were being presented to him. Like his colleague in Haikou, who had equipped the obstetric department with a baby scales but noted that 'until today it has been very difficult to convince the mothers of the usefulness of regularly weighing babies', he concluded that weighing and controlling the evolution of a newborn baby were practices that few would accept. He resigned himself to just providing milk (CADN. Série A, Légation de France à Pékin, 1923; CAOM.GGI.doc.40934, 1922, 1923; GGI.doc.41003, 1925).

Medical prescriptions and recommendations, issued by the French physicians, were thus subject to a variable compliance. French physicians suggested that these attitudes towards Western medications were related to Chinese stereotypes of Western medicine and their agents. 'He (the Chinese) has a strange idea of the foreign physician's power, he considers him as a kind of sorcerer, and he believes that in one visit, he will get rid of his disease; he is disappointed when he realizes that the treatment will last a long time' writes a French doctor in Haikou in 1912; while another notes 'If he resorts to the foreign physician, it is because he considers him as a thaumaturgist able to cure, in a few days, diseases that last for number of years or are incurable.' (CAOM.GGI.doc.32772, 1912; CAOM.GGI.doc.23859, 1906.)

In fact, the French physicians' interpretation, that the Chinese had particular expectations of Western physicians, was wrong. As the analysis of a wide corpus of Chinese physicians' biographies shows, a talent for diagnosis and performing miracles through treatment also appear to have been the qualities expected and most highly appreciated in a Chinese physician. According to Gong Pengshou, a famous physician of nineteenth-century Guangxi, a physician was precisely the one that could combine these qualities: 'What we mean by "physician" is someone who enables a dying person to get up again and to come back to life.'[7]

Were the different degrees of compliance indicated above as specific to the application of French medicine really that particular?

French medicine and its local competitors

According to both foreign narratives and medical texts produced in southern China, medication including natural substances was the most common therapeutic prescribed by Chinese physicians. This subtropical area has always been very rich in minerals, plants and animals, and it provided the Imperial Court with a great part of its drugs (Gong 1983: 96–98). At the beginning of the twentieth century, this area was still famous for its natural resources. Yunnan, in 1908, was considered by the French consul Soulié de Morant as the greatest drugs market for all of the Far East (CAOM.GGI.doc.19713, 1908). These substances, physicians noted, could be found everywhere, even in the hinterland: 'In Longtcheou, in addition to big well stocked pharmacies, we find a lot of little shops [...] Groceries in any village have shelves for drugs.' (CAOM.GGI.doc.65324, 1907.)

Chinese medical texts, written in the area between the eighteenth and twentieth centuries, confirm these observations. The analysis of five extracts related to the disease *huoluan* (literally 'sudden troubles') in local medical treatises written between 1751 and 1936 by authors from different social backgrounds shows that prescriptions including dried or fresh plants, minerals and parts of animals, crushed and infused, were at the forefront of therapeutics. We find in He Mengyao's *Progress in Medicine* (*Yibian*) the prescription of 13 kinds of decoction, two types of powder and two sorts of pills; acupuncture and moxabustion are only prescribed in one case (He 1994 [1751]: 287–93). We also find diet recommendations. In Huang Yan's *Subtle points in Medicine* (*Yixue jingyao* 1800: 29–31), we find the prescription for three different decoctions, one kind of pill and acupuncture for serious cases. In Liang Lianfu's *What the Ignorant in Medicine Should Know* (*Bu zhi yi biyao* 1881: 94–96), we have the prescription for seven different decoctions and diet interdictions; while in Pan Mingxiong's *Summary of Medicine of the Pingqin Room of Books* (*Pingqin shuwu yilue* 1865:13–16), there are two types of decoction and diet interdiction. An anonymous compilation of prescriptions (*Jingyan liangfang* 1936: 157) provides prescription for three kinds of decoction and diet recommendations as well.

This sample of local medical literature suggests that drugs, be it infused, reduced in powder or merged into pills, were the most common medication proposed by physicians, acupuncture being marginal and always reserved for very serious cases. Moreover, it reveals that physicians often suggested diet recommendations to their patients.[8]

Although Chinese nineteenth-century sources do not provide direct access to patients and physicians' discourses that could tell us something about how patients reacted towards physicians' prescriptions, physicians' biographies and books of medical case histories (*Yi'an*), which gather and document clinical cases, offer valuable insights into the dynamics between patients and physicians. Wang Ji in his *Stone Mountain Medical Case Histories*, for instance, reveals that patients, especially when they belonged to the upper classes, not only discussed Wang Ji's diagnosis but very often refused to comply with his prescriptions (Grant 2003: 86–91). Many anecdotes in Chinese physicians' biographies of the far south of China convey patients' scepticism and resistance to physicians' recommendations. The biography of Mo Xiancheng, a physician in Guangzhou, tells us that a soldier had come to visit him because he had a big mass under the knee. Mo Xiancheng had diagnosed a lymphangitis. The soldier did not believe him and did not comply with his recommendations. The biography of Cui Biyu, another physician in Guangzhou, tells of his patient Xie Jianxun, who vomited and bled, and refused to take the prescription that contained ginseng root, rhizome of *rehmannia glutinossa*, rhubarb and cinnaber. Finally, the biography of Zheng Jining, a physician of Xiangshan in Guangdong, provides no specific anecdote, but notes that if a patient had not followed his prescription or had modified it, he would never come back to visit him (*Gazetteer of Guangzhou* 1880: 451, 454; *Chongxiu Xiangshan xianzhi* 1880: 1668).

All these anecdotes show that it was far from uncommon for Chinese patients to question a Chinese physician's authority. A refusal to comply with a physician's recommendations might have been motivated by a personal understanding of the sickness that did not fit with the nature and expected effects of a prescription. Chinese medicine, far from constituting a coherent, unified and unchanged body of knowledge, was continually evolving within a dominant and stable conceptual scope. If ideas of *Yin* and *Yang*, and concepts related to the *Five Phases*, were generally shared by all physicians, a great diversity of conceptual approaches for understanding and treating diseases existed. Inevitably they provoked polemics and gave rise to opposing schools of thought.

At the same time, a refusal to comply with prescriptions might have been motivated by a phenomenon that went beyond the theoretical rifts within medicine proper: the widely shared belief that disease was caused by spirits (*gui*), requiring other therapeutic strategies. According to both foreign observers and Chinese scholars charged with drafting local gazetteers, sick people were not always confident about the work of physicians and their medications. In local gazetteers, the sentences 'Ill people don't take medicine' and 'Ill people don't believe in physicians' appear regularly as stereotypes. Moreover, rituals between healers and patients, or collectives processions, are sometimes well documented, and all respond to a demonic conception of disease that emerged in the first millennium before our era, and that prevailed in China despite the emergence of new ideas theorized and canonized at the beginning of the imperial period, under the Han dynasty (Unschuld 1985). Religious people, Taoists in particular, and above all the shaman (*wu*) – seen since the Shang Dynasty as having the power to diminish the bad effects of evils on human beings – were the healers most commonly consulted.

Epidemics were regarded as a collective punishment for the bad behaviour of the living, according to a number of different traditions (Maspero 1971: 89–220; Katz 1995: 49). To counter their impact, processions were a more frequent therapy than resorting to Chinese medications or to Western serotherapy. Processions in Guangzhou during the terrible plague epidemic of 1894, in Fuzhou (1902), in Beihai and Lianzhou (1910), in Haikou (1926 and 1927) and in Yunnan (1942), are well documented by foreign observers (CAOM.GGI.doc.22003, 29/05/1894; CAOM.GGI.doc.18319, 1902; Pouthiou-Lavielle 1910; CAOM.GGI.doc.32773, 18/6/1910; CAOM.GGI.doc.40934, 27/5/1930; Hsu 1952).

In addition to this ritual, usually performed in emergency to chase epidemics away, the festival of *Duanyang* seems to have crystallized the preventive efforts in the provinces of Yunnan, Guangxi and Guangdong. A festival to celebrate the fifth day of the fifth lunar month was extremely old, and must have had diverse functions in different places and at different periods.[9] At least during the Qing Dynasty, and into the beginning of the twentieth century in the far south, this festival functioned as a preventive and apotropaic ritual against epidemics, smallpox, skin diseases and disease in general, according to the demonic conception of disease, as this narrative suggests:

> For the festival of the 5th day of the 5th month [...] we put on the door the leaves of mugwort and calamus. When it is twelve, we write talismans with cinnabar on yellow paper that we past everywhere inside and outside the rooms, on doors and on windows, we drink liquor of realgar and we sprinkle it on the walls, to prevent, as we say, from disease and to keep insects and ants away.
>
> *(Gazetteer of Pingle, Jiang 1940: 89)*

Mugwort and calamus symbolize sword and tiger, respectively, conceived of as the best protectors against demonic creatures. Chinese words written in red on yellow paper are also intended to dominate evil demons.[10] Realgar, highly toxic, was sometimes sprinkled on the bodies of children, or, put in little flasks attached to one's body, was used as charms or talismans, according to the ancient belief that having the drug on oneself allowed the wearer to take advantage of its qualities (Obringer 1997: 78).

This short sketch of local therapeutic strategies thus confirms that when French physicians arrived in their posts, local people used to resort to different healers and to adopt and sometimes to oppose different therapeutic strategies, according to their own ideas about disease. Before the Guomindang regime took radical measures against Chinese medicine during the late 1920s (Xu 1997), introducing a regime of competition and mutual exclusion between physicians in China, it is very likely that the Chinese regarded French physicians as little more than an additional kind of healer. Like Chinese physicians, French physicians used pills, drug decoctions and moral recommendations, more or less effectively, provoking more or less compliance.

Conclusion

Reflecting on the issue of how French authority and power, through the figure of the physician and his prescriptions, took shape in southern China, this chapter first confirms that the different 'contact zones' between China and the rest of the world in nineteenth- and twentieth-century China hosted divergent colonial arrangements. Unlike their colleagues appointed in Guangzhouwan, who had to enforce coercive measures issued by the French administration, notably in time of plague epidemics, the physicians appointed in treaty-ports had neither the power nor the interest to act violently in introducing a 'hygienic modernity' that everywhere was likely to exacerbate hostility among the colonized and lead to a general distrust towards Western physicians (Turin 1971: 341–46; M. Lyons in Arnold 1988: 105–24; Benedict 1996: 131–49; Rogaski 2004).

If the political autonomy of Imperial and then Republican China limited the power of the French physicians, as Esserteau regretted in 1925, it undoubtedly contributed to limiting the phenomenon of resistance as well. Instead of imposing their practices, French physicians appointed in treaty-ports had to adapt them to render them more acceptable to their intended recipients. And, in view of the different initiatives taken, we have the clear impression that their actions have been more collaborative than authoritative. Everywhere, French physicians resigned themselves to vaccinate against smallpox in the spring only. Without going so far as to imitate the strategy of the Chinese physician Ding Ganren, who ascribed Chinese properties to Western drugs in terms of thermic influence and flavours,[11] according to Chinese ideas of pharmacology (Andrews 1997) some physicians began to alter the dosages of medicines they prescribed, to add elements to their therapy, or to superimpose their techniques on Chinese medical practices (CAOM. GGI.doc. 23859, 1906). Some physicians tried to render more familiar the environment where patients would be examined and where they would receive their prescriptions: as early as 1900, the out-patient department of the French hospital in Haikou was equipped with two little cupboards which exhibited Western surgical tools, and the Chinese medical treatises that constituted, as the local French physician was told, the private library of a Chinese physician (CAOM.GGI.doc.32756, 31/5/1900).

To facilitate the understanding of Western prescriptions, French physicians used to display in their hospitals notices translated into Chinese on the most common diseases and basic hygienic principles. In some places, drugs came to be delivered with labels in both French and Chinese. More generally, French physicians used the Chinese language with their patients when they had learnt it, or relied on the nursing staff – composed of Indochinese people at the beginning, nursing staff were progressively replaced by locally recruited people. While prescriptions were an expression of the French physician's authority, it was usually the nurses, able to speak Chinese, and the local dialect as time went by, who prepared and delivered drugs or administered injections. These cultural intermediaries undoubtedly played an important role in the acceptance of French medicine and authority, as this narrative suggests:

> Educated by his medical studies at the French medical school of Hanoi, and aware of the dangers of contamination in time of epidemic, [...], he (a Chinese nurse) first received an injection of preventive serum of Haffkine, and afterwards he did not hesitate to visit plagued people [...] furthermore, he made great efforts to convince his compatriots to be cautious in order to avoid the expansion of the disease, and he explained them the advantages of serum injection, leading thereby a lot of indigenes to benefit from Haffkine serum injections and from immunity it provides against plague.
> *(CAOM.GGI.doc.32779, 8/6/1909)*

All these initiatives reveal that beyond projects that were undoubtedly imperialist in character stood human agents, who did not always react in simple, conformist ways. Undoubtedly, interactions between the French dominant physician and the members of the dominated society could take very different shapes. At one extreme might be a hospital managed by a French physician who stayed only two years, under colonial authority. At the other extreme there was the experience of a physician like Feray, who had graduated in Chinese, spent 14 years in Haikou and Kunming before dying in the First World War, and, in addition to providing health care, had become familiar with Chinese conceptualizations of disease; organized vaccination rounds in Hainan with the assistance of local officials; and strove to maintain a school of medicine in Kunming, organizing lessons in Chinese, and using beef and pork organs for teaching anatomy as human dissection was not authorized (Feray, 1907, 1910; CAOM.GGI.doc.40894, 1908; CAOM.GGI.doc.32757).

Notes

1 French archives offer serial information on the social origin, the genre and ailments of the patients who resorted to French physicians for a period of 30 years. Produced by physicians who usually stayed in their post much longer than the two years required, they provide a precise knowledge of the social, political and cultural environment of the area. These archives are collected in the Centre des Archives d'Outre-Mer in Aix en Provence (CAOM), Centre des Archives diplomatiques in Nantes (CADN) and Centre des Archives du Ministère des Affaires étrangères in Paris (CAMAE). Local gazetteers are the richest source of information for a particular place. They offer insights into the issues of diseases, institutions and practices related to health and of the medical landscape of each location. Gazetteers and local medical treatises thus permit analysis of the culture of health in which Western medications were prescribed, understood, rejected or accepted.
2 All the quotations from French archives are in French. Translations by the author.
3 Emblematic is the figure of Wu Lien-Teh, educated in Cambridge, entrusted with the direction of the first institution of public health, the Manchurian Plague Prevention Service, created after the 1910–11 epidemic of pneumonic plague in Manchuria.

4 For an inventory of medications available in the French hospitals in China, see GGI. doc.40934, 1923; GGI.doc. 32792, 1922; GGI.doc.32792, 1914 and GGI.doc.18501, 16/03/1918. For inventory of serums and vaccines that physicians had available to them, see GGI.doc.2522, 20/10/1904; GGI.doc.40969, 19/4/1906; GGI.doc.40970, 26/3/1907; GGI.doc.42396, 14/2/1907; GGI.doc.18889, 05/04/1918; GGI.doc.40934, in all the reports made on the hospitals in Kunming and Mengzi.

5 This principle was observed until the Indochinese authorities reduced subsidies to the French hospitals settled in China and encouraged them to find new sources of income, authorizing, in 1913, the creation of paying out-patient departments and the selling of medications. Drugs were thus delivered with charge in Canton in 1916, while the principle of admitting charges for drugs was accepted in the French hospitals of Haikou (1912) and Kunming (1913). However, drugs – including serums and vaccines – remained free for the poor until these establishments ceased work.

6 These institutions had been created in France under this name since 1894 in the wake of the reflections about infant mortality, by physicians such as Burdin, Variot and Dufour.

7 Making good predictions and delivering miracles are the most often used praises in physician's biographies (Bretelle-Establet 1999: 530–31). See Gong Pengshou's biography, in Guo (1987): 2033–34.

8 This therapeutic order is not specific to the far south. Since the sixteenth century, acupuncture was no longer in favour in scholarly circles, and was forbidden at the Court in 1822. On the contrary, the prescription of drugs was very common. The use of natural substances for therapeutic purposes goes back to the Zhou dynasty (1121–1256). However, knowledge in this field developed later under the Sui and Tang dynasties, between the seventh and tenth centuries (Unschuld 1985: 114–15).

9 On this festival, see Bodde (1975): 75–138; Katz (1995): 66–67.

10 On the power of written characters in Chinese history, see Gernet (1994): 361–79.

11 In the second millennium, a science of drugs properties developed in the theoretical framework of *yin*, *yang* and the Five Phases (*wuxing*). In these representations, one drug has thermic properties such as 'cooling' and a special taste such as 'bitter' which were expected to play different roles in the body to the extent of alleviating symptoms.

8

WRITING HOME AND CHINA

Elisabeth Frey in Tianjin, 1913–14

Yixu Lu and David S. G. Goodman

Except for research into the German colony of Qingdao, the presence of Germany and Germans in China has, by and large, been neglected in both studies of China and German colonial studies.[1] When German influence and involvement in China has been an object of study, the source materials are usually official documents, press reports and popular fiction, with the Boxer Rebellion attracting most attention (Kuss and Martin 2002; Lu 2006). The German expatriate community outside Qingdao, especially their experience in everyday life in China at the beginning of the twentieth century, has rarely been the subject of study, although there was a significant German community in China during the late nineteenth and early twentieth centuries, located mainly in port cities such as Shanghai, Tianjin and Wuhan.

One of the Germans living in China at this time was Walther Frey, an architect who came to China in 1905 and left in 1938 having designed some of the more important public buildings in Beijing, Tianjin, Shanghai and Taiyuan.[2] Amongst other activities, Walther Frey was involved in the reconstruction of Qianmen in Beijing; the design and development of the North China Union Language School; the construction of Yan Xishan's munitions factory; and planning for an (eventually unbuilt) Houses of Parliament under Yuan Shikai's direction. His sister Elisabeth joined him in the autumn of 1913 in Tianjin, where he was working for the German architecture firm Rothkegel & Co.

Elisabeth was ambivalent about the length of her sojourn. In one letter she makes clear there is a three-year limit on her stay,[3] but at the same time does not envisage a firm date of return. She thus visits China neither as tourist with the expectation of being home again soon, nor as a migrant looking to establish a new home elsewhere. She has no official mission to perform duties abroad for the 'common good'. Nor is her journey to China simply for pleasure, since she is expected to run the household of her bachelor brother. Her stay was abruptly terminated by war, and she was evacuated from Tianjin in early December 1914, after Qingdao was occupied by the Japanese.

Elisabeth Frey wrote regularly to her mother in Stuttgart throughout her sojourn. Her 31 letters, written between 21 September 1913 and 7 July 1914, have been preserved by her family, and open an unusual perspective onto an encounter between two cultures – one that poses a number of enigmas and challenges ready categorisation. Undoubtedly the family's long-standing connection with China – another brother also worked there for German firms – influenced the contents of the letters: what the letters say and do not say, dwell on or ignore.

Elisabeth Frey's letters are regular, lengthy and consecutively numbered. It is clear that she is aiming for the kind of narrative continuity one would also expect in an epistolary novel. Against this, she is totally without any artistic pretensions. She writes in a fluent colloquial style and is quite unselfconscious as regards the reader expectations of the *Bildungsbürgertum*, or educated middle class, to which she clearly belongs. On one hand, there are affinities to epistolary fictions of the times – the effect of a sustained monologue over ten months that is not dependent on whatever may have been in the replies from home, titles for some of the letters to mark them as episodes in a continuing *reportage*, and great vividness in evoking what interests her. On the other hand, the relentless focus on the domestic and expatriate milieux, the lack of reference to anything written about China except her own brothers' letters, and the scarcity of descriptions of the exotic land she is in, when she clearly has the narrative fluency to give them if she wants to, set her discourse clearly apart from anything meant to reach a general readership.

The question of genre arises since these letters are not only private communications to a particular individual, nor are they meant as a literary form aimed at a general audience. On 1 February 1914, writing from Shanghai, Elisabeth reminds her mother that her letters should be carefully preserved for her own specific purposes, as a 'beautiful' souvenir for herself. Thus the letters have at least two quite distinct functions, with consequences for issues of genre. They fulfil the dual roles of a diary for herself and travelogues for the whole family back in Germany.

What makes Elisabeth Frey's account comparable with the epistolary novels still fashionable at the time is that – intentionally or not – it has a direction: it becomes the success story of a '*höhere Tochter*' ('daughter of the upper-middle classes'), whose social accomplishments allow her to blossom in the restricted expatriate ambience in China. Her emancipatory adventure would not have been possible in the social circles open to her in Stuttgart. When the correspondence breaks off, she has reached the apogee of her social success, so the structure of her whole narrative is not dissimilar to that of a letter-novel, lacking only the culmination of a '*standesgemäße Heirat*' ('socially appropriate marriage').

The issue of genre thus devolves into two sets of questions: first that of narrative perspective; second that of cultural stance in confronting China. The narrative perspective is more relevant to the underlying determinants of her individual project in producing this remarkable volume of continuous and consistent narrative. The cultural stance bears more on her membership of a colonial community that has behind it the crisis of the Boxer Rebellion of 1900; and to come its sudden disruption by the hostilities of 1914, and the attitudes to China this connotes. China, for the

German colonists, is thus an environment in which the menace of insurrection has been averted for good and all, and nothing threatens the steady aggrandisement of the colonial enterprise.

The two sets of questions are not entirely separate. Sometimes they overlap in the persona of the letters, at other times they diverge. Ideally, the issues they raise should be put in the context of other contemporary, 'authentic' letter collections. Since none is (currently) available, reference can be made to another body of German writing on China, the novels which were written in abundance at the time.

A minimalist, contrasting frame of reference, in terms of German fiction on China written by women in the early twentieth century, can be found in two narratives intended for the commercial market. The first, Elisabeth von Heyking's *Briefe, die ihn nicht erreichten* (*Letters that did not reach him*) initially appeared anonymously in 1903, and was one of the greatest commercial successes in the spate of writing with a Chinese setting that began with the establishment of the German colony in Qingdao in 1897. By 1925, it had seen over 100 reprints and its author was famous (Li 1992). One point of comparison with Elisabeth Frey was that von Heyking had lived in China for a substantial period, 1896–99, and had also moved in the upper regions of the expatriate community there, since she was the wife of the German envoy to the Qing court. But the novel is a tragic love story that ends with the Boxer Rebellion, and was written in 1903. Very surprisingly, given its popularity over two decades, Elisabeth Frey shows no sign of having read it. Its sharp contrasts with Elisabeth Frey's letters are useful in two senses. First, it fulfils a quite different set of reader expectations, allowing us to see where Elisabeth Frey's narrative project clearly diverges from writing intended for a market. Second, it is entirely critical of European colonialism in China. This goes so much against the prevailing mood of German fiction on China from these years that this factor – combined with the author's social status – may help explain why it first appeared anonymously. von Heyking's name did not appear on the title page until the novel had established itself as a best-seller.

The other novel, A. Harder's *Wider den Gelben Drachen* (*Fighting the Yellow Dragon*) of 1900 is a chauvinist version of the German *Bildungsroman*, or novel of individual development, and is much more in the mainstream of patriotic, colonialist fiction set in China from 1897 to 1914. It is very well researched, although it is not certain that the author spent any time in China (Lu 2006). Its main usefulness is to highlight the divergence of *Briefe, die ihn nicht erreichten* from the cultural stance of most contemporary fiction on China.

Any counterpointing of Elisabeth Frey's descriptions of China with comparable passages in *Briefe, die ihn nicht erreichten*, as far as cultural stance is concerned, has to take into account not only the difference between the personal narrative project and marketable fiction, but also von Heyking's departure from those prevailing cultural attitudes, which are much more forcefully conveyed in *Wider den Gelben Drachen*. The issue of genre raised by Elisabeth Frey's letters therefore occasionally involves a process of triangulation. This can lay no claim to precision, but is preferable to leaving them with no context but themselves or works by professional historians on German colonial activity in China, which necessarily focus on the general at the expense of the particular.

Elisabeth Frey writes China

First and foremost, Elisabeth Frey is in Tianjin to put her brother's house in order. This presents a formidable challenge and is one major reason why the central focus is on matters domestic, and why she seems to show so little interest in reporting on China at large. There are other reasons, to be explored in the next section. But from the outset, the household is the focus and her exotic surroundings very much the periphery. This throws the problems with Chinese servants into stark relief. She arrives to find an unsatisfactory situation, and it is to last for some months. Her casual acceptance of her brother's beating an unsatisfactory '*Kuli*' and her comments on the servant's then giving notice highlight a cultural divide that continually challenges her:

> Things have to move slowly, otherwise the manservant ('the boy') will quit. I'd regret that, he looks so neat and tidy, but I don't want to give too much praise yet. While Walther was still sick, he dismissed the coolie 'Li' with a box on the ears. He caught him in the act of bringing in clean glasses from the kitchen and putting them on the sideboard, then checking them to see if they were clean. It seems some of them weren't clean to his satisfaction. He held them up to the light and licked off the dirt with his tongue, then rubbed them on his jacket till they shone. This caused another major incident; Walther gave him a proper thrashing, so that he claimed afterwards he had lost his 'face' and could no longer stay in our service.
>
> *(Letter from Tientsin, 7 October 1913)*

Three months later, her insistence on German standards of cleanliness is still causing her great frustration:

> I am still not entirely satisfied with my kitchen. Granted it's a lot cleaner, and the new dinner service does look better, but the servants are just a filthy lot! Things never get properly cleaned, and if you ask one of them for a ladle or something, he pulls it out of the drawer, but, worrying that it might not be clean, he rubs it again with his own dish rag, which is a lot filthier. Then he is really pleased with himself and goes on thinking how clean he is!…Will I ever be able to get these louts to understand?
>
> *(Letter from Tientsin, 16 December 1913)*

Cleanliness and its absence is an obsessive theme, not only in Elisabeth's letters, but also in the bulk of German writing about China at the time. The language problem intrudes only casually into the following description of a violent altercation in the kitchen six months later. A more distanced reading could foreground the fact that she, who speaks scarcely any Chinese, is giving instructions to servants who speak nothing else:

> Had to bawl out the cook again on Friday! I told him he should clean everything up, put down clean paper and stick new white fringes along his shelves – you know how at home we have fringes of crocheted lace. So he cut the strips of paper, not very even, but clean all the same…But when I came out, he'd done nothing, just stuck on new strips and left all the dirt just sitting there. This put me in a blind rage; I called him in and ripped down everything he had done. You should have seen the expression in his eyes! Then he had to take down everything off the shelves; he got in a fury and slammed the things down on the table. Then I showed him I'd belt him one if he did it again – he speaks only Chinese. And, sure enough, the next time he slammed something down, I belted him on the hand, and told him in plain Swabian: if you don't stop that now, I'll fetch the Master! That worked – Walther has already given him one over the ear. Finally, he had to set about things properly until, in the end, there was no more dirt anywhere…Oh these Chinese!!! – sometimes you just have to let it all out, and then you feel better.
>
> *(Letter from Tientsin, 16 June 1914)*

Again, violence and the further threat of violence have to bridge the language barrier. There is a complex cultural interaction behind this letter. The servant does his best to please by carrying out a task he must find quite bizarre. Because he transgresses the imperative to cleanliness in a way he does not understand, Elisabeth flies into a rage. He responds in a similar emotional register, and Elisabeth not only hits him, but invokes her brother as a source of further punishment.

Narrative perspective and cultural stance both converge to express Elisabeth's dominant intention that she is there to create a wholly Swabian household in China, without the slightest concession to local customs or the local cuisine. Having any of her cooks prepare any local dishes in her kitchen is in the realm of the unimaginable.

Her servants, who are designated by their functions rather than their names, come and go, are dismissed, give notice, or just disappear without being registered as individuals. Rather, they are identified by the incidents they cause, whether comic or infuriating. They are essentially aspects of an ongoing problem that will never really be solved, although she does not speculate on any reasons for it. Not to have servants would be unthinkable, but the problems they present can be addressed only in the form of confrontations or frustrations.

A milder and more reflective view of Chinese servants is taken in *Briefe, die ihn nicht erreichten*. The author of the letters is accompanied in the USA by her Chinese servant Ta, and his interaction with American servants leads to comment on the latter's relative lack of reservation once outside China:

> He is much less reserved towards us here than in Peking. There we didn't really learn anything about the lives of our boys. They were always there when

they were needed, they did their work in silence, obviously knew all our little habits exactly – but at the moment when they left the house and went out into the street, they disappeared into a world unknown to us, and we didn't ever hear a word about this part of their lives. Only if they wanted to be absent for longer than usual, then we would get to hear that their mother or father was dying. In the beginning I was very moved by this, I always let them take time off, even offered them medications. But they simply had too many dying fathers and mothers – my reserves of compassion were called on so often that in the end they were exhausted.[4]

(von Heyking 1904: 67f.)

To read this elegantly written fiction against the robust Swabian tirades of Elisabeth Frey is instructive – if proper caution is exercised. Because the letter-novel is a love story that ends tragically, the narrative perspective is attuned from the start to a fineness of sensibility that often inclines towards the sentimental. In such a discourse, the frustrations Elisabeth Frey vents so uninhibitedly to her mother would be simply discordant.

Setting this difference aside, it is still worth looking at the way the 'servant problem' is constructed by both writers. von Heyking has no incompetent servants; Elisabeth Frey has nothing but. Nonetheless, von Heyking has her account culminate in an 'exhaustion of sympathy', directed at one chronic failing: long absences from duty. One might suspect this could extend back to some of the types of incident that provoke Elisabeth Frey's outbursts, but it suits the purposes of von Heyking's fictional persona to limit negative emotion to one strand in which compassion gives way to scepticism.

Both accounts allow the instrumental attitude of the colonial mistress towards her Chinese servants to become visible. von Heyking, however, makes this an object of reflection: once their tasks are done, they cease to exist as individuals unless they exhaust patience by not being there when needed, and perhaps – she implies – there is something wrong with this. Elisabeth Frey does not consider for a moment that she misses anything by knowing nothing of her servants as people. They are the imperfect resources of an always precarious domestic order, which must be upheld at all costs, and their chronic failings are instrumental. Curiosity goes no further.

This is not to denigrate Elisabeth Frey's unselfconscious accounts of her day-to-day struggle in favour of a fictional character carefully crafted to engage the sympathies of the gentle, perhaps gentrified reader. Fiction could just as easily swing the opposite way: in *Wider den Gelben Drachen* the protagonist is treacherously killed by his servant, Ah Fong, whose very life was saved as a child by the German missionaries, who had adopted him as an orphan (Harder 1900). Such murderous servant–master relationships are much more typical of the patriotic German fiction that centres on the Boxer Rebellion. But by 1913 the Boxer crisis was long past, and if a servant quits because he has lost face by being beaten, it means no more than that another spare part must be found for the (at best) unreliable domestic machine.

These accounts clearly establish that the usual relationship between German colonialists and their Chinese servants was plagued by misunderstandings and clashes, and that the characteristic colonial response was to cope with the otherness of the servants by instrumentalising it as much as possible. This is a trope of colonial writing in general, rather than German writing in particular. Elisabeth Frey stands out only because it simply does not occur to her that there is a complex persona or situation here that might deserve some enquiry or explanation. von Heyking knows there is, foreshadows how it might be explored, and then suavely resolves it in her persona's own favour.

In whatever guise it is presented, the 'servant problem' on the domestic front is not unrelated to the colonial powers' frustrations and rivalries in the commercial and diplomatic arenas. Elisabeth Frey's casual acceptance of the corporal punishment of servants is part of the wider climate in which the Chinese are violently exploited and resistance is construed as insolence.

For Elisabeth Frey, who is determined from the outset that her stay in China is going to be a success, the 'servant problem' is basically a chronic irritation, not a symptom of a wider malaise. Her last preserved letter from early July 1914 shows no awareness of the threat of war. Underlying the opposite time perspectives to those of von Heyking's crafted urgency is a colonial attitude to the subject people which has survived the Boxer Rebellion intact, and sets the tone for daily interactions.

Elisabeth's Frey's writing on China is not confined to the household, and it is rewarding to look at her very selective encounters with Chinese art forms. Elisabeth was musical, sang well and could play guitar and piano, but her encounter with Chinese music, in the form of the Peking Opera, was to be no more successful than her first Chinese banquet. After enjoying an excursion to the Temple of Heaven (of which more anon), she visits a theatre on her way back, with unfortunate consequences: Different factors come together here. She has just been lost in admiration at a triumph of Chinese architecture. This could, given her own considerable musicality, help render the encounter with the Peking Opera less shocking. It does not, nor does it encourage her at any later time to approach Chinese music in a less challenging form.

> I won't forget midday today in a hurry! On our way home, we came to a Chinese theatre, and of course I had to see it. You have no idea how stupid and incomprehensible we found it ! And with such hideous singing ! You know the women's roles are acted by men and they always sing in falsetto – the noise is enough to drive you mad! Oberlein and I soon had enough. When he entered, we were stared at for about five minutes because it seemed we were more interesting than what was happening on stage.
>
> *(Letter, On the train between Jinan and Pukou, 9 January 1914)*

Elisabeth's considerable narrative talent manages to include a great deal in a few lines. The alien art form elicits immediate rejection and contempt. To put the seal on the experience, Elisabeth and her male companion become themselves the object of unwelcome curiosity. To be oneself a spectacle amid such an outlandish spectacle is the final affront to her sensibilities, and they lose no time in leaving. What might be called an intercultural blackout is total, but underlying and perhaps reinforcing this alienation is conceivably the reversal of the traditional 'colonial gaze'. Elisabeth and her companion are not entertained. Instead of exercising the aloof, controlling superiority of the colonial gaze, she and her companion become an entertainment for their cultural inferiors.

Of course, this is conjecture. Elisabeth has been in China several months by now, and there is no way of telling whether her experience has been pre-formed by any number of warnings as to what to expect from a Peking Opera. But the trauma of becoming herself a spectacle within a spectacle does carry some conviction.

Reading books about China or translations from the Chinese play no part in Elisabeth's narrative. The one exception to her aesthetic indifference to the exotic is architecture. Viewing masterpieces of Chinese architecture, Elisabeth becomes genuinely rhapsodic (Letter, On the train between Jinan and Pukou, 9 January 1914), and this is readily understandable. Her father was an architect. Of her seven brothers, two are architects. On the other hand, there are a few instances when Elisabeth confronts situations in China, which appear spontaneous and get to be written without the determining influences already indicated. They all have an emblematic significance, since they demonstrate the 'colonial gaze' in its commonest form.

Elisabeth spent the New Year's period of 1913–14 in Shanghai with another of her brothers, who was then working there for the German company Bayer. She recounts an unpleasant transit in Nanjing from a train to a ship, which she apparently has to make unaccompanied, emphasising the 'stench' of the natives and the total chaos into which she is plunged:

> …You back home simply can't imagine what happens at a railway-station such as this. Pandemonium! You would think people were being killed, but, really, all that is happening is that everyone is trying to transfer their luggage and their families form one train to another. I could see only one other European besides myself.…There was a lot of pushing and shoving – hitting as well – and some Chinese had to put up with really hard blows from the police, because they did not get out of the way when I wanted to get through. The police are quite good in this respect. On the ferry I got a place right up front for the crossing. That was really great, with the wind gusting about your ears, so wonderfully refreshing. After the fug in the train and all the stinking Chinese also waiting for the ship, a really special delight!
>
> *(Letter from Shanghai, 19 January 1914)*

If violence in her household towards her own servants seemed acceptable as a last resort, a modern reader is surely struck by the fact that she finds it only right and proper, and worthy of only casual mention, that the [Chinese] police clear a way for *her* through the mass of Chinese travellers by beating them with cudgels. This seems to be the colonialist stance at its least humane. But it is not the only such example.

Later, having returned to Tianjin, she reports a fire in the Chinese part of Tianjin. She and her brother are relaxing late one evening when a friend (Oberlein) calls to invite them to the spectacle:

> Walther and I had made ourselves really comfortable and were lying around in our kimonos reading, when there was a ring at the door after midnight.... Oberlein appeared with the news that there was a great blaze in the Chinese city...We got into our street clothes again on the spot and dashed off in rickshaws to the fire....You really should have seen it! I had never seen such a great inferno – simply marvelous! A great storehouse full of bundles of thatch, coal etc. was on fire, also at least fifty to sixty bales of goods piled up and covered with mats. And of course all the adjoining houses had caught fire. Every time the wind shifted, another house caught fire. Fantastic to watch! We stood there for a couple of hours. And the carryings-on of the Chinese fire-brigade! We nearly died laughing. They don't waste much time on fighting the blaze with water – the main body of them simply stand around with torches and they let at least fifty banners flutter in the breeze, and to accompany this they set up a hellish din with great tin rattles to exorcise the demons. About one o'clock a pretty strong wind came up and made it blaze up even more, and the whole crowd marched in procession with their flags and lights around the fire once more, shouting their heads off the whole time. By then the fire-brigades had arrived and with steam-driven pumps and the Chinese hand-pumps they successfully beat the fire back – when we went home at two you could see that they had it under control.
>
> *(Letter from Tianjin, 16 June 1914)*

After eight months in China, Elisabeth has become so inured to regarding the Chinese as the non-human other, that she can see in this disaster only an entertainment. That lives may be being lost, especially when the wind strengthens and revives the fire, does not intrude on her thoughts. The centrepiece of the entertainment is the antics of the Chinese fire fighters: 'We nearly died laughing.' Here, as at the railway station in Nanjing, the colonial gaze seems to exclude all empathy. When she returns home with her brother and his friend Oberlein, they spend another hour quenching their thirst and chatting, and she rounds off the episode: 'That was our experience of tonight, great!'

Elisabeth Frey should not be singled out as having been especially callous, simply because her private letters happen to have been preserved. The superiority that the colonialist constantly assumes over the colonised majority, even where, as in Tianjin, there was not the same colonial jurisdiction as in Qingdao, simply seems to block out empathy, just as the immediate classification of the Peking Opera as 'stupid' permanently blocked for her any access to Chinese music. Within the circle of her family and the groups of expatriates with whom she mixed on a daily basis, Elisabeth comes across as good-humoured, affectionate and loyal to her peers. The problem is that, from the outset, the Chinese are so far from being her peers that she cannot recognise how distanced she is from them as human beings, even when directly confronted with their suffering.

Tempting as it is to ask why Elisabeth Frey could not even ask a question as to where those made homeless by the fire in Tianjin might find shelter, the answers do not bear on the question of genre. Elisabeth is not before a moral tribunal, and a successful novel of sentiment cannot be called as a crown witness against a collection of letters that is not marketing its own stock of feelings.

Elisabeth Frey's emancipatory fable

As already emphasised, Elisabeth's central interest is in her mission of creating a Swabian household in Tianjin, and that when she 'writes China', it is because something on the periphery has caught her attention, like the great conflagration across the city. The middle ground has been deliberately omitted to this point, because it is easier to access the questions it poses as to genre if viewed against both the centre and the margins.

Elisabeth is the epitome of the German upper-middle-class, unmarried woman. Her interests and accomplishments never stray from the acceptable limits laid down for her class. What does happen, however, is that she changes countries. This does not mean that she changes her social milieu, because German expatriate society in China offers – in early July 1914 still – almost a mirror image of her social ambience at home. It is the *almost* that is crucial. For there is a displacement of sufficient parameters to permit her stay in China to take on the allure of an adventure.

Her project, as realised in her letters home during 1913–14, is to transpose Swabia into a foreign environment with no concessions granted. Hence her obsession with making Chinese cooks reproduce cuisine as her family understands it, despite all the frustrations it offers. What makes up for the often thankless task, and what makes her defensive of her cultural stance, but never defeatist, is the simple fact that her letters home – on which, as we have seen, she places enormous value – are her own success story. In short, her narrative as a whole is a realisation of an identity that is, for her, significantly different from the one she left behind in Stuttgart.

As already noted, she takes considerable care to ensure her mother conscientiously preserves the entirety of her narrative against her return, as the body of letters is going to be her very own 'beautiful recollections' (Letter of 1 February 1914). This letter is written after she has been in China for some four months. She has had time to assess her surroundings, and her determination that her memories are to be 'beautiful' is no less firm than her resolve that her Chinese cooks are going to master Swabian cuisine. In point of fact, any unpleasant incidents are either part of the 'servant problem' – central, but chronic and to be coped with – or peripheral. 'Peripheral' in this context indicates things that bring her into confrontation with China at large. Unless the contact occurs within the privileged area of architecture with its family sanction, or else in the oasis of hygienic Qingdao, Elisabeth's stock reactions are physical flight, as with the Peking Opera, or the withdrawal into the colonial mind-set of impervious superiority, as in her accounts of the scene at the railway station or the fire in Tianjin.

In these terms, it is revealing that she reports nothing at all that is in the slightest bit unpleasant from the middle region, German expatriate society. It is likely that this is where her romance of emancipation is set. This has a great deal to do with implicit sexuality. In March 1914, over five months into the visit, she gives a humorous account to her mother of a declaration of love she has received from Herr Strufe, a merchant about ten years her senior:

> We keep making new acquaintances, from Shanghai, and a Herr Strufe, whom I had got to know on board, would also like to correspond with me. We had got along quite well and spent many pleasant hours together. He stayed for about eight days in Tientsin and invited Walter and me one evening to visit him in his hotel. The next evening I got a letter with a fairly explicit declaration of love and with the request to exchange letters with him in future…He is a very nice man and not as young as he might be – 38, now I think of it, but Elisabeth Frey does not fall in love so quickly and so easily. That's what I wrote to him too, and that we had to get to know each other better. You know, Mother, it was a hard letter to write – you know how I am – but I managed it. I had Walther read it first, because there were no secrets in it. I treated the whole affair with good humour, and this turned out to be the best I could have done. For yesterday I already received another letter from him, very pleasant in tone, in which he agreed with what I had said in my letter to him. He is now going home on leave – perhaps he will find some nice girl in Hamburg, where his mother lives. Back home there's such a wealth of choice – people who've been out here a long time lose sight of that. So we are going to exchange letters – I'm quite happy to do that – but certainly not very often. So there's no danger, Mother, my heart is far too tranquil about the whole thing. I get terribly spoiled here – it's a good thing that I'm already 28 and really sensible. All the young men and bachelors are mad about me, and that's really great fun.
>
> *(Letter, 30 March 1914)*

Coming a month after her programmatic statement that all her memories of China are to be pleasant ones, this letter reveals her as an astute strategist of success in the terms in which she has defined it. To take the ending first: she luxuriates in her attractiveness to the gentlemen of the colony, even though she is twenty-eight, something she might not have enjoyed so readily at home. In her last preserved letter (from July 1914), she is still playing the same game. She rejoices in the attention she gets from an officer who is 'certainly four years younger than I' (Letter, 7 July 1914).

The game began soon after she arrived in Tianjin with the disingenuous remark to her mother: 'It is really embarrassing here that everyone thinks I am so young, twenty or twenty-two. It's a laughing matter, but I don't go out of my way to correct them – they can think what they like.' (Letter from Tianjin, 8 October 1913.) Her status as an unattached woman, with no financial need to enter into marriage and with her brother as the most respectable of male protectors, puts her into a different situation from that in Stuttgart, and it becomes an experience of rejuvenation. Here she is a desirable, but heavily tabooed sexual object, and she enjoys it.

She is flattered by Herr Strufe's attentions, and, in an exigency, she might be tempted to take his suit more seriously. But she has sized up her situation accurately, and perceived what it offers her. In one sense, she has exchanged a secure niche in the family in Stuttgart for an equally secure one in the German community in China. But she is sensible of significant shifts, which work to her advantage and favour her project of accumulating a few years of precious memories.

'Rejuvenation' she takes with a certain touch of irony, since she is aware her admirers and suitors in China would be confronted with a much wider selection of genuinely younger women of her class back in Germany. More concretely and genuinely, she can run her own household in China without the supervision of a mother, mother-in-law or husband. Her brother Walther seems docility personified. When, in June, she can report home: 'This morning I was, for the very first time, quite satisfied when I walked through my household – it was the first time I did not have to bawl anyone out' (Letter from Tianjin, 16 June 1914) – a climax has finally been reached. This has been her goal from the outset, and it has often eluded her due to a fresh variant of the 'servant problem'. So much of what she writes has been leading up to this experience of emancipation, as she has construed it for herself, and in these terms it is easier to understand why prospects of marriage do not interest her much. She has a secure home back in Stuttgart, but there she is not mistress of the house. She is happy to flirt with eligible gentlemen, but their flattery falls short of the domestic independence that she went to China to enjoy. She knows this socialising is not a lifetime vocation, but it is an interlude few of her peers back in Stuttgart can indulge in with such a lack of anxiety.

Her emancipatory project is reinforced in two significant ways. Because of the scarcity of competition, she enjoys a heightened attractiveness. The second reinforcement comes through her ability to shine in society as a singer and musician. Early in her stay, she reports proudly that, in the sphere of artistic endeavour, she has virtually no competition among expatriate German girls: 'Now, I have done a lot to entertain them and they were effusive in their thanks at the end. Of course one is happy if one has something to offer – the other girls had nothing they could perform.' (Letter from Tianjin, 14 October 1913.)

She reports a whole series of musical triumphs to her mother, and by December, her self-confidence is boundless: 'My reputation has reached Peking. That will be very nice if I visit there. You are happy, too, aren't you, that I am such a celebrity here? I am supposed to perform here again at the New Year's Eve Ball, but if we're not here, I can well do without it.' (Letter from Tianjin, 9 December 1913.) In July, she reports on the ball given by the Consul and attended by the officers of the German naval ship *Tiger*. When she goes down a couple of days later to wave the ship goodbye, the officers invite her on board for a farewell drink. As her exclamatory tone makes explicit, this is the high-point of her social success:

> All the officers in Tientsin, the whole Consulate and a whole lot of other gentlemen were there – I as the only lady in the company. Gradually I am turning into a cheeky little devil! This comes from my successes – really I'm already too old for all this, but just in terms of years, not feelings. Back home, I was already on the shelf, here I'm suddenly young again. Oh, life is really beautiful, Mother! Today I'm setting out on another journey, and my heart leaps at the thought! You're happy for me too, aren't you, Mother!
>
> *(Letter from Tianjin, 7 July 1914)*

Unfortunately, Elisabeth's preserved letters end in July 1914. It would have been interesting to see how she coped with the events that led to her evacuation and eventual return to Germany via San Francisco in early 1915. Clearly, she has discovered the 'cheeky little devil' she suspected to be latent within her, and, moreover, she has done so without breaching any of the conventions incumbent on her social standing. The emancipation to which she joyfully lays claim would not have been likely back in Stuttgart, but she has still not had to cross any frontiers of respectability to attain it. She has simply made the most of the opportunities that her determination, her musical gifts and the restricted ambience of Germany-in-China have offered her.

To return to the issue of genre, Elisabeth has written her own success story, staked her claim to a revamped identity, fluently, vividly, but never venturing beyond the horizon of expectations shared with her mother/family. The tone is confident from the start and has reached a peak when the letters break off. This is why parallels with *Briefe, die ihn nicht erreichten* are instructive, but always have to be taken with a pinch of salt. For the two narratives are aligned, in terms of perspective, towards quite opposite ends. That one is explicitly fiction, while the other claims not to be, is perhaps a less important qualification. A good deal of von Heyking's actual experience in China has been used in her fiction; we simply cannot tell if there are fictional elements in Elisabeth Frey's letters and, if so, what they might be.

Writing China, writing Elisabeth

There are some key methodological questions posed by Elisabeth's letters home. To what extent are such 'first-hand accounts' already predetermined by educational factors and social circumstances? To what extent can these letters be accorded the status of 'authentic source materials'?

In terms of the predetermined (or otherwise) nature of 'first-hand accounts' it would require a great deal of courage to affix the label of 'transnationality' to any aspects of Elisabeth Frey's narrative. Her determination to transpose Swabia into Tianjin occupies so much of her energies that – with a few exceptions – she seems to regard her wider encounters with China and its culture as variations on the chronic 'servant problem'. What applies to cooking is readily extendable to other areas. In a relatively early letter from November 1913, she makes a kind of profession of faith in connection with her own cooking that can be readily applied to her other encounters with things Chinese: 'We had a hare I cooked myself. It really tastes quite different. The servants just can't manage such a beautiful sauce. Maybe if I show them how a few more times. But our way of cooking back home is just so often better.' (Letter from Tianjin, 28 November 1913.)

The closed mind, sealed by a deep conviction of superiority, is equally evident in the kitchen as in the Peking Opera. Only the area of architecture seems to have some openness, but this, after all, is the family profession, and her brother's admiration for Chinese architecture may have simply been annexed by her. As the letters stand, speculation cannot take us further.

The question as to the use of the letters as historical 'source materials' is complicated by the fact that they have a particularly strong agenda of their own. That Elisabeth 'writes China' so seldom is directly related to the fact that her prime concern is 'writing herself'. There is no need to doubt the veracity of her outbursts on the 'servant problem', since such problems were scarcely unknown in Stuttgart. In her few peripheral encounters with non-colonial China, her retreats, whether physical or into emotional detachment, are such a recognisable phenomenon in colonial writing in many languages that there seems little cause to question them.

For the middle ground, her interaction with her fellow expatriates, it is simply not possible at this distance to know whether there is a conscious or unconscious admixture of fiction in her narrative. Was everything in the region between unreliable servants at home and filthy streets in Chinese cities so unremittingly pleasant? This is where the question of genre is most tantalising, for if anything in her letters is reminiscent of the seamlessness of fictional plotting, it is the portrayal of Elisabeth's charmed life in expatriate circles.

For her narrative to be one of a consciously crafted emancipation that she will later treasure, an expatriate community free of factions, jealousies and unsavoury incidents is indispensable, and so it appears on paper. It is likely that no further account of life in the circles Elisabeth Frey described will ever emerge to put these letters into perspective. But, even if it is accepted that her letters have an agenda that has censored out many aspects of expatriate experience, their documentation of the colonial cultural stance in so many spontaneous ways gives them a value of their own beside the already published material on the colonial presence in China, written after the event and with scholarly detachment.

Notes

1 The most recent example of this negligence is the volume Ames *et al.* 2005.
2 The period of his sojourn was not continuous. He spent four and a half years from November 1914 in a prisoner-of-war camp in Japan.
3 She makes clear in her letter of 26 October 1913 that she expects to be back for the wedding of her brother Paul in three years' time.
4 Elisabeth von Heyking's *Briefe, die ihn nicht erreichten* (*Letters that did not reach him*) initially appeared anonymously in 1903.

PART III
Late colonialism and local consequences

9
MODERNISM AND ITS DISCONTENT IN SHANGHAI

The dubious agency of the semi-colonized in 1929

Yiyan Wang

Shanghai has a special place in modern Chinese art history, especially when it comes to the *avant garde* in art. 1929, for instance, was a year of great significance in this regard, for at least two reasons: China's First National Art Exhibition (FNAE) was successfully held there, and a debate over the directions of China's art modernization took place during and after the exhibition. The national exhibition marked the coming of age of modern Chinese art. The intense, polemical discussion during the exhibition over preferences as to artistic styles, primarily between the leading artist Xu Beihong (1895–1953) and the prominent literary figure Xu Zhimo (1896–1931), was to have a lasting impact on modern Chinese art and art practice.

The choice of Shanghai as the location of the FNAE was a clear sign that the city was significant in the trajectory of modern Chinese art. In the recent boom of scholarship on Shanghai in Chinese and English, it has been confirmed that the city in the early decades of the twentieth century was undoubtedly cosmopolitan, although these studies have taken different routes to arrive at that conclusion. In the late 1920s, Shanghai had become the most populous city in China and one of the major cosmopolitan centres in the world. Shanghai was a city that attracted hundreds and thousands of migrants from China and internationally (Lee 1999; Shih 2001; Wang 2007). There were, of course, many historical, political, social and economic factors at play. Whereas Shanghai's rapid growth and material modernity cannot be credited solely to the driving force or greed of colonial powers, the city's public space was mostly open and Western, characterized by Western architecture and Western cultural practices: high-rise buildings on the Bund, department stores, coffee houses, dance halls, public parks and a public transport system.[1] It was in Shanghai that modernism in Chinese literature and art took root and flourished, albeit briefly. The multiplicity of colonial ruling powers in Shanghai resulted in a cosmopolitan environment where relative stability and security in daily life were available for more people than elsewhere in China. Most significantly, China's intellectual and cultural elite increasingly gravitated towards Shanghai in the 1920s. The colonial presence and fragmented ruling powers in Shanghai provided sanctuary and protection for intellectual freedom to a large degree, and there emerged a relatively independent public sphere (Wagner 1995).Cosmopolitanism in Shanghai in the 1920s was 'a socio-cultural condition' that had arisen as a result of China's and the international socio-economic conditions of the time, with multiple colonial rules as the major contributing factor.[2]

Shanghai's relative industrialization and its material modernity, in particular the commercial publishing and printing industry, made it possible for writers, journalists and artists to earn income through freelance writing and translation. Individuals found that they could pursue intellectual ideas and interests while deriving much of their income from contributing to the increasingly large numbers of newspapers and journals published in Shanghai (Li, N. 2005; Li, Y. 2006). Writers and intellectuals also found it easier to find teaching positions in Shanghai, where increasingly more private universities had been established than in Beijing, for instance. In turn, the congregation of artists, writers and intellectuals and their creative activities enriched the city's cultural life and intellectual scope.

In contrast to Shanghai's relative stability and prosperity during this period, Beijing was in sharp decline, suffering from abuse at the hands of a succession of warlord rulers. The warlords were well known to be withholding the salaries of professors and public servants, in effect forcing them to leave Beijing to seek a living elsewhere. Beijing was losing the attraction to intellectuals that it had had during the May Fourth period (during the late 1910s to the early 1920s) (Wang 2007: 63–96). In the late 1920s, the Nationalist government had been concentrating on developing Nanjing as the national capital, which also contributed to the flocking of intellectuals to Shanghai or cities in its vicinity. Lu Xun, for instance, moved out of Beijing to Shanghai in 1928 as a temporary measure in the first instance, but ended up living there until his death in 1936. The relatively open social and cultural space made Shanghai a distinctive city, not only in China but also in the world. Its diversity of cultures was greatly enriched by domestic and international migrants, whether they were refugees, opportunists, adventurers, criminals, workers or people from other social groups. In the 1920s, the cosmopolitan cultural practice in Shanghai was 'naturally' conducive to the birth of artistic and literary modernism in China. All these factors had contributed to Shanghai's emergence as the site that brought about Chinese modernism in literature and art, however brief the careers of Chinese literary and artistic modernists, cut short by Japanese invasion (Shih 2001: 231–75)

The boom of artistic creativity in Shanghai in the 1920s was linked with the cosmopolitan conditions, which in turn also attracted artists returning from study overseas. The connection between cosmopolitanism and artistic creativity has been the subject of a number of studies (Lee 1999; Shih 2001; Laurence, 2003: 1–36; Danzker et al 2004; Yan 2006). Internationally, Paris in the nineteenth century was another city that cosmopolitanism served both as its primary identity and a driving force for artistic creativity, since a cosmopolitan environment tends to encourage the flow of ideas in different directions. In both Shanghai and Paris, colonialism was central in the making of the city and its creativity, although Paris was self-appointed as the capital of cosmopolitanism, whereas Shanghai was given the title 'Paris of the Orient'. In the discourse of the Chinese Communist Party, cosmopolitanism was associated with being bourgeois and therefore anti-proletarian. During the Maoist era, Shanghai's cosmopolitan practice was regarded as one of the many evils colonialism had brought to China. The positive social and cultural impact has only been reappraised by scholars in and outside China since the end of the Maoist era in the early 1980s.

Beginning at the dawn of the twentieth century, Western influences on art in China were palpable. The rapid development of printing industry and commercial publishing led to print media disseminating Western art works to a wide audience. Students also started going to Japan to study Western art and some of them would return in a few years. Galleries, artists' associations, art publications, newspapers that printed art works, and art news were flourishing. The artists in the group known as the Shanghai School were leaders in experiment and radical change with the traditional Chinese genre of ink-brush painting. Also in Shanghai, the first art school was established in 1911 to teach Western art and Western artistic techniques. For instance, Liu Haisu was self-taught by copying reprints of Western art works, especially those of van Gogh, from magazines in the early 1910s, and became a most respected and famous artist in a matter of a few years. He was also active in art education, very keen on disseminating Western artistic ideas and techniques. He was the first to use naked models for drawing class in 1914, an incident that shook social conservatives to the core. Sun Chuanfang, the Chinese warlord in charge of the Shanghai area at the time, issued a 'wanted circular' denouncing Liu Haisu's 'immorality'. In 1917, Liu Haisu was labelled by others as a 'traitor to art' for including sketches of nudes in a public exhibition of student work. And yet Liu Haisu was able not only to survive, but also to thrive as an artist and art educator in Shanghai, despite, and perhaps because of, the controversies he stirred up. By the late 1920s, Shanghai's art scene was booming as the city had emerged as the centre of artistic activities, surrounded by artists and art schools in nearby Hangzhou, Suzhou and Nanjing. In the 1920s, the results of China's art education and art modernization were visible: Hundreds of students had returned or were returning to China, primarily to Shanghai or its surrounding area, from their studies of Western art in Japan, Europe and America.[3] Dozens of art schools that taught primarily Western art techniques were operating in some of China's major cities. Most importantly, hundreds of artists were either practising Western art genres or concentrating on modernizing and regenerating traditional Chinese ink-brush painting. The FNAE in 1929 was a remarkable exposition of the achievements in the first phase of modern Chinese art, and its location in Shanghai was reflective of its burgeoning art scene.

The discourse of art modernization and the First National Art Exhibition

The idea of holding art exhibitions at the national level was on the mind of many elite thinkers since the early 1910s, and was discussed frequently in the public sphere.[4]

In 1925, at a meeting of art educators from 15 provinces organized by the Ministry of Education held in Shanxi University, Liu Haisu formally proposed that a national art exhibition be held. The proposal was accepted and Liu was appointed chairman of the organizing committee. However, it was not until January 1929 that the committee was able to make the decision to hold the exhibition in Shanghai, which was soon followed by a call for submission of exhibits from all provinces. Originally, the exhibition was planned to open on 20 March 1929, but it was later postponed to 10 April 1929, when the location was finalized at the 'National Products Exposition Hall' (*Guohuo zhanlan huichang*) on the street that was named after it (*Guohuo Lu*). More than 20 provinces responded and their enthusiasm was translated into over 1080 artists submitting 4600 art works, among which 549 artists and 1200 art works were selected. The committee also invited 342 artists to participate, who sent 1300 art works. Selected Japanese, European and American art works were also included in the exhibition. The exhibition had sections on Chinese calligraphy and painting, bronze and stone inscriptions, Western painting, sculpture, architecture, art and craft, and photography. Total exhibits amounted to 2328 pieces.[5]

In Shanghai, *Shenbao*, a popular local daily newspaper in the Republic era, publicised the announcement of the FNAE in its regular section of 'Education News' (*Jiaoyu xinwen*), where news about the Exhibition would appear regularly until after its completion. According to reports in *Shenbao*, on 10 April 1929, the FNAE opened to glowing reviews, and its closing ceremony on 3 May was well attended by many dignitaries and celebrities of the day. The exhibition certainly was all-embracing, and the open-mindedness of the selection committee was reflected in the variety of art genres, including those that belonged to Chinese traditions and those that were newly learnt from other parts of the world, especially from Europe. The FNAE was remarkable, for the 'national' exhibition nonetheless included works by foreigners and overseas Chinese.[6] In the opening remarks by Xu Zhimo, published in the first issue of *Meizhan* (*Art exhibition*), the official newsletter of the FNAE, he proudly proclaimed it a grand success in China's history of displaying art to the public, highlighting its unprecedented scale in the great number of entries; in its wide range of genres from paintings, sculptures, crafts to architecture; and in its inclusion of artists from inland provinces of China and foreign countries (Xu 1929: 1).

Members of the organizing committee for the FNAE included Li Yishi, Lin Fengmian, Lin Wenzheng, Xu Beihong and Xu Zhimo, in addition to Liu Haisu as chairman.[7] Except for Xu Zhimo, the others were all influential artists at the peak of their creative powers. Li Yishi, Lin Fengmian and Xu Beihong had recently returned after more than ten years of study of Western art in Europe. Although he did not venture to Europe until 1929, Liu Haisu had already established himself as a prominent oil painter and a formidable art educator since the 1910s. Although Xu Zhimo has largely been known to the general public as a romantic poet, translator and professor of literature, his role in the FNAE was pivotal. He had been an active art critic and instrumental in introducing Western art to China by allocating space in the magazines and newspapers he edited, and through his circle of friends, including Cai Yuanpei and Liang Qichao, who were powerful, leading intellectuals in China in the 1920s.[8]

The FNAE's ultimate patron was Cai Yuanpei, Minister of Education in the Nationalist Government and a devoted promoter of art and education through aesthetics. A leading intellectual, Cai was extremely tolerant and accommodating of different opinions and attitudes in approaches to art. However, the members of the selection committee for the FNAE had strong and divergent opinions about art styles and the relationship between art and China. Most notably, Xu Beihong resigned five days after the committee started meeting, announcing to the public that he had to leave Shanghai to take up his new position as president of the national art school in Beijing. It was widely believed, however, that his resignation was the result of his disagreement with the 'modernists' on the committee, namely Lin Fengmian, Liu Haisu and Xu Zhimo. The committee was divided into two camps, those who were in favour of a realist style (Xu Beihong and Li Yishi) and those who were embracing *avant garde* or modernist styles in general (Xu Zhimo, Lin Fengmian and Liu Haisu), to judge by their subsequent publications. It is not clear whether Lin Wenzheng, the general secretary of the FNAE, took a clear stance, but he was a strong proponent of the view that art should not be divided along national or cultural boundaries.

The terms of modernism and realism are adopted here retrospectively to refer to the roughly two kinds of attitude towards the style and function of art and literature that prevailed among the artists and intellectuals involved in the debate in the 1920s and the 1930s. 'Modernism' refers to the thoughts and cultural tendencies that are sympathetic to the wide range of experimental and *avant garde* trends in the arts that emerged from the middle of the nineteenth century, as artists rebelled against traditional historicism, and later through the twentieth century, with artists rejecting previous tradition and creating individual, original techniques.[9] With regard to the notion of realism, David Der-wei Wang sees it in this context as 'a shared notion among contemporary Chinese literati and artists that the foundation of artistic merit would necessarily be the authentic representation of the Real' (Wang, D. D.-W. 2001: 29). One reason for advocacy of the view that the Chinese had to connect mimic representations of the Real with artistic merit had to do with the belief that only a realist representation would be able to speak to the masses effectively. Clearly, the artists and intellectuals involved in the debates in the early decades of the Republic era were not using the terms 'modernism', '*avant garde*' or 'realism', and their attitudes towards the different approaches were not clear-cut either. However, modernism and realism serve very well as terms to categorize the basic differences.

Meizhan was the official periodical of the FNAE, which was published every three days, beginning on 10 April 1929. It was an open forum for news, information and intellectual discussions about art. Listed on the first page of each issue were the names of editors and contributors. The editorial team from the beginning to the end of the journal remained the same, as did the contributors. Xu Zhimo headed the list of editors, followed by Chen Xiaodie, Yang Qingqing and Li Zuhan. Among the list of 24 contributors were Cai Yuanpei, Feng Zikai, Lin Fengmian, Yang Xingfo and Xu Beihong, although not all contributors wrote for the journal. *Meizhan* finished publication on 7 May 1929. In addition to the ten issues published during the

FNAE, there was one 'additional issue' (*zengkan*) produced immediately afterwards. In the same year, all 11 issues of *Meizhan* were compiled together and published as a monograph under the title of *Meizhan huikan* (*Fine art exhibition journals combined*) by *Xinyue shudian* (Crescent Books), run by Xu Zhimo in Shanghai. *Meizhan* interpreted 'art' very broadly, and articles on all aspects of art and art practice, such as education, exhibition and circulation of art, were published. Artists were invited to comment on the FNAE, and their comments were also published.

It became clear after the exhibition was opened that Xu Beihong had resigned not in order to withdraw from the public sphere, but as an open protest against the modernist inclinations of the organizing committee. He also boycotted the show by not submitting any of his own art work. On 22 April 1929, in issue 5 of *Meizhan*, while the exhibition was becoming increasingly popular in Shanghai and nationally, Xu Beihong's essay 'Perplexity' (*Huo*) was published. It opened with a single statement of celebration, followed by the sarcastic comment that 'what is really worth celebrating about this inaugural national exhibition is that there are no works by the shameless artists such as Cézanne, Matisse, or Bonnard' (Xu, B. 1999a: 200–227). Its postscript, which was directed specifically at Xu Zhimo, betrays the true intention of its author, namely to bring their disagreement to the open and to rehearse the argument that Xu Beihong had apparently lost in previous discussions within the selection committee. In the same issue, there was also the first part of a rejoinder by Xu Zhimo (1999), entitled 'I also am perplexed' (*Wo ye huo*), of which the rest appeared in Issue 6. In Issue 7, Cai Yuanpei published an essay, 'On the relativity of art criticism', in an attempt to bring out the subjective nature of judgement on art merit while retaining his neutrality between the two Xus (Cai 1999). In support of Xu Beihong's viewpoint, Li Yishi, who had studied at the Glasgow Fine Art School and lived in Scotland and Europe for more than a decade, published an essay declaring 'I am not perplexed' (*Wo bu huo*) in Issue 8. Li Yishi forcefully reiterated Xu Beihong's view on the need for realism in art for China. Issues 9 and 10 saw Xu Beihong continue with one further commentary in response to Xu Zhimo's rejoinder. Still centreing on the metaphor of perplexity, he called it 'Perplexity unresolved' (*Huo zhi bujie*) (Xu, B. 1999b).

What is indeed perplexing and still largely unknown is what happened to the voice of the modernists. Xu Zhimo had actually written a much longer rejoinder of 6000–7000 characters. One of the other editors of *Meizhan*, also a respected and innovative ink-brush artist, Yang Qingqing, acknowledged that he had received it in a brief essay entitled 'Brief post-perplexity remarks' (*Huo hou xiaoyan*), saying that because that particular issue of *Meizhan* had already been typeset, he had to leave its publication until the next opportunity. It is not certain why Xu Zhimo's second rejoinder was not published in *Meizhan*, but it seems that Yang's claim was true and that the editors were running out of space, since Xu Beihong's 'Perplexity unresolved' was published only on 4 May, in Issue 9, and continued in the Additional Issue. To date, it is still unclear whether Xu Zhimo's second rejoinder was published at all. Given Xu Zhimo's reputation, status and connections in the top literary, artistic and political echelons in Shanghai and Beijing, let alone his being editor of other journals and newspapers, he should not have had difficulty in publishing it elsewhere, even if *Meizhan* had ceased publication. Research so far has not discovered any sources that contain Xu Zhimo's second rejoinder, or even a mention of it, except in Xiaoping Tang's recent monograph. Based primarily on information provided by a critic named Li Yuyi, Tang does not consider the FNAE an overwhelming success. He also has a different interpretation of Yang Qingqing's remarks on the 'perplexity' debate, believing that Yang was a peacemaker between the two Xus, and does not give the missing rejoinder further discussion (Tang 2008: 89–96). It is possible, as hinted by Xiaobing Tang, that in order to remain friends with Xu Beihong, Xu Zhimo decided to withdraw his second rejoinder. There have been another two highly informative and illuminating studies in English on the debate, one by David Der-wei Wang and the other by Zheng Shengtian. Neither mentions Xu Zhimo's second rejoinder (Wang, D. D.-W. 2001; Zheng 2004).

It is not clear whether the authors had full access to the Chinese sources, but one thing is certain: Xu Zhimo's articulation of the value and trend of artistic modernism has yet to be restored to the public domain, even if that particular piece of writing has not physically survived the turbulence of modern Chinese history. More significantly, not only did Xu Zhimo's second rejoinder go missing; Xu Zhimo as an influential and insightful art critic has been totally ignored in modern Chinese art history, despite his major contribution and the important roles he played in the early decades of the Republican era. To date, Xu Zhimo remains known almost solely as a romantic poet to the Chinese public and scholars inside and outside China, including the most recent work by Xiaobing Tang (Zhu and Ruilin 1989; Zhao and Ding 2002: 551–52, 557–68; Tang 2008: 95.) David Wang calls him a 'connoisseur' in his essay (Wang, D. D.-W. 2001: 37). All the same, it can be argued that Xu Zhimo was an art critic: he was the primary editor of and a major contributor to *Meizhan*; a major member of the selection committee of the FNAE and a key player in the decision making; Xu Beihong's 'Perplexity' essay has a postscript addressed specifically to him; Xu Zhimo wrote and delivered the opening remarks of the FNAE, which was also the first major essay published in *Meizhan*; he was listed as the first editor of *Meizhan* and his publishing house published *Meizhan huikan* afterwards. The omission, or rather, the erasure of Xu Zhimo's writing on art and of his contribution as an influential public intellectual and acute art critic from modern Chinese art history, is most meaningful when it becomes clear that the absence of Xu Zhimo's second rejoinder signifies the onset of misfortunes of Chinese modernist pursuits in art and literature in the past century.

Discussions about art among artists and intellectuals had been ongoing since the beginning of the twentieth century, but the 'perplexity' debate between the two Xus accentuated the major issues in Chinese art modernisation. The debate was really about whether modern Chinese art should welcome all styles and genres and whether artists' self expressions should be valued, or whether art should serve primarily a social function by communicating to the masses through accessible styles. Views expressed by the two Xus represented the different stances and divided opinions among Chinese artists and art critics, although it is not always clear that their stances were firmly demarcated.

In Xu Beihong's first 'Perplexity' essay, he dismisses the artistic merit of the works of artists such as Manet, Cézanne and Degas on the ground of commercialism and lack of solid techniques. But what really worries him is the harmful effect of those art works on an indiscriminating Chinese public and art scene (Xu, B. 1999a: 209). In Xu Zhimo's words,

> What is an artist? if not he who expresses his unique inspirational experiences through painting or sculpture? Techniques should have their place. Knowledge also has its use. But no one can produce what you and I would call art if he only has refined techniques and profound knowledge. Do you and I not seek in art the same things that we seek in life – the fresh expression of our spirit and the nobility of life itself?
>
> *(Xu Zhimo 1999: 209)*

Apparently, Xu Zhimo considered it most important that art be granted its own autonomy, and he saw art as expression of the self – as long as the artist was true to his emotions and true to the spirit of the moment. For Xu Beihong and his supporters, it was important that art works speak to the audience. Especially in China, the artist must fulfil his social responsibilities by producing art works that would enhance, instead of corrupt, social morals. To insist that art works must speak to the general audience entails a demand on the art form, namely, art works should imitate and reflect reality in order to articulate a 'truth' that serves a higher social purpose.

Xu Beihong had been studying art in Europe since 1919 and returned to Shanghai in January 1928. At the time when the organizing committee was formed, it was less than a year since his return. In Paris, he was deeply attracted to the academic realism of Europe's classical masters (such as Prud'hon, Delacroix and Rembrandt) and the genre's capacity to capture the grandeur and scope of significant historical events. He and his followers believed that Chinese art should imitate such social and historical realism in order to reach a wider audience and to encourage Chinese people to aspire for a better society. His view of artistic realism is, however, more succinctly spelt out by his follower, Li Yishi. 'I'm not perplexed at all', Li declared, insisting that an artist should be aware of his social responsibilities and that his works should not just be expressions of his own emotions or perceptions, as has been advocated by Xu Zhimo. This is how Li put it:

> Expressions of Cézanne and Matisse are indeed more than honest emotions on their part, but I am still against their spread in China, because we may plant harmful seeds there. In the past twenty years, people's thoughts have already been distracted. What we should be doing is to use the power of art to rectify their thinking while soothing their spirit. If indeed such art works as those by Cézanne and Matisse became popular in China, what a disaster that would be!
>
> *(Li 1999: 216)*

Echoing the view that stresses the social function of art, Xu Beihong subsequently painted two of his most representative works: *The Old Fool Trying to Remove the Mountain* and *The Five Hundred Martyrs of Hengtian*, the latter of which was actually created during the FNAE and in the midst of the debate with Xu Zhimo. Both paintings were *guohua*, ink-brush painting on paper, but showing strong influence of the academic realist style, with underlying references to what Xu Beihong perceived as the Chinese national spirit – perseverance, loyalty, determination. They would long remain exemplary works of *guohua* in the Maoist era, regarded as landmarks in establishing realism as the only legitimate and acceptable art style in the eyes of art establishment in China. Xu Beihong as the authoritative artist in that genre became a formidable institution.

The 1929 debate cut across all matters cultural, literary and artistic, but what mattered most to those involved was the national. In the end, it turned out that the nation needed 'realist' representations, so that expressions of the self would soon be suppressed. Regarding the outcome of this debate, David Der-wei Wang offers a most incisive comment:

> Xu (Zhimo) made himself the sounding board for the contesting voices of Chinese artistic modernity: realism or modernism, or something else? In the midst professions of perplexity, Chinese artists and art educators were trying to negotiate the real, and they were to learn that agencies such as exhibitions, art academies, pedagogical technologies, and political alliances all mattered.
> (Wang, D. D.-W. 2001: 38)

Privileging the Real had a lot to do with the intellectual concern for China, and 'the National', directly or indirectly, was a decisive element in the artistic choices of many artists and writers. Xu Beihong's public statements formally and publicly launched resistance to modernism as a possibility for modern Chinese art as early as 1929, a date that was much earlier than the commonly accepted wisdom that believes realism dominated the Chinese art scene only after Japanese soldiers arrived on China's doorstep, and after the Chinese Communist Party had endorsed realism as the legitimate style for the nation and the state (Gao Minglu 1998: 16). The institutionalization of the realist style in art and Xu Beihong as the foremost modern Chinese artist occurred long before the CCP controlled art and art practice, when Cai Yuanpei and those around him had the decisive power in the Nationalist government.[10] Most of the artists and intellectuals were concerned with the idea of China through realist representations, and remained dismissive of ideas such as art for its own sake or for the sake of the self for a long time to come. Considering that Xu Zhimo's views expressed in his essays on art were representative of Chinese modernists, and these views were largely absent to the public sphere, it is fair to say that the Chinese modernists had already lost their battle for legitimacy in China by the late 1920s, even though they appeared to have outnumbered the realists in terms of practising artists, both on the selection committee for the FNAE and in the works exhibited at the time.

Triumph of realism – the path chosen for the colonized

The 1929 events were highly indicative of what was at the centre of China's colonial experience – the complex relations between China and the colonial powers (the West and Japan), between nationalism and colonialism. The triumph of realism in both modern Chinese art and literature was largely an inevitable consequence of the global dominance of the West and China's decline since the nineteenth century. To be sure, the West's territorial expansion, military aggression and political control inevitably provoked resistance and sparked nationalist urges. However, at the same time, China's need to modernize meant it was imperative that it learnt from the West and Japan. China's humiliation and indignation at the hands of the colonial powers only led the Chinese to question what and how China should learn from the West, but it was never a matter of 'if'. Most importantly, in the context of intellectual history and cultural creativity, the colonial conditions were instrumental in bringing about the interchanges and confluences of cultures. One of the most visible consequences of the multiple colonial rules in China was the rapid transformation of Shanghai into a major cosmopolitan centre, where there were surely more opportunities for the exchange of, and experiments with, different ideas.

Two issues have surfaced in revisiting this aspect of modern Chinese art history: the cosmopolitan environment of Shanghai; and the agency of Chinese artists, intellectuals and the state function in that environment. Both were related to the colonial conditions of China and Shanghai at the time. The rise of modernist pursuits in art and literature in Shanghai was a result of the cosmopolitan cultural space. The existence of the foreign concessions in Shanghai was the precondition of the distinctive form of cosmopolitanism that flourished in Shanghai. Modernism has been known to incorporate 'fresh' elements from other cultures, and modernist expressions benefited a great deal from the cultural synergy. In other words, colonialism created conditions for cosmopolitanism, which in turn were transformed into creativity that transcended the boundaries of one's own cultural traditions and familiar milieu. Many great works of the twentieth century are products of cosmopolitan practice in major metropolises such as Paris and London. The FNAE held in 1929 in Shanghai was the height of artistic synergy for a long time to come.

What differentiates cosmopolitanism in the West and in China (or other cosmopolitan centres of the world which emerged as a result of the colonial expansion of the West in the nineteenth and twentieth centuries) is the element of nationalism embedded in the intellectual pursuits of the countries under colonial control. Although individual artists or writers may have favoured modernism, collectively, it seems, at least in the case of Chinese literature and arts, nationalist concerns would overtake the course of modernization, and artistic creativity for the expression of the self would lose legitimacy, now and then. The nationalist concern, as occurred in the Chinese art scene in the 1920s and in Chinese literature in the 1930s, would lead to the dominance of realism in artistic expression. Such a tendency, then, puts into question the nature of agency on the part of the colonized.

Given the debate that took place in April 1929, the subsequent disappearance of a substantial piece of writing by Xu Zhimo, one of the major proponents of modernist approaches to art, and the subsequent directions followed by modern Chinese art in the decades following that moment, on the whole, the exercise of agency on the part of the 'colonized' over the means and manner of their nation building was deceptive. It appeared that the artists and art critics had the capacity to decide which styles they would like to adopt and what kinds of subject matter they would like to present. However, the choices were more or less predetermined, because all those who participated in a 'colonial cosmopolitan' setting could only react to the dominance of colonial powers and Western influences.

To be sure, the artists and critics were highly proactive in their attempt to create a new art for the Chinese nation, and indeed they were able to pick, choose, reject and adopt as they wished. However, as Patha Chatterjee points out, there was not much room left for the colonized to imagine in their nation-building, given the overwhelming power of the models from the Europeans and the North Americans (Chatterjee 1993: 49). Precisely as a result of the modernity sought in reaction to Western dominance, modern Chinese literature and art travelled on similar paths. Despite having been written into separate histories to the present day, writers and artists were preoccupied with the desire to make China both strong and modern. Not only did their routes of development converge, but the interests, tastes, abilities and political inclinations of the participants also often overlapped. Modern Chinese literature and art also shared the same task of representing the nation, and were equally burdened by the weight of cultural traditions, which they had to transcend. In the brief modernist detours, the writing subject managed to speak about the self. But the nation was relentlessly overwhelming and in the end, for both literature and art, other alternatives were suppressed to give way to realism, a style considered most capable of connecting artistic representation to the masses of the modern nation. There is an important point to be made here: whether modernism or realism, when the colonized 'chose', they chose to respond to their circumstances, and the questions on their mind were too often framed against the deprived nation and the powers that dominated it. Last, but not least, realism was also institutionalized. The realists in art as well as in literature, in China at least, became the bureaucrats whose tastes and style would perpetuate and overpower until the reopening of Chinese social space to international influences at the end of the Maoist era.

Notes

1 A radically different view of Shanghai's development is provided by Meng Yue 2006: 212. She sees Shanghai more as a product of the cultural life of Jiangnan (southern Jiangsu region) in the areas surrounding Shanghai. For Meng Yue, Shanghai's cosmopolitanism resulted from the 'unruling powers' at work, connected to 'Chinese cosmopolitanism as both a rare historical value and a cultural and political practice, rather than a philosophy or a national ideological system'. This 'unruling' cultural practice had brought about Shanghai's decrease because choices were limited by two historical events: 'the first was the irreconcilable internal split between "retranslational" and "revolutionary" intellectuals

around 1917; the second was the ascension to power of the Jiang Jieshi (Chiang Kai-shek) faction of the GMD government through the 1927 anti-Communist coup, which largely limited the choices of being politically and culturally non-conformist while at the same time being cosmopolitan.' In either interpretation, the prolific literary and artistic output in Shanghai in the early decades demonstrates a cultural boom, which came to an abrupt decline only when the Japanese troops arrived uninvited.

2 Cosmopolitanism has been 'reactivated' in scholarly discussion in recent years by a wide range of social and political theorists, including Kwame Anthony Appiah 2006, Timothy Brennan 1997, Jacques Derrida 2001, and Steven Vertovec and Robin Cohen 2002. These recent works on cosmopolitanism deal mostly with major cosmopolitan centres located in developed countries, where the central issues are how to accommodate different cultural values in a multicultural, liberal democratic society and how to argue for equal rights and access to social progression for refugees, migrants or other under-privileged groups. Arguing primarily for a 'mid-way' to respond to challenges posed by globalization and the inadequacies of multiculturalism, these works are not directly related to the cosmopolitan Shanghai, where the central issue was the social and cultural conditions that allowed for the exchange, dissemination and acceptance of different intellectual ideas. In other words, it is the 'aesthetic cosmopolitanism' practised by the intellectual, literary and artistic elite that is under discussion in this chapter. However, these recent theoretical works are very effective in outlining the current understanding of cosmopolitanism. The introduction given by Steven Vertovec and Robin Cohen on cosmopolitanism is most useful and, in particular, their summary of how the notion of 'cosmopolitanism' could be viewed as: '(a) a socio-cultural condition; (b) a kind of philosophy or world-view; (c) a political project towards building transnational institutions; (d) a political project for recognizing multiple identities; (e) an attitudinal or dispositional orientation; and/or (f) a mode of practice or competence' (Vertovec and Cohen 2002: 9).

3 According to the list generated by Ruan Rongchun and Hu Guanghua, 434 students went overseas to study art or engage in art-related studies between 1887 and 1945 (see Ruan and Hu 2005: 292–303).

4 As early as 1912, Lu Xun raised the idea that a modern nation should build an art museum and stage art exhibitions in order to display and circulate art for public education (Lu 1956b: 1–5).

5 This summary is based on information provided by Takeyoshi Tsuruta in *Bijiutsu Kenkyu*, No. 349, 1974: 115–16. His description of the FNAE is the most detailed among the sources that I have come across. He provides the number of pieces of art work on display in each individual section. The total number of 2328 is the sum of the numbers of the seven separate sections Tsuruta provides. According to Zheng Shengtian, the total number of art works was 2346 (Zheng 2004: 181). Xiaobing Tang simply states that there were more than 2200 art works on display (Tang 2008: 90).

6 Judging by the circumstances, the 'foreign' works seemed to have been both works of less-known foreign artists, and reproductions of those European and Japanese masters the committee thought should be models for Chinese artists. Xu Beihong's first open letter mentioned his relief that the exhibition did not include certain 'despicable' Western artists. Tsuruta offers only a list of Chinese-style paintings for the FNAE (Takeyoshi Tsuruta in *Bijiutsu Kenkyu*, no. 349, 1974: 128).

7 These names are from various sources, primarily from Takeyoshi Tsuruta's publication in *Bijiutsu Kenkyu* no. 349, and articles collected in Lang and Shui 1999, Vol. 1. Xiaobing Tang's monograph *Origins of the Chinese Avant-Garde* (Tang 2008) offers refreshing and insightful interpretations of the exhibition and the debate. He does not, however, seem to have come across the primary and secondary sources dealt with here.

8 Xu Zhimo was associated with some members of the Bloomsbury group when he was a student at King's College, Cambridge from 1921 to 1922. It is believed that he stayed at Roger Fry's house during that time (Patricia Laurence 2003: 132). Roger Fry was an art historian, critic, painter and the Slade Professor of art history at Cambridge University, and an influential figure in English society at the time. After his return to

China, Xu corresponded with Fry and tried to arrange for Fry and G. L. Dickinson (Dean of King's College, Cambridge) to visit China to give public lectures on art and literature, entrusted by Cai Yuanpei and Liang Qichao on behalf of the Chinese government (according to Xu's letters to Roger Fry dated between August 1922 and June 1923 in the archive of King's College, Cambridge). The trip did not take place.
9 Based on the definition offered by www.huntfor.com/arthistory/c19th/modernism.htm
10 According to Michael Sullivan, Cai Yuanpei was not impressed with the artworks of Picasso when he visited the artist's Paris studio in 1915, since Cai 'found no example for China in Cubism' (Sullivan 1996: 32).

10

EQUALITY AND THE 'UNEQUAL TREATIES'

Chinese émigrés and British colonial routes to modernity

John Fitzgerald

China's 'Unequal Treaties' with Britain were unequal in more ways than one. They were procedurally unequal in that they were negotiated and signed under duress. In compelling territorial concessions and financial indemnities that infringed on China's sovereignty, they failed to uphold the principle of the equal sovereignty of states. And they were unequal in the sense that they were not in all respects reciprocal. A number of specific concessions embedded in the treaties, including the concession that Britons should be tried in China under British legal jurisdiction (extraterritoriality), applied to just one partner to the treaties. From the Treaty of Nanking in 1842 to the Boxer Protocol of 1901, Britain's treaties with China warrant the twentieth-century title of 'Unequal Treaties' (Dong 2005; Hou 2006).

Nevertheless, there was some ambiguity in the treaties themselves on the question of equality. To some Chinese residents overseas, Britain's treaties with China provided a quasi-legal foundation for claims for equality of treatment, for equality before the law, and, in specific contexts, for racial equality. The claims for legal and racial equality which the treaties enabled among Chinese settlers in British ports fed directly into broader debates on egalitarian ethics associated with modernity over the late nineteenth and early twentieth centuries. Founded as it was on the prior idea of the equality of sovereign states, the twentieth-century neologism 'Unequal Treaties' was a later product of these wider debates. Novel ideas of sovereign state equality, racial equality, and civic equality each needed to take root in China as part of the broader 'social imaginary of modernity' before the patently unequal treaties of the nineteenth century could come to be remembered in the twentieth century for what they were – unequal (Taylor 2004).

This chapter draws attention to the efforts of Chinese émigrés to Britain's Australian colonies in fighting for equality of treatment with British Australians. The long and bitter struggle for equality within Britain's Australian territories was catalysed by an assumption, embedded in the treaties, that Chinese subjects enjoyed equal rights of mobility. The British colonial infrastructure of the day provided clearly marked avenues for Chinese community leaders to present their case for equality of treatment, to build new kinds of social infrastructure under British rule of law, and, in the face of continuing discrimination, to develop successful business strategies that effectively evaded restriction by following the skeins of British colonial maritime networks stretching across the South Pacific to south-eastern China. We follow some of the routes along which Chinese émigrés elected to move, to trade, and to extend their social networks in distinctively 'equal' ways over the period from 1870 to 1930.

The chapter mounts four related arguments. First, the Treaties themselves provided a foundation for claims of equality of treatment. Secondly, claims for equality enabled by the treaties fed into broader debates among Chinese communities in Australia about the ethical foundations of human equality. Third, a preoccupation with equality on the part of Chinese émigrés in the British antipodes fed directly into debates within elite circles in China on the meaning and value of equality in the modern world order, illustrated in this case by Liang Qichao's six-month visit to Australia between October 1900 and May 1901. Finally, Britain's maritime trade routes through Oceania and East Asia provided readily available avenues for highly mobile Chinese Australian merchants to develop trans-national social networks, raise capital, conduct business, and introduce a new style of commercial egalitarianism into twentieth-century China.

Treaties and empires

The idea that sovereign states are *equally* sovereign was not embraced by the Chinese empire for some decades after the court signed the first of its treaties with Britain in 1842. Equality among states was a relatively new idea for China, as it was for many parts of the world. China was an old-world empire with a political centre that claimed suzerainty over its neighbors, and in which orthodox social, political, and diplomatic arrangements were grounded in Confucian notions of hierarchy. Britain was a new and different kind of beast, a modern nation-state with entrepreneurial capital, steam-powered industries, and parliamentary institutions driving its imperial ambitions. Despite its entrenched social hierarchies, Britain professed the equality of sovereign states and the equality of subjects before the law. Britain was one of a new breed of independent sovereign nations that operated under a system that Emmerich de Vattel called *The Law of Nations*. 'Nature has established a perfect equality of rights between independent nations', Vattel observed. 'A dwarf is as much a man as a giant; a small republic is no less a sovereign state than the most powerful kingdom' (de Vattel and Chitty 1758 [1883]).

At the time of composition, Vattel's *Law of Nations* signaled a revolution in the conceptualization of relations among states which was to have profound implications for old-world empires. These were being challenged not just by force of arms, but by far-reaching commercial, social, and cultural developments that undermined old-world social hierarchies and replaced them with new competitive hierarchies based on the acquisition of wealth, the practice of professions, and personal achievement. The encounter involved massive social, cultural, and political revolutions from which no monarchy or empire was exempted in Asia or in Europe.

China was not spared. In 1840, the British Government resorted to war to force the Qing empire to open its ports to trade in opium. British victory in the war was understood in Europe as demonstrating that China was a national state no different from any other (John Fitzgerald 1996: ch. 3). Recognition within China of the formal equality of states came only gradually over the closing decades of the nineteenth century through the day-to-day practice of diplomacy in the courts and councils of Europe, Japan, and the United States. One measure of this emerging recognition was the coining of the phrase 'Unequal Treaties' around the turn of the twentieth century to characterize the terms on which the Chinese empire entered into treaties with Britain and other countries following its defeat in the Opium Wars and the several wars that followed. Invocation of the word 'unequal' signaled growing recognition among Chinese elites that states *should* enter into formal negotiations on equal terms: growing recognition of the nominal equality of sovereign states; and growing recognition that equality was a legitimate principle underlying a broader political and social world view (Fitzgerald 2004).

The adoption of this twentieth-century neologism misrepresented the treaties as these were understood among certain Chinese communities overseas in the nineteenth century. China's nineteenth-century treaties with Britain indirectly established equal rights of mobility in reciprocal provisions allowing freedom of movement throughout the British Empire. Chinese émigrés transiting through Hong Kong or the aptly named treaty-ports in China were, in principle, entitled to move as freely as native Englanders through India, Canada, Australasia, and the British colonial settlements of Southeast Asia and the Pacific Islands. These treaty entitlements to equal rights of movement and abode made no provision for discrimination on the grounds of race. Indeed, the Unequal Treaties could be read to imply equality among peoples. It was not Chinese émigrés but states employing racial grounds for exclusion that contravened the treaties – the Australian colonies among them. Insofar as an ethic of equality was encoded within the treaties, they enabled a struggle for *equal recognition* within the British empire. The growing appeal of equality as an orthodox ethical ideal among Chinese elites can be traced through the efforts of Chinese community leaders in the Australian colonies to achieve the equality to which they felt entitled under the treaties.

Chinese émigrés and Britain's Antipodean colonies

In the 1870s, Chinese residents in Australia began to publish pamphlets and to petition Peking over their unequal treatment at the hands of colonial authorities. In the face of discriminatory immigration procedures, the petitioners referred explicitly to clauses of the treaties signed in Beijing and Tianjin, which established equal rights of movement for Chinese embarking from British treaty ports in China with those which Britons enjoyed embarking from their home ports in Great Britain and Ireland.

Among the petitions drafted by Chinese community leaders in colonial Australia was one presented to the Imperial Commissioners for forwarding to Sir Henry Loch, Governor of Victoria, in June 1887, and copied to Peking. It was a representative petition bearing 47 signatures and drafted by prominent Melbourne merchants. The petition presented two basic grievances. It complained first that a special tax of £10 per head had been imposed upon Chinese and Chinese alone, and second that special restrictions had been imposed on Chinese wishing to travel from one Australian colony to another in contravention of the treaties. The ground for each complaint was that the restrictions were 'in direct violation of all international law and usage, and in contravention of the Treaty engagements entered into by the Governments of the two Empires' (Victorian Legislative Assembly 1888).

Similar complaints were made in the following year. In June 1888, a group of Sydney businessmen, led by the prominent Sydney tea merchant Quong Tart, and representing 'Chinese residents in Australasia and New Zealand', petitioned an inter-colonial conference in Sydney. The petition led with an assertion of the liberties enshrined in the treaties:

> That by Article Five of the Treaty of Pekin…it was amongst other things, provided that the Chinese, in choosing to take service in the British Colonies or other parts beyond the seas, were to be at perfect liberty to enter into engagements with British subjects for that purpose, and to ship themselves and their families in British vessels at the open ports of China.
>
> *(Quong et al. 1888)*

Based on the provisions of the Treaty of Peking, the petitioners sought redress for restrictions on their freedom to travel to and from China and the Australian colonies, and argued for the repeal of restrictions on movement between the colonies themselves.

These treaty claims provided a quasi-legal foundation for broader claims of equality under British legal jurisdiction. One of the striking features of the public discussions surrounding presentation of the petitions is the way in which the ideal of equality moved between a legal notion of entitlement under contract, on the one hand, and a sense of fair play grounded in natural justice and divine right, on the other. To be sure, government representatives on each side negotiated around legal terms and precedents. Protests lodged by the Chinese Court on behalf of Chinese overseas typically referred to Britain's obligations under the Anglo–Chinese treaties; British negotiators did likewise in responding to claims by Chinese and Australian government representatives. But treaties could be revised to enshrine inequality. Under the Angell Treaty between the United States and China, signed in November 1880, Beijing conceded the right of 'the Government of the United States [to] regulate, limit, or suspend' the entry or residence of Chinese in the USA (Andrew Gyory 1998: 212–16). To Chinese communities in the British colonial world, the Angell Treaty presented a dangerous precedent.

Chinese community leaders in Australia also appealed to ideals of fair play, over and above Britain's treaty obligations, and to invoke a sense of natural justice that was based not merely on liberties enshrined in treaties, but on broader recognition of the equality of Chinese and Europeans as fellow human beings. Documents held in the Qing imperial archives in Beijing record this style of complaint. 'We are also human beings, living in this world, and we expect to be treated with justice', argued one Australian–Chinese petition sent to the Chinese Foreign Ministry in 1889. 'Why should people in Australia act in this unfair and harsh way, unprecedented in history?' Chinese were mistreated on the sole ground that 'the color of their skin is different from that of Europeans'. Why, the petitioners asked, were Chinese alone denied the universal rights otherwise bestowed on peoples? (Tongwen 1889). A further petition in the Qing Archives, presented by around 50 Chinese merchants in Australia in 1889, referred to the 'humiliation' and 'insults' heaped upon China and its people by the Australian colonies. 'Why are Chinese people looked down upon and treated differently?' they asked (Lei Dehong et al. 1889). Another petition, bearing around 40 signatures, linked its appeal to fair play to China's national claims for equal recognition. Local authorities in Australia, it reported, 'tolerate everyone except Chinese...Their prejudice, harshness and contempt are starkly obvious' (Kuang Qizhao 1889).

Similar arguments were mounted in defence of the principle of the equality of sovereign states. The three Melbourne businessmen who, in 1887 petitioned Sir Henry Loch about their rights under the 'Treaty engagements entered into by the Governments of the two Empires' assembled a wider range of arguments for equality of treatment in a passionately argued pamphlet, *The Chinese Question In Australia*, which was published some years earlier (Lowe et al. 1879: 28). In the pamphlet, as in their petition, the merchant leaders appealed to contracts and treaties, and highlighted the reciprocal obligations imposed on the Australian colonies to permit freedom of movement under the treaties. In the pamphlet, however, they went further to draw their readers' attention to the claims for state equality set out in Emmerich de Vattel's *Law of Nations*, which they expressly cited in print. They appealed to the universal ethical claim of human equality set out in the American Declaration of Independence – 'We hold these truths to be self-evident: that all men are created equal' – and they appealed to a universal ideal of 'human nature'. Their philosophical propositions were leavened with humor. Responding to claims that Chinese laborers depressed general wages by their willingness to work for little reward, for example, they argued that 'human nature is human nature all the world over; and the Chinaman is just as fond of money, and just as eager to earn as much as he can, as the most grasping of his competitors'. But their underlying purpose was serious. 'You do not endeavor to exclude Germans, or Frenchmen, or Italians, or Danes, or Swedes. There are men of all these nationalities here. Why then are Chinese colonists to be placed under a ban?' (Lowe et al. 1879: 9, 20, 23).

Beyond Australia, the treaties offered grounds for Chinese imperial authorities to monitor the treatment of Chinese abroad. In May 1887, the editor of the *Melbourne Argus* introduced a 'remarkable' article by China's Minister to London, the Marquis

Tseng (Zeng Jize, son of statesman Zeng Guofan). As Minister to London, the Marquis was, in effect, Minister to Britain's Australian colonies. In his article, the Marquis highlighted three areas in which the Chinese empire sought recognition of equality in the 1880s: equality of national sovereignty, equality of peoples, and recognition that China enjoyed its own regional sphere of influence equal to that of the Great Powers, a principle not entirely consistent with the principle of equal sovereignty (Tseng 1887).[1] In regard to the equality of peoples, the Marquis asserted that the empire would ensure that China's subjects abroad were treated with the respect accorded to other immigrants in the colonies and settler societies of Asia and the Pacific. One of the Marquis' strongest claims for equality of treatment with the Great Powers extended to what he called the 'outrageous' mistreatment of Chinese outside of China. *The Argus* introduced the Marquis' Tseng article in anticipation of a forthcoming visit by two Imperial Commissioners, General Wong Yung Ho (Wang Ronghe) and Commissioner U Tsing (Yu Qiong), who, the editor maintained, were coming to Australia to do the Marquis' bidding. *The Argus* conceded that the Marquis had mounted a strong case for the Commissioners' right to investigate the treatment of Chinese in Australia in order to ensure equality of treatment.

Liang Qichao and the question of equality

Paradoxically, the issue of equality underlay White Australian rejection of Chinese residents' appeals for equality of treatment. In May 1888, shortly after the Imperial Commissioners had left Sydney, New South Wales Premier Henry Parkes prohibited a further cohort of Chinese immigrants from disembarking from a vessel moored in Sydney Harbor, *The Afghan*, on the ground that he 'did not want to see any race here who were not entitled to all immunities, privileges and rights of citizenship – of equal marriage, equal salvation, with the best and truest of any of the races here already' (Russell and Chubb 1998: 95). As far as Premier Parkes was concerned, this was not a matter of racial inequality. Parkes dismissed the complaints of vulgar anti-Chinese agitators who claimed that Chinese were an inferior race. If anything, Parkes argued, Chinese immigrants were a class above the general riff-raff landing on Australian shores (Yarwood 1968: 90). But no matter how closely they read Britain's imperial treaties, or how forcefully they asserted their equal status as human beings, Chinese were to be denied the bounty of a free and equal people because, it was said, they did not appreciate equality. The eloquent appeals and petitions of Chinese residents required an unequivocal repudiation of the colony's Orientalist prejudices about the mandarins and mendicants from China who wanted to make Australia home. What was needed was a new-style person from China – a *xinmin* – who could embrace and embody the modern ethics of equality.

China's champion of the *xinmin* ideal, Liang Qichao, stepped ashore on the Fremantle docks in Western Australia in October 1900, and over the next six months toured Perth, Geraldton, Adelaide, Melbourne, Ballarat, Bendigo, and the New England district of New South Wales before embarking for Yokohama from the eastern port of Sydney six months later. At each point of call, Liang showed himself to be the kind of man who could redeem China's reputation and standing. His arrival was timely, coming shortly after the suppression of the Boxer Uprising in north China. As an outspoken critic of the 'backward' Boxers, Liang was greeted by colonial governors and welcomed by local mayors and members of parliament at several ports. He was invited to speak in temperance halls and churches. He was taken on tours of the premises by chairmen of hospital boards, governors of museums, newspaper proprietors, and directors of botanical gardens from Perth to Sydney. According to the Chinese press, on 12 January Liang was invited to a function at the Sydney Town Hall to celebrate Australian Federation in the company of Australia's first Prime Minister, Edmund Barton. Two days later, he called in person on the British Governor to discuss prospects for political reform in China. Lord Hopetoun expressed his earnest wishes for the success of the reform party (*Tungwah News*, 16 January 1901; Bob Nichols 1986).

During his stay in Sydney, Liang presented a series of weekly lectures on the subject of equality in the upstairs reading rooms of a local Chinese newspaper, the *Tung Wah News*. In his lectures, Liang focused on problems presented by Confucian notions of hierarchy for his mission of recasting person-to-person relations around the principle of equality, and for reforming China's system of government from a 'master–slave' style of administration to a political system enshrining the principle of the equal subject. 'A country is founded on equality,' he declared, 'and love [of country] arises from the way [people] treat one another.' The imperial court in Beijing treated its national citizens as 'personal slaves'. 'Westerners', by contrast,

> look upon their countries as the common property of rulers and people. It is just as though fathers, elder brothers, sons and younger brothers all worked together in managing a family's affairs. In this case, every single person is a patriot. Not so in China, where the country belongs to one family and every one else is a slave.

In the modern West, Liang proclaimed, no person or government could humiliate another without inviting resistance grounded in the principle of equality. In contrast to China, children in the West, whether rich and poor, male or female, were all taught from an early age to 'govern their own selves' (Liang Qichao 1928: 13–23; Vol 2).

Apart from a brief visit to American Hawaii, Liang had no experience of the West before arriving in Australia. In fact the characteristics of youth, vigor, public spiritedness, fairness, and equality that he famously attributed to the West in his early writings reflected many of the attributes that the editors of *The Tungwah News* attributed to Sydney during the course of his visit. The same might have been said of Fremantle, Adelaide, Melbourne, and many of the cities and towns that punctuated his Australian itinerary. On the back of the gold-fever of the mid-nineteenth century, Melbourne had developed as the world's fastest-growing city in the 1880s. The extensive rail yards, palatial residences, substantial community halls and churches, banks, zoos, parks, and gardens that Liang visited in Melbourne were in many cases products of his own lifetime (Davison 1978). Adelaide was one of the first electorates in the world to recognize the rights of women as voting citizens. And in Sydney and Melbourne, he observed a powerful labor movement that asserted the equality of workers in their dealings with employers and governments. Shortly after leaving Australia, Liang wrote an article celebrating the establishment of the country's first Federal Labor cabinet, commending it to his readers as the first national government of its kind in the world. To Liang's way of thinking this was an epochal event:

> The year 1904 will be remembered by the workers of the world and should be commemorated throughout the whole world. Why? Because this year witnessed the birth of the first national cabinet organized by a Labor Party…No leader of a Labor Party has ever held the authority to serve as prime minister or to organize a cabinet. The government that has been set up in Australia this year marks an historical breakthrough.
>
> *(Liang 1904)*

And yet Australia presented an anomaly that no person of Chinese descent could ignore. Chinese in Australia were humiliated by their failure to be counted as equal subjects and citizens. The concern over racial equality that drove generations of Chinese Australian petitioners then drove Liang Qichao as well. Over the years following Federation, new discriminatory legislation was introduced to further prohibit Chinese immigration, to prevent Chinese residents from becoming citizens, to ensure wives could not accompany their husbands, and generally to ensure that Chinese Australians could neither leave nor return to Australia on the same terms as White Australians. Two years after his return to Yokohama, Liang published a bitter critique of the White Australia policy. His preferred option was for British and Chinese Australians to recognize the fundamental equality and dignity of all. Why should Chinese acknowledge the equality of peoples when Westerners did not? In a resounding conclusion to an essay on the White Australia policy, he predicted that the day would arrive 'when we yellow people have attained sufficient power to transform White Australia into Yellow Australia' (Liang 1903: 69–70).

Modern civic associations and business networks

Despite its regulatory restrictions, Australia offered a stable legal foundation for business development, and provided a style of civic life conducive to free and open association. Chinese Australians appreciated the values that underlay this system no less than other Australians, and they fought to participate in public life as full and equal citizens. But after Federation, in 1901, they were compelled to move around more than other Australian residents by a suite of federal and state legislation restricting access to Australian citizenship for Chinese residents, preventing wives and children joining their husbands and fathers permanently in Australia, and, in some states, restricting ownership of property and investment in particular industries

(Paul Jones 1999). In light of these restrictions, commuting became a favored option for Chinese Australians attempting to run businesses and to raise families. In the face of discriminatory legislation, they extended their business operations to other British colonial sites in East and Southeast Asia, where a familiar British style of rule of law prevailed without the added burden of discriminatory restraints on property ownership, trade, and movement.

Chinese residents of British Australia were highly mobile, recording visits to and from Sydney over the late nineteenth and early twentieth centuries well in excess of their aggregate numbers. Around 100,000 people entered the Australian colonies from China between the 1840s and Federation in 1901 (S.-W. Wang 2001: 197). Thirty thousand Chinese immigrants and their descendents who remained in the country at the turn of the century were entitled by right of abode to travel from and to Australia, albeit with discriminatory certification. Over the first two decades of the twentieth century, around 28,000 registered Chinese departures and arrivals are recorded for New South Wales alone, overshadowing by three to four times the total registered Chinese population of the state.[2] Historian Paul Jones estimates that, over the four decades from 1901 to 1939, Chinese Australians made 80,000 journeys to or from Australia (Jones 2001: 217). Some may have been returning home to live out their final years, but most were commuting through Sydney *en route* to a variety of destinations in China, Hong Kong, Southeast Asia, and the islands of the south Pacific on business and family matters.

They were, on the whole, conservative risk-takers. When it came to risking capital, Chinese Australian entrepreneurs favored Hong Kong as their point of entry into the China market. In the Crown Colony, they could start up business ventures under British legal jurisdiction while making useful connections through Cantonese-speaking civic associations not unlike those they had set up for themselves in Australia. John Carroll has shown that Hong Kong's success as a regional hub for business and industry was founded on the local Chinese community's capacity for self-government (in dispute resolution, policing, health care, social welfare, and making representations to government) no less than upon the *laissez-faire* policies and rule of law of the British colonial administration (Carroll 2005). Across Hong Kong, an extensive institutional apparatus of Chinese hospitals, philanthropic associations, clubs, and churches developed alongside the colonial administration to provide social and business services to Chinese residents of the city. This development was matched on a modest scale in Australia by an institutional arrangement of churches, clubs, and societies that were set up to manage local community affairs and mount claims through the press and to the government for equality of treatment in addition to expanding business opportunities. Although smaller in scale, the complex of civic institutions that developed in Sydney was commensurate with the complex that developed in parallel in Hong Kong.

Chinese Australian entrepreneurs were conservative in another sense as well, preferring to expand their business operations by developing extensive networks of trust among fellow countrymen rather than by evolving into formal corporate hierarchies (Cochran 2006: 5–6). They innovated significantly, all the same, expanding inherited networks based on kinship and native place to embrace inclusive civic associations that reached beyond particularistic ties. The NSW Chinese Chamber of Commerce, the Sydney Presbyterian Chinese Mission, the Chinese Masonic Society, and the Australasian Kuo Min Tang (Nationalist Party or KMT) were each inclusive bodies that reached beyond the limited family networks on which the entrepreneurs founded their business ventures. Through participation in such clubs, churches, and societies, Sydney-based entrepreneurs extended their connections beyond Australia to embrace counterpart bodies in Hong Kong and southern China, as well as umbrella organizations such as the Tung Wah community hospital in Hong Kong, which provided social services for Chinese Australians moving to Hong Kong or transiting through the colony on occasional visits to their family villages (Sinn 1989; Carroll 2005: 60ff). Their involvement with inclusive civic associations extended their networks of trust, enhanced their credibility, and expanded their options for raising capital and doing business. Engagement with inclusive associations substantially expanded the range of social networks available to Chinese merchant families in Australia, Hong Kong, and China without risking the quasi-familial relationships of trust on which their firms were ultimately based.

Involvement with civic clubs and churches allowed the entrepreneurs to move effortlessly in elite circles extending from their home communities in Heungshan (Xiangshan; today Zhongshan) to Sydney and thence to sites in Hong Kong and Shanghai, where they arrived as strangers but rapidly established themselves as community leaders through their civic connections. Their elite status in turn enabled them to raise capital for investment from large and small investors in and beyond Australia; to press for freedom of trade and movement in and out of Australia, China, and the Pacific islands; to offer opportunities to other network members to travel, live, and work in Hong Kong, Shanghai, and Oceania; and to support their families and communities in Sydney and their home counties while extending their business ventures abroad. Their experience with churches and societies in Australia was an important factor enabling Chinese Australian entrepreneurs to scale up their operations to levels that exceeded all but a few comparable firms in Hong Kong and China.

One particular group of Chinese entrepreneurs from Heungshan County established a range of commercial organizations, political parties, and Christian congregations, through which they developed extensive business enterprises stretching from Sydney through the British Pacific Islands to Hong Kong and Shanghai (Chan 1999). They elected to do business through family firms operating under British rule of law, in association with new-style civic institutions that helped expand their social networks along British maritime trading routes. Chinese Australian merchants were among the earliest in the diaspora to recognize the value of inclusive clubs and societies for community management and business networking. Chinese merchants established the first Chinese Australian chamber of commerce in Sydney following the visit of Liang Qichao over the summer and autumn of 1900 and 1901.[3] Similarly, the underground Yee Hing network of New South Wales was transformed from a loose rural affiliation of secret-society lodges into a tightly focused urban institution with a prominent public profile in the early 1900s. When it went public in 1911, as the Chinese Masonic Association of New South Wales, the Yee Hing network was led by the wealthy wool-broker and investor James Chuey (Huang Zhu). And some of the earliest and most inclusive organizations of the day were Chinese-Christian church congregations, including the Sydney Presbyterian congregation under the pastoral care of the Reverend John Young Wai, whose parishioners included members of the Masonic Society and the KMT, as well as a number of the Heungshan entrepreneurs who went on to establish successful businesses in Hong Kong and China (Lee 2000: 2–10; Kuo 2005; Fitzgerald 2007).

Colonial maritime business and political networks

The integration of China's treaty-port economies with Britain's maritime networks in Australia, Southeast Asia, and the Pacific Islands provided opportunities for Chinese émigrés to travel, trade, and extend their community networks in distinctively modern ways. Banana-trading firms with links to the Pacific islands, for example, lay behind several of the great Chinese Australian firms that came to dominate retail trade in Shanghai in the Chinese Republic. The success of the Four Great Companies – Wing On, Sincere, Sun Sun, and Dah Sun – is well known among international business historians (Yong 1977; Yen 1998; Wilton 1998; Chan 1999; Z. Li 1999; Lee 2000; Cai 2005). The Chinese Australian entrepreneurs behind these firms made up the largest identifiable group of international investors in Shanghai before the Communists came to power in 1949 – by one account contributing one-third of total international investment – in addition to making substantial investments in Hong Kong, Singapore, Canton, and Tianjin (Z. Li 1999: 243). Today, the grand buildings they erected along Shanghai's Nanking Road remain stand-out attractions in one of the most prestigious retail districts in China. The earliest of these merchants started out as banana traders in Australia and British colonies in the Pacific Islands.

Sydney merchants imported bananas and tropical fruits from the Pacific Islands in return for trans-shipping processed foods and manufactured products, largely sourced from Hong Kong, to the islands. Green bananas were imported from Queensland and Fiji for ripening in Chinese Australian company storehouses in Sydney before being distributed state-wide and interstate through local company networks. It has been estimated that Chinese Australian producers and importers with ties to Fiji handled between a half and three-quarters of all bananas ripened and traded in Australia over the first quarter of the century (Yong 1977: 48–53).

The banana trade was the cornerstone of Chinese Australian venture capital in the White Australia era (Guo 1949: 4; Guo 1961: 4–5; Yong 1977: 48–50; Couchman 1995). One of the largest of the banana firms, Sang On Tiy (*Shengantai*), was founded in 1902 as a partnership among the three Sydney fruit merchandizing firms of Wing Sang, Wing On and Wing Tiy. Wing Sang (*Yongsheng*) and Wing On (*Yongan*) were the respective parent companies of the Sincere, Wing On, and, indirectly, the Sun Sun department store chains later established in Hong Kong and China. Founded in

1890 by Heungshan natives in Sydney, in its early years Wing Sang was the largest trader of Queensland bananas in southern Australian ports. In time, the firm expanded into owning and managing fruit plantations abroad, chiefly in Fiji, and it diversified locally into general importing and exporting. Partners in the firm included Ma Ying-piu (Ma Yingbiao), founder of the Sincere Department Store chain, and George Kwok Bew (Guo Biao), a maternal cousin of the Kwok brothers who founded the Wing On firm in Sydney, Hong Kong, and China, and a partner with Ma Ying-piu in Sincere. One of the Kwok brothers, James Gock Lock (Guo Le), was an employee of Wing Sang before he ventured out on his own in 1897 to establish the Wing On Fruit Store in Sydney. Within two years, James was joined in the venture by four of his brothers, who together built up the substantial Wing On commercial empire. One of the brothers, Philip Gockchin (Guo Chuan), spent three years in Suva managing the Sang On Tiy banana combine before joining his brother in Hong Kong and later founding Wing On's flagship Shanghai store.

The families that dominated the banana industry and, in time, the great diversified firms based in Hong Kong and Shanghai were, at the same time, closely associated with the leading echelons of the Australasian network of the KMT. The families enjoyed close relations with every level of the KMT party organization, ranging from small cells in the party's Pacific islands network to its central headquarters in Shanghai and, from 1924, in Canton. Sun Yatsen, the founder and lifetime leader of the KMT, held a personal portfolio of Wing On shares purchased by his wife in 1916. The Wing On Company in turn made substantial loans and donations to Sun Yatsen's central headquarters in Shanghai (Young 1998: 33–46; Fitzgerald 2007: 250, n.13). Family and business ties linking the Sydney firms to local party branches in the Pacific islands were more intensive still. George Bew was part owner of Wing Sang and Co and at the same time a partner in the Sang On Tiy banana-importing firm, a founding shareholder in Sincere, a cousin of the Kwok brothers who owned the Wing On firm, and, from 1916 to 1920, State Director of the New South Wales branch of the KMT. A founding partner of the rival Tiy Sang firm of Fijian banana growers, Peter Yee Wing, was elected party treasurer during George Bew's term as director and succeeded him in that office. Yee Wing succeeded George Bew as head of the NSW branch from 1920 to 1925, when he was selected to head the reorganized Australasian party headquarters for three successive terms, from the KMT's first regional party congress in 1925 to 1931. George Bew and Peter Yee Wing, who were responsible for much of Fiji's annual banana production, and for a large slice of Australian distribution, held the reins of the New South Wales and Australasian KMT over its first 15 years of operation(Chen 1935: 27–43, 62–65, 156).

Historically speaking, Sydney's claim to regional leadership of the Australian KMT was relatively slim. Chinese in Melbourne could claim a longer history of republican activity dating back to the work of the Revolutionary Alliance (*Tongmenghui*) at the turn of the century. But Sun Yatsen's Party Centre preferred Sydney as site for the party's Oceania regional headquarters in recognition of its extensive maritime links with the British Pacific islands and colonial Southeast Asia. It assigned the Sydney KMT branch network responsibility for establishing branches on merchant vessels servicing British colonial ports in Southeast Asia, including Singapore, where KMT activity was outlawed. Within a few years of its creation, the Sydney headquarters had recruited around 1000 merchant mariners through 15 sub-branches on merchant vessels sailing between Australia and colonial ports in East and Southeast Asia (Yong and McKenna 1990: 36–38).

Sydney's maritime links also extended to Pacific island settlements serviced by traders based in Sydney. In the case of the Pacific islands, the sea routes that linked KMT branches were the same channels through which Chinese island trading and migration networks were routed through Sydney. Pacific island merchants appreciated the party's attention. Although dominated by a small coterie of leading merchant families, the Australasian KMT headquarters welcomed merchants of modest means engaging in legitimate fields of trade within its jurisdiction. None responded more warmly than the owners of small and medium businesses in British Fiji and New Guinea, seeking to extend their home-town connections and kinship ties through institutional networks operating around the Sydney KMT headquarters. One prominent retired member of the KMT in Sydney recalled visiting the Australasian party headquarters shortly after alighting from a steamer from Fiji as a young man after the war in the Pacific. 'In Fiji I joined the KMT to extend my social networks', he told a gathering of KMT historians in October 2005. 'We all did. We joined the KMT to make connections in a city where we arrived as strangers.'[4]

The KMT also defended Pacific island communities in their dealings with White Australia. In the 1920s, a regulatory regime that had become familiar to Chinese Australians since Federation was extended to cover business and movement in and out of the South Pacific islands. Australian authorities used their League of Nations Mandate after the Great War to extend the administrative reach of White Australia to Pacific communities that had been relatively free from discriminatory constraints on movement, property ownership, and trade under German and British colonial administrations. The Australasian KMT network then expanded through the islands in the shadow of the Australian mandate, as a *doppelganger* of White Australia, helping Chinese residents to negotiate the tangled web of regulations governing Chinese migration and settlement in Australia's Pacific sphere of influence.

The KMT was particularly well suited to this role. Its uniquely privileged access to provincial governments in south China, and to the Nationalist Government of China after 1928, lent the party a degree of authority that no other Chinese Australian body could match. The KMT provided access to official Chinese and Australian government channels at the very moment when White Australian regulations were beginning to limit Chinese freedom of trade and movement in the south Pacific. In time, party members based in ports along Pacific island trading routes were able to draw on an extensive KMT maritime network to expand the range of their business connections in the Pacific islands and to approach government authorities to remove obstacles to investment, trade, and movement in the region. From the late 1920s, they were assisted by the Chinese Consulate in Sydney, which enjoyed *ex officio* membership on the Australasian KMT executive committee once the Consulate came under KMT Nationalist Government control in 1928.

A series of Australian government ordinances issued in the 1920s had the effect of severely limiting entry to the Pacific Islands of new arrivals from China and requiring all those leaving to apply for permission to return before departing. New arrivals were limited by a requirement that they secure a visa for entry. Although consistent with Britain's treaty obligations with China, this requirement facilitated discreet discrimination whereby visa applications could be ignored or rejected by British missions in the Far East without explanation. Henceforth, any Chinese departing with the intention of returning was required to apply for a Certificate of Identity and a Permit to Return, prior to departure. Permits for re-entry were handled more generously than visas for new arrivals. In 1928, the KMT approached the Chinese Consul-General in Melbourne, seeking clarification of the impact of the new commuting regulations on Chinese departures and returns to Fiji. In his formal response, the Governor of Fiji pointed out that no resident of repute had been denied re-entry after an absence of less than five years (Ali 2002: 65–70).

For Chinese residents of Fiji, the Governor's message was reassuring on two counts. First, it indicated that they could come and go as they pleased so long as they complied with fingerprinting and other intrusive requirements of the Governor's ordinance bearing on Permits to Return. The Governor's formal reply also showed that the KMT was capable of representing the interests of Chinese residents to government by virtue of its links with Australia, its status in dealing with the KMT Nationalist Government of China, and its position as an institution representing the Chinese residents of Fiji. In the following year, the Chinese Nationalist Government appointed a resident vice-consul to Fiji, the first of several KMT government representatives to serve on the islands before the Pacific war. The arrival of C. L. Cheng as resident vice-consul in 1930 further cemented the Sydney KMT's position in Fiji (Ali 2002: 81).

In the former German territories of New Guinea, the establishment of KMT branches coincided with Australian occupation of Germany's Pacific territories during the Great War. Again, the Party's expansion was enhanced by its role in formal dealings with Australian government authorities over migration and mobility. The KMT was called upon to represent the entire community in negotiating with crown authorities over travel, property, and family reunion regulations, which hit residents hard following Australia's military occupation of German territories in 1914 and the formal transfer of sovereignty from Germany to Australia after the war. The Australasian KMT office in Sydney then relished the opportunity to expand its operations into Australia's mandated Pacific territories (Wu 1982).

The Four Great Companies

The long arm of the British empire beckoned enterprising Chinese Australian businesses to spread their investment along a chain of British ports stretching from Sydney and Suva to Hong Kong and Shanghai, with the result that well connected émigrés from Heungshan County drew on their local networks to develop substantial enterprises in East Asia and the Pacific islands. Less well connected laborers and tradesmen who did not enjoy direct access to these networks took up share-holding partnerships with friends or firms that did. The results were impressive. As noted, Heungshan merchant firms with roots in Australia came to own and manage some of the most prominent commercial, industrial, and financial enterprises in the Republic of China, including one of its two largest textile enterprises, several hotels, banks and insurance companies, and the country's most prestigious department stores.

Department stores for Chinese customers were an innovation of the Australian retail pioneers who founded the Sincere (*Xianshi*) and Wing On (*Yongan*) department store chains in Hong Kong, Canton, and Shanghai from the turn of the century. Ma Ying-piu and his partners opened their first Sincere Department Store in Hong Kong in 1900, the first in Canton in 1912, and their grandest store of all in Shanghai in 1917. The Gock brothers' Wing On Company opened for business in Hong Kong in 1907 before setting up a flagship store in Shanghai in 1918. In time, these department store chains were joined by two other Chinese Australian retail firms along Nanking Road in Shanghai, the Lee and Liu families' Sun Sun Department Store (*Xinxin*) in 1926, and The Sun Company Store (*Daxin*) opened by the Choy (*Cai*) family in 1931. To Shanghai residents, the four Chinese Australian stores came to be known as the Four Great Companies. All of their founders hailed from Heungshan County in Guangdong, but their business roots lay in Sydney, where they retained extensive personal and business connections, raising much of their capital from investors in Australia and offering opportunities to fellow Heungshan natives (and fellow Australians) to experience life and work in Shanghai (Chan 1999: 66–68).

The share-raising strategies of the Four Great Companies followed the well worn path of smaller Chinese Australian business ventures, which set a local precedent for shareholding partnerships in successful business ventures within Australia. The successful expansion of Chinese Australian general stores in New South Wales was as remarkable in its own way as the growth of the Four Great Companies in Hong Kong and Shanghai. Kwong Sing and Co, for example, was founded in the NSW country town of Glen Innes in 1886 by a businessman known locally as Wong Chee. Wong later transferred management of the store to a Heungshan native of Shekki district, Percy Young (Kwan Hong Kee), who expanded the business into a department store with the aid of nephews sponsored to Australia. By the 1940s, each of the departments of the Glen Innes store was managed by a different member of the Young (Kwan) family. By mid-century, the Young family owned and operated a dozen stores in ten regional centers in New South Wales.[5]

Kwong Sing's founder, Wong Chee, helped to launch another retail store chain in northern New South Wales when he introduced Sydney-born Harry Fay (Louie Mew Fay; Lei Miaohui) to the owner of the Hong Yuen general store in Inverell. By 1916, Fay had become a managing partner of Hong Yuen, and over the following two decades sponsored family members to work in the Inverell store, encouraging them to take up shares in the business. By the early 1930s, he was employing 60 permanent staff and claimed an annual turnover of £100,000. By the 1940s, Hong Yuen shareholders had expanded their operations to other regional towns in New South Wales, including Moree, Texas, and Warialda.

The expansion of the Kwong Sing and Hong Yeun family networks in rural NSW paralleled the expansion of the Four Great Companies in Hong Kong and China on a scale commensurate with the demography of rural NSW and the relatively limited financial and human resources of the families that controlled them. The parallel is not merely fortuitous. The Glenn Innes business pioneer Wong Chee is better known in Chinese business history as Wong Poon Narm (Huang Bingnan), one of the five original partners who founded the Sincere Department Store in Hong Kong in 1900, the Canton store in 1912, and the Shanghai store in 1917. Early in the 1920s, he famously parted company with Sincere to join Liu Xiji and Charles Lee in forming the Sun Sun Company, which opened its first department store in Shanghai in 1926 (Sincere Co. Ltd 1924: 5–6, 11–12, 209–13). By this time, Wong was operating well beyond his immediate family circle. Along with the Mas, Kwoks, Lees, Choys, Lius, and other prominent merchant families in Sydney, he expanded his available pool of potential investors to communities in Australia and abroad who were willing to risk their savings in larger international business ventures. By the time the Four Great Companies were canvassing share-holding investments around Australia, the practice of making low-risk investments in profitable commercial ventures through extended networks of trust was well established among Chinese Australians (Chan 1999: 66–67; Li 1999: 245).

Networks of colonial modernity

Studies of Chinese colonial modernity typically focus on single enclaves of multiple colonial powers within China, such as Shanghai before Liberation; or highlight larger territorial spheres of influence dominated by a single colonial power, such as German and later Japanese Shandong. These instances of incursions into Chinese territory and infringement of Chinese sovereignty were sanctioned and enabled by the Unequal Treaties. If we shift our focus beyond China, and China-centered histories, to a broader trans-national frame of reference embracing multiple sites of colonial domination within and beyond China, governed by a single colonial power in Great Britain, we find that the treaties sanctioned and enabled struggles for dignity and equality within the framework of colonial modernity.

Life in China's treaty-ports under the Unequal Treaties could be humiliating for Chinese residents subject to the policing powers and administrative whims of foreign colonial authorities, and exposed to the everyday taunts of colonial racism. Life was no less humiliating for Chinese residents of British settler societies in the Australian colonies, or in New Zealand and the British colonial enclaves of the Pacific Islands. But in these cases, the Unequal Treaties provided a point of leverage for pressing claims for freedom of movement and for equality of treatment under British rule of law.

Making a living was no simple task for Chinese émigrés in the face of the ideology of white supremacism that reigned in Britain's Pacific territories. The Unequal Treaties made the task a little easier by asserting freedom of movement for Chinese émigrés departing from Britain's ports in China for other British ports abroad.

In this sense, the treaties legitimated and catalysed broader claims for equality of treatment and equality before the law, which were passionately debated in reading rooms, town halls, church congregations, and in the Chinese and English language presses of the day. Claiming freedom of association and assembly, Chinese community leaders organized modern civic associations and political parties – most notably the KMT – to press formal claims for equality of treatment before colonial and later federal government authorities in Australia. More often than not, their claims were overruled by authorities acting in breach of the treaties or surreptitiously circumventing them. Still, taking advantage of residual rights of movement and abode earned on arrival, Chinese Australians became prodigious commuters and entrepreneurs, identifying business opportunities at every port of call along Britain's maritime sea lanes, and developing extensive social networks stretching from Sydney to the Pacific islands, to Hong Kong and Canton, and to Shanghai, where they helped to shape China's modern commercial revolution.

A specific history of Chinese colonial modernity mapped around the maritime routes linking British enclaves and colonies in and beyond China inevitably bumps up against the margins of a liberation narrative that ends at China's shores. The history of China's colonial émigrés in the British Pacific then invites reflection on the adequacy of the standard liberation narrative for accommodating transnational stories. The stories of the émigrés who made their homes in Britain's maritime empire can also be told as liberation narratives. Certainly they were no less humiliated by the experience of colonial racism than their stay-at-home counterparts in Wuhan or Changsha. Indeed, because they understood what it meant to be humiliated, they inspired, funded, and in notable cases led the revolutionary movement to overthrow the Qing empire and to restore China's national sovereignty and territorial integrity. At the same time, they explored transnational remedies that were ultimately closed off by China's national liberation. Mobile Chinese émigrés who passed through Australian ports took advantage of the opportunities that colonial modernity afforded to craft their own modalities of liberation within the framework of the British empire. Wherever they set foot, they brought with them not only their skills, and their capital, but also their passion for equality and dignity.

Notes

1 *The Argus*, 30 May 1887 (Tseng 1887). This article first appeared in the *Asiatic Quarterly Review* in January 1887 and was republished in the *London and China News* before appearing in *The Chinese Recorder* in April. See also *The New York Times*, 18 February 1887.
2 The registered population possibly disguised replacement migration, as Chinese returning to China were permitted to nominate substitutes (Markus 2004). The failure of US exclusion laws to achieve their stated purpose is explored by McKeown (2003).
3 Nanjing historian Cai Shaoqing maintains that the NSW Chinese Chamber of Commerce, founded in 1903, was the second in the world after Hong Kong (Cai 2005). On the Chamber's changes of form and title over time, see Yong (1977): 83, 117, 120ff.
4 Kuo Min Tang History Workshop, Sydney KMT Headquarters, 15 October 2005.
5 Kwan family stores were established in Glen Innes, Emmaville, Texas, Stanthorpe, Casino, Coffs Harbour, Ballina, Kyogle, Werris Creek and Bundarra (Wilton 1998: 106).

11
HONG KONG AND THE NEW IMPERIALISM IN EAST ASIA, 1941–66

Prasenjit Duara

The goal of this chapter is to try and understand the transformation of imperialism in East Asia in particular, but also as a global phenomenon from the 1930s until the present. Hong Kong, especially after the Second World War, represents one modality of this fundamental change. The transformations in other imperialist-dominated societies have rarely led to the same developments as in Hong Kong, but the dynamics of these imperialisms are not dissimilar in principle. One of the questions I shall be asking is how and why the transformation of imperialism in Hong Kong ended up with a more developed capitalist society.

Changes in the form of imperialism were a response to competitive pressures among the imperialists from the early twentieth century and the somewhat later demands for independence and development in the colonial or subordinated areas. This change was most clearly evidenced in the Japanese puppet state of Manchukuo (1932–45). The British Empire experienced these pressures acutely after the First World War, but was only significantly transformed after the Second World War, when Hong Kong emerged as the new jewel in the crown in the 1950s. At the same time, however, the opportunity for the colony of Hong Kong to successfully realize the new imperialist ideal had to do with the conditions of the Cold War. Indeed, the Cold War itself was an expression of the transformed imperialism inasmuch as the Soviet Union and the United States launched novel means of subordinating allies and dependencies.

The Cold War scenario created new circumstances that advantaged a place like Hong Kong. Distanced from the two superpowers and balancing the relationship between China and Britain, Hong Kong gained considerable leverage. Because of these circumstances, Hong Kong was able to overwhelm imperial control and overtake the metropolitan country according to several economic indices. As such, the imperial relationship was not merely transformed, but transmuted into something that the original term could no longer fully capture.

The new imperialism

The inter-war era was characterized by a new environment for imperialist competition and domination: British 'free-trade imperialism' was weakened by new imperialist rivals and threatened by the rise of nationalism in the colonies and semi-colonies. Of course, the threat of nationalism in the colonized world affected as much the new imperialist rivals such as Germany, Japan and the USA, among others. These latter-day rivals developed the new imperialism by creating regional formations or economic blocs in which colonies or subordinate territories were often reconstituted as nominally sovereign states, but which were militarily dependent upon the metropole. The new imperialism reflected a strategic reorientation of the periphery to be part of an organic formation designed to attain global supremacy for the imperial power. As Albert Lebrun declared after the First World War, the goal was now to 'unite France to all those distant Frances in order to permit them to combine their efforts to draw from one another reciprocal advantages' (Marshall 1973: 44). Yet France itself would find it very hard to implement this new formation.

With the simultaneous rise of rights consciousness in the colonies and dependencies and the increased need for resource and social mobilization within them, it was more efficient for the new imperialists to foster modern and *indirectly* controlled institutions in the dependencies. The goal was to control these areas by dominating their institutions of mobilization, such as banks, the transportation infrastructure, and political institutions, which were created to resemble those of the metropole (such as legislative councils, institutions of political tutelage, and political parties like the communist parties or the Concordia in Manchukuo). In short, the new imperialists attended to the modernization of institutions and, thus, identities. They often espoused cultural or ideological similarities – including sometimes anti-colonial ideologies – even while racism and nationalism accompanied the reality of military–political domination.

Subordinate states were militarily dependent upon and economically mobilized for the sake of the metropole, but it was not necessarily in the latter's interest to have them economically or institutionally backward. Thus this imperialism occasionally entailed a separation of economic and military/political dimensions. In some situations, as in the Soviet Union–Eastern Europe and the Japan–Manchukuo relationships, massive investments and resources flowed into the client states, thereby breaching the classical dualism between an industrialized metropole and a colony focused on the primary sector (Duara 2003, 2006).

The older imperial powers of Britain and France recognized the value of economic growth in the empire for competitiveness during the First World War, when colonial troops and resources played a vital role. In Britain, Joseph Chamberlain's neo-mercantilist ideas of colonial development and of 'imperial preference' began to be taken more seriously after the First World War. But as a consequence of entrenched ideas of colonial self-sufficiency, post-war capital needs at home and, not least, demands for protection by British industry, only once before 1940 did expenditure on colonial development creep above 0.1 per cent of British gross national product.

(Constantine 1984: 25, 276; Havinden and Meredith 1993: 148–59) Similarly, we have noted the post-First World War transformation of French attitudes toward the colonies summed up in Albert Lebrun's words. But while the French government extended imperial preference and implemented reforms, particularly with reference to legal and political rights in Africa during the 1930s, investments in economic and social development projects were insignificant until the creation of the Investment Fund for Economic and Social Development in 1946 (Marshall 1973: 224–26).

The establishment of Manchukuo in 1932 marked the first major effort at the transformation of the metropole–colony relationship. Indeed, it was especially after the establishment of Manchukuo that Japanese exploitation of colonies such as Korea was accompanied by sharp increases in their productive capacity. The Japanese economic bloc, built throughout the 1930s and intensified during the Pacific War, resembled the German New Order built upon states that were essentially German puppets or had German military governors. Moreover, since the entire occupied zone became subordinated to Japanese war needs, Japan's defeat similarly represented a failure of the new imperialism. Nonetheless, Japan's initial experience with Manchukuo and the colonies in the 1930s reveals the lineaments of a more functional version of the new imperialism not entirely driven by wartime needs. Compared with the older European imperial powers, for instance, the accumulated per capita British investment in India was only $8 compared with Japanese investment in Korea of $38 in 1938 (Park 2003: 19).

I have dealt elsewhere with the details of the new imperialism – or the 'imperialism of free nations'. Suffice it here to make a few summary points. First, it was not until 1945 that the Soviet Union, the United States and the older European powers attained the relatively crystallized version of its various features that we see in a place like Manchukuo before the 1937 occupation of China and the Pacific War. In particular, the developmental aspects – or the developmental state pioneered in Manchukuo – was not a feature of any of the pre-Second World War imperialisms. Second, while both Japanese and German imperialism was marked by abominable cruelties, the German New Order was clearly not based upon the rhetoric of racial equality in relation to East Europeans. The Japanese rhetoric of the equality of Asians and deliverance from European imperialists had, as we shall see, an important impact, even though it was negated in practice by the Japanese conquerors (Duara 2006).

While colonial development was not high on the agenda, Britain still had to respond to the dynamics produced by the new circumstances after the First World War. It was motivated to create an economic zone by the decline in the value of the pound sterling following the steep wartime debts it ran up with the USA. By the 1930s, Britain became increasingly dependent on the colonies' resources to stabilize the pound in relation to the dollar and other hard currencies, and its balance of payments. In 1931, Britain went off the gold standard and created the Sterling Zone to enable protectionism in trade and commerce between it, its dependent territories, and other countries that maintained the external value of their currencies in a fixed relationship to sterling (Hinds 2001: 11, 29).

The Second World War piled up the UK's debt to the USA ever more sharply and, especially after 1947, British colonial authorities engaged in a process of colonial resource mobilization and control over colonial finances by integrating the remaining colonies even more closely to the metropole. The idea was to maximize colonial exports to counter the drain on Britain's gold and dollar reserves which became especially rapid after it attempted to float the pound sterling in 1947; the Korean War led to further devaluation of the sterling (FO 371/53630, 476 File HKRS 163-1-761; Hinds 2001: 121).

For its part, Britain was obliged to undertake two policy measures. One was to introduce social welfare and development programmes in the colonies, with the goal of preparing them for political self-governance, although not independence. A Social Welfare Advisory Committee was set up in 1943 to advise the Colonial Office (Tang 1998: 50). The second policy was to invest more in the dollar-generating sectors of the colonial economies, including building up their infrastructure and capital needs.

This implicit contract with the colonies represented what I consider the British variant of the new imperialism. However, in most cases it worked against the interests of the colonies, because Britain did not have the economic resources to introduce adequate welfare and development programmes; moreover, its interest in restricting the use of dollars and fear of US investment, and hence influence, in the colonies also limited colonial development. At the same time, this was a period when political unrest and demands for independence were working against closer integration. In other words, *political self-governance and closer economic integration*, the central features of the new imperialism, began to militate against each other. After 1955, when it was clear that the major sterling surplus colonies, Nigeria, Ivory Coast and Malaya, were not going to be happy with self-governance in an empire where the metropole still called the shots, Britain gave up hope of empire and prepared to finally allow full convertibility for the pound sterling by the mid-1960s (Hinds 2001: 146, 197).

Yet, as Catherine Schenk has shown, where and for whatever reasons it continued to have colonies, Britain continued to exercise tight control over – or tried to reserve the right to control – colonial monetary policies. Hong Kong turned out to have the largest sterling reserves of any colony in the 1960s; its reserves rose from £140–60 million in the last few years of the 1950s to £363 million by October 1967. This amounted to over 10 per cent of the UK's total sterling liabilities to the overseas Sterling Area. This growth was the result of the combination of the successful industrialization of Hong Kong with the colonial monetary system that required 100 per cent sterling reserves (Schenk 1994: 7). Roger Louis has pointed out that Hong Kong remained as autocratic a colony as any until the final years of the transfer with respect to its power to tax and administer justice, in its police force, and in defense of its frontiers (Louis 1997: 1053). However, the critical financial support provided by Hong Kong for Britain declined after the devaluation of the pound sterling in 1967.

The consequences of the 1967 pound devaluation on colonial relations between Britain and Hong Kong have been closely studied by Schenk. Initially, London insisted on its imperial prerogative by unilaterally devaluing the pound by 14 per cent and letting the colony simply bear the sharp fall in the value of Hong Kong's extraordinarily large reserves of £400 million. But precisely because Hong Kong could plunge sterling into still further decline by its control of such large reserves, and because of the dwindling military power of UK in the colony, the Hong Kong government was able to 'strike back', establish its financial autonomy, and shift the balance of power between it and Britain (Schenk 2004).

Wartime Japanese occupation, 1942–45

I pick up the story of British imperialism in Hong Kong during these mid-century years with the Japanese occupation of Hong Kong. The Japanese occupation of Hong Kong demonstrated the same harshness and a common pattern of occupation as in many other parts of China. At the same time, Hong Kong's distinctive position as a Chinese region, and as a colony with links to other European colonial possessions in Southeast Asia, gave it a special role in the Japanese conception of its wartime empire. Just as significantly, the impact of the rhetoric and state-building practices of the Japanese new imperialism had far-reaching consequences for British policies and attitudes in the colony during the post-war period. But for the recent work of Philip Snow, which has inspired my own explorations, this impact has been largely ignored in the historiography (Snow 2003). My purpose in exploring this impact is to suggest that the new imperialism was a complexly interrelated regional and even global phenomenon.

The Japanese invasion in December 1941 followed the sequence established in Manchukuo and other parts of China. After several weeks of stupefying violence and rape by Japanese troops and their Triad allies, the military courted the elites and middle classes to collaborate with them under the banner of a reformist pan-Asianism (Snow 2003: 91–102; Tsang 2004: 125–30).[1] As in Manchukuo and Central China, Japanese local agents initially mobilized local 'peace restoration' committees, called Rehabilitation Advisory Committees, in Hong Kong (Brook 2005; Mitter 2000). Later in 1942, these were replaced by the Chinese Representative Council and the Chinese Co-operative Council, into which they inducted the leading Hong Kong elites such as Robert Kotewall (Law Kuk-wo), Chow Shou-son, Robert Ho-tung and Aw Boon-haw, the Tiger Balm king. As they restored and expanded local institutions, the Japanese added many Chinese and other Asians, Portuguese and Eurasians to all levels of government and social organizations (Ward 1943: 18–22).

Writing about the occupation of Hong Kong in 1943, soon after having left it, US Consul Robert Ward leaves us with a record of the impressions of the early years of Japanese rule. He notes with considerable concern what he regards as the military, administrative and ideological successes of the occupation. For Ward, the ideological appeal of pan-Asianism was paramount and most threatening. He saw its appeal, particularly to the poor and dispossessed, in the overturning of the European-dominated world order, in terms similar to the way analysts regard the appeal of

Muslim fundamentalism today. In perhaps the most dramatized episode of pan-Asianism, the Japanese military forced British men to pull rickshaws carrying Chinese and Indians. For the elites and middle classes, Ward notes the importance of the massive expansion of the institutional infrastructure of government, explicitly comparing the situation under British colonial rule before 1942 unfavourably with the situation in 1943 (Ward 1943: 18–33; HKN 3/29/1942).

In the pre-1942 system, the entire administration was run by British members of the civil service, and there were only four Chinese members – appointed by the Governor – in the Executive and Legislative Councils. There were no local administrative or representative agencies. In contrast, the military government established 18 District Bureaux as 'self-government' agencies under the four-member Chinese (or Hong Kongese) Representative Council. These bureaux were staffed by Chinese heads and deputy heads, hundreds of Chinese employees, and as many as 3000 ward leaders under them. In addition, the major trades were represented by a 22-member Chinese Co-operative Council. The Japanese also reopened the Chinese Seamen and Associated Seafaring Trades Union, which had been closed down after the crippling 1925 Seamen's strike, and created fishing and marketing co-operatives. By 1943, this and other unions were being reorganized, probably to make them more amenable to the will of the regime (Ward 1943: 35; Snow 2003: 124–25; HKN 2/26/1942; 3/2/1942).

The 18 bureaux represented a cross between the *baojia* surveillance system and a modern mobilization agency. They were principally engaged in security, rice rationing for the population, repatriation of refugees from the mainland, creating annual budgets, and, not least among Japanese concerns, public health. The organization of community representation resembled the corporatist structures of the Concordia Society in Manchukuo. As elsewhere, Japanese control over this structure was ensured by the presence of Japanese officials in senior administrative positions, as well as by an alternative hierarchy for surveillance of Chinese officialdom. In Hong Kong, this was housed in the three Area Bureaux created not long after the institution of the District Bureaux. The Area Bureaux were directly responsible to the Governor (Lt. Gen.) Isogai Rensuke's headquarters (*sotokubu, zongdubu*). Despite the controlling scaffold, Ward had this to say about the appointment of so many Chinese: 'Of course, they are all answerable to Japanese officials but it will not be long before the adequate performance of the tasks which have been put on them becomes a matter of personal "face;" and thereafter their self-respect; their own view of themselves cannot but be inextricably engaged in their being good servants of the Emperor of Japan.' (Ward 1943: 35: HKN 3/7/1942; 3/22/1942.)

Hong Kong was also conceived to play an important role in the grand plan of the Co-prosperity Sphere. It would serve not only as the financial and trans-shipment centre between the northern and southern parts of this empire, but also as the demographic, cultural and, indeed, ideological hinge. According to the Governor, 'The ultimate objective is to build Hong Kong into an entrepot where Asiatics from Nippon, China, Manchukuo, Philippines, East Indies, Malaya and other places can enjoy harmony and mutual prosperity on an equal footing.' (HKN 10/14/1942.)

Thus it was to become not only the major centre for ship-building, repair, fuelling and trans-shipment, but also a point at which the different communities from Asia would articulate their relationship with the Japanese centre. Records of the meetings between Chinese merchants and Japanese representatives reveal a cautious interest among the former in developing access to new markets and resources in Southeast Asia that participation in a Japanese empire might provide (HKN 12/10–12/1942). It is thus rather ironic that the Japanese empire and control of Hong Kong broke down precisely at this point.

The Japanese army in Hong Kong came to be divided between the China faction and the Southeast Asia faction. The early state-building initiatives represented the efforts of the China faction, who saw reforms in Hong Kong as an opportunity to consolidate their power in the mainland. As the war drew on, their influence was eclipsed by the dominance of the Southeast Asia group, who saw the colony rather more as a portal and supply base for penetration into Southeast Asia. As the pursuit of war increasingly overtook all other goals, the army became ruthlessly demanding of the population. Japanese business and military interests rode roughshod over local interests and concerns. By 1944, the military police and the Triads once again unleashed a reign of terror upon the local populace (Snow 2003: 89, 149–56, 215–28). The appeals of pan-Asian unity were long forgotten, and Ward's early fears came to be seen as baseless and utterly incapable of realization.

Yet the Japanese occupation changed everything. The wartime propaganda against European racism and the subsequent movement towards decolonization would make it difficult for the British to sustain their racist policies and institutions, even though attitudes of superiority would return once they were comfortably lodged back on the Peak by the 1950s. During the immediate post-war administration of Governor Mark Young in 1946–47, there were considerable attempts at reform. The 1918 Ordinance barring Asians from living on the Peak was repealed; mixed marriages were legalized; Chinese police were recruited; and some members of the Urban Council were now elected and it gained jurisdiction over education, welfare, public works and town planning. Most striking was the creation of 18 self-governmental entities known as 'neighbourhood groups' (*kaifongs*) (Lethbridge 1969: 123–25; Snow 2003: 289–95).

To be sure, the creation of neighbourhood groups was never linked to the Japanese-period bureaux. Indeed, they were regarded as age-old Chinese self-governing institutions that had fallen into desuetude since at least 20 years before the Pacific War began. In 1949, the newly established Social Welfare Officer sought to revive these voluntary organizations, and by March 1952 there were, once again, 18 fully established neighbourhood group 'welfare associations'. According to the Social Welfare Board report, the goal was not merely to enable them to provide relief or charity, but to include a 'whole network of constructive services designed to help in practical ways their own welfare and to maintain that improvement. Thus they brought together the old traditional idea of welfare with the modern Western tradition of social welfare.' (CO 1023/126 Social Welfare Office, Report from 1948–52: 18–20.) Aline Wong's work furnishes some evidence that the District

Bureau system was directly incorporated into the neighbourhood groups system in 1949. In the district of Shamshuipo, for example, the funds left for maintaining the former District Bureau Forces were immediately converted into the foundation fund of the Shamsuipo neighbourhood group in 1949, when the government proclaimed complete responsibility for the District Bureau Force over the whole Colony (Kan 1970: 113).[2]

In fact, the neighbourhood groups were scarcely modern welfare units in the Western sense, at least not until the 1970s. Similarly to the Japanese-period bureaux, they represented a combination of the old *baojia* system of surveillance, Chinese local elite-sponsored community and temple organizations, entities providing basic medical services and education, and a channel to mediate the views of the government and the population. But they received no funds from the government, nor did they have any power except for the aura of state sanction. They provided for themselves through collective subscriptions, fees and contributions from local leaders, much like village temple committees in imperial times (Wong 1972: 79; Tang 1998: 58). Indeed, they were introduced at a time when the refugee population was on the rise, and surveillance, particularly with regard to infiltration by communist agents and Triads, became once again an important function (CO 1023/126, Social Welfare Office Report 19). The neighbourhood groups were doubtless a response to the growing awareness of colonial state's responsibilities, but they were also consistent with the British version of the new imperialism: to introduce new measures of surveillance and mobilization without increasing governmental expenditure.

The Hong Kong Contract

For various reasons, Hong Kong reflected a different type of 'implicit contract' from the other British colonies. While Britain was beginning by the 1950s to despair of empire in these other regions, colonial dominion in Hong Kong was not only waxing, it began to achieve more than it dreamed of promising. Much of it had to do with the understanding of the second post-war Governor, Sir Alexander Grantham (1947–57), who expected Hong Kong to revert to Chinese rule in 1997, and was more interested in cultivating PRC non-interference and permitting economic growth than granting municipal or legislative rights. Grantham's vision was unlike that of Sir Mark Young, who, humiliated by his experience of imprisonment in Stanley during the Occupation, had been committed to ultimately creating a self-governing citizenry within the empire that would remain loyal to the British and shun Chinese national affiliation (the more typical British implicit contract).

As the Cold War settled in and the British elite began to feel more secure in the immediate political future under Grantham, colonial attitudes became apparent once again. Democratic reforms were rolled back, non-locals were increasingly recruited to the police force, and the 'Peak mentality' returned among the Europeans (Snow 2003: 291–92, 318–26). As attested by James Hayes and others with intimate knowledge of colonial society, the British in Hong Kong in the 1950s still represented a colonial society in which the expatriate elite held themselves to be a superior race living apart from the natives (Hayes 1990: 6–10).

At the same time, however, under the changed global circumstances, colonial attitudes and decision-making structures could be quite compatible with competitiveness in a capitalist world. Indeed, in the absence of a strong national movement, the implicit contract with the colony involving autonomy within the imperial system was carried through by the local colonial government. This government appears to have developed a powerful sense of responsibility for, and interest in, the territory. A cursory glance through the tension- and sarcasm-filled pages of the Colonial Office archives through the 1950s and 1960s shows that the interests of the colony were as staunchly – and successfully – supported by the local colonial government in their exchanges with their metropolitan masters in the Treasury, as any nationalist government might be (BT 64/4562 1953–54).[3]

I am not sure it is productive to ask why there was a turnaround in the attitude of the colonial bureaucrat. Perhaps it was less fundamentally an attitudinal transformation as much as a structural and a discursive one. Hong Kong was the one place where the new imperialism could in fact be realized and, if we assume that professional bureaucrats do strive to achieve their goals, they were certainly able to achieve it here. Yet it was not without an often bitter struggle against metropolitan authorities. One of the goals of the remainder of this chapter is to examine the transformation of the conditions of the job of the local colonial officials. To what extent, and why, did local colonial officials defy metropolitan authorities in promoting the interests of Hong Kong?

At least two factors were at work here. First, I refer not only to the obvious discursive effects of decolonization, but also to the emergence of multilateral global organizations and international conventions that applied new norms and standards of global development to Hong Kong. Brimming over with equal doses of sarcasm are the responses in the archives to upstart ex-colonials named Qureishi and Lokanathan, from agencies such as SEATO or ECAFE, pressing colonial bureaucrats to accord with these standards.[4] The second refers to the ambivalent and necessarily ambiguous goals of the new imperialism previously alluded to. The new imperialism was *theoretically* designed to benefit both metropole and colony: it was a non-zero-sum game strategy. Yet it was an imperialist arrangement, and whenever it could the metropole would squeeze the dependency. From his vantage point, the colonial bureaucrat could see the bigger picture and sometimes succeeded in persuading the authorities, although often without stating his case.

Indeed, one of the most important instruments of local colonial power was arrogated silently. In 1948, the Treasury determined that its control over Hong Kong finances would cease and a system of consultation and supervision would be exercised over colonial finances, including the requirement of Colonial Office approval for the annual estimates and certain important items. Although this was referred to as 'financial devolution', as K. C. Ashton from the Colonial Office was to reveal in 1956, Treasury control over Hong Kong finances remained more stringent than in the colonies of Africa and the Fiji Islands. This control was made possible because, unlike the other colonies, there was an absence of 'an unofficial majority in the Legislative Council' (read nationalist demands) (CO 1030/392, Financial Devolution of Hong Kong, original 1948, revisions 1956).

However, Ashton also noted that, although Grantham never asked for financial devolution, in practice he ignored the entire system of consultation and regulation. Thus annual estimates (or the budget) were presented to the Colonial Office only after the legislature voted on them and when they were virtually unalterable. Later, we will see how the Governor was also able to protect the currency interests of local traders against stringent sterling regulations. The Ashton note frankly admitted that this kind of *de facto* financial autonomy of the Governor and the nominated legislature may have been better for the empire than publicized devolution, which could have incited more radical politicians to constitutional reform. It was hardly desirable to give 'the vote and influence to the working classes as distinct from the business classes, because the working classes might be expected to require more of a welfare state and hence a great increase in government expenditure'.[5]

Grantham's policies were successful from the perspective of the new imperialism. Hong Kong would serve the imperial metropole in the empire's efforts to stay financially viable: it would generate dollar resources and, as we shall see, provide opportunities for UK citizens and corporations in the financial markets. In return, the colony acquired local control over other financial matters and a limited degree of self-governance. Although there were many irritants and loopholes in this contract, the balance it struck seemed to work for both metropole and elites in the dependency. While perhaps the success of the new imperialism was related to its inevitable finitude, it worked because of the absence of nationalist pressures to demand more than the contract could deliver.

Hong Kong and the Cold War

This brings us to the historical force behind the weakness of nationalism in Hong Kong – the Cold War. In its ideal expression, the Cold War represented a logical culmination of the new imperialism: two superpowers sought to gain the loyalty of theoretically sovereign nation-states, which would, however, be militarily dependent upon the hegemonic power and subject to its political, economic and ideological strategies. Of course, historical reality was much messier; first there were rivalries within each camp and the British did not give up hope of superpower status until the Suez crisis of 1956 and the Taiwan Straits crisis of 1958 (Tsang 2006: 10, 194). In this respect, the Soviet–PRC split was much more consequential in realigning the balance of power. Second, there was the historical force of nationalism operating not only within each bloc, but also outside it through the non-aligned movement (the rhetoric of which was perhaps more powerful than its politics), which resisted the hegemons and their strategies. Finally, the very polarization of the hegemons itself permitted certain key players such as Hong Kong to leverage their status as intermediaries and contested spots between the two powers.

With the advent of the Korean War, the principal battles of the Cold War moved from Europe to East Asia. One might say that the Cold War had its hottest moments in East Asia, Korea, Vietnam and Malaya, among others. Until 1950, the USA did not show much interest in the British possession of Hong Kong, which they believed would be returned to China. But with the shift in the theatre of the Cold War, and in particular after the USA launched the Seventh Fleet in the Taiwan Straits, the USA became more committed to British control of Hong Kong. Once the safety of Hong Kong was assured, the British rhetoric of the Cold War escalated and Hong Kong was declared to be the Berlin of the East: the bastion that had to be defended if the world was not to fall to Communism. In addition, of course, protecting Hong Kong was also crucial to protecting the British Empire, because the turn to communism in Hong Kong would surely affect the growing unrest of the European empires in Southeast Asia (Tsang 2006: 60–87). In this way, colonial interests became folded into the Cold War vision of 'freedom' and prosperity.

The domino theory surfaced as the communist-led insurgency in Malaya erupted in 1948 and the Vietnamese communists successfully battled the French. By 1950, British troop strength in Hong Kong was increased from a few thousand to 30,000. Hong Kong during the 1950s and 1960s was equally the seat of covert operations as of free trade. At different times, and sometimes simultaneously, the KMT, as party; the secret agency of the ROC government in Taiwan; and the Ministry of Defence on the island ran – often uncoordinated – operations in Hong Kong. These included sabotage, recruiting and coordinating secret agents in the PRC, consolidating secret societies, running training centres, accumulating arms and explosives, and the like. US agencies such as the CIA conducted covert operations, and others such as the USIS or the Free Trade Union Committee of the American Federation of Labor sought to work through cultural agencies and working class groups. PRC partisans in Hong Kong infiltrated society at every level from the secret societies to glee clubs, but especially organizations of students, teachers and working groups in the transport industry (FO 371/105354, 561; File HKRS163-1-909, 581; File HKRS163-1-931; Wong 1972: 106–9; Tsang 2006: 60, 167–75).

Yet what made Hong Kong different from Berlin was that the British rulers did not wish to foment resistance against the PRC. Rather, Grantham sought to produce a dependence of the PRC upon Hong Kong, so that the colony could be left to develop in peace until its (in his opinion) inevitable transfer to China in 1997. Officially, he sought to maintain a policy of neutrality. In effect, that meant that the British authorities would not meddle with the clandestine operations on either side unless they became too visible (Tsang 2006: 165). As we have seen, however, Hong Kong did become the site in which the battles of the Cold War were waged at a political and ideological level. While the colonial authorities were not interested in conducting the political war, they saw economic development and the ideology of market freedom as the surer path to drive local nationalists away from alliance with communists.

Indeed, it was not only its position in the new imperialism, but the relative weakness of nationalism in Hong Kong that gave it a special advantage in the world economy and success in the free market. This weakness derived in great part from the Cold War itself as the political energies of the territory's population were split between the PRC and ROC. Indeed, popular movements embodying the spirit of nationalist resistance to continued British rule were by no means in short supply immediately after the Second World War in Hong Kong. But the colonial question became obscured after the onset of the Cold War (Li 2000). Moreover, the colonial government also rejected Mark Young's 1946 plan to develop a special Hong Kong identity as a democratic self-governing people. In other words, the kinds of nationalist passions that often pressured the nation-state to denounce formally unequal relationships and impose strict restrictions on economic relationships both within and with other nations were weak, if not absent, in Hong Kong. Revealingly, Hong Kong did not have a central bank. To be sure, as a colony, it did suffer from London's Sterling Area restrictions, but at the same time the local colonial state exercised sufficient autonomy – significantly, by leveraging its economic position between the PRC and the USA – to gain enormous currency advantage that would make it a global financial centre.

The Hong Kong gap: the ideology of the non-ideological

The local state in Hong Kong had not only become deeply committed to Hong Kong, but it became perforce much more interventionist than it had been. One of the curiosities of the new imperialism was the insistence of the colonial state that it continued to represent *laissez faire* government even when it was interventionist. To be sure, the state intervened mostly for the commercial and financial capitalists, but the emergent industrial interests also benefited from its activities.

Most scholars are agreed that, with regard to the infrastructure of society, Hong Kong was a most active state. Thus the creation of massive public housing and roads, port facilities, waterworks and other public amenities were designed ultimately to sustain the capitalist growth of this society. Public housing was especially symbolic of this effort. The scheme was triggered by the dangerous fires that periodically devastated the vast squatter colonies along hill slopes and mud flats; the Shek Kip Mei fire of 1953 was the most immediate trigger. Alan Smart argues that the government programme of resettlement was principally a response to Cold War imperatives because the PRC made much of the colony's neglect of the Chinese population during these fires. Yet the subsidized and concentrated mass housing programme became an important ingredient of the cheap labour force that worked in the growing numbers of export-oriented factories in the colony (Castells *et al.* 1990; Faure 2003: 27–31; Smart 2007).

Most scholars also agree that Hong Kong was – as we have seen – no welfare state, and was singularly free of financial regulation. Yet absence of regulation did not signify non-intervention. Indeed, the local state had to intervene consistently to oppose both metropolitan and international financial strictures on the economy.[6] During the 1950s and 1960s, this produced the well known 'Hong Kong gap'.

Colonial bureaucrats recognized that Hong Kong's most valuable economic legacy from the preceding century of colonial rule was the strength of regional capitalism.

Historical networks formed by native banks and local merchants, often organized along native-place lines, had sustained Hong Kong as an *entrepot* and a centre for remittances to China from Southeast Asia and elsewhere. To be sure, these regional networks scarcely existed apart from British imperial corporations and colonial institutions. As Hamashita has shown, the major Western banks spread their activities and connected the region (China and Southeast Asia) by aligning themselves with Chinese remittance and trade networks, and developed a symbiotic relationship with them.

Indeed, the networks also flourished because of their participation in the Sterling Area, which guaranteed monetary stability and preferential access to Hong Kong goods in the Sterling Area markets, including the UK (Schenk: 9) From as early as 1952, British Parliamentary records voiced noisy complaints about cheap goods from Hong Kong flooding the British market and disadvantaging British industrial producers (BT 64/4562). Since, however, sterling was being strengthened by the dollar earnings of Hong Kong entrepreneurs earned precisely by its economic competitiveness, the government in UK could not pressure the colonial government to the same degree as it might have earlier to restrict imports from Hong Kong (Schenk: 81).

The colonial government actively protected local businesses, including native banks and merchant networks, from the restrictive sterling policies of the metropole. As a result, Hong Kong saw the operation of two currency systems: one referred to the large, usually foreign banks and firms subject to the fixed exchange rate and sterling policies of the British government; the other to the local and regional networks that utilized a market exchange rate with the US dollar that was necessary for Hong Kong to function in its historical role as an *entrepot*.

In a narrow sense, Hong Kong acquired its importance as an international financial centre because of this peculiar structure, or what came to be known as the 'Hong Kong gap': the colony could benefit from the Sterling Area while at the same time significant groups – most notably local bankers and merchants – possessed the capacity to avoid the financial strictures imposed by colonial rule. The differential between the value of the dollar according to the fixed exchange rate and its floating market value invited vast amounts of capital from all over the world to gain advantage from currency arbitrage. This inflow also financed, to some extent, the industrialization of Hong Kong, which in turn added to its dollar and sterling earnings from export (Schenk: 82–85).

The immediate agents and beneficiaries of the Hong Kong gap were the local merchant and banking communities involved originally in the *entrepot* trade. Merchants from South China had taken over the *entrepot* trade from the Europeans as early as the 1870s. Goods brought in by large ships from Europe and the USA were reshipped to other parts of East and Southeast Asia in smaller Asian boats and ships. During the war, this trade had abruptly diminished, but the trans-shipment trade returned with renewed strength and expanded coverage. Indeed, the argument made to allow Hong Kong merchants to retain 75 per cent of their earnings in US dollars (and surrender 25 per cent at the official exchange rate) warned that, unless merchants received dollars at the market value, they would be outcompeted in the predominantly US dollar-dominated *entrepot* trade by merchants from Macao and other ports that did not have the same constraints (CO 1030/292; Schenk: 21–23, 103).

Although trans-shipment from Hong Kong suffered as a result of the US- and UN-sanctioned embargo on strategic exports to China after the Korean War, these merchants networks were able to by-pass many of these constraints. They also benefited from the growth of industry in the PRC and the attendant export of industrial goods destined for overseas markets via Hong Kong during the mid-1950s and especially the 1960s. PRC companies built up large trade surpluses and demanded payment in sterling rather than in dollars because of the status of the USA as a political and economic foe. (Schenk: 40–41, 85). Thus the alignments of the Cold War contributed still further to the Hong Kong gap by creating a politically influenced demand for pound sterling to be exchanged in the free market rather than at the official rate.

Conclusions

This study has deliberately focused on a macro-perspective to shed light on some of the critical continuities and discontinuities of imperialism. As such, it has neglected accounts that allow us to see how local groups adapted to and shaped colonial society, such as the studies of empire in Cooper and Stoler's (1997) *Tensions of Empire*. A fuller understanding will require supplementation by such accounts; for instance, local agency, particularly of the financial and mercantile bourgeoisie, was surely important in grasping how the colonial government in Hong Kong developed the local commitment it did, and why it took the particular form of *laissez faire* that it did.

At the same time, the structure of the new imperialism cannot be easily dismissed. We have seen how the colonial government actively protected local interests in the free dollar market when the Treasury in London sought to curb, if not outlaw, this market in Hong Kong. One clue to the answer may lie in the fact that, while colonial authorities in Hong Kong were able to successfully resist these efforts in the dollar market, it was not able to prevent the interdiction on converting gold into dollars. Many British citizens also profited from the conversion of pounds into dollars in the Hong Kong free market; but the market in gold was restricted principally to Asian merchants (Schenk: 118). This suggests that the colonial government was successful where there were also benefits for metropolitan citizens.

Moreover, local circumstances cannot be divorced from global developments. Perhaps the most distinctive circumstance of Hong Kong was the weakness of political nationalism, which can in great part be traced to the Cold War that sustained the CCP–KMT rivalry. It seems doubtful that the local colonial authorities would have been able to balance local and metropolitan interests in the way they did if nationalism had been an active force in Hong Kong. Few nationalist financial authorities or central banks could tolerate the kind of dual system that undercut its sovereign authority.

While post-war nationalism in the new states led to certain patterns of industrial development often involving autarky, the peculiar structure of power in Hong Kong composed of absent nationalism and divided sovereignty (between Great Britain and local elites) led it towards a different economic path. It was a path that resulted in its status as an international financial centre, a global economic hub and agent of globalization. This status was undoubtedly a result of exceptional circumstances, but it turned out to be highly futuristic. Is it significant that, for almost 20 years in the post-war era, the Hong Kong education system did not educate its citizens in the history of Hong Kong, and that today the Shanghai high school history texts have also tried to downplay national pedagogy by omitting references to Mao Zedong and the Nanjing massacre?

The Hong Kong model of early globalization was fed by the convergence of the colonial doctrine of *laissez faire* and the Cold War ideology of 'freedom'. Behind these slogans was an active if selective strategy of intervention to ensure the conditions of capitalist competitiveness. These conditions did not entail a welfare state that was prevalent in the mature capitalist societies. The slogans also diverted attention away from the fundamentally non-democratic character of this neo-colony. The swollen labour force that crowded the colony worked long hours and in unhealthy conditions; they had minimal legal protections and weak bargaining power. The colonial government had secured the conditions for their maximal utilization. Was this the historical condition of 'freedom' that won the Cold War?

Notes

1 Robert Ward claims that much of the Japanese violence was directed against Westerners, and that the military stepped in to control the rape with the provision of military prostitutes and strict laws that applied to the Japanese troops. He also notes that gang warfare between the Triads and the Green Gang claiming adherence to the KMT was widely prevalent during these years (see Ward 1943: 15–17). Certainly, the Japanese military utilized the Triads extensively.
2 See Shamsuipo District Kaifong Welfare Advancement Association Annual Report (1st issue) January 1951 (Hong Kong).
3 See for instance the attached note from the Hong Kong office in Britain to the Financial Secretary of Hong Kong, which asked for an elucidation on paragraph 6 'to show what disadvantages would result if the Colony walked out of the sterling area. Needless to say I did not get what I asked for.' (476 File HKRS163-1-761)
4 See the exchanges regarding SEATO in FO 371/ 111883 and FO 371/ 111882. See also 449 File HKRS163-1-711 for the exchanges regarding ECAFE.
5 David Faure has a most illuminating perspective on the question of social welfare in Hong Kong. His research reveals that the Colonial Office in the 1950s urged Hong Kong to spend more of its resources on welfare, but that opposition to this expenditure, and increased taxes, actually emerged from the local elites in the legislature. In his opinion, the Grantham regime did not do too badly in having to chart its way between 'appeasing their superiors without as much as toeing the welfare-state line' (Faure 2003: 35).
6 For complaints from regulators of the Bretton Woods system and the UN, see 449 File HKRS163-1-711; 756 File HKRS163-1-1199; FO 371/111883.

12

THE HAPLESS IMPERIALIST? PORTUGUESE RULE IN 1960s MACAU

Cathryn Clayton

In the winter of 1966–67, the tiny city of Macau, which had been governed by the Portuguese since the mid-sixteenth century, was shaken by a series of anti-government demonstrations led by students sporting red armbands and brandishing little red books. These Cultural Revolution-inspired demonstrations cumulated in a riot in which Portuguese forces killed eight Chinese residents, wounded over 200, and made 62 arrests.[1] But by January 1967, as a direct result of the violence, the Portuguese administration had been forced to apologize for its actions and capitulate to a series of demands placed upon it by Chinese residents of Macau and by the Chinese Communist Party. Although the People's Republic of China did not assume formal control of Macau until 1999, many observers view the '123 Incident' – as these events were immediately dubbed, since the deaths occurred on 3 December 1966 (12/3) – as the point at which the Portuguese lost effective sovereignty over the city. From then on, Macau became known as a 'half-liberated area'.

The 123 Incident has been interpreted as a classic case of (Chinese, communist) anti-colonial protest meeting (foreign) colonial violence: a crisis that revealed the true brutality of colonialism and the true strength of the Chinese people united under Maoism. Despite the political expediency of this interpretation, which has served a number of different agendas in the past four decades, it does not tell us much about what spurred a portion of Macau residents to action at that particular time and place. Neither does it illuminate the specificities of Portuguese rule in Macau that led to this particular denouement – in contrast, for example, to the British in Hong Kong, who crushed similar (though more violent) unrest a few months later. While some have attributed this difference to a distinctly Portuguese style of colonialism, this attribution begs the question of how that style arose.[2] And while some have suggested that the 123 Incident represented the effective end of Portuguese colonialism in Macau, this characterization ignores the extent to which the 123 Incident and its aftermath can instead be seen as an intensification of the

Macau administration's long-standing policy of compromise with the Chinese state. Drawing on interview material collected as part of an oral history project funded by the University of Macau, this chapter takes the 123 Incident as a lens through which to examine the practices of Portuguese governance in Macau in the last half-century of its rule. In these interviews, eyewitnesses to and participants in the events of 1966–67 suggest that the strength of the Portuguese presence in Macau lay not in its tanks and guns, but in its apologies and capitulations.

Colonialism, Portuguese style

To the extent that there was something we might call a Portuguese style of colonialism in Macau, it was not something irreducibly Portuguese as much as it was the product of the unique historical circumstances that shaped the imperial ambitions and colonial ideologies of the Portuguese expansion in East Asia. In the mid-sixteenth and early seventeenth centuries, Macau was a key node in Portugal's 'seaborne empire' (Boxer 1969) – an empire born of the desire to overcome the Muslim realms that controlled the overland trade routes between Europe and Asia (and that had, until the mid-thirteenth century, controlled Portugal as well) by monopolizing the sea trade in spices and other luxury goods with Asia and by forging political alliances with the Christian kingdoms that were believed to exist in the East.[3] These goals meant that, unlike the European empires that succeeded it (and unlike the Portuguese empire in Africa or America), the Portuguese in Asia had little interest in controlling land or natural resources; the *Estado da Índia*, as the empire from Goa to Nagasaki was called, consisted of a series of relatively autonomous fortified port cities strung across the Indian Ocean and the South China Sea, connected only fractiously and tenuously to one another and to Lisbon.

As one such city, Macau experienced its 'golden age' between 1580 and 1640, when (among other factors) restrictive trade policies in Ming China and Edo Japan provided the conditions for the Portuguese to play a profitable role in the traffic in Chinese goods across Asia. When, in the decades that followed, Portugal's hold on Asian trade routes began to disintegrate due to changing conditions in Japan and China and attacks by the Dutch and the British, Macau entered a period of decline from which it never truly recovered. The British establishment of Hong Kong in 1842 was the final blow to Macau's status as a commercial hub. Without the land area, population, resources or technology for modern industry, the Portuguese administration of Macau turned to activities deemed illegal or immoral elsewhere: the traffic in coolies, opium and gold, and (most notoriously) gambling, which was legalized in 1850 and since the 1960s has accounted for more than half of government revenue. The Portuguese in Macau also never abandoned, as did the British and the Dutch elsewhere, its dependence on monopolies: throughout the twentieth century, the Macau government financed itself by selling to the highest bidder monopoly rights over one of several industries (gambling, or the sale of opium, gold or electricity) in return for a percentage of the profits.

Portugal's governance of Macau was also shaped by its interactions with the Chinese state. When Jorge Álvares first set foot on Lingding Island in the Pearl River Delta in 1513, the Ming dynasty was a force to be reckoned with. Despite the much-vaunted superiority of their ships and firepower, the Portuguese skirmished several times with Ming naval forces and lost. It was not until 1557 that they managed to establish a self-governing settlement on Chinese soil, and then only as a result of negotiations between Portuguese traders, local Chinese merchants and Ming officials. They were allowed to remain in Macau at the pleasure of the emperor, governing only themselves and the few Chinese who converted to Christianity, in return for an annual ground rent, a supply of foreign goods and technologies, and military assistance when called for. At the first sign of truculence, the Chinese state could (and on occasion did) simply close the border gate and order its subjects to leave the walled city, depriving the Portuguese of food, water and services.[4] In this sense, some historians have suggested obliquely or overtly that, prior to 1849, the Portuguese in Macau resembled not so much colonizers as counterparts of the other 'barbarian' populations on China's borders, subject to the Ming and Qing policy of 'using foreigners to control foreigners' (Fok 1996; Tang 1997).

This changed in 1849, when, in mimicry of the British next door in Hong Kong, Macau's Governor Ferreira do Amaral declared Macau a free port, ordered the cessation of ground rent payments, expelled the Chinese customs officials, and demanded legal jurisdiction over all Chinese residing within the city. Despite this attempt to assert its status as a colonizing power, by the mid-nineteenth century Portugal was hardly in a position to pose a threat to the Qing (except through its alliance with Great Britain, which was troubled at best). Thus, regardless of the treaty that the Qing finally signed in 1887 granting Portugal the right to occupy and govern Macau in perpetuity, little changed in terms of Macau's dependence on China or of Portugal's willingness to toe the lines drawn by the Chinese state. Repeatedly throughout the twentieth century, Portugal attempted projects that displeased the Qing, the Nationalist Party, or the CCP – such as building a new port, delimiting Macau's northern boundary, even celebrating the 400th anniversary of Portuguese rule – and was forced to abandon its plans. This state of colonial dependence was summed up in an image prevalent in the mid-1990s: that of the Portuguese Governor of Macau seated at a table with Stanley Ho (who held the gambling monopoly) on his right and the head of the New China News Agency (Xinhua she, the PRC's official representative in Macau) on his left: whenever he wanted to do anything, the joke went, he had to turn to his right to ask for the money to do it, and to his left to ask for permission to spend it. In this sense, by the standards of other modern imperial formations in China, colonialism Portuguese style (in Macau at least) gives new meaning to the term 'semi-colonialism': it was 'semi' as in 'sort-of' colonialism, a condition in which the answer to the question of whether China or Portugal held supreme authority over Macau could change from moment to moment, from situation to situation.

But the twentieth-century ideology of Portuguese colonialism made a virtue of this apparent weakness. This ideology, which became known as 'lusotropicalism', held that Portuguese expansion was an enterprise not of economic exploitation, but of racial and cultural mixing that was more humane and progressive than its northern European counterparts. It suggested – almost in so many words – that tiny Portugal had been able to colonize so much of the world because it made love, not war.[5] In place of the ideologies of free trade, the rule of law, and racial purity that characterized the British imperial project, lusotropicalism extolled the organic power of *mestiçagem* (mixing), which had created societies that, although materially impoverished, were characterized by an unusual degree of intercultural tolerance and hybridity. Although this rhetoric bore little relationship to the actual practice of Portuguese colonialism, which was just as brutal, racist and extractive as any other (Anderson 1962; Boxer 1963), the rhetoric does matter to an analysis of Portuguese governance in Macau. It matters to the extent that it legitimized the Eurasian community from Macau, indispensable in the day-to-day administration of the Portuguese empire in Asia since the sixteenth century, who are today known as the Macanese but many of whom identify proudly as 'Portuguese of the Orient'. It matters insofar as it was invoked to legitimize the Portuguese state's policies of neglect – benign or malign, depending on your perspective – which by the 1960s had left Macau without a robust economy, a well ordered society or a well educated populace. And it matters because this rhetoric informed (and still informs) the actions and views of many Portuguese and Macanese in coming to grips with the violence of the 123 Incident and its meaning.

Macau in 1966

This, then, was Macau in 1966: a city of fewer than 200,000 residents (more than 95 per cent of whom identified as Chinese) crammed into less than 20 square kilometres, with low standards of living, little modern industry, and high rates of poverty and illiteracy.[6] Public coffers were nearly empty. The Catholic church and Chinese civic associations – not the state – ran schools, a hospital and other social services for the vast majority of Chinese residents. The colonial administration was run by a handful of military men who depended on a small coterie of Macanese and local Chinese interlocutors to keep them in touch with their Chinese subjects, and to maintain the fragile balance of interests between the two business syndicates, comprised of two groups of ethnic Chinese elites, which controlled the two largest and most lucrative monopolies. One monopoly was the gold trade, which was the domain of a small clique of merchants led by Ho Yin and Chui Tak-kei, 'red capitalists' who headed Macau's Chinese Commerce Association and who had close ties with Zhou Enlai, Liao Chengzhi, Tao Zhu and other 'moderates' in the Chinese Communist Party. The other was the gambling franchise, which the Portuguese administration had taken away from Ho Yin's associates in 1962 and awarded instead to a group of Hong Kong-based financiers headed by Stanley Ho, which, although sometimes labelled 'right wing' in contrast to the Ho Yin group (see Hanna 1969), professed little ideology beyond the pursuit of profit. As Macau was one of the few places in Asia where either of these activities could be undertaken legally,[7] both were enormously profitable enterprises. Competition between the two syndicates for control of both monopolies was vicious: by July 1966, the pressure both sides brought to bear on the Portuguese administration was so intense that Governor António Lopes dos Santos resigned his post and returned to Portugal (Fernandes 2006). The metropole to which he returned, meanwhile, had the lowest standard of living in Europe, little industry, and a rate of illiteracy that far exceeded that of Macau.[8] The António de Oliveira Salazar dictatorship (known as the Estado Novo), while clinging to its colonies as the basis of Portugal's greatness, was at the same time fighting a losing battle to hold on to them: in 1961, Portugal lost Goa, Damão and Diu to the Indian army, and began a long, brutal and costly war against independence fighters in Angola, Mozambique and Guinea-Bissau.[9] The Estado Novo's right-wing ideology meant that Portugal had not only outlawed trade unions and censored the press, both at home and in the colonies, but also refused to recognize the PRC, even 17 years after its founding.

Meanwhile, although China considered Macau to be its territory, the Portuguese presence made the city too important as a source of gold, commodities and information for the CCP, under embargo by the West and no longer on speaking terms with the USSR, to repossess it.[10] Conversely, Macau depended too heavily on the mainland for water, food, electricity and profitable (though largely illicit) trade to want to provoke a showdown. It had a strong Nationalist Party presence in the form of labour unions, guilds, schools, charities and triad associations, and, since 1949, a growing CCP presence in the form of neighbourhood associations, labour unions, schools and a *de facto* embassy (Nam Kwong Company). By the early 1960s, a balance of interests among all parties seemed to have been reached, and Sino–Portuguese relations seemed to be undergoing a rapprochement as small groups of Portuguese and Macanese civilians were invited to tour the PRC. But, as the country became swept up in the Cultural Revolution in 1966, in Macau this balance began to tip. In leftist schools, regular course content was replaced with the teachings of Mao Zedong, and 'struggle sessions' came to occupy more and more classroom hours. More importantly, Ho Yin's authority as the acknowledged representative of the Macau Chinese community to the Portuguese administration was challenged by a coalition of workers, students and teachers from more radical Maoist organizations. Ho Yin is reported to have told the Acting Governor of Macau, Colonel Carlos da Mota Cerveira – who ruled Macau between July and November 1966 – that this group was beginning to call him a 'lackey of the Portuguese'.[11]

The 123 Incident

The events of 3 December 1966 neither began nor ended on that date.[12] In July of that year, a leftist association on Taipa – one of Macau's two outlying islands – had applied to the government for a permit to demolish two abandoned buildings in Taipa Village and build an elementary school in their place. On 15 November, after four months of waiting in vain for a response, a group of about 100 Taipa residents began demolishing the buildings in question, permit or no permit. Their work came to the attention of the Administrator of the Islands, Rui de Andrade, who ordered the Taipa police to put a stop to it. A small number of unarmed policemen went to the scene, where the workers lobbed stones and insults at them. Meanwhile, the acting governor asked Chui Tak-kei from the Chinese Chamber of Commerce to intervene; he did, and by 11 a.m. the crowd had dispersed. But some two hours later, the workers resumed their demolition work. Police were again sent to the scene, armed this time with rattan shields and rubber truncheons, and eventually managed to clear the work site. In the process, however, there were several injuries on both sides, and the police made six arrests.[13]

The incident instantly became city-wide news as the local Chinese papers ran stories and photographs condemning the 'bloody conflict provoked by the Portuguese authorities'. Groups of students and workers visited the wounded in the hospital to witness first-hand the effects of Portuguese brutality, and an *ad hoc* committee of Taipa residents presented the government with a list of demands, including reparations to the wounded, the immediate release of detainees, the punishment of Andrade and the police chief, immediate authorization for work to continue on the school, and the destruction of all rubber truncheons, which were believed to be especially dangerous implements that 'injure internally, not externally'.

On 30 November, the Taipa incident became national news as the mainland Chinese media reported on the incident for the first time, accusing the Portuguese of 'Fascist atrocities against Chinese nationals' (*HK Star*, 1 December 1966). Macau's CCP-run newspaper, the *Macau Daily*, began using the language of ultra-leftist radicalism: the Portuguese authorities were 'ruthless imperialists'; the patriotic Chinese of Macau, guided by Mao Zedong thought, would rise up and refuse to be bullied. That same day, a group of 60-odd students and workers demonstrated in front of the seat of government (the Palácio do Governo) in support of the Taipa residents' petition, shouting slogans and reading aloud from Mao's Little Red Book. The demonstrations escalated until, on Saturday 3 December, student protestors demanded an audience with the governor and tried to charge up the stairs into his office. As the police tried to stop them, the rumour that the Portuguese police were throwing Chinese schoolchildren off the second floor of the Palácio do Governo flew through the streets, and the crowd outside grew to more than 2,000. Riot police were brought in with water cannons and tear gas, which simply escalated the conflict. Public buildings and monuments downtown – symbols of Portuguese rule – were attacked by groups of mostly young men, who trashed the public records office, toppled a statue of a Macanese military hero in the main square, and tried to storm police headquarters. The army was called in and martial law declared as tanks rolled through the narrow streets. By nightfall on Sunday 4 December, eight Chinese had been killed (five of whom were under the age of 20), scores wounded and dozens arrested. And the new Governor of Macau – Brigadier-General José Manuel Nobre de Carvalho, veteran of colonial administrations in Cape Verde and Angola, who had arrived in Macau only ten days *after* the Taipa clash, and who had not even been told about the rising tensions until a few hours before his boat docked in Macau – had agreed to the Taipa residents' demands.

But over the next few weeks, Nobre de Carvalho was presented with list after list of escalating demands from the Macau Chinese Students' Association, the 'All Circles Committee' (comprised of the leaders of local leftist organizations), and the Guangdong Province Foreign Affairs Office. The first two groups pressed for a formal apology, punishment of government officials, reparations, a promise never again to use force against the people of Macau, and an admission that the Portuguese state had committed 'fascist crimes' against the Chinese people. Guangdong upped the stakes by demanding the expulsion from Macau of all organizations and individuals with ties to the Nationalist Party (and its regime on Taiwan), and the extradition of seven Nationalist Party spies whom the Portuguese had captured in Macau waters in 1963.

Almost as quickly as these demands were presented, the Governor agreed to them. By Christmas 1966, four Portuguese officials had been dismissed, the spies handed over to the People's Liberation Army, and the display of Nationalist Party flags in Macau prohibited. The administration borrowed over $2 million from local merchants to cover the cost of compensating the victims and their families. The police not only stopped carrying rubber truncheons, they virtually stopped policing; public order was kept by civilian teams organized by neighbourhood associations and the Chinese Chamber of Commerce. The only sticking point was the wording of the apology: in Lisbon, Salazar refused to allow Portuguese soldiers to be called 'criminals'.

Over the next few weeks, as Macau residents, encouraged by compatriots from across the border, paraded through the streets carrying Mao posters and chanting revolutionary slogans, the Governor tried to negotiate between the adamantly anti-communist Salazar, who (still smarting from the loss of Goa) insisted that capitulation would spell the end of Portuguese sovereignty over Macau, and the equally adamant Chinese communists, who insisted that the demands be met unconditionally. Chinese gunboats circled the waters around Macau and mass rallies clogged the city's streets. Rumours flew: the Communists were going to cut the electricity and poison the water; the PLA was preparing to invade; hordes of Red Guards were massing on the border; the Portuguese were preparing to abandon Macau. The Hong Kong Government, which was keeping a close eye on the events in Macau, drew up secret plans to accommodate the entire Portuguese garrison (some 1000 soldiers) in case of a wholesale evacuation.[14] Thousands of Macau residents fled the city, and the economy came to a standstill. On 25 January, groups of Macau Chinese residents mounted the 'Three No's' campaign, paying no taxes, selling no goods, and providing no services to the Portuguese. A few days later, Salazar allowed the Governor the autonomy to decide his own course of action, and on 29 January 1967, Nobre de Carvalho and two aides, dressed in civilian clothes, were escorted into the Chinese Chamber of Commerce conference room and seated at a table under a portrait of Mao Zedong, where they signed an 'admission of guilt', were served tea, and were escorted out again past cheering crowds.

Beijing made it clear that, as of the signing, it considered the case closed. But over the next months, the tension, the marches, demonstrations and minor clashes continued.

A letter written in July 1967 by a Portuguese civil servant in Macau to a friend in Mozambique describes a situation of near anarchy: leftist organizations 'control traffic, close streets to transit, do whatever they want' – organizing mass rallies against the Catholic Church, detaining the British consul, covering the home of a wealthy Macanese merchant with graffiti and big-character posters – 'while we [sit here], arms crossed'.[15] Finally, in August 1968, the CCP sent an envoy to Macau to urge local communists to quell their activism and allow Macau's political and economic situation to return to normal. But back in Lisbon, Salazar was reported to have said that, in the wake of the Governor's actions in Macau, 'there still existed the outward signs of [our] sovereignty: the flag, the currency, a few officials. But…we were no longer sovereigns: we were merely the administrators of a 'joint venture' [*condomínio*] under foreign supervision' (Nogueira 1986: 217). This attitude was evident in the Portuguese administration's response in the years that followed, when, as two of our interviewees put it, the Portuguese administration virtually abandoned any aspect of government that pertained to the Chinese in Macau. Even in the late 1990s, as the handover approached, many residents of Macau felt that the formal transfer of sovereignty would not make much difference to their lives: for, ever since the 123 Incident, the Portuguese in Macau had been 'merely actors in a stage play directed by Beijing'.[16]

Remembering Portuguese rule

In 2005, my colleague Agnes Lam and I received funding to prepare an oral history of this key crisis point in the twentieth-century history of Macau. Nearly 40 years after the events, and six years after the end of Portuguese rule, we began asking eyewitnesses and participants to evaluate the causes of the 123 Incident. One of the key points of contention that emerged across our interviews was the question of whether the 123 Incident was a manifestation of the Cultural Revolution or an expression of local grievances. This was not a question that we asked our interviewees; in fact, initially I found it a singularly unsatisfying way of thinking about the problem, for how can the Cultural Revolution be understood except by picking apart how local interests became caught up in the rhetoric and practices of a revolution that proclaimed itself not just national but global in scale? But it was a question that virtually all of our interviewees seemed bent on answering; and in thinking about this insistence, I realized that for many of them, assessing the causes of the 123 Incident was a way of assessing the effects of Portuguese rule.

While a majority of respondents attributed the conflict to outside forces – a kind of 'spillover' of the Cultural Revolution that had been orchestrated by Red Guards from across the border – a significant and articulate minority emphasized local factors that had little to do with Maoist radicalism. A retired Portuguese naval officer, António, began our interview by asserting that he believed the 123 Incident 'had nothing to do with the Cultural Revolution'. According to him, the whole thing had been orchestrated by Ho Yin and his cronies as a last-ditch (and ultimately successful) attempt to prevent the Portuguese from taking the gold concession away from them; the local 'communist' elites, he argued, were simply using the Cultural Revolution to further their own capitalist ends (see also Fernandes 2006). In his comments, António portrayed Macau as a place where Ho Yin was the one truly in charge: he was the administration's only channel of communication with the Chinese in Macau and in the PRC; he ran the banks, controlled the dockworkers' and transport unions; financed the private hospital and the biggest charities in town; he even paid for the police uniforms. In António's view, the Portuguese administration had been hamstrung by its own *laissez faire* approach to governance and its near-total reliance on monopolies run by one or two powerful Chinese individuals. Threatening to give the gold concession to outsider Stanley Ho in return for a higher percentage of the profits was an ill-conceived attempt to assert an authority that the Portuguese had never had; the 123 Incident was Ho Yin's way of reminding them that, although they were nominal sovereigns of Macau, he personally was the one who held real power.

Other interviewees, ethnic Chinese men who had been active participants in the rioting, denied that their actions had been orchestrated either by Ho Yin or the Red Guards; instead they cited frustration with the irrational, inefficient and discriminatory everyday practices of Portuguese governance. They recalled endless bureaucratic delays and absurd, inflexible regulations, such as the rule that all government documents and all public signs – including those on public toilets – be written only in Portuguese, despite the fact that the majority of Macau residents could not read Portuguese because the government had made no effort to facilitate Portuguese-language instruction in schools. 'When you go to a public toilet and you don't know which one is for men and which for women, it does cause you some inconvenience!' laughed one. Others cited more immediate causes as the 'real' reasons behind the incident: recent conflicts between street hawkers and the police, sporadic tensions between the taxi drivers' union and the government, and brewing resentment over an unpopular 1964 tax hike. These accounts suggest that the 123 Incident gave expression not to Maoist fervour or even to anti-colonial sentiment *per se*, but to frustrations with specific ill-conceived policies, the arrogance and intransigence of individual governors, and the corruption and incompetence of low-level bureaucrats.

This image of the Portuguese in 1960s Macau as a weak, inefficient and irrational governing power resonates with the image that emerged in eyewitness descriptions of the conflict itself: the Portuguese in Macau, far from being ruthless imperialists (as the CCP would portray them), or faultless imperialists (as the lusotropicalists would have it), were hapless imperialists. The narratives of military men, protesters and observers alike ring with irony as they describe Portuguese police trying to dispel the crowds by using fire hoses that didn't have enough water pressure; throwing tear gas canisters rusted shut from years of storage in humid armouries and then standing downwind; trying to defend themselves with rattan shields eaten through by termites; and, tragically, firing live ammunition when rubber bullets would have more than sufficed.

Virtually all our respondents, including those who counted the 123 Incident as a 'victory' for the Chinese people, invoked comparisons with Hong Kong, and described the British response to the 1967 'disturbances' as quick, efficient and decisive – a stark contrast to the risible frailty of the Portuguese state. Rather than a wholesale condemnation of Portuguese rule, however, many of our interviewees suggested that, while the state's frailty and its distance from the everyday lives of the vast majority of Chinese residents of the city had been a key cause of the unrest, in the longer term these same factors had in fact been a kind of comparative advantage, for the Portuguese administration as well as for the residents themselves.

One Macanese interviewee, José, an architect who had served in city administration in the 1960s, felt that the frailty of the state had engendered in Macau a unique and resilient local culture characterized by the commonality of 'human warmth and decency' (renqing) across ethnic lines, which had in fact prevented the 123 Incident from playing out even worse than it did.[17] He and several other Portuguese and Macanese interviewees noted that the boycott of January 1967 was largely ineffective because their Chinese friends and colleagues would sneak around Red Guard patrols to bring them whatever they needed from the market; the only ones who suffered, they insisted, were the bigots and crooks who actively mistreated the local Chinese. As he put it, 'Macau is a small place. These things – kill, revolt, boycott – cannot work because we've been living under the same roof for many years. People have grown up together. No matter what is the militancy, the aggressiveness of an ideology, [in Macau] the human side prevails'. In this sense, José drew a contrast with mainland China, and to a lesser extent Hong Kong, as vast, inhuman places with strong states where militant ideologies could and had prevailed over basic human decency, with devastating results. The difference, however, lay not so much in the formal ideologies or structures of Portuguese rule as in the 'smallness' of Macau, in terms both of its physical size and of the empathies and intimacies that had been engendered by the irrelevance of the state to the daily lives of most of its residents.

The fact that a Macanese ex-government official would express such lusotropically inflected views of the warm and cosy effects of Portuguese rule may not be surprising; but even those interviewees who argued that the 123 Incident was caused by the Portuguese administration's inexcusable neglect of the welfare of Chinese residents, and who viewed the Governor's capitulation as the Chinese people's victory over colonialism, noted with irony that this 'victory' had simply ensured that the Portuguese state withdrew even further from the governance of its Chinese subjects. Yet they also suggested that this withdrawal was not necessarily a bad thing, for it had enabled (or obliged) Macau – in contrast to Hong Kong or the PRC – to maintain the 'old-fashioned' social institutions and practices that could now be claimed as markers of authentic Chineseness. The administration's tendency to look after its own (the Portuguese and Macanese) meant that there was an enormous amount of leeway for individuals and civic associations to develop the economy, as well as education and social welfare programmes. In the 1990s, Macau had more civic associations – native-place associations, lineage associations, tradesmen's associations, temple associations, charity associations – per capita than any other city in China. Many of these claimed to perpetuate 'authentically' Chinese traditions, rituals and social relationships that had all but disappeared in the rest of China. They also represented a staggering diversity of perspectives – from Hong Kong, Taiwan, overseas Chinese communities and multiple diverse regions within the PRC – on what 'authentic' Chineseness could look like.

And, ironically, in 'defeat' at least one Portuguese official, too, found victory. Franco Nogueira, Salazar's foreign minister, summed up his view of the effects of the 123 Incident in a journal entry he made in early 1967: 'They say that there were fireworks [after the Governor signed the admission of guilt] and that a crowd of ten thousand Chinese celebrated. The Governor has ended up a hero. None of the crisis was blamed on him: he has just taken office and cannot be held responsible for the actions of the previous administration. [...] This whole episode has ended up being a success for us – and has consolidated Macau' (Nogueira 1986: 217–18). Nogueira's startling conclusion that Portugal's strength as a colonial power lay in weakness provides a stark contrast to Salazar's lament for the end of Portuguese sovereignty over Macau; but perhaps even more startling is the degree to which Nogueira's comments resonate with those of the Chinese and Macanese residents of Macau who asserted that the Governor, by signing the 'admission of guilt', had not humiliated himself, the Portuguese nation and Europeans everywhere, but had done the only thing that made any pragmatic sense. It was even, suggested one Macanese woman we interviewed, a noble act: by sacrificing his personal dignity as a representative of Portuguese colonial power, Nobre de Carvalho had 'saved' Macau.

Conclusion

The 123 Incident of 1966–67 has often been invoked to ridicule the Portuguese colonial apparatus for being so lacking in wealth, power, ideology and political acumen that it all but collapsed at the first sign of unrest. Yet this view fails to consider that the 123 Incident was neither the first nor the last time that Macau's Portuguese administrators found compromise and capitulation to be not just their only recourse, but also their best strategy for political survival. It does not acknowledge the paradoxes of Portuguese rule in Macau, in which weakness could very well be a form of strength and humiliation a form of triumph.

In listening to the latter-day interpretations of the long-term social and cultural impact of the 123 Incident on Macau and its residents, and to the terminology through which individuals of various ethnic, class and occupational positions narrate its causes and effects, we may hear a more nuanced and ambivalent appraisal of Portuguese rule in Macau. The unexpected convergences between lusotropicalists who extol Macau's spirit of intercultural tolerance and Chinese cultural nationalists who credit Portuguese colonialism with enabling 'traditional' Chinese culture to flourish in Macau complicate the notions of colonialism, sovereignty and legitimacy that underpin the modern system of nation-states. Indeed, they suggest that the *longue durée* of the Portuguese presence in China cannot be understood through the simple fiction of alien domination and native subjugation that the term 'colonialism' implies; instead, this presence depended on compromise and negotiation, on the persistence of and interplay between partial and uncertain sovereign claims.

Notes

1. Different sources provide different numbers of wounded: Huang (1987) and Huang (1999) give 107, while Fernandes (2006), drawing on official Portuguese reports, gives 212.
2. It also ignores sharp differences among the forms of Portuguese rule in Africa, South Asia, and East Asia; unfortunately a discussion of these differences is outside the scope of this paper.
3. The following summary of the Portuguese in Asia draws on Chang (1934); Boxer (1969); Souza (1986); Pearson (1987); Boyajian (1993); Subrahmanyam (1993); Tam (1994); Alden (1996); Coates (2001).
4. Both Chinese and Portuguese sources suggest that everyone involved understood that the Portuguese remained in Macau at the sufferance of the emperor (see Boxer 1984: 27; Chen 1996: 6).
5. Gilberto Freyre, the Brazilian social scientist who first developed the theory of lusotropicalism, attributed the character of Brazilian society to the 'procreative fervor' of Portuguese settlers (see Freyre 1966 [1933]).
6. The 1960 census puts the population of Macau at 169,299. However, in a 1967 speech in Lisbon, former governor Lopes dos Santos suggested that by then the real population was closer to 270,000 (Lopes dos Santos 1968: 145).
7. The Bretton Woods Agreement of 1944 'sought to ensure consistent fixed exchange rates in terms of gold by restricting gold sales to regulated markets operating at a fixed official price of US\$35/oz' (Schenk 1995: 388). Because Portugal never signed the Agreement, gold could be bought and sold legally in Macau at free market prices.
8. Perry Anderson notes that, in the 1950s, the average income in Portugal was \$210 per year, and over 40 per cent of the population aged seven or above was illiterate (Anderson 1962: 83–88).
9. According to Barreto (2002), these wars lasted 13 years, consumed 50 per cent of all public spending, and employed around 200,000 armed forces personnel – more than 2 per cent of Portugal's entire population – at any one time.
10. The CCP, for example, had expressly left Macau and Hong Kong off the list of 23 targets for anti-colonial revolution around the world that it drew up in 1965 (see Van Ness 1970).
11. '*Incidentes em Macau: Relatório Respeitante aos Factors Decorridos em Macau no Período Compreendido entre os Dias 15 e 25 de Novembro de 1966*,' by Carlos Armando da Mota Cerveira (Arquivo Histórico Ultramarino MU/GM/GNP/028E-06-15-40), p. 9.
12. In the following account I draw on Dicks (1984); Lam and Pinto (1996); Castanheira (1999); Carvalho (2004); Fernandes (2006); interviews and contemporary newspaper accounts from Macau and Hong Kong.
13. Reports vary as to the number wounded in the Taipa Incident: Macau's leftist Chinese-language paper, *Macao Daily*, claimed 34 Chinese injuries; the police claimed seven Chinese residents and two policemen were injured badly enough to require medical attention, while the *Hong Kong Star* reported that 13 policemen and two residents were injured.
14. 'Evacuation of Macao', 20 January 1967, FCO 40/71, Public Record Office, London.
15. '*Carta particular de Francisco V. de Morais ao Dr. Manuel de Castilho*', PIDE/DGS, SC/CI(2) 867, Torre do Tombo, Lisbon.
16. The words of one of our interviewees, a Macanese intellectual who was in high school in 1966.
17. Yan Yunxiang defines *renqing* as 'a basic emotional empathy and understanding of others and, related to this, a set of moral obligations and social norms' that has deep roots in Confucian moral codes (Yan 1996: 3).

BIBLIOGRAPHY

Abbas, A. (2000) 'Cosmopolitan descriptions: Shanghai and Hong Kong', *Public Culture* 12(3): 769–86.
Alden, D. (1996) *The Making of an Enterprise: The Society of Jesus in Portugal, its Empire, and Beyond, 1540–1750*. Palo Alto, CA: Stanford University Press.
Ali, B. N. K. (2002) *Chinese in Fiji*. Suva: Institute of Pacific Studies, University of the South Pacific.
Ames, E., Klotz, M. and Wildenthal, L. (eds) (2005) *Germany's Colonial Pasts*. Lincoln, NE/London.
Andall, J. and Duncan, D. (2005) 'Memories and legacies of Italian colonialism', in J. Andall and D. Duncan (eds) *Italian Colonialism. Legacy and Memory*. Oxford: Peter Lang, pp. 9–27.
Anderson, B. (1991) *Imagined Communities*. London: Verso.
Anderson, P. (1962) 'Portugal and the end of ultra-colonialism', *New Left Review* 16: 84–102.
Anon. (1910) 'Jinggao guozhong zhi tan shiye zhe', *Guo feng bao* 2 November, reproduced in Jiu Shanghai de zhengquan jiaoyisuo 265–73.
Anon. (1918) *Lun Shanghai quyinsuo* [*On the Shanghai quyinsuo*], 'Cang, Jingji zhanzheng yu jingji tixie' ['Economic war and economic guidance and help'], *Yinhang zhoubao* [*Bank Weekly*] 3 December (2): 47.
Anon. (1936) *Jingyan liangfang (Excellent Prescriptions)*.
Anon. (1963) *Diplomatic History in Qing Dynasty*, Vol. 186. Wen Hai Publisher.
Andrew, D. T. and McGowen, R. (2001) *The Perreaus and Mrs. Rudd: Forgery and Betrayal in Eighteenth-Century London*. Berkeley, CA: University of California Press.
Andrews, B. (1997) 'Tuberculosis and the assimilation of germ theory in China, 1895–1935', *Journal of the History of Medicine and Allied Sciences* 52: 114–57.
Andrews, E. M. (1985) *Australia and China: The Ambiguous Relationship*. Melbourne: Melbourne University Press.
Andrews, J. F. and Shen, K. (1998) *A Century in Crisis: Modernity and Tradition in the Art of Twentieth-Century China*. New York: Guggenheim Publications.
Appiah, K.A. (2006) *Cosmopolitanism: Ethics in a World of Strangers*. New York: W. W. Norton & Co.
Arendt, H. (1951) *The Origins of Totalitarianism*. New York: Harcourt Brace.
Arnold, D. (1988) *Imperial Medicine and Indigenous Societies*. Manchester/New York: Manchester University Press.

—— (1993) *Colonizing the Body, State Medicine and Epidemic Disease in Nineteenth Century, India*. Berkeley, CA: University of California Press.
Austin, D. (2004) 'Kingdom-minded people': the contributions of Chinese business Christians toward the transformation in society', PhD dissertation, University of Queensland.
Barlow, T. (ed.) (1997) *Formations of Colonial Modernity in East Asia*. Durham, NC: Duke University Press.
Barreto, A. (2002) *Social Change in Portugal, 1960–2000*, Working Paper WP 6–02. Lisbon: Instituto de Ciências Sociais, Universidade de Lisboa.
Bassi, U. (1929) *Italia e Cina: Cenni Storici sui rapporti diplomatici e commerciali*. Modena: E. Bassi & Nipoti.
Ben-Ghiat, R. and Fuller, M. (eds) (2005) *Italian Colonialism*. London: Palgrave.
Benedict, C. (1996) *Bubonic Plague in Nineteenth Century China*. Palo Alto, CA: Stanford University Press.
Benson, S. (1930) *Diaries*, Add. 6798 6 December 1928–5 August 1930. Cambridge: Cambridge University Library, Department of Manuscripts.
Benvenuti, G. M. (2000) *Un Italiano nella Cina dei Boxer: Lettere (1900–1901)*, Nicola Lablanca (ed.). Modena: Panini.
Bergère, M.-C. (1986) *L'Age d'or de la bourgeoisie Chinoise, 1911–1937*. Paris: Flammarion.
—— (1998) *Sun Yat-sen* (Janet Lloyd, trans.). Palo Alto, CA: Stanford University Press.
—— (2009) *Shanghai: China's Gateway to Modernity* (Janet Lloyd, trans.) Palo Alto, CA: Stanford University Press.
Bertinelli, R. (1983) 'La Presenza Italiana in Cina dal 1900 al 1905', *Rivista di Studi Orientali* LVII: 185–229.
Betta, C. (2003) 'From Orientals to imagined Britons: Baghdadi Jews in Shanghai', *Modern Asian Studies* 37(4): 999–1023.
'Betty' (1905) *Intercepted Letters*. Hong Kong: Kelly and Walsh. [Reprinted in Barbara-Sue White (ed.) (1996) *Hong Kong: Somewhere Between Heaven and Earth*. Hong Kong: Oxford University Press.]
Bickers, R. (1998) 'Shanghailanders: the formation and identity of the British settler community in Shanghai 1843–1937', *Past & Present* 159: 161–211.
—— (1999) *Britain in China: Community, Culture and Colonialism, 1900–49*. Manchester: Manchester University Press.
—— (2004) 'Settlers and diplomats: the end of British hegemony in the International Settlement, 1937–45', in Christian Henriot and Wen-hsin Yeh (eds) *In the Shadow of the Rising Sun: Shanghai under Japanese Occupation*. Cambridge: Cambridge University Press.
—— (2006) 'Purloined letters: history and the Chinese Maritime Customs Service', *Modern Asian Studies* 40(3): 691–723.
—— (ed.) (2008a) 'Chinese customs section', *Journal of Imperial and Commonwealth History* 36: 221–311.
—— (2008b) 'The Chinese Maritime Customs at war, 1941–45', *Journal of Imperial and Commonwealth History* 36: 295–311.
Bickers, R. and Henriot, C. (eds) (2000) *New Frontiers: Imperialism's New Communities in East Asia 1842–1952*. Manchester: Manchester University Press.
Bickers, R. A. and Wasserstrom, J. N. (1995) 'Shanghai's "Dogs and Chinese Not Admitted" sign: legend, history and contemporary symbol', *China Quarterly* 142: 444–66.
Biener, A. S. (2001) *Das Deutsche Pachtgebiet Tsingtau in Schantung, 1897–1914*. Bonn: Institutioneller Wandel durch Kolonialisierung.
Bocca, G. (1961) *Italia e Cina nel Secolo XIX*. Milano: Ed. Comunita.
Bodde, D. (1975) *Festivals in Classical China*. Princeton, NJ: Princeton University Press.

Bonah, C. and Rasmussen, A. (eds) (2005) *Histoire et médicament, aux 19e et 20e siècles*. Paris: Glyphe.
Borgnino, R. L. (1936) 'La "Concessione" Italiana in Cina', *Augustea* 1936: 363–66.
Boxer, C. R. (1963) *Race Relations in the Portuguese Colonial Empire, 1415–1825*. Oxford: Clarendon Press.
—— (1969) *The Portuguese Seaborne Empire, 1415–1825*. London, Hutchison.
Boxer, C. R. (ed. and trans.) (1984) *Seventeenth-century Macau in Contemporary Documents and Illustrations*. Hong Kong: Heinemann (Asia).
Boyajian, J. (1993) *Portuguese Trade in Asia under the Habsburgs, 1580–1640*. Baltimore, MD: Johns Hopkins University Press.
Brennan, T. (1997) *At Home in the World: Cosmopolitanism Now*. Cambridge, MA: Harvard University Press.
Bretelle-Establet, F. (1999) 'Resistance and receptivity: French colonial medicine in Southwest China, 1898–1930', *Modern China* 25(2): 171–203.
—— (1999) 'La santé en Chine du Sud', PhD LCAO, University Paris, 7.
—— (2002) *La santé en Chine du Sud, 1898–1928*. Paris: CNRS Asie Orientale.
—— (2009) 'From extending French colonial control to safeguarding national prestige: the French medical dispensaries in southern China', in Iris Borowy (ed.), *Uneasy Encounters: Medicine and Health in China, 1900–1937*. Frankfurt am Main: Peter Lang, pp. 63–92.
Bridge, C. and Fedorowich, K. (eds) (2003) *The British World: Diaspora, Culture and Identity*. London: Frank Cass.
Brocheux, P. and Hemery, D. (1995) *Indochine, la colonisation ambiguë*. Paris: La Découverte.
Brook, T. (2005) *Collaboration: Japanese Agents and Local Elites in Wartime China*. Cambridge, MA: Harvard University Press.
Brooks, B. J. (2000) 'Japanese colonial citizenship in Treaty Port China: the location of Koreans and Taiwanese in the Imperial Order', in R. Bickers and C. Henriot (eds) *New Frontiers: Imperialism's New Communities in East Asia*. Manchester: Manchester University Press.
Brooks, C. (1989) *Mortal Remains. The History and Present State of the Victorian and Edwardian Cemetery*. Exeter: Wheaton.
Brunero, D. M. (2006) *Britain's Imperial Cornerstone in China: The Chinese Maritime Customs Service, 1854–1949*. London: Routledge.
Buck, D. (1978) *Urban Change in China. Politics and Development in Tsinan, Shantung, 1890–1949*. Madison, WI: University of Wisconsin Press.
Cai, S. (2005) 'Aozhou niuxiuwei xueli zhonghua shanghui yanjiu 1901–43' ['A study of the New South Wales Chinese Chamber of Commerce in Sydney, Australia, 1901–43'], *Lishixue yanjiu* [*Historical Research*] 4: 198–204.
Cain, P. J. and Hopkins, A. G. (2001) *British Imperialism, 1688–2000*, 2nd edn. London: Longman.
Cai, Y. (1999) 'Meishu pinglun de xiangduixing' ['On the relativity of art criticism'], in Lang Shaojun and Shui 1999 (eds) *Ershi shiji Zhongguo meishu wenxuan* [Selected Writings on Art in China in the Twentieth Century], Vol. 1. Shanghai: Shanghai shuhua chubanshe, pp. 195–97.
Caizhengbu caizheng kexue yanjiusuo, Zhongguo dier lishi dang'anguan (eds) (1997) *Guomin zhengfu caizheng jinrong shushou dang'an shiliao* (1927–37), Nationalist government finance, banking and tax revenue archival materials. Beijing: Zhongguo caizheng jingji chubanshe.
Cang, S. (1922) 'Woguo jinri jingji shang zhi bingyuan' ['Origins of our country's current illness'], *Yinhang zhoubao* [*Bank Weekly*] 6(7): 1–2.
Canis, K. (1997) *Von Bismarck zur Weltpolitik. Deutsche Außenpolitik 1890 bis 1902*. Berlin: Wiley-VCH Verlag GmbH.

Cao, S. (2002) 'Origin of Siming Assembly Hall Case: analysis of Siming Assembly Hall property ownership', *Archives and Historical Studies* 4.
Cardano, N. and Porzio, P. L. (eds) (2004) *Sulla Via di Tianjin: Mille Anni di Relazioni tra Italia e Cina. Un quartiere Italiano in Cina*. Roma: Gangemi.
Carroll, J. (2005) *Edge of Empires: Chinese Elites and British Colonials in Hong Kong*. Cambridge, MA: Harvard University Press.
Cartier-Bresson, H. (1956) *China in Transition: A Moment in History*. London: Thames & Hudson.
Carvalho, R. L. D. (2004) 'Depoimento', in F. Lima and E. Cintra Torres (eds) *Macau Entre Dois Mundos*. Lisbon: Fundação Jorge Alvares and Editorial Inquérito.
Cassel, P. K. (2008) 'Rethinking extraterritoriality in China: In the crucible of personal and territorial jurisdiction', paper delivered to AAS Meeting, Atlanta, 3–6 April.
Castanheira, J. (1999) *Os 58 Dias Que Abalaram Macau*. Lisbon: Publicações Dom Quixote & Livros do Oriente.
Castells, M. Goh, L. and Kwok, R. Y.-W. (1990) *The Shek Kip Mei Syndrome: Economic Development and Public Housing in Hong Kong and Singapore*. London: Pion.
Cesari, C. (1937) *La Concessione Italiana di Tien-Tsin*. Roma: Istituto Coloniale Fascista.
Chan, W. K. K. (1999) 'Selling goods and promoting a new commercial culture: the four premier department stores on Nanjing Road, 1917–37', in Sherman Cochran (ed.) *Inventing Nanjing Road: Commercial Culture in Shanghai, 1900–1945*. Ithaca, NY: East Asian Program, Cornell University.
Chang, T. (1934) *Sino-Portuguese Trade from 1514–1644: A Synthesis of Portuguese and Chinese Sources*. Leyden: E.J. Brill.
Chatterjee, P. (1993) *The Nation and its Fragments: Colonial and Postcolonial Histories*. Princeton, NJ: Princeton University Press.
Chen, B. (1949) *Chen Bulei huiyi lu* [*Chen Bulei's Memoirs*]. Shanghai: Ershi shiji chubanshe, II.
Chen, G. (ed.) (1938) *Xianggang zhinan* [*Guide to Hong Kong*]. Changsha: Shangwu.
Chen, M. (ed.) (1996) *Zhonguo Weisheng Fagui Shiliao Xuanbian* [Selected Articles of Public Health Regulation]. Shanghai.
Chen, W. (1996) 'Historical materials on Portugal and Macau in "The Veritable Records of the Ming"', *Revista de Cultura* (Chinese edition): 155–64.
Chen, Z. (1935) *Zhongguo guomindang aozhou dangwu fazhan shikuang* [*Historical Outline of the Development of Chinese KMT Party Affairs in Australasia*]. Sydney: Zhongguo guomindang zhu ao zongzhibu.
China Maritime Customs (1878) *Provisional Instructions for the Guidance of the In-door Staff*. Shanghai: Statistical Department of the Inspectorate General.
—— (1879) *Inspector General's Circulars. First Series: 1861–1875*. Shanghai: Statistical Department of the Inspectorate General.
—— (1913) *Decennial Reports on the Trade, Industries etc of the Ports Open to Foreign Commerce and on the Condition and Development of the Treaty Port Provinces: 1902–1911*, Vol. II. Shanghai: Statistical Department of the Inspectorate General of Customs.
—— (1924) *Decennial Reports on the Trade, Industries etc of the Ports Open to Foreign Commerce and on the Condition and Development of the Treaty Port Provinces: 1912–1921*, Vol. II. Shanghai: Statistical Department of the Inspectorate General of Customs.
—— (1938a) *Documents Illustrative of the Origin, Development and Activities of the Chinese Customs Service. Volume III. Inspector General's Circulars, 1911 to 1923*. Shanghai: Statistical Department of the Inspectorate General of Customs.
—— (1938b) *Documents Illustrative of the Origin, Development and activities of the Chinese Customs Service. Volume VI: Despatches, Letters, Memoranda, etc., 1842–1901*. Shanghai: Statistical Department of the Inspectorate General of Customs.

Cicchiti-Suriani, A. (1951) 'La Concessione Italiana di Tient Tsin (1901–51)', *Rassegna Italiana di Politica e Cultura* 31(October): 562–66.
Coates, T. (2001) *Convicts and Orphans: Forced and State-Sponsored Colonizers in the Portuguese Empire, 1550–1755*. Palo Alto, CA: Stanford University Press.
Cochran, S. (2006) *Chinese Medicine Men: Consumer Culture in China and Southeast Asia*. Cambridge, MA: Harvard University.
Cohen, P. (2007) 'In economics departments, a growing will to debate fundamental assumptions', *New York Times* 11 July.
Cohen, P. A. (1997a) *Discovering History in China*. New York: Columbia University Press.
—— (1997b) *History in Three Keys: The Boxers as Event, Experience and Myth*. New York: Columbia University Press.
Collin, J. (1999) 'Entre discours et pratique, les médecins montréalais face à la thérapeutique, 1869–90', *Revue d'histoire de l'Amérique française* 53(1): 1–36.
Como, B., Discepolo, B. and Machetti, G. (eds) (2006) *Tianjin Yidali fengqingqu Jianzhu yu zhengxiude lishi yu huigu* [*Tianjin: Il Quartiere Italiano: Architettura e Restauro tra Storia e Memoria*]. Beijing: Ed. Graffiti.
Constantine, S. (1984) *The Making of British Colonial Development Policy, 1914–1940*. London: Frank Cass.
Cooper, F. (2005) *Colonialism in Question: Theory, Knowledge, History*. Berkeley, CA: University of California Press.
Cooper, F. and Stoler, A. L. (eds) (1997) *Tensions of Empire: Colonial Cultures in a Bourgeois World*. Berkeley, CA: University of California Press.
Cooper, F. and Stoler, A. L. (1997a) 'Between colony and metropole: toward a research agenda', in F. Cooper and A. L. Stoler (eds) *Tensions of Empire: Colonial Cultures in a Bourgeois World*. Berkeley, CA: University of California Press.
Cornet, C. (2004) 'The bumpy end of the French concession and French influence in Shanghai, 1937–46', in Christian Henriot and Wen-hsin Yeh (eds) *In the Shadow of the Rising Sun: Shanghai under Japanese Occupation*. Cambridge: Cambridge University Press.
Couchman, S. (1995) 'The Banana Trade: Its Importance to Melbourne's Chinese and Little Bourke Street, 1880s–1930s' in Paul Macgregor (ed.) *Histories of the Chinese in Australasia and the South Pacific*. Melbourne: Museum of Chinese Australian History, pp. 75–87.
—— (2004) *After the Rush: Regulation, Participation and Chinese Communities in Australia 1860–1940*. Special edition of *Otherland*, Melbourne.
Crossette, B. (1999) *The Great Hill Stations of Asia*. New York: Basic Books.
Cui, W. (ed.) (1922) *Xi Shangzhen*. Shanghai: Funü zhiye yanjiu she, Part 1.
Cui, Z. (2005) *Shanghai Diplomacy during the Russo–Japanese War, Historical Studies: History of Imperialism's Invasion to China*.
Danzker, J.-A. B. et al. (eds) (2004) *Shanghai Modern: 1919–1945 Ostfildern-Ruit*. Germany: Hatje Cantz.
Davison, G. (1978) *The Rise and Fall of Marvellous Melbourne*. Melbourne: Melbourne University Press.
De Antonellis, G. (1977) 'L'Italia in Cina nel secolo XX', *Mondo Cinese* 19(July–September): 51–59.
DeBary, W. T. and Luffrano, R. (comp.) (1960) *Sources of Chinese Tradition*. New York: Columbia University Press, 2: 107.
DQSLXJ (1986) *Deguo qinzhan Jiaozhouwan shiliao xuanbian 1897–1898* [Selected Materials on the German Occupation of the Jiaozhou Bay 1897–98], Qingdaoshi bowuguan, Zhongguo di yi lishi dang'anguan and Qingdaoshi shehui kexue yanjiusuo, (eds). Jinan.
Deist, W. (1976) *Flottenpolitik und Flottenpropaganda. Das Nachrichtenbureau des Reichsmarineamts 1897–1914*. Stuttgart.

Deng, M. (1986) *The History of Imperialism's Invasion in China*, Vol. 2. Beijing: Renminchubanshe.
Dernburg, B. (1907) *Zielpunkte des deutschen Kolonialwesens*. Berlin: Ernst Siegfried Mittler und Sohn.
Derrida, J. (2001) *On Cosmopolitanism and Forgiveness*, trans. Mark Dooley and Michael Hughes. London: Routledge.
Des Voeux, G. W. (1903) *My Colonial Service in British Guiana, St. Lucia, Trinidad, Fiji, Australia, Newfoundland, and Hong Kong with Interludes*, Vol. 2. London: John Murray.
Dicks, A. (1984) 'Macao: legal fiction and gunboat diplomacy', in G. Aijmer (ed.) *Leadership on the China Coast*. London: Curzon Press.
Dikötter, F. (2004) *Narcotic Culture, A History of Drugs in China*. Hong Kong: Hong Kong University Press.
Dirks, N. B. (1992) 'Introduction: Colonialism and culture', in Nicholas B. Dirks (ed.) *Colonialism and Culture*. Ann Arbor, MI: University of Michigan Press, pp. 1–25.
Dirlik, A. (1978) *Revolution and History: Origins of Marxist Historiography in China, 1919–1937*. Berkeley, CA: University of California Press.
Dong, W. (2005) *China's Unequal Treaties: Narrating National History*. Lanham, MD: Lexington Books.
Dou, J. (1943) *A Study of the Organization of Fellowmanship*. Cheng Chung Book Co., Ltd.
Duara, P. (1995) *Rescuing History from the Nation. Questioning Narratives of Modern China*. Chicago, IL: Chicago University Press.
—— (2003) *Sovereignty and Authenticity: Manchukuo and the East Asian Modern*. Lanham, MD: Rowman and Littlefield.
—— (2006) 'Nationalism, imperialism, federalism and the case of Manchukuo: a response to Anthony Pagden', *Common Knowledge* 12(1): 47–65.
Eckart, W. (1989) *Deutsche Ärzte in China 1897–1914. Medizin als Kulturmission im Zweiten Deutschen Kaiserreich*. Stuttgart.
Ennis, T. E. (1936) *French Policy and Developments in Indochina*. Chicago, IL: University of Chicago Press.
Esherick, J. W. (1987) *The Origins of the Boxer Uprising*. Berkeley, CA: University of California Press.
Esherick, J. W. (ed.) (2000) *Remaking the Chinese City: Modernity and National Identity, 1900–1950*. Honolulu: University of Hawai'i Press.
Fainzang, S. (2001) *Médicaments et société*. Paris: PUF.
Fanon, F. (1967) *The Wretched of the Earth*. Harmondsworth: Penguin.
—— (1986) *Black Skin, White Masks*. London: Pluto Press.
Faure, D. (2003) *Colonialism and the Hong Kong Mentality*. Hong Kong: Centre of Asian Studies.
Feng, Z. (1947) 'Min yuan lai zhi jiaoyisuo' ['Stock exchanges since the founding of the Republic'), in Zhu Sihuang (ed.) *Minguo jingji shi* [*Economic History of the Republic*], Shanghai.
Feray (1907) 'Historique et pratique de la vaccine', *Annales d'Hygiène et de Médecine Coloniale* 498–514.
Fernandes, M. S. (2006) *Macau na Política Externa Chinesa, 1949–1979*. Lisbon: Imprensa de Ciências Sociais.
del Ferro, G. V. (1901) 'L'Italia nella questione cinese', *Rivista politica e letteraria* October.
FCO (1967) 'Evacuation of Macao', 20 January, 40/71. London: Public Record Office.
Fileti, V. (1921) *La Concessione Italiana di Tien-tsin*. Genova: Barabino e Graeve.
Fitzgerald, J. (1996) *Awakening China: Politics, Culture and Class in the Nationalist Revolution*. Palo Alto, CA: Stanford University Press.

—— (2004) 'Gendering the social imaginary: modernity, nationalism, and representations of egalitarian sentiment in 19th and 20th century China', paper presented to conference on *New Gender Constructs in Literature, the Visual and the Performing Arts of Modern China and Japan*. Heidelberg: University of Heidelberg.

—— (2007) *Big White Lie: Chinese Australians in White Australia*. Kensington: UNSW Press.

Fok, K. C. (1996) 'The "Macau formula" at work: an 18th century Qing expert's view on Macau', in A. de Saldanha and J. dos Santos Alves (eds) *Estudos de História do Relacionamento Luso-Chinês*. Macau: Instituto Português do Oriente.

Foucault, M. (1976) *Discipline and Punish: The Birth of the Prison*. New York: Pantheon Books.

—— (1980) *Power/Knowledge: Selected Interviews & Other Writings 1972–1977*. New York: Pantheon Books.

Foucault, M. (1984) 'Des espaces autres' (Conférence au Cercle d'études architecturales, 14 mars 1967), in *Architecture, Mouvement, Continuité*, No. 5, Octobre: 46–49; also available in Michel Foucault (Édition établie sous la direction de Daniel Defert et François Ewald) *Dits et Ecrits 1954–1988, IV, 1980–1988*. (Paris: Editions Gallimard, 1994), pp. 752–62.

—— (1990) *The History of Sexuality*. New York: Columbia University Press.

—— (1997) 'Il faut defendre la societe', Cours au College de France (1975–76). Paris.

Freyre, G. (1966) *Casa-Grande e Senzala: Formação da Família Brasileira sob o Regime de Economia Patriarcal*, 13th edn. Rio de Janeiro: José Olympio.

Fuma, S. (1989) 'Shanhai – shinmatsu shanhai no kindaika to tsuka mondai' ['Shanghai – problems of modernization and charitable cemeteries at Shanghai at the end of the Qing era'], in *Kōza tenkanki ni ōkeru nigen No. 4 – Toshi no wa* [*Studies in the Rise of Mankind No. 4 – What are Cities?*]. Tokyo: Iwanami.

Gao, M. (ed.) (1998) *Inside Out: New Chinese Art*. San Francisco, CA: San Francisco Museum of Art.

—— (ed.) (2002) *Inside Out: New Chinese Art*. Berkeley, CA: University of California Press.

Gernet, J. (1994) *L'intelligence de la Chine, le social et le mental*. Paris: Gallimard.

Gillingham, P. (1983) *At the Peak: Hong Kong Between the Wars*. Hong Kong: Macmillan.

Gilman, S. (1985) *Difference and Pathology: Stereotypes of Sexuality, Race and Madness*. Ithaca, NY: Cornell University Press.

Giolitti, G. (1922) *Memorie della mia vita*, with a study by Olindo Malagodi, 2 vols. Milano: F.lli Treves.

Goldman, M. and Lee, L. O.-F. (eds) (2002) *An Intellectual History of Modern China*. Cambridge: Cambridge University Press.

Gollwitzer, H. (1962) *Die Gelbe Gefahr. Geschichte eines Schlagwortes*. Göttingen.

Gong, C. (1983) *Zhongguo lidai weisheng zuzhi ji yixue jiaoyu* [*Medical Teaching and Health Establishments in Chinese History*]. Beijing: Weisheng bu kejiao.

Goodman, B. (1995) *Native-Place, City and Nation: Regional Networks and Identities in Shanghai, 1853–1937*. Berkeley, CA: University of California Press.

—— (2000) 'Improvisations on a semicolonial theme, or, how to read a celebration of transnational urban community', *Journal of Asian Studies* 59(4): 889–926.

—— (2002) 'Democratic calisthenics: the culture of urban associations in the new republic', in Merle Goldman and Elizabeth Perry (eds) *Changing Meanings of Citizenship in Modern China*. Cambridge, MA: Harvard University Press.

—— (2004a) 'Semi-colonialism, transnational ties, and press culture in early Republican Shanghai', *China Review* 4(1).

—— (2004b) *Native Place, City, and Nation: Regional Networks and Identities in Shanghai, 1853–1937*, trans. Song Zuanyou. Shanghai Classics Publishing House.

—— (2005a) 'Unvirtuous exchanges: women and the corruptions of the stock market in early Republican China', in Mechthild Leutner and Nicola Spakowski (eds) *Women in China: The Republican Period in Historical Perspective*. Münster: LIT Verlag, pp. 351–75.

—— (2005b) 'The new woman commits suicide: press, cultural memory and the New Republic', *Journal of Asian Studies* 64(1): 67–101.

Gramada, G. [pen name of George Sokolsky] (1921) 'The gambling in produce exchanges', *North China Daily News* 6 December.

Grant, J. (2003) *A Chinese Physician, Wang Ji and the Stone Mountain Medical Case Histories*. New York: Routledge.

Grantham, A. (1965) *Via Ports: from Hong Kong to Hong Kong*. Hong Kong: Hong Kong University Press.

Guo, A. (1987) *Zhongguo fensheng yiji kao*. Tianjin: Kexue jishu chuban.

Guo, C. [Phillip Gockchin] (1961) *Yongan jingshen zhi fazhan ji changcheng* [*The Growth and Ripening of the Wing On Spirit*]. Hong Kong: NP.

Guo, L. [James Gocklock] (1949) *Huiyilu* [*Memoirs*]. NP: Wing On Company.

Guo, Y. (ed.) (1989) *Tianjin gudai chengshi fazhan shi Tianjin gudaichengshi fazhanshi* [*History of the Development of the Ancient City of Tianjin*]. Tianjin: Tianjin Guji Chubanshe.

Gyory, A. (1998) *Closing the Gate: Race, Politics, and the Chinese Exclusion Act*. Chapel Hill, NC: University of North Carolina Press.

Hanna, W. A. (1969) *A Trial of Two Colonies*, American Universities Field Service East Asia Series, Vol. XVI, Nos 1 and 2. Macao.

Harder, A. (1900) *Wider den Gelben Drachen*. Bielefeld and Leipzig: Verlag von Velhagen & Klasing, pp. 528f.

Havinden, M. and Meredith, D. (1993) *Colonialism and Development: Britain and its Tropical Colonies, 1850–1960*. London: Routledge.

Hayes, J. (1990) 'East and West in Hong Kong: vignettes from history and personal expeience', in Elizabeth Sinn (ed.) *Between East and West: Aspects of Social and Economic Development in Hong Kong*. Hong Kong: Center for Asian Studies, University of Hong Kong.

—— (1995) '"Good Morning Mrs Thompson!" A Chinese–English word book from 19th century Sydney', in Paul Macgregor (ed.) *Histories of the Chinese in Australasia and the South Pacific*. Melbourne: Museum of Chinese Australian History.

He Mengyao (1994) *Yibian* [*Progress in Medicine*]. Renmin weisheng chubanshe.

Headrick, D. R. (1981) *The Tools of Empire: Technology and European Imperialism in the Nineteenth Century*. New York: Oxford University Press.

—— (1988) *The Tentacles of Progress: Technology Transfer in the Age of Imperialism, 1850–1940*. New York: Oxford University Press.

Henriot, C. (1993) *Shanghai 1927–1937. Municipal Power, Locality, and Modernization*. Berkeley, CA: University of California Press.

—— (2007) 'Scythe and sojourning in wartime Shanghai', *Karunungan – A Journal of Philosophy* 27(September).

Henze, P. B. (2000) *Layers of Layers of Time: A History of Ethiopia*. New York: Palgrave.

Hersey, J. R. (1982) 'A reporter at large: homecoming', *The New Yorker* 10 May: 49–66.

Hevia, J. L. (2003) *English Lessons: The Pedagogy of Imperialism in Nineteenth-Century China*. Durham, NC: Duke University Press.

Hinds, A. (2001) *Britain's Sterling Colonial Policy and Decolonization, 1939–1958*. Westport, CT: Greenwood Press.

Hiroyuki, H. (1994) 'Shinmatsu shanhai shime kōshō no "unkan nettwaku" no keisei: kindai chūgoku shakai ni okeru dōkyō ketsugo ni tsuite' ['The formation of the "coffin sending network" of the Siming Gongsuo in late-Qing Shanghai: a study of native-place ties in modern China'], *Shakai-Keizai Shigaku* [*Socio-Economic History*] 59(6).

Holdsworth, M. (2002) *Foreign Devils: Expatriates in Hong Kong*, with additional text by Caroline Courtauld. Hong Kong: Oxford University Press.
Hong, J. and Zhang, J. (1989) *Jindai Shanghai jinrong shichang* [*Financial Markets in Modern Shanghai*]. Shanghai: Shanghai renmin chubanshe.
Horowitz, R. S. (2006) 'Politics, power and the Chinese maritime customs: the Qing restoration and the ascent of Robert Hart', *Modern Asian Studies* 40: 549–81.
Horowitz, R. S. (2008) 'The ambiguities of an imperial institution: crisis and transition in the Chinese Maritime Customs, 1899–1911', *Journal of Imperial and Commonwealth History* 36(2): 275–94.
Hou, Z. (2006) 'Bupingdeng gainian yu jindai zhongguo de bupingdeng tiaoyue' ['The concept of inequality and the Unequal Treaties in modern China'], *Zhongguo shehui kexueyuan yanjiushengyuan xuebao* [*Journal of the Graduate School of the Chinese Academy of Social Sciences*] No. 2.
Hövermann, O. (1914) *Kiautschou. Verwaltung und Gerichtsbarkeit*. Tübingen: J.C.B. Mohr.
Hsu, F. L. F. (1952) *Religion, Science and Human Crisis*. London, Routledge.
Hu, S. (1986) *A Retrospect in Seventeen Years, Our Political Advocacy*. Yuan Liu Publishing Ltd.
Hu, S. (nd) *Autobiography in My Forties*. Shanghai: Dong Ya Library.
Huang, H. Z. (1987) *Macau History*. Hong Kong: Commercial Press.
Huang, Q. C. (1999) *General History of Macao*. Guangzhou: Guangdong Education Press.
Huang, Y. (1800) *Yixue jingyao* [*Subtle Points in Medicine*]. Shanghai: Cuiying shuju yinhang.
Hubatsch, W. (1983) *Grundriß der deutschen Verwaltungsgeschichte, Bd. 22: Bundes-und Reichsbehörden*. Marburg: JG Herder.
Hunt, M. H. (1993) 'Chinese national identity and the strong state: the Late Qing–Republican crises', in Lowell Dittmer and Samuel S. Kim (eds) *China's Quest for National Identity*, Ithaca, NY: Cornell University Press, pp. 62–79.
Hunter, J. (1984) *The Gospel of Gentility: American Women Missionaries in Turn-of-the-century China*. New Haven, CT: Yale University Press.
Iijima, W. (2000) *Pesuto to Kindai Chugoku* [*Plague and Modern China: The Institutionalization of Public Health and Social Change*]. Tokyo: Kemmbun Shuppan.
—— (2005) *Mararia to Teikoku* [*The Hidden History of Malaria; Colonial/Imperial Medicine and Integrated Regional Order in 20th-Century East Asia*]. Tokyo: University of Tokyo Press.
Iser, W. (1974) *The Implied Reader: Patterns of Communication from Bunyan to Beckett*. Baltimore, MD/London: Johns Hopkins University Press.
Jennings, E. T. (2003) 'From Indochine to Indochic: the Lang Bian/Dalat Palace Hotel and French colonial leisure, power and culture', *Modern Asian Studies* 37(1): 159–94.
Jiang, G. (ed.) (1940) *Pingle xianzhi* [*Gazetteer of Pingle*].
Jiang, H. (1994) *Jiaoyisuo xianxing ji*, reprinted in Tang Zhesheng (ed.) *Jiaoyisuo zhenxiang de tanmizhe – Jiang Hongjiao* [*Jiang Hongjiao, Sleuth of Secret Stock Market Truths*], Zhongguo jinxiandai tongsu zuojia pingzhuan congshu, Vol. 7. Nanjing: Nanjing chubanshe.
Jindai Lishi, Y. (1981) *Case of Chinese Killed by Russian Soldier in 1904*, Jindai Lishi Yanjiu [Modern Chinese History Studies] Vol. 43. Zhonghua Books Company.
Johnston, T. and Erh, D. (1994) *Near to Heaven: Western Architecture in China's Old Summer Resorts*. Hong Kong: Old China Hand Press.
Jones, A. F. (2001) *Yellow Music: Media Culture and Colonial Modernity in the Chinese Jazz Age*. Durham, NC: Duke University Press.
Jones, F. C. (1940) *Shanghai and Tientsin*. London: Humphrey Milford.
Jones, P. (1999) 'Alien Acts: the White Australia policy, 1901 to 1939', PhD dissertation. Melbourne: University of Melbourne.
—— (2001) 'Chinese in modern Australia', in James Jupp (ed.) *The Australian People: An Encyclopedia of the Nation, Its People and their Origins*. Melbourne: Cambridge University Press.

Kan, A. L.-C. (1970) 'The kaifong (neighborhood) associations in Hong Kong', dissertation. Berkeley, CA: University of California.
Kantocho, R. T. C. (1923) *The Research Unit for the System of Land in Guandong Kantoshu Jijyo (The Basic Situation of Guandong) Manmo Buka Kyokai* Dairen: 'The outline of the basic situation of land system in Guandong', pp.1–4.
Kantokyoku, B. (1937) *(Guandong Government, Documentation Branch) Kantokyoku Shisei Sanjyunen Gyoseki Chosa Shiryo* (The Thirty Years Administration of Guandon Government) Dairen.
Karl, R. E. (2002) *Staging the World: Chinese Nationalism at the Turn of the Twentieth Century*. Durham, NC: Duke University Press.
Karl, R. (2005) 'On comparability and continuity: China, circa 1930s and 1990s', *Boundary* 32(2): 169–200.
Katz, P. (1995) *Demon Hordes and Burning Boats: The Cult of Marshal Wen in Late Imperial Chekiang*. Albany, NY: State University of New York Press.
Kelly & Walsh (1893) *Hand-Book to Hong Kong, Being a Popular Guide to the Various Places of Interest in the Colony, for the Use of Tourists*. Hong Kong: Kelly & Walsh.
Kelly, J. D. (1997) 'Gaze and grasp: plantations, desires, indentured Indians, and colonial law in Fiji', in Lenore Manderson and Margaret Jolly (eds) *Sites of Desire, Economies of Pleasure: Sexualities in Asia and the Pacific*. Chicago, IL: University of Chicago Press, pp. 98–122.
Kennedy, D. (1996) *The Magic Mountains: Hills Stations and the British Raj*. Berkeley, CA: University of California Press.
Kermogant, A. (1907) 'L'assistance médicale en Indochine', *Annales d'Hygiène et de Médecine Coloniale* 24–43.
Killy, W. (ed.) (1993) *Literaturlexikon: Begriffe, Realien, Methoden*, Vol. 2. Gütersloh/München: Bertelsmann.
King, A. D. (1976) 'Culture, social power and environment: the hill station in colonial urban development', *Social Action* 26(3): 195–213.
Kleinman, A. (1982) 'Patients treated by physicians and folk healers: a comparative outcome study in Taiwan', *Culture, Medicine and Psychiatry* 6: 405–23.
Kong, X. (1997) 'Die Jiaozhou-Krise und die Reform-Bewegung von 1898' ['The Jiaozhou crisis and the reform movement movement of 1898'], *Berliner China-Hefte* 12: 42–56.
Koseisho, K. E. (1980) *(The Public Health Department, Ministry of Social Welfare) Keneki Seido Hyakunenshi (A Hundred Years of the Quarantine System)*. Tokyo: Gyosei.
Kreissler, F.(2000) 'Exil ou asile à Shanghai? Histoire des réfugiés d'Europe centrale (1933–45)', 3 vols. Thèse d'Etat, Université Paris VIII.
Kronecker, F. (1913) *15 Jahre Kaiutschou, Eine kolonialmedizinische*. Berlin: Studie.
Kuang, Q. (1889) *Correspondence from Kuang Qizhao to the Zongli Yamen Regarding the Report by Chinese Merchants of Harsh Treatment in Australia (19th day of 8th month of Guangxu 14)*. Beijing: First National Archives.
Kuhn, P. (2009) *Chinese Among Others: Emigration in Modern Times*. Lanham, MD: Rowman and Littlefield.
Kuo, M.-F. (2005) 'The "imagined Chinese community" in the carnivals of 1897', paper presented to Postgraduate Conference, School of Social Sciences, La Trobe University.
Kuss, S. and Martin, B. (eds) (2002) *Das Deutsche Reich und der Boxeraufstand*. München: Iudicium.
Kwan, M. B. (1996) 'Mapping the hinterland: treaty ports and regional analysis in modern China', in Gail Hershatter, Emily Honig, Jonathan N. Lipman and Randall Stross (eds) *Remapping China: Fissures in Historical Terrain*. Palo Alto, CA: Stanford University Press, pp. 224–41.

—— (2001) *The Salt Merchants of Tianjin: State-making and Civil Society in Late Imperial China*. Honolulu: University of Hawai'i Press.

Ladds, C. (2007a) 'The world of the Chinese maritime customs', in Robert Bickers, Catherine Ladds, Jamie Carstairs and Yee Wah Foo (eds) *Picturing China 1870–1950: Photographs from British Collections*. Bristol: Chinese Maritime Customs Project Occasional Papers, pp. 5–8.

—— (2008a) '"The Life Career of us all": Britons and Germans in the Chinese Customs Service, 1854–1917', *Berliner China-Hefte: Chinese History and Society* 33: 34–53.

—— (2008b) '"Youthful, likely men, able to read, write and count": joining the foreign staff of the Chinese Customs Service, 1854–1927', *Journal of Imperial and Commonwealth History* 36: 227–42.

Lam, A. and Pinto, R. (1996) *Macau Um Dois Tres*. Macau: Teledifusão de Macau.

Lang, S. and Shui, Z. (eds) (1999) *Ershi shiji Zhongguo meishu wenxuan* [*Selected Writings on Art in China in the Twentieth Century*], 2 vols. Shanghai: Shanghai shuhua chubanshe.

Lanning, G. and Couling, S. (1921) *The History of Shanghai*. Shanghai: Kelly and Walsh for Shanghai Municipal Council.

Lary, D. (1974) *Region and Nation: The Kwangsi Clique in Chinese Politics, 1925–1937*. Cambridge: Cambridge University Press.

Lassere, M. (1994) 'L'espace urbain et la mort: la création d'un cimetière communal à Grenoble (XVIIIe-XIXe siècles)', *Cahiers d'Histoire* 39(2): 119–32.

Laurence, P. (2003) *Lily Briscoe's Chinese Eyes: Bloomsbury, Modernism, and China*. Columbia, SC: University of South Carolina Press.

Lee, C. C.-C. (2000) *Li Chengji xiansheng fangwen jilu* [*The Reminiscences of Charles Cheng-Che Lee*], interviewed and recorded by Lai Chi-Kong. Taipei: Institute of Modern History of Academia Sinica.

Lee, O.-F. L. (1999) *Shanghai Modern: The Flowering of a New Urban Culture in China, 1930–1945*. Cambridge, MA: Harvard University Press.

Lee, R. (1989) *France and the Exploitation of China 1885–1901*. Hong Kong: Oxford University Press.

Lee, R. P. L. (1980) 'Perceptions and uses of Chinese medicine among the Chinese in Hongkong', *Culture, Medicine and Psychiatry* 4: 345–75.

Lee, V. (2004) *Being Eurasian: Memories across Racial Divides*. Hong Kong: Hong Kong University Press.

Lee, S.-M. and Emily, M. H. (2005) *A Phoenix of South China: The Story of Lingnan (University) College, Sun Yat-sen University*. Hong Kong: Commercial Press.

Lei, D. et al. (1889) *Report to Zongli Yamen from Chinese Merchants Regarding Exorbitant Taxes Imposed on Chinese in Australia (1st day of 7th month of Guangxu 14)*. Beijing: First National Archives.

Lenin, V. I. (1968) 'Imperialism, the highest stage of capitalism', in James E. Connor (ed.) *Lenin on Politics and Revolution: Selected Writings*. New York: Pegasus.

Léonard, J. (1981) *La médecine entre les savoirs et les pouvoirs*. Paris: Montaigne.

—— (1992) *Médecins, malades et société dans la France du XIXe siècle*. Paris: Centre National des Lettres.

Lethbridge, H. J. (1969) 'Hong Kong under Japanese occupation: changes in social structure', in Ian C. Jarvie and Joseph Agassi (eds) *Hong Kong: A Society in Transition*. London: Routledge Kegan & Paul.

Leutner, M. and Mühlhahn, K. (1991) 'Die "Musterkolonie" – Die Perzeption des Schutzgebietes Jiaozhou in Deutschland', in Mechthild Leutner and Kuo Heng-yü (eds) *Deutschland und China: Beiträge des Zweiten Internationalen Symposiums zur Geschichte der deutsch-chinesischen Beziehungen*. Berlin/München: Minerva, pp. 399–423.

Leutner, M. and Mühlhahn, K. (eds) (1997) *'Musterkolonie Kiautschou'. Die Expansion des Deutschen Reiches in China. Deutsch–chinesische Beziehungen 1897–1914. Eine Quellensammlung.* Berlin.
Levenson, J. R. (1971) *Revolution and Cosmopolitanism: The Western Stage and the Chinese Stages.* Berkeley, CA: University of California Press.
Levich, E. W.(1994) *The Kwangsi Way in Kuomintang China, 1931–39.* Armonk, NJ: M.E. Sharpe.
Lewis, W. (1989) 'The quest for William Henry Donald (1875–1946)', *Asian Studies Association of Australia Review* 12(1).
Li, C. (1992) *Der China-Roman in der deutschen Literatur 1890–1930.* Regensburg.
Li, C. (2000) 'Zhanhou guomin zhengfu dui Xianggang wenti zhi chuli – Wang Shuixiang shijian gean yanjiu' ['The management of the Hong Kong question faced by the post-war KMT government: a study of the Wang Shuixiang Incident'] in Hong Kong, Macau and Modern China Scholarly Seminar Collection Editorial Board (ed.) *GangAoyu Zhongguo xueshu taohuilun wenji.* Taipei: Guoshiguan.
Li, D. (2004) 'Popular culture in the making of anti-imperialist and nationalist sentiments in Sichuan', *Modern China* 30: 470–505.
Li, E. (1963) *Wan Qing de shouhui kuangquan yundong* [*The Mining-Rights Recovery Movement in the late Qing-period*]. Taibei.
Li, G. (ed.) (1879) *Guangzhou fuzhi 1880* [*Guangdong Gazetteer*].
Li, N. (2005) *Wanqing, minguo shiqi Shanghai xiaobao yanjiu: yizhong zonghede wenhua wenxue kaocha* [*A Study of Minor Newspapers in Shanghai in the late Qing and Republican Period: an Interdisciplinary Investigation of Culture And Literature*]. Beijing: Renmin wenxue chubanshe.
Li, W. (1986) 'Yizujie' ('The Streets of the Italian Concession'), in Tianjinshi zhengxie wenshi ziliao yanjiu weiyuanhui (ed.) *Tianjin zujie (The Italian Concession).* Tianjin: Tianjin Renmin Chubanshe, pp. 134–45.
Li, Y. (1999) 'Wo buhuo' ['I am not bewildered'], in Lang Shaojun and Shui Zhongtian (eds) *Ershi shiji Zhongguo meishu wenxuan* [*Selected Writings on Art in China in the Twentieth Century*], Vol. 1. Shanghai: Shanghai shuhua chubanshe, pp. 214–17.
—— (2006) *Zujie wenhua yu 30 niandai wenxue* [*Concession Culture and Literature in the 1930s*]. Shanghai: Sanlian shudian.
Li, Z. (Lai Chi-Kong) (1999) 'Jindai Guangdong xiangshan shangren de shangye wangluo chutan' ['Preliminary analysis of the commercial networks of the modern Huengshan merchants of Guangdong'], *Zhongguo haiyang fazhan shilun wenji* [*Essays on the History of Chinese Maritime Development*] 7: 233–55.
Liang, L. (1881,1936) *Bu zhi yi biyao* [*What the Ignorant in Medicine Should Know*]. Zhenben yishu jicheng.
Liang, Q. (1903) 'Bai aozhou zhi fanduilun' ['A theory to counter White Australia'], *Xinmin congbao* [*The New Citizen*] 34, 24 June.
—— (1904) 'Aozhou xin neige yu ershi shiji qiantu zhi guanxi' ['The new Australian cabinet and its significance for the future of the twentieth century'], in *Yinbingshi quanji* [*Complete works of the Ice-Drinker's Studio*].
—— (1910) 'Jinggao guozhong zhi tan shiye zhe', in *Guo feng bao* 2 November, reproduced in *Jiu Shanghai de zhengquan jiaoyisu*: 265–73.
—— (1928) *Yinbingshi wenji* [*Collected Essays from the Ice-Drinkers' Studio*], 22 vols. Shanghai: Shangwu yinshjuguan.
Liang, Y. (2003) *Study on Shanghai Governors – Figures in a Changing Society 1843–1890*, trans. Chen Tong. Shanghai Classics Publishing House.
Lima, F. and Cintra Torres, E. (2004) *Macau Entre Dois Mundos.* Lisbon: Fundação Jorge Alvares and Editorial Inquérito.

Liu, H. (1987) *Shanghai Modern History*. East China Normal University Publishing House.
Liu, L.(1995) *Translingual Practice: Literature, National Culture and Translated Modernity China 1900–1937*. Palo Alto, CA: Stanford University Press.
—— (ed.) (1999) *Tokens of Exchange: The Problem of Translation in Global Circulation*. Durham, NC: Duke University Press.
Liu, S. (ed.) (1975) *Minguo renwu xiaozhuan* [*Brief Biographies of Notables in the Republic*], Vol. 17. Taipei: Zhuanji wenxue chubanshe.
Liu, Z. (2004) *Jindai Shanghai huashang zhengquan shichang yanjiu* [*Research on the Chinese Stock Market in Modern Shanghai*]. Shanghai: Xuelin chubanshe.
Lo, S. H. (1995) *Political Development in Macau*. Hong Kong: Chinese University Press.
Lopes dos Santos, A. (1968) 'Conjuntura de Macau', in *As Províncias do Oriente: curso de extensão universitária ano lectivo de 1966–1967*. Lisboa: Instituto Superior de Ciências Sociais e Política Ultramarina.
Lorin, A. (2004) *Paul Doumer, Gouverneur général de l'Indochine 1897–1902: le tremplin colonial*. Paris: L'Harmattan.
✓ Louis, W. R. (1997) 'Hong Kong: The Critical Phase, 1945–49', *American Historical Review* October.
Lowe, K. M., Cheong, C. H. and Mouy, L. A. (1879) *The Chinese Question in Australia, 1878–79*. Melbourne: F.F. Bailliere.
Lu, D.(1964) 'Jiang Jieshi, Zhang Jingjiang deng zuo jiaoyisuo jingji de wuzheng' ['Material evidence for Jiang and Zheng's involvement in the stock market'], in *Wenshi ziliao* (*Literature and History Materials*) 49: 156–58.
Lu, S. (1922) *Jiaoyisuo xianxingji* [*Revelations of the Stock Exchange*]. Shanghai: Zhonghua tushu jicheng gongsi.
Lu, X. (1956a) *Lu Xun lun meishu* [*Lu Xun on Art*], Zhang Wang 张望 (ed.). Beijing: Beijing renmin meishu.
—— (1956b) 'Ni bobu meishu yijianshu' ['Opinions on the development of fine art'] in Zhang Wang (ed.) *Lu Xun lun meishu* [*Lu Xun on Art*]. Beijing: Beijing renmin meishu, pp. 1–5.
—— (1999) 'Ni bobu meishu yijianshu' ['Opinions on the development of fine art'] in Lang Shaojun and Shui Zhongtian (eds) *Ershi shiji Zhongguo meishu wenxuan*. Shanghai: Shanghai shuhua chubanshe, Vol. 1.
Lu, Y. (2006) 'German colonial fiction on China: the Boxer Uprising of 1900', *German Life and Letters* 1: 78–100.
Lyons, T. P. (2003) *China Maritime Customs and China's Trade Statistics 1859–1948*. Trumansburg, NY: Willow Creek.
Ma, Y. (1999 [1921]) 'Shanghai jiaoyisuo qiantu zhi tuice' ['Conjectures about the Future of Shanghai Stock Exchanges'], lecture at Wusong zhongguo gongxue, reprint, *Ma Yinchu quanji*, v. 1, Hangzhou: Zhejiang renmin chubanshe, 1999, and *Shanghai zongshanghui yuebao* [*Journal of the Chinese General Chamber of Commerce*] 1(3): 20–21.
McElderry, A. (2001) 'Shanghai securities exchanges: past and present', *Occasional Paper Series in Business History* 4 (January).
McKeown, A. (2003) 'Ritualization of regulation: the enforcement of Chinese exclusion in the United States and China' *American Historical Review*, 108(2): 377–403.
Macleod, L. (1988) *Disease, Medicine and Empire, Perspectives on Western Medicine and the Experience of European Expansion*. London: Routledge.
Mao, H. (2006) 'Recommendation of officials during the 1898 Reform Movement', *Historical Research* 6. http://en.cnki.com.cn/Article_en/CJFDTotal-LSYJ200606005.htm
Marks, S. (1997) 'What is colonial about colonial medicine? And what has happened to imperialism and health?' *Social History of Medicine* 10(2): 205–19.

Markus, A. (2004) 'Reflections on the administration of the 'White Australia' immigration policy', in Sophie Couchman *et al.* (eds) *After the Rush: Regulation, Participation and Chinese Communities in Australia 1860–1940* (special edition of *Otherland*, Melbourne).
Marshall, D. B. (1973) *The French Colonial Myth and Constitution-making in the Fourth Republic.* New Haven, CT: Yale University Press.
Martin, B. (1996) *The Shanghai Green Gang: Politics and Organized Crime, 1919–1937.* Berkeley, CA: University of California Press.
Maspero, H. (1971) *Le Taoïsme et les religions chinoises.* Paris: Gallimard.
Matzat, W. (1985) *Die Tsingtauer Landordnung des Chinesenkommissars Wilhelm Schrameier.* Bonn.
—— (1986) 'Wilhelm Schrameier und die Landordnung von Qingdao', in Heng-yü Kuo and Mechthild Leutner (eds) *Beiträge zu den deutsch-chinesischen Beziehungen.* München: K.G. Saur Verlag, 33–66.
Maybon, C. B. and Fredet, J. (1929) *Histoire de la Concession française de Changhai.* Paris: Plon.
Miners, N. J. (1987) *Hong Kong under Imperial Rule, 1912–1941.* Hong Kong: Oxford University Press.
Minzhenbu (1911) *Minzhenbu Fanyi Jilu*, Beijing, Vol. 5 (The Ministry of Civil Administration).
Mitter, R. (2000) *The Manchurian Myth: Nationalism, Resistance, and Collaboration in Modern China.* Berkeley, CA: University of California Press.
—— (2008) *Modern China: A Very Short Introduction.* Oxford: Oxford University Press.
Mittler, B. (2004) *A Newspaper for China?: Power, Identity, and Change in Shanghai's News Media, 1872–1912.* Cambridge, MA: Harvard University Asia Center.
Mohr, F. W. (1911) *Handbuch für das Schutzgebiet Kiautschou.* Qingdao: W. Schmidt.
Monnais-Rousselot, L. (1997) 'Médecine coloniale, pratiques de santé et sociétés en Indochine française (1860–1939), Une histoire de l'Indochine médicale', PhD dissertation, Université Paris 7.
Morse, H. B. (1920) *The Trade and Administration of China*, 3rd revised edn. New York: Russell & Russell (reprinted 1967).
Mühlhahn, K. (1996) 'Kolonialer Raum und Symbolische Macht: Theoretische und methodische Überlegungen zur Analyse interkultureller Beziehungen', in Mechthild Leutner (ed.) *Politik, Wirtschaft, Kultur: Studien zu den deutsch-chinesischen Beziehungen.* Münster: LIT, 461–90.
—— (1998) 'Deutsche Vorposten im Hinterland. Die infrastrukturelle Durchdringung der Provinz Shandong', in Hans-Martin Hinz and Christoph Lind (ed.) *Tsingtau. Ein Kapitel deutscher Kolonialgeschichte in China, 1897–1914.* Berlin: Deutsches Historisches Museum, pp. 146–58.
—— (2000) *Herrschaft und Widerstand in der „Musterkolonie' Kiautschou: Interaktionen zwischen China und Deutschland, 1897–1914.* München: Oldenbourg.
Nagaki, D. (1989) *Kitazato Shibasaburo to sono Ichimon* [*Kitazato Shibasaburo and his Students*]. Tokyo: Keio Tsushin.
Nagayo, S.(1980[1902]) *Shoko Shishi* [Autobiography of Nagaya Sensai], reprinted by Heibonsha: Tokyo.
Nankaidaxue zhengzhixuehui (1926) (ed.) *Tianjin zujiejitequ* [*The Tianjin Concessions*]. Shizhengfucongshu, Tianjin: Shangwuyingshuguan.
Nathan, C. F. (1957) *Plague Prevention and Politics in Manchuria: 1910–1931.* Cambridge, MA: Harvard University Press.
Ngo, T.-W. (ed.) (1999) *Hong Kong's History: State and Society under Colonial Rule.* London: Routledge.
Nichols, B. (1986) *Bluejackets and Boxers: Australia's Naval Expedition to the Boxer Uprising.* Sydney: Allen & Unwin.

Nie, Q. (1922) 'Lun jiaoyisuo zhi libi yu woguo qiyejia jinhou ying you zhi juewu' ['Stock market pros and cons and what our country's entrepreneurs should understand in the future'], *Shanghai zongshanghui yuebao* 2(4).
Nocentini, L. (1904) *L'Europa nell'Estremo oriente e gli interessi italiani in Cina*. Milano: Hoepli.
Nogueira, F. (1986) *Um Politíco Confessa-se (Diário: 1960–1968)*. Porto: Livraria Editora Civilização.
Norem, R. A. (1936) *Kiachow Leased Territory*. Berkeley, CA: University of. California Press.
Nozinski, M. (1990) *Outrage at Lincheng*. Macomb, IL: Glenbridge.
Obringer, F. (1997) *L'Aconit et l'Orpiment, Drogues et poisons en Chine ancienne et medieval*. Paris: Fayard.
Osborne, M. A. (1994) *Nature, The Exotic and the Science of French Colonialism*. Bloomington, IN: Indiana University Press.
Osterhammel, J. (1986) 'Semi-colonialism and informal empire in twentieth-century China: towards a framework of analysis', in Wolfgang J. Mommsen and Jürgen Osterhammel (eds) *Imperialism and After: Continuities and Discontinuities*. London: Allen & Unwin.
—— (1997) *Colonialism: A Theoretical Overview*, Shelley L. Frisch, trans. Princeton, NJ: Markus Wiener.
Otte, T. G. (2007) *The China Question: Great Power Rivalry and British Isolation 1894–1995*. Oxford: Oxford University Press.
Pan, M. (1865) *Pingqin shuwu yilue* [*Summary of Medicine of the Pingqin Room of Books*].
Park, S. (2003) 'Exploitation and Development in Colony: Korea and India', *Korean Journal of Political Economy* 1–1.
Pavoni, R. (1997) *Reviving the Renaissance: The Use and Abuse of the Past in Nineteenth-Century Italian Art*. Cambridge: Cambridge University Press.
Pearson, M. N. (1987) *The Portuguese in India*. Cambridge: Cambridge University Press.
Petrie, G. F. (1912) 'An epidemiological review of the epidemic of pneumonic plague in northern China', *Report of the International Plague Conference held at Mukden*, April 1911, Manila.
Pistolese, G. E. (1935) 'La Concessione Italiana di Tien-Tsin', *Rassegna Italiana*, A. XIII, Special Volume (XLI) 'L'Italia e L'Oriente Medio ed Estremo', August–September: 305–10.
Pollack, S. *et al.* (2000) 'Cosmopolitanisms', *Public Culture* 12(3): 577–89.
Porter, R. (1997) *The Greatest Benefit to Mankind, A Medical History of Humanity from Antiquity to the Present*. London: Harpercollins.
Pouthiou-Lavielle (1910) 'Considérations sur la peste à Pakhoi pendant le mois de mai 1910', *Bulletin de la société médico-chirurgicale de l'Indochine*, 1(10): 507–16.
Pratt, M. L. (1991) 'Arts of the contact zone', *Profession 91*. New York: MLA: 33–40.
—— (1992) *Imperial Eyes: Travel Writing and Transculturation*. New York: Routledge.
Pyenson, L. (1985) *Cultural Imperialism and Exact Sciences. German Expansion Overseas, 1900–1930*. New York: Lang.
—— (1993) *Civilizing Mission. Exact Sciences and French Overseas Expansion, 1830–1940*. Baltimore, MD: Johns Hopkins University Press.
Qi, L. 'Shanghai Huashang Zhengquan Jiaoyisuo gaikuang' ['Overview of the Shanghai China Merchants' Securities Exchange'] in Zhongguo renmin zhingzhi xieshang huiyi (ed.) *Jiu Shanghai de jiaoyisuo*, pp. 39–42.
Quong, T. *et al.* (1888) 'To the Honorable the Representatives of the Australasian Colonies, meeting in Conference upon the Chinese Question in Sydney, June, 1888', petition presented by Quong Tart and others, New South Wales Legislative Council, Conference on Chinese Question: Proceedings of the Conference held in Sydney in June 1888, Minutes of the Proceedings, papers laid before the conference. Sydney: Government Printer.

Reed, R. (1976) *City of Pines: The Origins of Baguio as a Colonial Hill Station and Regional Capital.* Berkeley, CA: Center for Southeast Asian Studies, University of California.

Reinhardt, A. (2002) 'Navigating imperialism in China: steamship, semicolony, and nation, 1860–1937', Ph.D. Dissertation, Princeton University.

—— (2008) 'Decolonisation on the periphery: Liu Xiang and shipping rights recovery at Chongqing, 1926–38', *Journal of Imperial and Commonwealth History* 36: 259–74.

Rennie, D. F. (1865) *Peking and the Pekingese, During the First Year of the British Embassy at Peking.* London: John Murray.

Ristaino, M. R. (2002) *Port of Last Resort: The Diaspora Communities of Shanghai.* Palo Alto, CA: Stanford University Press.

Rogaski, R. (2004) *Hygienic Modernity: Meanings of Public Health in Treaty-Port China.* Berkley, CA: University of California Press.

Ruan, R. and Hu, G. (2005) *Zhongguo jinxiandai meishushi 1911–49* [*The History of Chinese Modern Art 1911–49*]. Tianjin: Tianjin renmin meishu chubanshe.

Russell, R. and Chubb, P. (1998) *One Destiny! The Federation Story: How Australia became a Nation.* Ringwood: Penguin.

Said, E. (1993) *Culture and Imperialism.* New York: Pantheon Books.

Schenk, C. R. (2001) *Hong Kong as an International Financial Centre: Emergence and Development, 1945–1965.* London: Routledge.

Schenk, C. R. (1994) *Britain and the Sterling Area: From Devaluation to Convertibility in the 1950s.* London: Routledge.

—— (1995) 'The Hong Kong gold market and the Southeast Asian gold trade in the 1950s', *Modern Asian Studies* 29(2): 387–402.

—— (2001) *Hong Kong as an International Financial Centre: Emergence and Development, 1945–1965.* London: Routledge.

—— (2004) 'The empire strikes back: Hong Kong and the decline of sterling in the 1960s', *Economic History Review* LVII(3): 551–80.

Schrecker, J.E. (1971) *Imperialism and Chinese Nationalism: Germany in Shantung.* Cambridge, MA: Harvard University Press

Seelemann, D. A. (1982) 'The social and economic development of the Kiaochou Leasehold (Shantung, China) under German administration, 1897–1914', PhD dissertation, Toronto.

Selle, E. A. (1948) *Donald of China.* New York: Harper & Brothers.

Shan, K. and Liu, H. (1996) *Tianjin: Zujie zheshui yanjiu.* Tianjin: Tianjin Renmin Chubanshe.

Shandong, S. (ed.) (1961) *Shandong Jindaishi ziliao* [*Materials on Modern Shandong History*], 3 vols. Jinan.

Shanghai Archives (ed.) (2001) *Board Meeting Minutes of the Industrial Services Bureau*, vols 15 and 16, *Board Meeting Minutes by Municipal Committee.* Shanghai: Social Science Publishing House.

Shanghai shi difang xiehui (1933) *Shanghai shi tongji* [*Statistics for Shanghai Municipality*]. Shanghai.

Shanghai renmin yinghang shanghai shi fenhang (ed.) (1978) *Shanghai qianzhuang shiliao* [*Materials on Shanghai Native Banks*]. Shanghai: Shanghai renmin chubanshe, 1978 reprint of 1960 edn.

Sheng, X. (1975) *Archives for Political Campaigns of Sheng Xuanhuai*, several vols. Beijing: Wenhai Publishing House.

Shigehisa, K. (1993) 'Concepts of disease in East Asia', in K. Kiple (ed.) *The Cambridge World History of Human Disease.* Cambridge: Cambridge University Press, pp. 52–59.

Shih, S.-M. (2001) *The Lure of the Modern: Writing Modernism in Semicolonial China, 1917–1937*. Berkeley, CA: University of California Press.
Sihn, K.-H. (2006) *Jilbyeong-ui Sahoisa* [*The Social History of Disease*]. Paju: Sallim Publishing.
Sincere Co. Ltd (1924) *Twenty Fifth Anniversary*. Hong Kong: Commercial Press.
Sinn, E. (1989) *Power and Charity: The Early History of the Tung Wah Hospital*. Hong Kong: Oxford University Press.
Smart, A. (2007) 'The origins of public housing in Hong Kong: Cold War geopolitics and the limits of colonial power', paper presented at the AAS conference, Boston.
Snow, P. (2003) *The Fall of Hong Kong: Britain, China and the Japanese Occupation*. New Haven, CT: Yale University Press.
Sournia, J. C. (1992) *Histoire de la medicine*. Paris: La découverte.
Souza, G. B. (1986) *The Survival of Empire: Portuguese Trade and Society in the South China Sea, 1630–1754*. Cambridge: Cambridge University Press.
Spence, J. (2001) *The Search for Modern China*. New York: W. W. Norton & Company.
Spurr, D. (1993) *The Rhetoric of Empire*. Durham, NC and London: Duke University Press.
Stanley, A. (1908) 'Health and hospitals', in Arnold Wright (ed.) *Twentieth Century Impressions of Hongkong, Shanghai, and Other Treaty Ports of China: Their History, People, Commerce, Industries, and Resources*. London: Lloyds Greater Britain Publishing Company.
Steinmetz, G. (2007) *The Devil's Handwriting: Precoloniality and the German Colonial State in Qingdao, Samoa, and Southwest Africa*. Chicago, IL: Chicago University Press.
Stichler, H. C. (1989) 'Das Gouvernement Jiaozhou und die deutsche Kolonialpolitik in Shandong 1897–1909. Ein Beitrag zur Geschichte der deutsch-chinesischen Beziehungen', PhD dissertation, Humboldt Universität zu Berlin.
Stoler, A. (1995) *Race and Education of Desire: Foucault's History of Sexuality and the Colonial Order of Things*. Durham, NC: Duke University Press.
Stoler, A. L. (2006) 'On degrees of imperial sovereignty', *Public Culture* 18(1): 125–46.
Stoler, A. L. and MacGranahan, C. (2007) 'Refiguring imperial terrains', in Ann Laura Stoler and Carole McGranahan (eds) *Imperial Formations*. Santa Fe, NM: Oxford School for Advanced Research Press, pp. 3–44.
Subrahmanyam, S. (1993) *The Portuguese Empire in Asia, 1500–1700: A Political and Economic History*. London and New York: Longman.
Sullivan, M. (1996) *Art and Artist of Twentieth-Century China*. Berkeley, CA: University of Berkeley Press.
Sun, Y. (1923) *Guofu Quanji* [*The Complete Works of the Founding Father*]. Taibei: Zhongguo Guomin Zhongyang Weiyuanhui, Vol. 1. Sanminzhuyi Lecture 2: 19.
Sun, Y.-S. (1927) *San Min Chu I: The Three Principles of the People*, trans. Frank Price. Shanghai: Institute of Pacific Relations.
Taiwan Sotokufu Minseibu Eiseika (1898) *Public Health Department of Japanese Colonial Government in Taiwan Meiji Nijyukune Taiwan Pesutobyo Ryukou Kiji* [*The Pandemic of Plague of 1896 in Taiwan*]. Taihoku.
Tam, C. (1994) *Disputes Concerning Macau's Sovereignty between China and Portugal, 1553–1993*. Taibei: Yongye Press.
Tang, Kaijian [湯開建] (1997) 'Tian Shengjin "An Yue shugao' zhong de Aomen shiliao"' [田生金《按粵疏稿》中的澳門史料] ['Historical materials on Macau in Tian Shengjin's "Memorials from Guangdong"'], *Revista de cultura* (Chinese edn) 33: 45–53.
Tang, K.-L. (1998) *Colonial State and Social Policy: Social Welfare Development in Hong Kong 1842–1997*. Lanham, MD: University Press of America.
Tang, X. (2008) *Origins of the Chinese Avant-Garde: The Modern Woodcut Movement*. Berkeley, CA: University of California Press.

Tang, Z. (ed.) (1994) *Jiaoyisuo zhenxiang de tanmi zhe–Jiang Hongjiao* [*Jiang Hongjiao, Sleuth of Secret Stock Market Truths*]. Zhongguo jinxiandai tongsu zuojia pingzhuan congshu, v. 7. Nanjing: Nanjing chubanshe.

Tang, Z. (ed.) (1981) *Kang Youwei zhenglunji* [*The Political Writings of Kang Youwei*]. Beijing.

Taylor, C. (2004) *Modern Social Imaginaries*. Durham, NC: Duke University Press.

Thomas, N. (1994) *Colonialism's Culture: Anthropology, Travel and Government*. Princeton, NJ: Princeton University Press.

Thomas, W. A. (2001) *Western Capitalism in China*. Aldershot: Ashgate.

Thompson, R. R. (1995) *China's Local Councils in the Age of Constitutional Reform, 1898–1911*. Cambridge: Cambridge University Press.

Thompson, V. E. (2000) *The Virtuous Marketplace: Women and Men, Money and Politics in Paris, 1830–1870*. Baltimore and London: Johns Hopkins University Press.

Tianjin, S. K. L. Y. (ed.) (1987) *Tianjin jianshi* [*An Introductory History to Tianjin*]. Tianjin: Renmin Chubanshe.

Tong, H. (1921) 'Controversy over the Shanghai Stock and Produce Exchange', *Millard's Review*, 22 January

Tsai, W. (2005) 'Port of call: case study of Tongzhou', paper presented at conference on the Maritime Customs and Modern China, Nanjing.

Tsang, S. (2004) *A Modern History of Hong Kong*. London: I. B. Taurus.

—— (2006) *The Cold War's Odd Couple: The Unintended Partnership between the ROC and the UK, 1950–1958*. London: I. B. Taurus.

Tseng, M. (Zeng Jize) (1887) 'China, the sleep and the awakening', *Chinese Recorder and Missionary Journal* 18(4 April): 146–53.

Tsin, M. (1999) *Nation, Governance, and Modernity in China: Canton, 1900–1927*. Palo Alto, CA: Stanford University Press.

Tsuruta, T. (ed.) (1974) '*Materials on Chinese Painters of the Last Hundred Years, Compiled by Takeyoshi Tsuruta*' Part II, based on Tsuruta's publications in *Bijiutsu Kenkyu* nos 293, 294, 303, 307.

Turin, Y. (1971) *Affrontements culturels dans l'Algérie colonial*. Paris: Maspero.

Unschuld, P.U. (1985) *Medicine in China, A History of Ideas*. Berkeley, CA: University of California Press.

Uthemann, W. and Fürth, U. (eds) (1911) 'Tsingtau. Ein kolonialhygienischer Rückblick', *Beiheft 4 der Beihefte zum Archiv für Schiffs-und Tropenhygiene* 15: 5–39.

Van Ness, P. (1970) *Revolution and Chinese Foreign Policy: Peking's Support for Wars of National Liberation*. Berkeley, CA: University of California Press.

Vandervort, B. (1998) *Wars of Imperial Conquest in Africa, 1830–1914*. London: UCL Press.

de Vattel, E. and Chitty, J. (eds) (1758 [1883]) *The Law of Nations, Or, Principles of the Law of Nature, Applied to the Conduct and Affairs of Nations and Sovereigns: From the French of Monsieur de Vattel*, with additional notes by Edward Ingraham. Philadelphia, PA: T.W. Johnson and Co.

Vaughan, M. (1991) *Curing their Ills: Colonial Power and African Illness*. Palo Alto, CA: Stanford University Press.

van de Ven, H. (ed.) (2006) 'Robert Hart and the Chinese Maritime Customs Service', *Modern Asian Studies* 40: 545–736.

Vertovec, S. and Cohen, R. (eds) (2002) *Conceiving Cosmopolitanism: Theory, Context, and Practice*. Oxford: Oxford University Press.

Vittinghoff, N. (2002) *Die Anfänge des Journalismus in China (1860–1911)*. Wiebaden: Harrasowitz.

von Heyking, E. (1904) *Briefe, die ihn nicht erreichten* [*Letters that did not reach him*]. Berlin.

Wagner, R. G. (1995) 'The Role of the foreign community in the Chinese public sphere', *China Quarterly* 142: 423–43.
Wagner, R. (ed.) (2007) *Joining the Global Public: Word, Image, and City in Early Chinese Newspapers*. Albany, NY: State University of New York Press.
Wakeman, F., Jr. (1991) 'Models of historical change: the Chinese state and society, 1839–1989', in Kenneth Lieberthal (ed.) *Perspectives on Modern China. Four Anniversaries*. Armonk, NY: M.E. Sharpe, 68–102.
Wakeman, F. (1995) *Policing Shanghai, 1927–1937*. Berkeley, CA: University of California Press.
Wakeman, C. and Light, K. (2003) *Assignment Shanghai: Photographs on the Eve of Revolution*. Berkeley, CA: University of California Press.
Wallerstein, I. (1974) *The Modern World System: Capitalist Agriculture and the Origins of the European World-Economy in the Sixteenth Century*. New York: Academic Press.
Walsh, W. B. (1943) 'The Yunnan myth', *Far Eastern Quarterly* 2: 272–85.
Wang, D. D.-W. (2001) 'In the name of the real' in Maxwell K. Hearn and Judith G. Smith (eds) *Chinese Art, Modern Expressions*. New York: Department of Asian Art, Metropolitan Museum of Art, pp. 29–59.
Wang, E. (1921) *Jiaoyisuo daquan* [*The Complete Stock Exchange*]. Shanghai: Jiaoyisuo yuan shuqi yangchengsuo [Stock Market Employee Summer Training Institute].
Wang, S. (1987) *Deguo qinlüe Shandongshi* [*The German Expansion in Shandong*]. Beijing.
Wang, S.-W. (2001) 'Chinese immigration 1840s–1890s', in James Jupp (ed.) *The Australian People: An Encyclopedia of the Nation, Its People and their Origins*. Melbourne: Cambridge University Press.
Wang, X. (2007) *Zhishifenzi de neizhan: Xiandai Shanghaide wenhua changyu (1927–1930)* [*In-fights among the Intellectuals: The Cultural Spheres in Modern Shangahi, 1927–30*]. Shanghai: Shanghai renmin chubanshe.
Wang, Y. (2007) 'Venturing into Shanghai: the *flâneur* in two of Shi Zhecun's short stories', *Modern Chinese Literature and Culture*. 19(2): 34–70.
Wang, Z. (1922) *Qingdao*. Qingdao.
Ward, R. S. (1943) *Hong Kong under Japanese Occupation; A Case Study in the Enemy's Techniques of Control*, prepared by American Consul, detailed to the Far Eastern Unit, Bureau of Foreign and Domestic Commerce, Department of Commerce, Washington, DC.
Warner, T. (1998) 'Der Aufbau der Kolonialstadt Tsingtau: Landordnung, Stadtplanung und Entwicklung', in Hans-Martin Hinz and Christoph Lind (eds) *Tsingtau. Ein Kapitel deutscher Kolonialgeschichte in China, 1897–1914*. Berlin: Deutsches Historisches Museum, pp. 84–95.
Wasserstrom, J. N. (2000) 'Locating old Shanghai: having fits about where it fits', in J. W. Esherick (ed.) *Remaking the Chinese City: Modernity and National Identity, 1900–1950*. Honolulu: University of Hawaii Press, pp. 192–210.
Weber, M. (1985) *Wirtschaft und Gesellschaft*. Tübingen: Mohr.
Welch, I. (2003) 'Alien son: the life and times of Cheok Hong Cheong, 1851–1928', PhD Dissertation, Australian National University.
Welland, S. S.-L. (2006) *A Thousand Miles of Dreams: The Journeys of Two Chinese Sisters*. Lanham, MD: Rowman & Littlefield.
Wesley-Smith, P. (1994) 'Anti-Chinese Legislation in Hong Kong', in Ming K. Chan (ed.) *Precarious Balance: Hong Kong between China and Britain*. Armonk, NY: Sharpe.
Wilton, J. (1998) 'Chinese stores in rural Australia', in Kerrie L. MacPherson (ed.) *Asian Department Stores*. Richmond, UK: Curzon.
Wolfe, P. (1997) 'History and imperialism: a century of theory, from Marx to postcolonialism', *American Historical Review* 102(2): 388–420.

Wong, A. K. (1972) *The Kaifong Associations and the Society of Hong Kong*. Taipei: Orient Cultural Service.
Woodhead, H. G. W. (1925) *The Truth about the Chinese Republic*. London: Hurst.
—— (1934) *A Journalist in China*. London: Hurst and Blackett.
Wright, A. and Cartwright, H. A. (eds) (1908) *Twentieth Century Impressions of Hongkong, Shanghai, and other Treaty Ports of China: Their History, People, Commerce, Industries, and Resources*. London: Lloyds Greater Britain Publishing Company.
Wright, S. F. (1950) *Hart and the Chinese Customs*. Belfast: The Queen's University.
Wu, D. Y. H. (1982) *The Chinese in Papua New Guinea: 1880–1980*. Hong Kong: Chinese University Press.
Wu, J. (2001) 'Observation to 2nd Siming Assembly Hall Incident', *Historical Studies* 4.
Wu, L.-T. (1959), *Plague Fighter: The Autobiography of a Modern Chinese Physician*. Cambridge: W. Heffer & Sons.
Xianggang yongan youxian gongsi ershiwu zhounian jinianlu (1932) [*Commemorative Record of the Twenty Fifth Anniversary of the Hong Kong Wing On Company*]. Hong Kong: Wing On Publishers.
Xie, K. (1920) *Ershi'er nian lai zhi Jiaozhouwan* [*Jiaozhou Bay in the last 22 Years*]. Shanghai.
Xiong, Y. (1988) 'Discourse on the Anti-Russia Campaign in Shanghai', in Tang Zhenchang et al. (eds) *Study on History of Shanghai March*. Xuelin Press.
Xu, B. (1999a) 'Huo' ['Perplexity'], in Lang Shaojun and Shui Zhongtian (eds) *Ershi shiji Zhongguo meishu wenxuan* [*Selected Writings on Art in China in the Twentieth Century*], Vol. 1. Shanghai: Shanghai shuhua chubanshe, pp. 200–202.
—— (1999b) 'Huo zhi bu jie' ['Perplexity unresolved'], in Lang Shaojun and Shui Zhongtian (eds) *Ershi shiji Zhongguo meishu wenxuan* [*Selected Writings on Art in China in the Twentieth Century*], Vol. 1. Shanghai: Shanghai shuhua chubanshe, pp. 218–22.
—— (1999c) 'Huo zhi bu jie (xu)' ['Perplexity unresolved' (continued)], in Lang Shaojun and Shui Zhongtian (eds) *Ershi shiji Zhongguo meishu wenxuan* [*Selected Writings on Art in China in the Twentieth Century*], Vol. 1. Shanghai: Shanghai shuhua chubanshe, pp. 223–25.
Xu, X. (1997) 'National essence' vs 'science': Chinese native physicians' fight for legitimacy, 1912–37', *Modern Asian Studies* 31(4): 847–77.
—— (2008) *Trial of Modernity: The Judicial Reform in Early Twentieth-Century China, 1901–1937*. Palo Alto, CA: Stanford University Press.
Xu, Y. and Billingsley, P. (2000) 'When worlds collide: Chinese bandits and their 'foreign tickets'', *Modern China* 26(1).
Xu, Z. (1929) 'Meizhan bianyan' ['Opening remarks on the First National Art Exhibition'], *Meizhan* 1(10 April): 1.
—— (1999) 'Wo ye huo' ('I also am perplexed') in Lang Shaojun and Shui Zhongtian (eds) *Ershi shiji Zhongguo meishu wenxuan* [*Selected Writings on Art in China in the Twentieth Century*], Vol. 1. Shanghai: Shanghai shuhua chubanshe, pp. 203–13.
Yan, J. (Yen Chuan-ying) (ed.) (2006) *Shanghai meishu fengyun: 1872–1949 Shenbao yishu ziliao diaomu suoyin (Arts in Shanghai, 1872–1949*: an index of articles, reviews, advertisements, and news items published in Shenbao newspaper. Taipei: Academia Sinica.
Yan, Y. X. (1996) 'The Culture of Guanxi in a north China village', *China Journal* 35: 1–25.
Yang, L. (2007) 'Die Ereignisse von Gaomi und der Widerstand der Bevölkerung gegen den deutschen Eisenbahnbau', in Mechhild Leutner and Klaus Mühlhahn (eds) *Kolonialkrieg in China. Die Niederschlagung der Boxerbewegung*. Berlin: Ch. Links, pp. 49–59.
Yang, Q. (1999) 'Huo hou xiaoyan' ['Some brief remarks after perplexity'], in Lang Shaojun and Shui Zhongtian (eds) *Ershi shiji Zhongguo meishu wenxuan* [*Selected Writings on Art in China in the Twentieth Century*], Vol. 1. Shanghai: Shanghai shuhua chubanshe, pp. 226–27.

Yang, T. and Xuezhuang, W. (1978) *The Anti-Russia Campaign in 1901–1905*. Beijing: China Social Sciences Press.

Yang, T. (2000) 'Jiang Zhongzheng xiansheng he Shanghai Zhengquan wupin jiaoyisuo', *Jindai Zhongguo* [*Modern China Bimonthly*] 139 (October).

—— (2002) 'Perspectives on Chiang Kai-shek's early thought from his unpublished diary' in Mechthild Leutner (ed.) *The Chinese Revolution in the 1920s*. London and New York: Routledge.

Yarwood, A. T. (1968) *Asian Migration to Australia: The Background to Exclusion 1896–1923*. Melbourne: Melbourne University Press.

Yeh, C. V. (2006) *Shanghai Love: Courtesans, Intellectuals, and Entertainment Culture, 1850–1910*. Seattle, WA: University of Washington Press.

Yeh, W.-H. (2007) *Shanghai Splendor: Economic Sentiments and the Making of Modern China, 1843–1949*. Berkeley, CA: University of California Press.

Yen, C.-H. (1998) 'Wing On and the Kwok brothers: a case study of pre-war Chinese entrepreneurs' in Kerrie L. MacPherson (ed.) *Asian Department Stores*. Richmond, UK: Curzon.

Yersin, A. (1908) 'Notes sur une épidémie de peste à Nha Trang', *Annales d'Hygiène et de Médecine Coloniale* 11: 442–44.

Yip, K.-C. (1995) *Health and National Reconstruction in Nationalist China*, Ann Arbor: Association for Asian Studies, University of Michigan.

Yong, C. F. (1977) *The New Gold Mountain: The Chinese in Australia 1901–1921*, Adelaide: Raphael Arts.

Yong, C. F. and McKenna, R. B. (1990) *The Kuomintang Movement in British Malaya, 1912–1949*, Singapore: Singapore University Press.

Young, J. (1998) 'Sun Yatsen and the department store: an aspect of national reconstruction', in Kerrie L. MacPherson (ed.) *Asian Department Stores*, Richmond, UK: Curzon.

Yu, H. (1947) 'Min yuan lai woguo zhi zhengquan jiaoyi' ['Domestic securities trading since the first year of the Republic'], in Zhu Sihuang (ed.) *Minguo jingjishi* [*Economic History of the Republic*]. Shanghai.

Yue, M. (2006) *Shanghai and the Edges of Empires*. Minneapolis, MN: University of Minnesota Press.

Zhang, J. (1994) 'Wan Qing zikai shangbu shulun' ['On the self-opened commercial zones in the late Qing-period'], *Jindaishi yanjiu* [*Research on Modern History*] 5: 73–88.

Zhang, S. (1991) 'Li Hongzhang yu Jiaozhouwan' [Li Hongzhang and the Jiaozhou Bay], in Liu Shanzhang and Zhou Quan (eds) *Zhong De guanxi shi wencong* [*Essays on the History of Sino–German Relations*]. Qingdao, pp. 66–80.

Zhang, Y. (1986) 'Qingdao de shili juan' ['The sphere of influence of Qingdao'], in Institute of Modern History, Academia Sinica (ed.) *Jindai Zhongguo quyushi yantaohui lunwenji* [*Essays of the Conference on Regional Modernisation in Modern China*]. Taibei, pp. 801–38.

Zhao, L. and Ding, Y. (2002) *Zhongguo youhua wenxian 1542–2000* [*Oil painting in China and Chinese writings on art, 1542–2000*]. Changsha: Hunan meishu chubanshe.

Zheng, S. (2004) 'Waves lashed the Bund from the west: Shanghai's art scene in the 1930s', in Jo-Anne Birnie Danzker *et al.* (eds) *Shanghai Modern: 1919–1945*. Ostfildern-Ruit: Hatje Cantz, pp. 174–98.

Zhu, B. and Ruilin, C. (eds) (1989) *Zhongguo xihua wushinian: 1898–1949* [*Fifty Years of Western Paintings in China: 1898–1949*]. Beijing: Renmin meishu chubanshe.

Zhu, S. (1947) *Minguo jingji shi* [*Economic History of the Republic*]. Shanghai.

Zhu, T. (ed.) (1989) *Jiu Zhongguo jiaoyisuo jieshao*. Beijing: Zhongguo shangye chubanshe.

Zhu, Y. (1998) 'Jindai Shanghai zhengquan shichang shang gupiao maimai de sanci gaochao' ['Three peaks of stock-purchasing in modern Shanghai's securities markets'], in *Zhongguo jingjishi yanjiu* [*Research on China's Economic History*].

Zhu, Z. (1994) 'Zhengquan wupin jiaoyisuo jianshu' ['Brief account of the Securities and Commodities Exchange'], in Zhongguo renmin zhengzhi xieshang huiyi Shanghai shi weiyuanhui wenshi ziliao weiyuanhui (ed.) *Jiu Shanghai de jiaoyisuo*. Shanghai: Shanghai shi zhengxie wenshi ziliao ziliao bianji bu.

Zou, Y. (1980) *Jiu shanghai renkou bianqian de yanjiu* [*A study of population change in old Shanghai*]. Shanghai: Shanghai renmin chubanshe.

INDEX

Note: Page numbers in *italic* type indicate maps or figures; those followed by 'n' indicate a note.

123 Incident 212–13, 216–19; oral history project 219–22

Adelaide, Australia 187
administration 27; role of Europeans 28
advisors, foreign 28, 35
Aglen, Sir Francis 29
All Circles Committee 218
Álvares, Jorge 214
Amaral, Ferreira do 214
American Declaration of Independence 184
American Federation of Labor 207
Anderson, Ron 14
Angell Treaty 183
architecture: Chinese 106, 158, 164; Italian 99–102; in Tianjin 17; Walter Frey 18
Area Bureaux, Hong Kong 202
art 157–8; in Shanghai 167–77
Ashton, K. C. 205–6
Asia, pan-Asianism 201–2
Asiatic Petroleum Company 33
Australia: Chinese Australian businesses 188–90; civic life 187–90; and Pacific islands 191, 192–3; treatment of Chinese émigrés in 18, 19, 180–1, 182–7, 195–6
Austria-Hungary: colonialism in China 2; Tianjin concession 93, *93*
automobile industry 60
Aw Boon-haw 201

babies 144
Balfour, Arthur 90
banana trade 190–1
baojia-system 48, 204
Barton, Edmund 186
Bassi, Ugo 103

Beihai *136*; French medicine in 137; police bureau 139
Beijing: decline of 168; Diplomatic Body 9
Beijing Guanhua Bao (*Beijing Mandarin Paper*) 50–1
Belgium: Tianjin concession *93*; treaty rights in China 2
benign colonialism 102–4
Benvenuti, Guiseppe Messerotti 104, 105–6
Bickers, Robert 9, 10, 15, 25–36
Birns, Jack 25
Blake, Henry 87
Bonetti (architect) 101
Borgnino, Rinaldo Luigi 102–3
bourgeoisie, Chinese 4, 5
Bowen, George 84
Boxer Protocol (1901) 180
Boxer Rebellion (1900) 12, 47, 94, 103–4, 106n3, 119, 138, 139, 151, 152, 156
boycotts: anti-Japanese 63; Hong Kong (1925–6) 90–1; Macau 221; Qingdao 49–50
breastfeeding 144
Bretelle-Establet, Florence 18, 134–50
Briefe, die ihn nicht erreichten (*Letters that did mot reach him*) (von Heyking) 153, 155–6, 157, 163
Britain 1, 7, 8; British Settlement, Shanghai 109; business relations with Germany in China 29; commercial trade agreement with Japan 90; importance in China 31; informal empire 26, 28, 35–6; a the new imperialism 199–201; post-war debt to United States 200; Sterling Zone 199–201; Tianjin concession *93*, 101

bubble of (1921–2) 57, 58, 63, 65–6, 70–3
Bubbling Well Road Cemetery *see* BWC (Bubbling Well Road Cemetery), Shanghai
Building Code, Tainjin 99–100
burial grounds *see* cemeteries
Burma, hill stations 82
BWC (Bubbling Well Road Cemetery), Shanghai 113, *114*, 115, 117, 126–8, *129*

Cai Yuanpei 170, 171, 172, 175
Canton *136*; French medicine in 139, 140; police bureau 139; retail development 194, 195
capitalism: capitalist imperialism 3; and morality 63, 69–73
Carlotto, Ermanno 103
Carpine, Giovanni da Pian del 103
Carroll, John 10, 16–17, 21n11, 188; Peak residential segregation study 16–17, 81–91
Cartier-Bresson, Henri 25
Carvalho, José Manuel Nobre de 217, 218, 222
Casabianca, Dr. 140
Cecchetti, Adolfo 99
cemeteries: and the Shandong Railway Company 46; Shanghai case study 17, 108–30
Cerveira, Carlos Mota 216
Ceylon, hill stations 82
Chamberlain, Joseph 85, 198
Changyi Guild 49
charitable missions 8
Chatterjee, Partha 177
Chen Bulei 63
Chen Duxiu 57–8
Chen Guofu 63, 74n13
Chen Hongming 5
Chen Xiaodie 171
Cheng, C. L. 193
Cheung Chau 90, 91
Chiang Kai-shek (Jiang Jieshi) 83, 178n1; Madame Chiang Kai-shek 90; and stock exchanges 59, 63, 64, 73, 74n13
China: colonial modernity in 195–6; defeat by Japan (1895) 51; hill stations 82, 83, *see also* People's Republic of China
China Enterprise Society 64
'China-centered studies' 7
Chinese Co-operative Council, Hong Kong 201, 202
Chinese Commerce Association, Macau 215, 217
Chinese Committee, Qingdao 49–50

Chinese Communist Party 4, 215, 219; and art 169, 175
Chinese General Chamber of Commerce 89
Chinese Maritime Customs Service *see* CMCS
Chinese Representative Council, Hong Kong 201
Chinese Seamen and Associated Seafaring Trades Union 202
Chinese staff of CMCS 30–1
cholera 142
Chow Shou-son 201
Christianity, and cemetery policy in Shanghai 116
Chuey, James (Huang Zhu) 190
Chui Tak-kei 215, 217
churches, Chinese 189, 190
CIA 207
Cicchiti-Suriani, A. 95, 96
civic life, in Australia 187–90
Clayton, Cathryn 20
cleanliness, and German attitude to China 154–5
CMCS (Chinese Maritime Customs Service) 8, 13, 15, 25–7, 35–6; Hart's role 27–32; Nanning case study 32–5, *see also* treaty-ports
Co-prosperity Sphere 202
coal mining *see* mining industry
Cohen, Paul 6–7
Cold War 197, 204; and Hong Kong 206–8
Colonial Office, British 84, 86, 87, 89, 90, 91, 200, 205; and Hong Kong 84, 85
colonial states, military dependence of 198
colonialism 37; benign 102–4; colonial formations 7–9; colonial institutions 8–9; colonial studies 11–12; ending of 2–3, 20n3; informal 26, 28, 35–6; multiple colonialisms 11–12; and realist art 176–7; resistance to in Qingdao 44–53; terminology of 3–7, *see also* semi-colonialism
Committee of Concerned Asian Scholars 6
commuting, by Chinese communities in Australia 188, 196
Concordia Society 202
Confucianism: destruction of library at Gaomi 46; and hierarchy 181, 186
Consular Bodies 9
contact zones 104–5
Cooper, Frederick 11
cosmopolitanism 178n2; in Shanghai 167–9, 176

cremation 113; Sikhs 118
criminal law, in Kiaochow 41
Crispi, Francesco 95
Crusens, High Judge 41
Cui Biyu 146
'cultural colonization' 6
Cultural Revolution 216, 219, 220
Customs College 30–1
customs revenues 13, 29

Dah Sun 190, *see also* Four Great Companies
Dai Jitao 61, 74n6
Dalian (Darien), Russian/Japanese administration of 29
death *see* cemeteries
decolonization 2, 203, 205, *see also* independence movements
department stores 190–1, 194–5
Des Voeux, William 82, 84–5
Detring, Gustav 30
dietary advice 144, 146
Ding Gangren 148
Diplomatic Body, Beijing 9
Diplomatic Corps 13
discrimination *see* racial discrimination
District Bureaux, Hong Kong 202, 203–4
domestic life, colonial 18
Doumer, Paul 32, 136, 137
drugs: medical 140–2; traditional medicine 145–6
Du Yuesheng 83
Duanyang festival 147
Duara, Prasenjit 8

economics; and morality 69–73
education 37; art schools 169; Customs College 30–1; German-Chinese College, Qingdao 52, 53; Hong Kong 211; missionary schools 30
Egypt, role of European experts/advisors 28
Ehrlich, Paul 141
electricity industry, Qingdao 40
entrepot trade, Hong Kong 209–10
epidemics 135–6
equality: and racial discrimination in Australia 182–7, 195–6; of sovereign states 180, 181–2, 184–5; and the 'Unequal Treaties' 180–1, 182
Esserteau, Dr. 138, 148
Ethiopia 95, 107n9
ethnography, and racial segregation 43
Eurasians: in Hong Kong 88–9, 91; in Macau 215
Europeans, expert/advisory role of 28

Executive Council, Hong Kong 83, 84, 85, 90, 202
extraterritoriality 10, 12–13, 30, 180; and stock exchanges 67

Fairbank, John 6
families, in colonial society 43
Far Eastern Review 13
Fashoda Iincident (1898) 29
Fay, Harry (Louie Mew Fay, Lei Miaohui) 194
FC (French Concession), Shanghai: and cemeteries 108, 109, 110, 112, 113, 115, 116, 117, 118–20, 124; and stock exchanges 66–7
Feng Zikai 170
Feray, Dr. 139, 149
feudalism 4
fiction: based on stock markets 71–2; epistolary 152; German 153–4
Fifth Memorial (Kang Youwei) 44
Fiji 190, 191, 192, 193
Fileti, Vincenzo 94, 103, 104, 106
fires: Shek Kip Mei fire, Hong Kong 208; in Tianjin 159
First World War 2, 8, 39, 198; and Italy 102
Fitzgerald, John 19, 180–96
FNAE (First National Art Exhibition), Shanghai (1929) 19, 167, 169–77
Foreign and Colonial Office, British 17
foreign nationals 14
Foucault, Michel 92–3, 98–9
Four Great Companies 190, 193–5, *see also* Dah Sun; Sincere; Sun Sun; Wing On
France: attitude to colonies 198, 199; colonial troops 118; colonialism in China 1, 2, 32, 135–6, *136*; FC (French Concession), Shanghai 108, 109, 110, 112, 113, 115, 116, 117, 118–20, 124; medicine 17–18, 134–49; Tianjin concession *93*
French Mixed Court 9
French Municipal Council 109, 115, 119, 129
Frey, Elisabeth, letters home from China 18, 151–64
Frey, Walther 18, 151
fruit trade 190–1
Fry, Roger 178n8
Fuzhou, treaty-port status 1

Gallina, Giovanni 95, 96
gambling 70, 74n5; in Macau 213, 214, 215
Gaomi, German military action in 46, 47

Gascoigne, William 85
Germany: business relations with Britain in China 29; colonialism in China 1, 2, 7, 8, 15–16, 20n12, 29, 37–54; Elisabeth Frey's letters home from Tianjin 18, 151–64; German law in Kiaochow 41–2; naval forces 39, 40, 54n1; New Order 199; Pacific territories 193; Tianjin concession 93, 101
Giolitti, Giovanni 95
Gock brothers 194
Gock Lock, James (Guo Le) 191
Gockchin, Philip (Guo Chuan) 191
gold trade 215, 219–20
Gong Pengshou 145
Goodman, Bryna 1–22, 124; Chinese stock exchanges study 16, 57–77
Goodman, David S. G. 1–22; German colonial life in Tianjin 18, 151–64
governance, colonial 7–8, 9–11, 15–16
governmentality, colonial 37
Grantham, Sir Alexander 91, 204, 205
greed 72–3
Guangdong 135, *136*; *Duanyang* festival 147; and French colonialism 2; French medicine in 134
Guangdong Guild 49
Guangdong Province Foreign Affairs Office 218
Guangxi 33, 34, 135, *136*; *Duanyang* festival 147; and French colonialism 2; French medicine in 134
Guangzhou (Canton) 10; treaty-port status 1
Guangzhouwan 1, 18, 135, *136*; status of French doctors in 137–8, 148
guilds: in Kiaochow 49; and securities trading 59
guohua (national painting) 175
Guomindang (Kuomintang; Nationalist Party) 52, 193; and finance 61; and hypo-colonialism 4; and judicial system 14; and treaty revision 2

Haikou *136*; French medicine in 137, 149
Hainan *136*
Haiyang Guild 49
Hankou, administration 7–8
Hanoteaux, Gabriel 135
Haoli 46–7
Harder, A. 153, 156
Hart, Sir Robert 26, 27–32
Hayes, James 204
He Mengyao 145
healing, and religion 147

Hennessy, John 83
Henriot, Christian 9, 10, 17, 108–33
Hersey, John 93
heterotopia 98, 99
Heungshan County, entrepreneurs from 189, 191, 193–4
Hevia, James 7
hierarchy, Confucian notions of 181, 186
hill stations 81, 82–3
HJC (Hungjao Cemetery), Shanghai 113, 115, 120, 123–4, 126, *127*
Ho Fook 90
Ho Kai 86–7
Ho Kam Tong 87–8, 89
Ho, Stanley 214, 215, 220
Ho Tung, Robert 87, 88, 89, 90, 201
Ho Yin 215, 216, 219, 220
Hong Kong: administration 7; and Chinese Australian businesses 188, 189, 194, 195; and the Cold War 206–8; colony status 1, 2; financial devolution 205–6; and the Hong Kong Contract 204–6; and the Hong Kong gap 208–10; 'Hong Kong model' of colonialism 12; Japanese residents 89–90; Japanese wartime occupation 91, 201–4; and migration 10, 20n11; and minority communities 10; and the new imperialism 197, 210–11; Peak residential segregation study 16–17, 81–2, 83–91, 203; post-war relationship with UK 19–20; retail development 194, 195; sterling reserves of 200–1; transfer to PRC (1997) 2
Hong Yuen 194, 195
housing *see* Peak, Hong Kong, residential segregation study
Huang Chujiu 68
Huang Yan 145
Hughes, A. J. 76
Hundred-days Reform 45
Hungjao Cemetery *see* HJC (Hungjao Cemetery), Shanghai
hypercolonies 4, 92
hypo-colonies 3, 4, 92

identity 9–11; and colonial governance 15–16
Imperial Maritime Customs Service *see* CMCS (Chinese Maritime Customs Service)
independence movements 200, *see also* decolonization
India, hill stations 81, 82, 83
India Office 91
Indochina, French colonialism in 135, 137

Index **251**

ink-brush painting 169, 175
insider information 60
International Mixed Court 8–9
International Settlement *see* IS
Investment Fund for Economic and Social Development 199
iron industry, Germany 40
IS (International Settlement), Shanghai 108, 109, 110, 115, 116–17, 121
Italy 8; concession in Tianjin 17, 92–106; and the First World War 102; Italo-Ethiopian War 95
Ivory Coast 200

Jaeschke 46, 47
Japan 20n12; cemeteries in Shanghai 116, 121; colonialism 1, 2, 8, 29, 30, 199; commercial trade agreement with Britain 90; defeat of China (1895) 51; immigration to Shanghai 108; involvement in Chinese stock exchanges 59, 61–6, 63–5; Japanese residents in Hong Kong 89–90; role of European experts/advisors 28; Second World War occupation of China 2; Sino-Japanese War (1894–5) 135; Tianjin concession *93*; wartime occupation of Hong Kong 91, 201–4
Jews: and cemetery practice in Shanghai 117, 120; migration to Shanghai 108, 120
Jiang Hongjiao 65, 71, 72
Jiaozhou *see* Kiaochow
jingji (economics) 69, 76n39
Jiyan Guild 49
Jones, Paul 188
Journal of the Chinese Chamber of Commerce 70
judicial system: and colonial powers 8–9; and Guomindang government 14; in Kiaochow 41–2, 51, 55n3

Kang Youwei 44, 45
Karl, Rebecca 5, 51
Kennedy, Dane 82
Kiaochow (Jiaozhou) 1; German leasehold territory 1, 38–56; German/Japanese administration of 29, *see also* Qingdao
kidnapping 14, 22n15
Kikungshan (Jigongshan), hill station 82, 83
King, Anthony 82
KMT (Kuo Min Tang,; Guomindang; Nationalist Party): Australasian 189, 190, 191–3; operations in Hong Kong 207
Knutsford, Lord 84–5

Korea 199; migrants 10
Korean War 207
Kotewall, Robert (Law Kuk-wo) 201
Kowloon 85
Kronecker, F. 42
Krupp, Friedhelm 40
Kuhn, Philip 11
Kuliang (Guliang), hill station 82
Kuling (Guling), hill station 82, 83
Kunming *136*; French medicine in 137, 139, 140, 141, 149; police bureau 139
Kwok Bew, George (Guo Biao) 191
Kwok brothers 191
Kwong Sing and Co. 194, 195

Ladds, Catherine 28
Lam, Agnes 219
lashing 41, 51
Lau Chu-pak 90
Law of Nations, The (Vattel) 181, 184
Lay, Horatio Nelson 29
Lebrun, Albert 198, 199
Lee, Charles 195
Lee, Vicky 89
legal system *see* judicial system
Legislative Council, Hong Kong 83, 84, 86, 87, 88, 89, 90, 91, 202, 206
Lenin, V. 3–5
Léonard, J. 141
Li Bingheng 45
Li Hongzhang 30, 45
Li Yishi 170, 171, 172, 174
Li Yuyi 173
Li Zuhan 171
Liang Lianfu 145
Liang Qichao 19, 51–2, 170, 181, 185–7, 189
Liao Chengzhi 215
liberation narratives 196
Lin Fengmian 170, 171
Lin Wenzheng 170, 171
Lincheng Incident (1923) 14
Little, L. K. 31
Liu, Lydia 37
Liu Xiji 195
Lo Man-kam 91
loans, foreign, to China 29
Loch, Sir Henry 183, 184
Lokawei Cemetery, Shanghai 115, 116, 118
Long, Walter 90
Longzhou 135, *136*; French medicine in 137, 139; police bureau 139
Louis, Roger 200
Lu Shouxian 71–2

Lu Xun 168
Lu, Yixu 18, 151–64
Lui Haisu 169, 170, 171
Lüshun (Port Arthur) 1
lusotropicalism 8, 214–15

Ma Yinchu 57
Ma Ying–piu 190, 194
Macanese people 216, 221
Macau 1, 8, 20, 212–22
Macau Chinese Students' Association 218
MacDonnell, Richard 81
Malaya 200, 208; hill stations 82
Manchukuo 8, 197, 199, 202
Manchuria, Japanese occupation of 30
Manhao 135
Mao Zedong 5, 216, 217, 218
Marinelli, Maurizio 17, 92–107
Marzoli, Egidio 101
masonic associations, Chinese 189, 190
May, Henry 86, 87, 88, 89, 90
Maze, Frederick 31
medical missions 8
medication, attitudes to 134, 142–5, 146
medicine 37; French 17–18, 134–49; and racial segregation 42–3; traditional 145–8
Meizhan 171–3
Melbourne, Australia 19, 186–7
men, role in colonial society 43
Meng Yue 10, 12, 177n1
Mengzi 135, *136*, 138; French medicine in 137, 139, 142
Mexico, treaty rights in China 2
Michelagnoli, Mario 96
migration 108; by Chinese to Australia 188; immigration of foreigners to Shanghai 108
Mikami Tayotsung 74n6
Miners, Norman 90
Ming Ddynasty 214
mining industry 2, 8, 135; Shandong province 38–9, 45, 50
miscegenation 88–9, 215
missionaries: and hill stations 83; missionary schools 30
Mo Xiancheng 146
modernism 171; in Shanghai 19, 167–77
modernity: colonial 195–6; multiple models of 13
Mokanshan (Moganshan), hill station 82
monopolies, in Macau 213, 216
morality, and economics 69–73
morphine 140
Morse, H. B. 29
Mouillac 140
movement, freedom of, of Chinese émigrés 182–5, 195–6
Mu Ouchu 70
Mühlhahn, Klaus 15–16, 37–56
music: Chinese 157–8; Elisabeth Frey's performances 162–3
Muslims, and cemetery policy in Shanghai 117, 118–20, *119*, 130
Mussolini, Benito 105

Nam Kwong Company 216
naming, of colonial spaces 101–2
Nanhai, police bureau 139
Nanjing 168
Nanjing Decade (1927–37) 14
Nanjing, Treaty of 1, 108, 180
Nannin, CMCS case study 32–5
'national humiliation' 2
nationalism: and art 176–7; Chinese 51–2, 54; weakness in Hong Kong 206–8
Nationalist Party *see* Guomindang
natives, status in Kiaochow legal system 41
Naval Ministry, German 39–40, 54n1
'neighbourhood', Italian concession in Tianjin 17, 92–106
neighbourhood groups, Hong Kong 203–4
neo-Renaissance architecture 101, 107n7
New Cemetery, Shanghai *see* Pashienjao (Baxianqiao) Cemetery
New Guinea 192
new imperialism 198–201; and Hong Kong 197, 201–11
new policy, Shandong 47–9
New South Wales: Chinese Chamber of Commerce 189; retail development 194–5; Yee Hing network 189–90
New Zealand 195
newborn babies 144
newspaper publishing 168
Ng Choy 83, 84
Nie Qijie 58, 65, 70
Nigeria 200
Ningbo Cemetery, Shanghai 124
Ningbo, treaty-port status 1
Nocentini, Ludovico 95
Nogueira, Franco 222
oil industry 33
opium trade 34
Opium Wars 1, 182
oral history project, Macau 219–22
Oriental Trust Guarantee and Exchange Company 61
Osaka Fuji Weaving and Spinning Association 64
Osterhammel, Jürgen 1, 5, 11

Ottoman empire, role of European experts/advisors 28
overseas Chinese communities 10

Pacific islands 191, 192–3, 195
Pan Mingxiong 145
pan-Asianism 201–2
Paris 168–9
Parker, Henry 185
Pashienjao (Baxianqiao) Cemetery ('New Cemetery'), Shanghai 111, 112, *112*, 113–14, 119
Peak, Hong Kong, residential segregation study 16–17, 81–2, 83–5; 1904 Peak District Reservation Ordinance 85–7; 1918 Peak District Ordinance 87–9; repeal of ordinances 90–1, 203
Peking Daily News 51
Peking Opera 157–8
Peking, Treaty of 183
pharmacology, development of 140–2
Pistolese, G. E. 96
plague 135–6, 137–8, 142, 143, 147, 149n3
police forces: creation of local police bureaux 139; SMP (Shanghai Municipal Police) 35, 118
Pollock, H. E. 86
Polo, Marco 103
Poma, Cavalier 95
Pootung Cemetery, Shanghai 111, 113, 121–2, *122*, *123*
population: migration of 10, 108; Shanghai 109–10; of Tianjin 96
Port Arthur (Lushun) 1
Portugal, and Macau 1, 8, 20, 212–22
positions (journal) 6, 7
postcolonial studies 11
Pratt, Mary Louise 104–5
PRC (People's Republic of China): and Hong Kong 207, 208, 210; renaming of colonial places 102
press, political 50–1
printing industry 168, 169
processions, response to disease 147
public health 135–6, 140, 141; and hill stations 82, 83; Hong Kong 88; in Kiaochow 42–3, *see also* sanitation
public opinion, in Kiaochow 50
publishing industry 168, 169
punishment, judicial 41–2

Qing state 35; administration 27
Qingdao: care of Chinese population 48, 49; German colonialism in 1, 7, 8, 15–16, 37–54
Quong Tart 183

racial discrimination: in Australia 182–7, 195–6; Qingdao 41–3, 44, 51; in stock markets 60
racial mixing 8, 214–15
racial purity 43
Raggi, Salvador 94–5
railways 8; French developments in China 1, 32, 135; Nanning 32, 34; Shandong province 38–9, 45–7, 50
realism, in art 171, 172, 175, 176–7
reforms: of (1901) 139; Hundred-days Reform 45; Reform Movement 51
Rehabilitation Advisory Committees, Hong Kong 201
Reinhardt, Anne 14
religion: and cemetery management 116; and healing 147
Renaissance, neo-Renaissance architecture 101, 107n7
resistance to colonialism; Qingdao 44–53
retailing, department stores 190–1, 194–5
Revelations of the Stock Exchange (Jiang Hongjiao) 65, 71, 72
Revolutionary Alliance (*Tongmenghui*) 191
Reygondaud, Dr. 142
Ricci, Matteo 103
rights consciousness 198
Rights Recovery Association, Shandong 50
rivers 33
ROC government, Taiwan 207, 208
Rogaski, Ruth 92
Rothkegel & Co. 151
rubber industry 60, 74n5
Ruffinoni, Daniele 103
Ruskin, John 107n7
Russia: colonialism in China 1, 2, 29; emigration to Shanghai 108, 120; Tianjin concession *93*, 94

Salazar 218, 219, 222
salvarsan 141, 142, 143
Sang On Tiy (*Shengantai*) 190, 191
sanitation 42–3, 82, *see also* public health
Sanjiang Guild 49
Schrameier, Wilhelm 53
science 37
Securities and Commodities Exchange 62, 64, 65
securities trading *see* stock exchanges
segregation: in housing 16–17; in Kiaochow 41–3; and racism 41–3, 44, *see also* Peak, Hong Kong, residential segregation study
semi-colonial/semi-feudal characterization of China 4, 5, 92

semi-colonialism 1, 3–6; in Macau 214; of Shanghai 65–6, *see also* colonialism
serums 141–2
servants, Chinese, in Elisabeth Frey's letters 154–7
Severn, Claude 90
Sforza, Carlo 100
Shandong: 'new policy' 47–9, *see also* Kiaochow; Qingdao
Shandong Mining Company (*Shandong Bergbau-Gesellschaft*) 45
Shandong Railway Company (*Shandong Eisenbahn-Gesellschaft*) 45–7
Shanghae Cemetery 110, 111, 113, 121
Shanghai: administration 7–8; cemeteries case study 17, 108–30, *111*, *112*; cosmopolitanism in 167–9, 176; establishment of institutions in 35; judicial system 8–9; and migration 10, 108, 168; and modernist art 18–19, 167–77; population 109–10; retail development 190, 194, 195; 'Shanghai model' of colonialism 12; Shanghai studies 11; stock exchanges 15, 16, 57–73; treaty-port status 1, 2, *see also* SMC (Shanghai Municipal Council); SMP (Shanghai Municipal Police)
Shanghai China Merchants' Securities Exchange 62, 64
Shanghai Cotton Exchange 64
Shanghai Federation of Charity Organizations 125
Shanghai General Chamber of Commerce 68
Shanghai Night Market Commodities and Securities Exchange 63
Shanghai Public Benevolent Cemetery *see* SPBC
Shanghai School (artists) 169
Shanghai Stock and Bonds Trading Association 59, 62
Shanghai Stock Exchange 60
Shantung Road Cemetery (Shanghae Cemetery) 121
Shao Lizi 67–8
Shek Kip Mei fire, Hong Kong 208
Shenbao newspaper 170
Shenk, Catherine 200–1
Shih, Shu-mei 5–6, 13
shipbuilding industry 40, 203
Siam, role of European experts/advisors 28
Siemens 40
Sikhs 118, 130
Simao *136*; French medicine in 137
Simla hill station 81, 82, 91

Sincere (Xianshi) 190, 191, 194, 195, *see also* Four Great Companies
Sino-French War (1894–5) 135
Sino-Japanese War (1894–5) 135
smallpox 141, 143, 144, 148
Smart, Alan 208
SMC (Shanghai Municipal Council) 35, 109, 112–13, 115, 116–17, 117–18, 120, 121–3, 124–6, 128, 129
SMP (Shanghai Municipal Police) 35, 118
Snow, Philip 201
Social Welfare Advisory Committee 200
Sokolsky, George 66
Soldiers' Cemetery, Shanghai 113, 122–3
Song Ziwen 31
sovereign states, equality of 180, 181–2, 184–5
Soviet Union, repudiation of Russian treaty rights in China 2
space, conceptualisation of 92–3, 98–9
SPBC (Shanghai Public Benevolent Cemetery) 128
speculation: 1921–22 bubble 57, 58, 63, 65–6, 70–3; rubber industry 60, 74n5
Stalin, Joseph 4–5
Standard Oil 33
steam-shipping industry 14
sterling: devaluation 200–1; Sterling Area 208, 209; Sterling Crisis 20; Sterling Zone 199–200
stock exchanges 15, 16, 57–9, 69–73; Chinese reaction to 63–9; early Shanghai stock market 59–63
Stock and Produce Exchange 65
Stock and Shareholders Association 60
Stoler, Ann 38
Stubbs, Reginald 89
student protests, Macau *see* 123 Incident
Stuttgart 152
Suez Crisis (1956) 20, 206
suicide, stock-market induced 70, 71–2, 76n46
Sun Chuanfang 169
Sun Company Store (*Daxin*) 194
Sun Sun (*Xinxin*) 190, 194, 195, *see also* Four Great Companies
Sun Yat-sen 3, 4, 5–6, 52–3, 92, 191; and stock exchange development 59, 61, 74n6, 75n13
Suzhou, treaty-port status 2
Sydney 19; Chinese businesses in 183, 194; KMT branch 191–2; Presbyterian church 190; visit of Liang Qichao 185–7
syphilis 141, 142, 143

Taipa 216–17
Taiping rebellion 35; and migration 10
Taiwan: Japanese occupation of 1, 30; and migration 10; ROC government 207, 208
Taiwan Straits crisis (1958) 206
Taixichen 42
Takeyoshi Tsuruta 178n5
Tang Shaoyi 95
Tao Zhu 215
Tardieu, Dr. 144
Temple of Heaven 157, 158
terminology of colonialism 3–7
textile industry 64
Thomas, Nicholas 11
Thomas, W. A. 60
'Three Principles of the People' (Sun Yat-sen) 3
Tiadongchen 42
Tianjin 12, 30; colonial domestic life 18; Elisabeth Frey's letters home from 18, 151–64; fire in 159; German military actions 47; Italian concession in 17, 92–106; maps 93, 97; treaty-port status 2
Tirpitz, Alfred von 39, 39–41
Tokyo Securities Exchange 59, 61
Tongrenfuyuantang *see* TRFYT (Tongrenfuyuantang)
transculturation 105
Treaty of Nanjing (Nanking) 1, 108, 180
Treaty of Peking 183
treaty system 9
treaty-ports 1, 2, 8, 12; Chinese quality of life in 195–6; and diplomatic representation 9; status of French doctors in 137, 138, 148; stock exchanges in 66, *see also* CMCS (Chinese Maritime Customs Service)
TRFYT (Tongrenfuyuantang) 124–5
Trotsky, L. 4–5
Truppel, Oskar von 48, 49
Tseng, Marquis 184–5
Tung Wah hospital, Hong Kong 189
Tungwah News, The 186

'Unequal Treaties' 1, 180–1, 182, 195
United States 207; American Declaration of Independence 184; Angell Treaty with China 183; Britain's post-war debt to 200; United States Court for China 9
universities, in Shanghai 168
utopia 98, 99

vaccination 141–2, 143–4, 148
Vadon, Dr. 140
Vallet, Dr. 140
variolization 143–4
Vattel, Emmerich de 181, 184
Victoria Peak *see* Peak
Vietnam 208
Vietnamese cemeteries 115, 118
Viga, Giovanni 95
violence: colonial conflicts 7, 45–7; in Tianjin 18; to Chinese servants 155, 157
von Heyking, Elisabeth 153, 155–6, 157, 163
von Strauch, E. A. W. 33–4, 35

Wai, John Young 190
Waldersee, General-feldmarschall von 47
Wang, David Der-wei 171, 173, 175
Wang Daxie 140
Wang Ji 146
Wang Xuewen 4
Wang, Yiyian 19, 167–79
Ward, Robert 201–2, 203
warlords 168
Wei Yuk 86–7
Weihaiwei (Wieihai) 1
Weng Tonghe 44–5
West Cemetery, Shanghai 115
West River system 33
Wider den Gelben Drachen (Fighting the Yellow Dragon) (Harder) 153, 156
Wilden, General Consul 66–7
Wilhelm II, Kaiser of Germany 43
Wing On (*Yongan*) 190, 191, 194, *see also* Four Great Companies
Wing, Peter Yee 191
Wing Sang (*Yongsheng*) 190, 191
Wing Tiy 190
women: Chinese 105; in colonial society 43; residence in hill stations 82; right to vote 187; and stock market investment 63, 71–3, 75n17, 76n46
Wong, Aline 203–4
Wong Chee (Wong Poon Narm) 194, 195
Wong Shing 84, 85
Woodhead, H. G. W. 101
Wu Lien-Teh 149n3
Wuzhou, CMCS 32

Xiamen, treaty-port status 1
Xiaoping Tang 173
Xinhai Revolution 52
xinmin 185
Xu Beihong 167, 170, 171, 172, 174, 175

Xu Yuan 66–7
Xu Zhimo 167, 170, 171, 172–3, 174, 177

Yang Qingqing 171, 172, 173
Yang Tianshi 61
Yang Xingfo 171
Yangzi river 33
Yee Hing network 189–90
'yellow peril' 43
Yishifengqingqu 98, 99, 101
Yiyan Weng 19
Young, Percy (Kwan Hong Kee) 194
Young, Sir Mark 91, 203, 204, 208
Yu Xian 45
Yu Xiaqing 61, 62, 64
Yuan Shikai 48, 52

Yunnan 135, *136*; *Duanyang* festival 147; and French colonialism 2; French medicine in 134; rebellion against French 138; traditional medicine 145

Zhang Jian 65
Zhang Jingjiang 61, 63
Zhang Rumei 45
Zheng Jining 146
Zheng Shengtian 173
Zhou Enlai 215
Zhou Fu 48
Zikawei Cemetery, Shanghai 115
Zongli Yamen 44, 45
Zou Yiren 109
zujie (concession) 98